THE
HUMAN SITUATION

*The Gifford Lectures
delivered in the University of Glasgow
1935–1937*

By

W. MACNEILE DIXON

GORDON PRESS

New York
1973

First Published 1937

Library of Congress Catalog Card Number 73-10996

International Standard Book Number 0-87968-062-8

GORDON PRESS
P.O. Box 459
Bowling Green Station
New York, N. Y. 10004

Printed in the United States of America

CONTENTS

Part I

Part II

5

CONTENTS

PREFACE

I AM greatly indebted to my friends, Professor Dewar of Reading and Miss Maude G. May of Glasgow, for many corrections and suggestions while the following pages were passing through the press.

W. M. D.

PART I

I

INTRODUCTION

The most singular and deepest themes in the History of the Universe and Mankind, to which all the rest are subordinate, are those in which there is a conflict between Belief and Unbelief, and all epochs, wherein Belief prevails, under what form it will, are splendid, heart-elevating and fruitful.   All epochs, on the contrary, when Unbelief, in what form soever, maintains its sorry victory, should they even for a moment glitter with a sham splendour, vanish from the eyes of posterity, because no one chooses to burden himself with the study of the unfruitful.

Goethe

I

INTRODUCTION

Had Emil Meyerson been alive I should not now be addressing you. He had accepted the invitation to succeed His Grace, The Archbishop of York, as Gifford Lecturer in this University. From him, had he survived, you would have had a survey of modern thought such as I cannot hope to rival. By his scientific attainments, his subtle and searching intellect, he was brilliantly equipped for such a survey. Few among the thinkers of our time possessed in as high a degree that delightful lucidity of thought and expression which seems to be a birthright of all Frenchmen. To your misfortune an amateur takes the place of a tried and laurelled veteran.

If it be said, and it is no more than the truth to say, that I owe my position here to the friendship of my colleagues, I would wish this to be added, that I take more pleasure in the regard of my friends than in any honour that could be done me. And yet their choice is, indeed, a great and signal honour. Possibly—it is a conjecture—I was invited to deliver this course of lectures partly at least in the hope that if I could not be so profound as my predecessors, I might, for that reason, be more easily followed. My colleagues may have had the Founder's intention in mind. The 'Deed of Gift' clearly sets forth his wish that the Gifford Lectures should be 'popular discourses'. 'Popular' I take to be within the compass of the plain man's understanding. Some Gifford Lecturers have ranked his mental powers and accomplishments very high, so high, indeed, that I have wondered at times whether I had myself attained to them. You would wish me, I fancy, to avoid the 'holy jungle of transcendental metaphysics', as Swinburne irreverently called it, the tangled wilderness of technical and inconclusive debate. You would prefer discourses as little in the manner of Spinoza or Hegel as possible. If such be your wish, I am in the heartiest sympathy. You might even go so far as to hope that I am in a state of innocence in respect of philosophy. However that may be, I am certainly in an embarrassing position. Before some of my colleagues my philosophical errors will be an open book, before others my scientific, before others again my theological errors; more especially as it will be my aim to reduce the issues that confront us to their simplest terms. I do not propose to apologise for these errors. I have never believed in excuses, and I have hopes that they may possibly in a measure cancel each other out. Were it possible I should gladly avoid the Chinese puzzle of metaphysics. Alas, we cannot. For, however little we are conscious of it, we are one and all metaphysicians, good or bad, generally indeed bad, yet inveterate metaphysicians.

The best we can do, the most I can promise you, is to employ familiar words, the words of our daily speech, and to use them in the sense to which we are all accustomed. I shall abide, as far as I can, by the tradition of our country and our ancestors.

Ours are not the first, nor yet the wisest heads which have pondered the riddle of the painful earth, and we shall not succeed where our betters have failed. But just as none of us can live any life save his own, none of us can wholly transfer his burdens to another's shoulders. We must in some measure in these days think for ourselves, as we must breathe for ourselves, and walk for ourselves. Happier, it may be, are those who can with serenity leave this troublesome business of thinking to others. *Denken ist schwer*, and it is not everyone who has a good head for thinking. Let the mind once awake, however, and nothing, whatever vexation or labour is entailed, can extinguish its curiosity or stay its tormenting propensity for enquiry. Not a few men have at times breathed the wish that God or nature had upon the great fundamental problems of life broken the spell of silence. Yet, perhaps, we should not desire it, since it may well be for the benefit of both mind and soul that it remains unbroken.

I would remind you that we have on this journey to part company with the friends of revealed religion.

> O well with him who hath secured his wealth
> Of thoughts divine, and wretched he whose care
> Is shadowy speculation on the gods.

To those who sail across the great ocean under the colours of revealed religion we dip our flag in greeting—and a good voyage to them.   Ours is a stormier course, the course prescribed by the founder of the Lectureship.

I propose to speak my mind.   I cannot believe you would wish me to say what I did not think, or think what I did not say. Nothing is to be gained by concealment or equivocation.   If you find my conclusions unpalatable, you are not without resource. You have only to assure yourselves that I am totally mistaken, which may, indeed, very likely be the truth.   And—who knows?—I may learn wisdom, and come to think differently.   I would have you regard these occasions as conversations.   My views will be at your disposal for consideration, not necessarily for acceptance.   If they have no inherent persuasiveness I would not have you accept them.   There are in the realm of thought no absolute authorities, no dictators.   No man, living or dead, can claim oracular powers.   Mine is a personal view.   All philosophies are in the end personal.   You can no more escape your philosophy than you can escape your own shadow, for it also is a reflection of yourself.   Systems of thought are the shadows cast by different races, epochs and civilisations.

> China and Ind, Hellas and France,
> Each hath its own inheritance;
> And each to Truth's rich market brings
> Its bright, divine imaginings.

All reasoning is in a manner biassed, and the bias is due to the nature, surroundings and education of the thinker.   We are none of us merely logical or calculating machines.   Mathematical reasoning is more nearly impersonal than any other type, but, as Aristotle pointed out, you do not ask it of the statesman.   And the matters with which we are to deal are not susceptible of mathematical demonstration.

Like myself, you have probably not seldom, in listening to discourses, found yourselves more interested in the man than in his deliverances, putting the question, for example, how far his true mind was revealed in them, or how far he merely wore the official costume of his party or profession.   How much more interesting are men than their utterances, and how much more revealing! I am inclined to think you would greatly prefer me to tell you point-blank what I believe than trouble you with the arguments for or against my beliefs.   And, indeed, within the time at our disposal, I cannot deal with the innumerable disputed questions either in science or philosophy. Few, if any, are the points upon which there is agreement. I can do little more than outline my own preferences, and the conclusions to which, in my judgment, among the many matters in debate, they appear to lead.

And it may be best for your protection and guidance to make, at the outset, a confession of some of these personal preferences. Of the more highly praised virtues (save courage and magnanimity) I am, as far as one can oneself judge of such things, deficient in appreciation, and the heaven of my choice would, I fear, contain but few saints or examples of moral perfection. Indeed I am not sure that it would contain any ; it would be mainly peopled by agreeable sinners, not too unlike myself for companionship. How sad are the virtuous, and how cheerful and light-hearted so often the profane. How gay and gallant, how amusing so many of the rascals! My affections have, I suppose, betrayed or undermined my moral principles. Holiness is a strong perfume, and a little of it goes a long way in the world. I have never been very clear whether it was compatible with laughter, and I should be very loath to bid an eternal farewell to laughter. For I am one of those people who love good sense, and yet love sheer nonsense in as great, almost in a higher degree. It affects me like champagne. I find it most exhilarating. Perhaps I should not, but I find even the frenzied illogicality of the world amusing. And my private opinion is that only if you can appreciate nonsense can you appreciate sense.

Again I am less enamoured of truth than of beauty. Beauty I know, or think I know, when I meet with it. Of truth I am never so sure. And if I could spend the course of everlasting time in a paradise of varied loveliness, I do not fancy my felicity would be greatly impaired if the last secret of the universe were withheld from me.

None the less my natural sympathies—though I fear they might not one and all recognise me as a friend—lie with the men of religion rather than with the ethical idealists, for whom, I confess, I have small regard and with whom I feel little sympathy. Putting the world to rights has never appealed to me as an occupation for which I felt myself in any degree or fashion fitted, nor have I believed those who were foremost in the endeavour peculiarly qualified for the undertaking. The world has gone its own imperturbable way despite their efforts, and the many-fountained Utopias and rose-scented Commonwealths will be established only, I believe, on the arrival of the Greek Kalends, when dreams come true. In what century did Nature change her ways, and in what year was human nature born again? When did disagreement die, and who has written the epitaph of injustice? In all ages the prophets and moralists have upbraided and denounced their fellow creatures. I desire to be excused their honourable society. I will sit on no jury for the arraignment of the human species. There is more than a morsel of truth in the saying, 'He who hates vice hates mankind.'

Qui vitia odit, homines odit.

I have, indeed, my own strong likes and dislikes, as you will presently discover, but I can find in myself no kind of superiority to my neighbours, which would justify me in censure of their ways or works. 'No man can justly censure another', wrote Sir Thomas Browne, 'because no man truly knows another.' And again, 'For my conversation it is like the Sun's with all men, and with a friendly aspect to good and bad.'

I propose, with your permission, in this first series of discourses to set forth, as briefly and clearly as in me lies, the undisputed and indisputable facts of the human situation, the circumstances in which we actually find ourselves. Of Schopenhauer it was said, 'He is not a philosopher like the rest; he is a philosopher who has seen the world.' The point is a cardinal one. There is no hope for those who will not face the facts, who philosophise, however well and wisely, in a desert, in an imaginary world conjured up in the solitude of their studies. To give any kind of interpretation of human life you must first try 'to see it steadily and see it whole'. 'I wish to make the world my book of study,' said Montaigne. It is also my wish. And I propose to allow my thoughts to revolve, as in the curve of an ellipse, around two foci; to ask, in the first place, What kind of world is this that we in fact inhabit? And later to discuss some among the possible and alternative interpretations of things as they are.

We begin, then, with every man's experience. Neither philosophy nor science operates in a vacuum. Beneath them lies our common and immediate knowledge of the world and ourselves. We did not make our natures, nor their surroundings. We find them. Here we are, eating and drinking, conversant with health and disease; here we are among our neighbours, thinking and feeling, hoping and fearing, enjoying and suffering, in a state of being not of our choosing; and it is of this very remarkable, this astonishing situation that we desire to reach some explanation, some interpretation, if explanation or interpretation be at all possible.

No doubt you will detect errors, even contradictions, in my reasoning. I comfort myself by remembering that no thinker of my acquaintance, however eminent, is free of them. Not the mathematically-minded Plato or Spinoza, not Descartes, nor Kant nor Leibniz. Their works, one and all, sparkle with contradictions of the most flagrant, delightful and encouraging variety. And why? It was said of Confucius that he had 'no foregone conclusions, no arbitrary predeterminations, no obstinacy and no egotism'. How charming to meet with is a mild and amiable comprehension of human character and human beliefs, which rejects all pedantry, all dogmatism, all doctrinaire types of thought, and is willing with perfect urbanity and good humour to hear and consider the views of an opponent. I should like to have known Confucius. He was evidently a gentleman. Yet I am satisfied he had his secret wish. Every heart has its secret wish, and the systems even of the most renowned philosophers betray it. Goethe describes the formidable look with which Napoleon disposed of superfluous persons without a word. They were 'pierced through by his glance, and saw themselves already shot or beheaded'. So with the famous monarchs of the mind. They terrify you with their authority, their look subdues you. Exalted like Oriental sultans, they sit on their golden thrones, and their subjects do obeisance before them. You are vanquished by their imposing air, or crushed by their powerful dialectic. How royal is their gesture, how incomparable their technique!

There is, however, no need for alarm. Pluck up your heart, approach a little nearer, and what do you find; that they have human wishes and weaknesses like yourself. You may discover that Kant smoked, played billiards and had a fancy for candied fruit. The discovery renders him at once less awe-inspiring. Look a little closer, and you perceive that this magnificence of demeanour is a mask. This terrifying apparatus conceals a preference for a certain conclusion. You may even find that the systems throw more light upon the preferences of the philosophers who construct them, or upon the race to which they belong, than upon the matters they discuss. The Jew, for example, is clearly apparent in the philosophy of Spinoza, and English blood and êthos in the Utilitarians. Differences of opinion are deeply rooted in the differences of our nature, in the original pattern of our souls. There never yet was a philosopher, whatever they may have said, no, nor man of science, whose conclusions ran counter to the dearest wishes of his heart, who summed up against them, or condemned his hopes to death. How honestly Darwin confessed the lurking presence of the desire to prove his theory true. 'I remember well the time when the thought of the eye made me cold all over. . . . The sight of a feather in a peacock's tail whenever I gaze at it, makes me sick.' What a danger lies in wait for our logic, when our affections or our interests are aroused.

I ask for no more than your conclusions on the great matters of human life and destiny. Let me know them, and I shall not trouble you to set out the arguments. I can myself supply them. Our desires attract supporting reasons as a magnet the iron filings. You will say, 'Then you are yourself prejudiced.' I fear most certainly. Yet there is a limit. We shall none of us be easily persuaded that we can believe the outrageously absurd because it takes our fancy. We must endeavour to proceed warily, and with what detachment we can muster. We should aim, I venture to think, now and always, at a conclusion, if such there be, which will satisfy the whole of our nature. And for two reasons. It is neither sensible nor scientific to take a part for the whole. 'The nature of man is his whole nature,' said Pascal. I accept that position. To strip the human being, for example, of all his attributes save his logical or calculating powers is an unwarrantable mutilation. Nature made him what he is. You cannot pick and choose. Nature is asserting herself in him, and you must take account not of one or two, but of all her assertions. On every side to-day you meet with an exaltation of the intellect at the expense of the spirit. You may trust, it is said, your thoughts, but not your aspirations. In your ideals you employ, it seems, a private script, a language unknown to nature; in your logic, on the other hand, nature herself speaks. This is, in effect, the great two-handed sword with which Spinoza struck terror into the hearts of his adversaries. With this selfsame sword science confidently lays about her to-day. You see the design. Nature is rent asunder. You enthrone the measuring, weighing, calculating faculty of the human creature. His remaining attributes are irrelevant. But who told you that nature had drawn this line? Where did you learn of this preference? Nature has no preferences. If she has given us deceiving souls, how can you argue that she has given us trustworthy intellects? It was the opinion of Coleridge that deep thinking and deep feeling were inseparable, and that the 'Euclidean understanding' failed, and must fail, to comprehend in isolation the sum of reality. If nature misleads us in the one case, she very probably misleads us in the other, and if that be so, it were best to wind up the debate, and turn our attention to stocks and shares. We should at least, then, aim at a conclusion which the intellect can accept and the heart approve.

And for a second reason. If you satisfy the heart alone, the understanding stands to its arms, and with justice protests: if the understanding alone, the heart is in revolt, and with equal justice refuses to be satisfied. For of what are we in search? Peace of mind. We desire to be at home in a friendly world, we desire a reconciliation, a harmony between ourselves and our surroundings. It might well, indeed, be asked, how came we at all to entertain the notion that life should present to us a countenance wreathed in perpetual smiles, why should we expect unearned, eternal good, a world good throughout, good for everyone, at all times and for ever? Apparently we do expect it as a birthright. And men ardently pursue truth also, assuming that it will be angel's bread when found.

Yet again, whence and why this determination to discover truth, irrespective of any certainty that it will prove either pleasant or profitable? A strange quest surely, and a strange conviction that the truth will not disappoint or betray us. Is there any guarantee that the truth, if it could be ascertained, would coincide with the good? Many philosophies have been built upon the assumption that the true and the good are one and the same. Much may be said for that thesis. None the less it is an assumption, an essay of faith. The universe contains secrets, which, if discovered, would astound men, but whether with terror or delight, who can tell us? Some thinkers, like Spinoza, have been driven to the desperate expedient of asserting that the true must be the good, however villainous in our eyes it appears. Every species of wickedness and folly, every kind of agony, physical and mental, must be called good simply because it exists. To my mind if we propose to use the words 'good' and 'evil', we must use them in a human and intelligible sense. I care not what great names are subscribed to this type of doctrine, this jugglery which merely changes the names, but leaves the pains and aches. For me it has no validity. Not a few men have clung passionately to the hope we all share that the nearer to the truth the nearer to happiness, yet so far the fruit of the tree of knowledge seems to have added little to human felicity. Indeed, some powerful thinkers have declared that he 'who increaseth knowledge increaseth sorrow', and that truth is a synonym for disillusion. Julian the Apostate was of opinion, and it is not a manifestly absurd belief, that the happiness of mankind would be increased by a return to earlier and more primitive conditions, that the human race should endeavour to forget its gains, and retrace its steps in time. Julian's thought, that the Golden Age lay behind us, has its echoes in Rousseau, and reverberates through the Christian scheme itself. The miseries of man arose, the story goes, from the eating of the fruit of knowledge. But the peculiar and mysterious fact is that however poisonous, we continue to crave for it, to believe it the healthiest diet, and to consume it with eager appetites; even to be convinced that it is medicinal, a sovereign remedy for all our diseases.

Let us, to begin with, agree upon something. And we can at least agree, borrowing the words of Cromwell, on the eve of Dunbar, that 'We are upon an engagement very difficult'. For the first and last of all life's complicated circumstances, the presiding fact, utterly astonishing, even stupefying, is that we are wholly in the dark about everything. Blank ignorance is our portion. In reasoning from our experience of nature and ourselves we have all the evidence there is. We can add none. There remains, then, the reasoning itself, which is philosophy. People often complain that philosophy is useless. This, however, is merely to vilify our own minds. Philosophy is nothing but men's thinking. The evidence fails us, and the reasoning fails us, and 'Nature nothing careth', as said Galileo, 'whether

her abstruse reasons and methods of operating be, or be not, exposed to the capacity of men.' In a measure, no doubt, nature responds to examination and study. We learn, and have learnt something of her history and habits. Yet upon the matters that most deeply concern us we have in reality no more information than our ancestors of the Stone Age. Without exception all the thoughts men have entertained upon this very singular experience we call 'life' are speculations, and no more than the purest speculations, hazardous guesses at the authorship and significance of the mystery play in which we are actors. ' "What is truth?" said jesting Pilate, and would not stay for an answer.' And what, indeed, is truth? For, so strange is our plight that even were you and I in possession of the truth, we could not know with certainty whether it was the truth or not. There is in the Pacific Ocean a vast expanse, a lonely solitude, without islands, which sailing vessels dread, and never willingly traverse. There variable winds baffle the mariner. You may lose your way, sail in its immensities for a hundred years, and never sight land. On such an ocean the ship of human enquiry contends continually with contrary winds. We would, indeed, think rather poorly of the world if we could understand it, if it were so trifling an affair as to be easily compassed by our petty understandings. Of that we are in no danger. Life and the world 'beggar all description', let alone comprehension.

Recall the systems which propose to instruct us, the philosophies realistic and idealistic, atomistic, theistic, atheistic, pantheistic; recall the innumerable doctrines, Buddha's doctrine, Plato's doctrine, the doctrines of Aristotle, Epicurus, Dante, Hegel ; recall the religions, Zoroastrianism, Hinduism, Mahommedanism, Christianity, the gods of the Egyptians, the Greeks, the Mexicans and Peruvians, all the creeds and theories, the attempts to draw a map of human nature they respectively present, their accounts of the relations of man to the source and origin, or creative principle of things—all held, be it remembered, by men anxious for the truth, by wise men and good; and is there any need to argue that no .pillar of fire has been vouchsafed to mortals as a guide through the wilderness, no revelation of the Most High, final, convincing, sufficing? If the truth be with Christ, it is not with Voltaire, if with Buddha it is not with Epicurus, if with Dante it is not with Nietzsche. Opinions, creeds, faiths, not one commands instant and unhesitating acceptance. All, whatever the part they have played in human history, however powerful the influence they have exercised on men's minds, however numerous their adherents, are tapestries wrought in the loom of human thought. The theologians of all ages and races have formed an image of God after their own fancies, and nothing could be more improbable than that He resembles in the least particular their conceptions of Him.

> The Ethiop gods have Ethiop lips,
>   Bronze cheeks and woolly hair;
> The Grecian gods are like the Greeks,
>   As keen-eyed, cold and fair.

In the great matters it is now common knowledge that we have no knowledge, unless it be sufficient to advise us of the utter folly of all dogmatism. Reason, for all the flourishing of her trumpets, has had no greater success in illuminating the grand problems than the imagination. From the central keep of the world's mystery its arrows fall idly back, as from the walls of the medieval castle the bolts of the archers.

All periods have their own methods of approach to the siege, in all there is a certain etiquette of opinions. And to-day you are not in the mode, in the best company unless you speak the language of science. Your accent is looked upon as provincial, and excludes you from intellectual society. In the armour of its vast prestige science bestrides the modern world 'like a Colossus', and

> we petty men
> Walk under his huge legs and peep about
> To find ourselves dishonourable graves.

'Every philosophy', in Hegel's words, 'belongs to its age, and is subject to its limitations.' Well, we shall have to present ourselves at the Vatican of Science, which occupies to-day the same position among the kingdoms of thought as did the Church in the Middle Ages. *Roma locuta, causa finita.* Science has delivered judgment, the case is closed. We shall have to enquire at this oracle as well as at the others, remembering that even oracles, like Churches, change their minds. In an authoritative scientific work of the date 1905 I read not long since the sentence, 'Ether is the fundamental postulate of physics'. In an equally authoritative work upon modern physics, dated 1934, I could not find the word 'ether' at all, the 'fundamental postulate' did not even occur in the index. The Victorian men of science supposed themselves near to plumbing the depths of the ocean of being. Our contemporaries do not think so. On the contrary, they declare that their predecessors were dredging the merest shallows. In the history of mind king succeeds king and dynasty follows dynasty. This continuous flux of thought I find encouraging as well as disconcerting. The dogmatisms at least are dead. We have discovered, too, something of real importance, that men are not only subject to the social conventions of their generation and country, but to those also of current opinion. They think in the manner of their times, and can no more escape it than they can escape the idiom of their mother tongue. Prisoners we are of our age, which is not of our choosing any more than our parentage or country.

And how persistent is the illusion that in our present way of looking at things, we have, if not the final truth, certainly the direct, the only avenue of approach to it. And yet the ways of thought which governed men's minds, which appeared inevitable five thousand years ago, are as strange and unfamiliar as the speech and institutions of that time. Did I say five thousand years? I should have said five hundred. Look back to the opinions universally held in Europe in 1435. The beliefs of savages excite our amusement. Ours will amuse our successors a few hundred years hence, and theirs, no doubt, be recalled with amazement a millennium later. Our business is not to solve problems beyond mortal powers, but to see to it that our thoughts are not unworthy of the great theme.

Briefly and broadly the issue is what it has always been, and always will be, the age-long issue between Naturalism and Supernaturalism. In the end everything melts into the cosmic background. All enquiries lead to the one enquiry. The great debate circles round a few words—good and evil, the soul, immortality, God. Interesting, is it not, that religion, though never more discredited, still remains a matter of universal interest? As in the late war there were engagements and encounters on many lands and many seas, which would in themselves have been senseless and unintelligible save in their relation to a single and central issue—the victory of Germany or the Allies, so in the

22

mental world the various disputes and conflicts in many fields, which appear wholly remote from religion, are in fact closely related to a single fundamental issue. They are skirmishes or affairs of outposts. To understand them you must look to the centre. You may isolate such matters as Evolution or Relativity Theory for special study, as you may study the campaign in East Africa or in Mesopotamia, but their real interest lies in the light they may throw upon the still profounder problems of human life and destiny. All turns upon your answer to the simple, penetrating question, the first in the Scottish Catechism, 'What is man's chief end?' The answer is equally admirable— 'Man's chief end is to glorify God, and to enjoy Him for ever.' Unhappily the answer leads to still further enquiries. How is God to be glorified and how enjoyed? There you have the hinge of the human situation. According to your convictions life becomes shallow or significant, to be borne with anger, indifference, disdain, or with eager anticipation. Death, for example, wears a different countenance if you regard it as the final destruction of us and all other creatures, or as an incident in a journey, a night of repose between days of activity. 'Human affairs', said Plato, 'are hardly worth considering with any great seriousness, and yet we must be in earnest about them.' We need not contest the point. What else, indeed, is there to be in earnest about? And if human affairs are not important, what else is important? Our interests are first in ourselves, and in the gods only in so far as they are associated with our lives and destinies. The Epicurean gods have no value for men, or for any beings save themselves. Nor is there any consolation to be drawn from supposing human affairs subservient to some other and grander scheme, of which we know nothing—a puppet show for the amusement of an audience of angels—a cog-wheel in a design without meaning or interest for us. You may re-member the argument of the old theology that the pot may not complain to the Potter, or ask 'Wherefore hast thou made me thus?' With this Oriental attitude of mind which identifies the will of a despot with righteousness, the Western man has little sympathy. He replies, 'If the Potter chooses to make creatures who can think and feel, sentient and reflective pots, they enter immediately into rights of their own. You cannot, even if a God, create sentient beings, and stand clear of respon-

23

sibility for their undeserved miseries. To make pots that suffer
and have no compensation for their sufferings, that are steeped
in ignorance of the cause of their wretchedness, is not from any
human standpoint defensible, and assuredly provides no reason
for praising their creator.' 'Is it not possible', asks Dostoievsky,
'to eat me up without insisting that I should sing the praises of
my devourer?' To my way of thinking, justice is justice, and
tyranny is tyranny, whether a sultan's or a God's.

How often it is proclaimed that Naturalism, or Materialism, is
dead. Yet its ghost continues to haunt the philosophers.
Perhaps it has not been buried with the proper rites. In my
opinion a very powerful case can be made out for Naturalism, and
its opponents have good reason to view its strength with apprehension. It has an ally in the human heart, there is something
in us which approves and accepts it. Let us say that there is
something in us hostile to religion, and something in us friendly
to it. 'The soul is naturally Christian,' said Tertullian. Yes,
and it is naturally Pagan. It is divided against itself. Religion
knows it well, this double mind: Psychology is well aware of it.
But this division is not of our making. It is from nature, 'the
outward man', in the phrase of Paracelsus, that we inherit this
double-mindedness. Man mirrors the world and is involved in
its duality, in the balanced rhythms which permeate the whole
fabric of things. We shall meet the swaying forces, the crossing
currents in many forms and guises. 'If man is good,' it has been
asked, 'why does he do evil? If evil, why does he love the good?'
Nature has decreed that he should desire incompatible things—to
have, for example, the approval of others, and yet go his own
unhindered way. He seeks unity and peace with his neighbours,
and at the same time to be the controller of their lives. Nature
urges him to exert all his powers, and in an instant their exercise
precipitates him into a struggle with the interests of others. He
is at once the lover and the rival of his fellows. We are very
strange creatures, so strange that, in my opinion at least, not a
philosopher of them all has written the first sentence in the book
of the soul. 'Four thousand volumes of metaphysics', said Voltaire, 'will not teach us what the soul is.' 'You will not find its
boundaries', said Heraclitus, 'by travelling in any direction, so
deep is the measure of it.'

Allow, since you cannot deny, that this strange being, man, is nature's architecture. Allow, as you must allow, that she has not limited his desires to material goods, or mere physical well-being. Look how he is willing to sacrifice them, *vitam impendere vero*, to stake his life for the truth, for his soul's satisfaction—a remarkable peculiarity in a worm of the dust. This worm will die for his creed, his country, his honour; a very delicate matter to account for by chemical reactions. To find the way to truth men have endured thirst and hunger, meditated in caves, on mountain tops, scourged themselves, stood motionless on pillars, undertaken lacerating pilgrimages, dedicated themselves to eternal silence, tortured their minds and bodies to destruction. Strange inhabitants are we of a world so strange that at one moment the heart aches at its loveliness, at another aches at its miseries, so strange that when we think of death we are in love with life, when of life we are enamoured of death. What kind of beings are we in fact? Whatever we are, never forget that we are nature's children, her contradictions are ours, ours also her talents and graces.

Questions in plenty throng upon us, questions to which no convincing answers have been given—the origin of things, the existence of God, time and space, the nature of mind, the meaning of life, the fate of the soul. Plato cannot inform us, nor Newton, nor Kant, nor Darwin. What is our business in the world, if we have any, and how are we to occupy ourselves while its tenants? An idle question, no doubt, for most men anxiously engaged, as the majority are engaged, in the task of keeping body and soul together, clinging to life with apparently no other aim save clinging to life.

But can we indeed be said to have any task in the world at all? Is it to seek pleasure and happiness, or, setting these aside, to prepare ourselves for another and wholly different world to come?—a question which has sharply divided opinion. If to find happiness here is the wise man's endeavour, how best to secure it? If in another place, of what kind is it likely to be, and how are we to prepare ourselves for it? Should we concern ourselves with the lives of others, to secure their happiness, or pursue our own independently, seeking, after the manner of some ascetics and quietists, an existence as far withdrawn as possible from the activities of human society? If, on the other hand, it is of the community and our neighbours we should chiefly think, should we endeavour to provide what they tell us would satisfy them, or what we, armed with superior wisdom, know would be much better for them, since by the grace of God we always have that knowledge? How easy are generalisations, and how futile. Does kindness to animals, for example, which we are all persuaded is a duty, include kindness to the wolf and the scorpion, the locust, the tsetse fly and the mosquito? Controversy upon most matters of consequence appears likely to be acute and prolonged.

How, we may further ask, are the proper principles of living to be discovered at all? If you propose to take nature as your guide, tell us what morality is taught by nature. What is her own morality? Has she in fact any? If not, is there a divine revelation enjoining us to eschew her ways, as perhaps antiquated, and to substitute other and better ways? We hear much of the preference of men for goodness, truth and beauty. Is this noble preference any more than an idiosyncrasy, an eccentricity, an interesting feature of the human species, distinguishing it among other animals, as his trunk distinguishes the elephant, or his hump the camel? Is it of any more intrinsic importance than a preference, let us say, for classical architecture over Gothic, or a vegetarian over a carnivorous diet?

Times so remarkable as those in which we are privileged to live brighten the intelligence. They are more than remarkable, they are revolutionary. Since the Renaissance there has been no such upheaval of thought, no such revaluation of values as in the century upon which we have entered. Now as then, within about fifty years, within the span of a single lifetime, all the old conceptions, the previous beliefs in science, in religion, in politics, have been wholly transformed; a change has taken place, we might almost say, in the inclination of the earth's orbit. We might fancy our planet had passed through some zone of cosmic disturbance. We are surrounded by specialists the most brilliant in every branch of human enquiry. But for a conspectus, a unifying creed, the plain man knows not where to look, and is plunged in a sea of perplexity. He reads one book to find its conclusions flatly contradicted by the next he opens. One is reminded of the celebrated summing up by Mr. Justice Maule. 'Gentlemen of the jury—If you believe the evidence of the plaintiff in this action, you will no doubt find for the defendant; if on

26

the other hand you believe the evidence of the defendant, you will no doubt find for the plaintiff. But if, like myself, you believe the evidence of neither, God help you all! Gentlemen of the jury, you may consider your verdict.'

Physics, upon which all the other sciences must necessarily build, introduces the modern man to new and bewildering, if not contradictory concepts. He hears of a finite but unlimited universe, of wrinkled and twisted space-time. He is told of electrons and protons constituting the atom, whirling in unimaginable orbits at inconceivable speeds, and before he has accommodated his mind to their fantastic dances they are joined by neutrons and positrons in a system of which the mathematical framework is still more complicated. If he supposes himself to understand the character of energy—a very foolish supposition on the part of any man—he must add to it the conception of negative energy. He must enlarge his mind to embrace the possibility of half a dozen geometries, which would have made Euclid stare and gasp; he must attempt to visualise cosmic rays, and 'waves of probability', and be aware, while he is attending to his income tax forms, that he is a dweller in an exploding or stampeding universe.

Time was when man was the chief object of his own attention, interest and study. We have changed all that. Nature has usurped the pride of place, and we are told to think of ourselves as mere incidents in a process. The modern view fuses man and things. Men are merely things of one kind among innumerable things of other kinds. That light travels at the rate of 186,000 miles a second rather than at 146,000, makes me neither glad nor sorry, any more than does the proportion of the electrons to the protons in an atom of oxygen; but that we are glad or sorry at any time, or at any thing, is, it seems, utterly irrelevant. What is of real importance is to know that there are six thousand white corpuscles and five million red corpuscles in a cubic millimetre of the blood of each one of us.

Time was when man's presence on the earth gave it dignity amid the heavenly host, when the intellectual systems magnified mankind, exalted the mind and assigned it great place in the hierarchy of creation. 'What a piece of work is man! How noble in reason! how infinite in faculties! in form and moving, how express and admirable! in action how like an angel! in apprehension how like a god!' Hamlet was, of course, mad, and only a madman could say such things. One must admit that it is hard for the plain man to accept what the philosophers and men of science tell him is the truth. Hamlet's bright angel wears, in their picture of him, a very bedraggled appearance. He comes last instead of first, and his god-like apprehension is merely a curious sparkling deposit left by the tides of matter upon the shore of time, or a kind of pearl secreted by a wounded oyster. Too much chlorine, too much or too little sulphur make us or mar us. Carbon, hydrogen, oxygen, nitrogen, or their combinations under colloidal conditions—there you have the whole history, a complete account of mankind. In them are to be found the spirit of Plato and of Shakespere, the brain of Newton and Beethoven, the hopes and fears and affections, the saints and heroes, the wars and civilisations, the religions and sciences, the cathedrals and the poems and the pictures.

If this is what is meant by explanation or enlightenment offered by our times, the plain man may well exclaim, 'Heaven keep us in our wits. Perhaps we are as mad as Hamlet. His madness would not be noticed among us—we are as mad as he.' Nevertheless, towards some such conclusions, unless I am mistaken, the finger of modern knowledge seems to point. Much has been said in their support. You will not be out of the fashion if you adopt them. True it is that they have not been demonstrated. It is not what science has proved, but what she threatens to prove, that so alarms the friends of religion and of the soul. 'You cannot', it is one of Chatham's sayings, 'you cannot make war with a map.' It might with equal truth be said, 'You cannot refute a programme'. And this ambitious programme has a long journey before it. For myself I have not been able to persuade myself and have not been persuaded that this our age has found the philosopher's stone, that the sublime futility, the grand *reductio ad absurdum* it offers us is the final truth.

> Nay, come up hither. From this wave-washed mound,
>   Unto the farthest flood-brim look with me;
> Then reach on with thy thought till both be drowned :
>   Miles and miles distant though the last line be,
> And though thy soul sail leagues and leagues beyond,—
>   Still, leagues beyond those leagues there is more sea.

Were the soul of man easily alarmed, it would long ago, one thinks, have perished out of the earth   It has stood its ground against the giants and dragons, the material powers and terrors, amid which its lot is cast. It has survived the denunciations of prophets and the wrath of kings. You would not say that it was born in the purple, you would not say it has had an easy journey since the birth of time. But an enduring heart has been given by the gods to mortals. The human soul is inured to hardships. Its resilience is not spent, nor its natural strength abated.

It is a sword of Spain, the ice-brook's temper.

No stranger to bad news, it will not cower and shudder under the disdain or contempt of this or any future day. Our modern teachers appear, I sometimes feel, apprehensive lest man should prove a greater enigma than they can deal with, or indeed, perhaps, than they desire him to be. They have, in my judgment, good reasons for their misgivings. The truth about him may be very remote from their notions, may lie elsewhere than they would have us believe. Man may be more interesting and important than they suppose, possibly even a star of some magnitude in the celestial universe.

II

THE NEW THOUGHT

Idle Charon

The shores of Styx are lone for evermore,
 And not one shadowy form upon the steep
 Looms through the dusk, far as the eye can sweep,
To call the ferry over as of yore;
But tintless rushes all about the shore
 Have hemmed the old boat in, where, locked in sleep,
 Hoar-bearded Charon lies; while pale weeds creep
With tightening grasp all round the unused oar.

For in the world of Life strange rumours run
 That now the soul departs not with the breath,
But that the Body and the Soul are one;
 And in the loved one's mouth now, after death,
The widow puts no obol, nor the son,
 To pay the ferry in the world beneath.

Eugene Lee Hamilton

II

THE NEW THOUGHT

Before going forward let us look back. It almost seems, I have said, as if our earth had during the last fifty years passed through a zone of cosmic disturbance. A somewhat similar disturbance took place four centuries ago, of which the convulsion we have ourselves experienced may be regarded as a continuation, a second shock of the same earthquake, or a second rising of the tide, such as takes place at certain points on our southern coast, more especially marked during the season of 'Springs.' The sea rises upon the land, retires, and before ebbing rises once again.

Four centuries ago, at the Renaissance, a change swept over European thought, the first great lift of the flood, whose second rising our own times have witnessed. Out of the great deeps emerged powerful forces transforming and revitalising human life. As it were upon bridges of unparalleled discoveries and inventions associated with the names of men like Columbus, Copernicus, Galileo, our ancestors crossed from the medieval to the modern world. The dawn, of which signs had already appeared in the eastern sky, brightened into daylight, and a fresh enthusiasm for life took possession of the hearts of men. The Renaissance ushered in a new day, the birthday of the modern world. Europe stood 'on the top of golden hours' and human nature seemed born again.

The poet Keats, in one of his letters, uses an arresting phrase, in respect of sixteenth-century literature: he speaks of 'the indescribable gusto of the Elizabethan voice', and quotes the Shakesperian line,

Be stirring with the morrow, gentle Norfolk.

That indescribable gusto, detected by the poet's ear, that buoyancy of language reflects the spirit of the early Renaissance, the spirit that was abroad in Western Europe. Day had come again after the long medieval night. The sun had risen, the windows of the darkened house were thrown open, and emancipated human nature walked out into the broad, fragrant daylight of an April morning. This buoyancy and gusto meet you everywhere in the national achievements. You see it in the canvases of the Italian painters, you hear it in the drama of·Shakespere and his fellow playwrights; each nation, after the fashion of its peculiar genius, reflects the light from its own mirror.

To accomplish anything you need an interest, a motive, a centre for your thought. You need a star to steer by, a cause, a creed, an idea, a passionate attachment. Men have followed many guiding lights. They have been inspired by love of fame and love of country. They have pursued power, wealth, holiness. They have followed Christ, Mahomet, Napoleon. Something must beckon you or nothing is done, something about which you ask no questions. Thought needs a fulcrum for its lever, effort demands an incentive or an aim.

No one, I fancy, will deny that knowledge has been the aim of our day and generation, the pursuit of knowledge and the increase of knowledge. Never has it been sought with greater determination and perseverance, and never with greater success. We cannot sufficiently admire the scientific achievements of our time. Our admiration, though we are prone to overlook it, is an admiration for man and his native power, his audacity and fearlessness, his imagination and industry, his ingenuity and understanding. Yet how great is the irony of things. How often our efforts lead to what we least expect. These notable victories of the mind, from which so much was hoped, have had for result not so much increased happiness as disquiet, have made for dejection rather than rejoicing. We know more than ever was known, and are convinced that we know nothing of what we most wish to know. We distrust more utterly than has ever been mistrusted the very intellect which has achieved so many and so signal triumphs. While our control over nature's energies approaches the miraculous, anarchy reigns in the moral and aesthetic, as well as in the intellectual sphere. One opinion is as good as another opinion. God and the soul are set aside as outworn superstitions, and the denial of any future life rings the passing bell of Christianity. Even the believers in unlimited human progress, that child-like and charming nineteenth-century

34

creed, are beginning to have their doubts. Christianity, or what remains of it, has suffered a sea-change, and is fast melting, if it has not already wholly evaporated, into humanitarianism. What is now left of the old theology in the circles of the educated and intelligent? What do we now hear of the Fall of man, the plan of salvation, the sacrifice of Christ, the redemption of the world through the shedding of blood, of predestination, of the blessings in store for the believer, the torments that await the infidel? Who now believes, as did St. Augustine, in the damnation of unbaptised infants, or that a man's actions in time determine his destiny throughout eternity? The old order is dissolving before our eyes, and the times ahead do not promise to be very settled and comfortable. 'The sea of faith' was 'once at the full',

> and round earth's shore
> Lay like the folds of a bright girdle furl'd,
> But now I only hear
> Its melancholy, long, withdrawing roar,
> Retreating, to the breath
> Of the night-wind, down the vast edges drear
> And naked shingles of the world.

How is this situation to be accounted for? In respect of religion, we need not travel far to obtain the answer.

The decay of religious faith is due to the increase of our positive knowledge. It cannot be ascribed to any degeneration in human nature, or to any change in human hearts. Men's hearts are where they have always been, nor are they now more inclined than formerly to vice rather than virtue. But in respect of the world in which we live we are vastly better informed than our predecessors. The new wine has burst the old bottles, and we no longer ask 'What does God think of me?' but 'What do I think of God?' 'I desire', said St. Augustine, 'to know nothing but God and the soul. Did I say nothing else? Nothing whatsoever.' (*Deum et animam scire capio. Nihil ne plus? Nihil omnino.*) But if God and the soul are extinct conceptions, as extinct as the Ptolemaic astronomy, or Strabo's geography, if they have no more than an antiquarian interest, if by the words 'God' and 'Heaven' we but 'give to airy nothing a local habitation and a name', of what then are we to think? During the past century the rising tide of knowledge carried away all the old land-

35

marks, the guiding lights by which Christian Europe had steered its course, and the ship of religion is now labouring in a heavy sea.

Lord Melbourne thought it undesirable to mix up religion with private life. Few, I fancy, would agree with him. A religion which is to live, most would say, must be fitted into the whole system of the believer's thought, directing as well as inspiring his every decision, both public and private. It should provide him with a touchstone, a way of looking at nature, the world and himself, which harmonises his ideas and meets his daily requirements. The principles of a man's religion should be in the most intimate relation with his secular occupations and undertakings, and these principles so clearly defined as to assist and support all his judgments. A consummation devoutly to be wished, but no easy matter to-day.

The failure of science, as anyone can see, is its failure to minister to the needs of the soul. The soul lies outside its orbit, its purview, its range of interests. The failure of religion in our time lies, on the other hand, in its inability to meet the needs of the intellect, to answer the innumerable and pressing questions we daily ask and must ask ourselves. Poetry is in like case, it offers no assistance to the perplexed intelligence. But that assistance is not asked of poetry. No one goes to Chaucer or to Keats for moral directions. Men, however, ask much more of religion than of poetry. They may be mistaken in respect of its function in their lives, but they ask for its guidance in human affairs. And the genius even of Christianity, the genius even of that world-inspiring poem, fails to solve the intellectual perplexities, and often the moral perplexities by which they are beset amid the infinite complexity of the modern world. Can anyone tell us whether Christ would have approved of the pattern of our present civilisation at all, and if not, how are we to escape from it? Would He have approved of costly and magnificent churches, of gorgeous ritual and music, of the theatre and the picture house, of all the ordered scientific and social activities amid which we spend our days? Can anyone tell us unequivocally what would have been His attitude to our systems of education, our horse-racing, commerce and athletics, the possession of property, to wealth, the lending of money at interest, to birth control, to the sterilisation of criminals or the unfit, to our legal system, to capital punishment? Is it possible with the help of Christian principles to dis-

36

entangle the moral issues involved and to say what should be done in respect of these and a thousand other such things? Is it possible to apply Christian principles to taxation, to systems of government, to international finance, to the adjustment of tariffs and bank rates? What do they dictate to a great nation in respect of its dealings with others? Should it seek or sacrifice its advantages in trade, encourage the presence of foreign blood, the admixture of white and black, give or refuse its blessing upon mixed marriages? Should it abandon or maintain its advantages in geographical position, in wealth of coal and metals? Neither a man nor a nation can preserve its own gains and interests without loss to others. Should America or England dilute their currency or go off the gold standard when it suits them, irrespective of the effects upon their neighbours? These are matters of life and death to their populations. It is not war only which is a matter of life and death, as the simple suppose. Economic sanctions, of which we have heard so much, make war by starvation instead of bullets. Trade and commerce are matters of life and death to millions.

These and similar questions are not in our times to be evaded, and generalisations in the manner of the Beatitudes do not answer them. You are, moreover, not in a Christian world. Has Christianity any firm and workable proposals to make in dealing, let us say, with Japanese competition, or Russian state atheism and its propaganda, upon diplomatic and international exchanges with races which have no regard for its ethics or ideals? And if no clear direction in their difficulties is given by Christianity, is it any wonder men say it has shot its bolt, that it has ceased to be the pole-star, as its adherents hoped, by which the ship of humanity would for all time steer its course?

You will say Christianity was never meant by its Founder to solve our intellectual problems, but to be a refuge from the distresses to which mankind is exposed, and you are, no doubt, right. Yet when men are continually assailed by such problems in the struggle for existence, is it surprising that a religion which fails to answer their questions loses its hold upon them? The truth is that Christianity did not, as is commonly supposed, convert Europe. On the contrary, Europe transformed Christianity. It was an Eastern and ascetic creed, a creed of withdrawal from life rather than of participation in its fierce conflicts and competi-

37

tions, and was so understood in the early centuries. But the Western races were not prepared to abandon the world. Their energies were too great, the natural man in them unsubduable. So it came about that Christianity came to terms with the West, and the accommodation resulted in an ill-defined compromise. The world, indeed, is not our home, which is God, they said, but we are here by His will and inscrutable purpose. Let us meanwhile apply Christian principles to its amelioration. Thus it was that Europe translated Christianity into a world-reforming faith, which, losing its original character, and becoming entangled in the multifarious interests of mankind, evaporated into humanitarianism, and took upon itself an intellectual burden never contemplated by its Founder, a burden it was unfitted to bear. For the souls afraid, mortally afraid of life—and how many they be, and have reason to be—Christianity came with healing in its wings. But to the lovers of life and the world, fascinated by the wide range of its vital and vivid interests, its sunlit landscape, the brave show of its human figures and enterprises, Christianity had no clear message. 'One world at a time,' men said, 'and the present is the present.'

Take a single illustration. Let us ask, 'What has Christianity to say of love between the sexes?'—surely a subject of central importance. Apparently not a word, or a derogatory word. The Fathers have little pleasant to say on women or love-making. They commend and exalt celibacy. Chrysostom spoke of women as a 'desirable calamity', and we are all familiar with St. Paul's remarks on marriage. Yet here you have a subject which more than any other has occupied the attention of the poets and artists, indeed all mankind, a passion which is at the root of life itself, which exceeds all others in strength, of which, as Stendhal said, 'all the sincere manifestations have a character of beauty,' which has provided the kernel for all the great stories of the world, with which every literature teems, which gives rise to half, and more than half, of all the pains and pleasures of life, plays a leading part in every activity, creates family relationships, running through human existence like the veins through the body, omnipresent, entering into association with every side of our conduct and on every day we live, leading to crimes, treacheries, self-sacrifice, heroism, eternally occupying the thoughts of society, and present in all its conversations. Upon this transcendent theme with its endless ethical ramifications, a strange silence reigns in the Christian documents.

And there is a similar silence in respect of the animal world. Their status in God's creation is overlooked. They are not thought of as concerned in the Fall, as sinful, as in need of grace or redemption, or as having any share in a future life. Presumably in heaven we shall never meet with them, and some of us will miss our favourites, birds, or dogs or horses. If animals were not, like ourselves, sufferers, condemned like us to death, that silence might somehow be explained. But death, we are told, entered the world through sin, and though not partakers in sin they partake of death, its consequence. Nor does it appear that they have rights of any kind, nor we any duties in respect of them. We may, it seems, treat them according to our good pleasure.

It must, indeed, be allowed that for the most part the philosophers regard them with a like indifference. Kant could find no better reason for the kind treatment of animals than the fear that lack of sympathy with them might blunt our human sympathies. How much nobler were Plutarch's sentiments! See the admirable passage in his *Life of Marcus Cato*. The poets without exception stand by them.

> If aught of blameless life on earth may claim
> Life higher than death, though death's dark wave rise high,
> Such life as this among us never came,
>   To die.[1]

For a time, following upon the Renaissance, all went very well. So brightly shone the star of the new knowledge that an astonishing optimism prevailed. The thrill of the new discoveries and the mental activities they engendered roused expectation of noble days to come. Equipped with the new-found instruments men determined to build a stately fabric of enduring civilisation. Presently everything would be explained and the forces of nature mastered. Mankind was on the eve of surprising the last secrets of the universe. A new highway offered itself for the fulfilment of human aspirations. The world was rapidly advancing towards a state of greater prosperity and universal contentment. 'Hunger and thirst will be unknown,' cried Winwood Reade, exultingly, 'population will mightily increase, and the earth will be a garden.'

[1]A. C. Swinburne, *At a Dog's Grave*.

The dear child! So simple was the faith of the rationalist, as simple as that of the medieval Christian. As simple? No, much simpler. The early Christians had never been hypnotised by such nursery dreams. With far less knowledge, by comparison, indeed, with none, theirs was a far deeper comprehension of the malady that afflicts the human race, a far deeper insight into the true nature of existence. They perceived that from its ephemeral character alone life upon earth, however ameliorated, however adorned, was utterly insufficient to satisfy that incomprehensible entity, the human soul. By the side of the nineteenth-century rationalists the early Christians were in knowledge, indeed, children, yet in wisdom, in their intuitive understanding immeasurably superior. The early Christians had abandoned hope in the present dispensation, and turned their thoughts to another and a better world. We have abandoned hope of any other, and perforce must make the best of the present—no very agreeable prospect. The kind-hearted humanitarians of the nineteenth century decided to improve upon Christianity. The thought of Hell offended their susceptibilities. They closed it, and, to their surprise, the gates of Heaven closed also with a melancholy clang. The malignant countenance of Satan distressed them. They dispensed with him, and at the same time God took His departure. A vexatious result, but you cannot play fast and loose with logic. We shall never understand the Middle Ages until we realise how profoundly they strove to find a deeper meaning, a sacred significance in all things. 'They never forgot', as has been said, 'that all things would be absurd if their meaning were exhausted in their function and place in the phenomenal world, if by their essence they did not reach into a world beyond this.'

Medieval man was intensely conscious of the surrounding mystery, a consciousness overpowered in our time by the scientific spirit of curiosity. Everything, all that meets the eye in the external world, the whole of nature and of human life, seemed to him unintelligible, senseless and void unless it could be interpreted in some transcendental sense, unless it were informed by some deeper meaning than the bodily senses revealed. This is, of course, the essence of religion. If things can be interpreted without remainder in terms of material particles and forces, their mystery and meaning vanish, and with them go most human values, religion with the rest. The Middle Ages trusted the inward vision, which discerned behind nature a certain something more divine than nature, *in recessu divinius aliquid*.

Ours is by contrast an age of reason, which deals only, as is the ambition of modern physics, in 'observables', the positive knowledge of the senses. And with what astonishing success! Within fifty years, within the life of a single generation, thoughts never before harboured in a human brain have flooded in from every quarter of the heavens. A legion of enquirers, roused to feverish activity, hurried to amaze us. Geologists told us the story of the earth in the making in far distant aeons. They spoke with decision of events upon which no eye had ever rested. The spade, that commonplace, unromantic instrument, became an open-sesame, a magic power, placing upon the map of the past regions not less marvellous than those discovered by the galleys of Columbus, buried cities and civilisations older far than the pyramids or the Pharaohs, remains of prehistoric man, and skeletons of ungainly monsters which roamed the earth before a human foot had trod the stage. The arrival of man upon the scene became an affair of yesterday. The mathematicians began to calculate the starry distances in light years, and the new clocks, radium, thorium, uranium, imperturbable, unimpeachably accurate, ticking through the centuries, provide for us a cosmic calendar, which dates the laying of the earth's foundations. Pasteur revealed the undreamt of universe of micro-organisms, revolutionising the whole art of medicine. Three hundred million malaria parasites can exist in a single drop of water. Mendel, a simple parish priest, whose name does not even appear in a cyclopaedia of 1891, threw open the gates to the study of heredity, setting forth the laws which govern its mysterious configurations. We heard for the first time of the wonders of the blood. Did you know that every corpuscle it contains passes every minute through the heart, that after three or four weeks the red corpuscles pass through the veins into the spleen, and die there? It is their cemetery. Did you know there was such a thing as 'heavy water', and of various kinds, deadly to some forms of life, but in which certain bacteria flourish? Have you heard that the earth is enclosed in a ceiled vault, or several vaults, on whose outer side rages a tempest of cosmic rays? What marvels have we not seen with our own eyes, which have already ceased to be marvels. The conquest of the air by daring pilots, of the stratosphere, of the submarine depths. Musicians in Paris or Berlin sing and play to us in our own homes, and the 'I will' of a royal bride in Westminster Abbey is heard, at the moment it is uttered, round the circumference of the globe. Electricity, a power hardly known to exist a hundred years ago, save as the dreaded lightning, is already so tamed and harnessed as to be little more than a poor beast of burden, a domestic slave, that sweeps our rooms, runs our errands, and does the meanest chares.

If anyone pictures ideas as shadowy, innocent harmless things, mere *epiphenomena*, let him look around. All these perturbations are due to their disruptive power. These disturbances cannot be traced to the action of material forces, to earthquakes or the shifting of climatic zones. They are the result of thinking. It is thought which has turned the world upside down, shy, retiring, invisible, unobtrusive thought, that insubstantial, airy nothing. And of all its doings none is perhaps more far-reaching, more disruptive than its most recent. The mind, turning its remorseless searchlight upon the whole scene of existence, proceeded to a scrutiny, an inspection of itself.

The new psychology is a stripling, hardly of age, yet it has penetrated to a region, a basement below the level of conscious thought, a region which can never again, as it had previously been, be overlooked. This hidden portion of ourselves, as complete a secret from each of us as the emotions and motives of our neighbours, this irrational area is now known to be, if not, indeed, the whole of us, yet so large a part that we shrink back in alarm. The action behind the scenes of thought is now declared to be of greater importance than that enacted upon the intellectual and conscious stage. In the murky basement is to be found the entity, whatever it be, which determines our preferences, our likes and dislikes, and in large measure dictates our behaviour. Imagining ourselves reasoning beings, supposing ourselves to weigh this or that argument or consideration, in the mental balance, we are in reality, it seems, swayed by instincts and impulses of which we know nothing. We drag after us the whole history of our family and race, of our animal inheritance. Primitive impulses, loves, hates, fears, jealousies are the coiled springs that move us. The human puppets dance to ancestral tunes. The old simple account of a man's character as governed by his conscious thought, by the association of ideas, and a preference of pleasure over pain, that old simple story is clean gone. It has been superseded by a new conception of the conscious mind as the waving sunlit surface of a tropical forest, beneath which lie the unseen depths of twisted roots and tangled undergrowth. It is a haunted darkness. There dwells an obscure brood of obsessions, repressions, conflicts, phobias. Our flitting dreams, once a subject for idle gossip, we now read as indicative of impulses and tensions in this half-discovered country. The Tavistock clinic, founded in 1920, for the treatment of mental disorders, morbid fears and anxieties, social delinquencies, neurasthenia and similar maladies, has had, within a few years, astonishing success. It is estimated that from such afflictions there are in England alone three million sufferers, and that the cost to the country may be reckoned at forty millions annually. Pursue these enquiries, and the endless ramifications of sex energy, in regions seemingly remote from its influence, emerge to disconcert and humiliate us. To avert our eyes is in vain. It lurks, this ghost, this sheeted spectre, in every corridor; it participates in every human undertaking. Repressed or denied, it takes instant revenge, and gives rise to a legion of miseries and disorders, mental and physical. We can no longer refuse to recognise its pervading presence and ceaseless activities. Sex affairs, free-love, birth control, sterilisation, are in consequence the talk of debating societies, of salons and tea-tables, in a fashion that would have scandalised our parents.

Do not imagine that you have here mere superstition or charlatanism. 'This is the greatest error in the treatment of sickness,' wrote Plato, two thousand years ago, 'that there are physicians for the body and physicians for the soul, and yet the two are one and indivisible.' We are only in the vestibule of this enquiry, which will carry us far. The exploration of these uncharted depths, these psychic gulfs and currents, will occupy generations long after we are gone. The repercussions of the knowledge already gained of this underworld are only beginning to be felt in medicine. It will not end there; they will be felt much further afield, in our legal system, in our treatment of social offenders, in our estimates of human conduct. It has only lately dawned upon us that transgressors of the social code are as often sufferers as malefactors. How many twisted minds there are, how many

43

sick souls in the world, bitter, disappointed, irascible, nervously miserable, a scourge to themselves and their neighbours, to whom, not knowing what ails them, the struggle for life, the competitions, the anxieties are a horror which they can neither face nor avoid.

And when all this is realised, as clear as the sun at noonday, what changes in our notions of moral responsibility, in our ethical demands, in our religious views will necessarily follow? Had Dante known that disorders of the pituitary gland may lead to crime, that iodine supplied to the thyroid would transform a cretinous idiot into a healthy child, had he known that the genes in the chromosomes supplied by one or other parent gave an ineradicable bias to a child's nature and character, would he have assigned human creatures to heaven or hell for their behaviour in this life with the same solid and unhesitating conviction? Eternal damnation following upon deficiency in phosphorus or iodine, upon some hereditary twist!

How profoundly such knowledge as we have already gained must modify our views upon human life, how profoundly affect the foundations of religion and morals, and the whole structure of society! A revolution is at hand, or rather we are in the midst of it, beside which the revolutions of history, of wars and world-wide conflagrations will in times to come be seen as ephemeral incidents in the Odyssey of the human spirit. Has anyone yet studied the infective power of ideas, their modes of transmission or magnetic fields? Does anyone understand the psychology of religious revivals, of mass suggestion, of tidal waves of emotion? Yet these have sent armies of crusaders to Jerusalem, built and destroyed cities, made and unmade great kingdoms. We are still children, gazing through penny telescopes at the majestic heavens. Under the new lights, penetrating the interior of the mind, the whole history of religious experience will be rewritten, the mystic visions, the conversions. The biographies of remarkable men, of geniuses and leaders and saints, will be studied anew. The secret motives, the springs of action, will be laid bare, the part played in the great drama of the world by inspirations and oracular dreams, by prophets and visionaries.

In the light of this accumulated knowledge from a hundred regions the old view of the world has fallen into ruins. That old view had no eye for the picture, now drawn for us with such terrible distinctness, of a nature without interest in man, in whose heart or purpose he had no privileged place, since it possessed neither heart nor purpose; a picture of air, earth and sea spawning millions of living things, like a maniac spinning frantically a gigantic wheel, scattering sparks of momentary life, senselessly and for ever. There are not less than two million species of animals now existing, and if extinct species could be added the number would rise to I know not how many more. We are, it seems, merely creatures among innumerable other creatures, tribes beyond enumeration, from bacilli to elephants, inhabiting for a moment the wrinkled surface of a burnt-out star. Upon this orgy of mad fecundity the heavens, which no longer declare the glory of God but the curvature of space, look impassively down, fortunate in that they are insensitive and have no share in earth's misery. They look down upon the interminable procession of the living to join the countless hosts of the dead, forty millions of human beings laid yearly in their graves.

> To-day the Roman and his trouble
> Are ashes under Uricon.

Nature, we are told, had no more thought of us than of the sands upon the sea-shore, but turning in her eternal circles, age after age, produced all manner of combinations and complexities, from stars and suns to organic compounds and living creatures, a riot of things, no one of which had priority in her mind, for mind she had none, only the power of producing it, a singular paradox. We are parts of the pattern, if pattern it can be called, animals like other animals, and condemned like them to perish, no more likely to live again than the shark or the cobra, animals shorter lived than some, more brutal than many, sustaining our existence for the most part on the flesh of others, neither a pleasant nor a poetic subject for meditation.

Few have the courage to proclaim the conclusions they have reached. They bear their knowledge with 'quiet desperation', or with the reflection that the burden will presently fall from their shoulders.

> If here to-day the cloud of thunder lours,
>   To-morrow it will hie on far behests;
> The flesh will grieve on other bones than ours
>   Soon, and the soul will mourn in other breasts.

45

'Man is the product of causes', asserts Lord Russell, 'which had no prevision of the end they were achieving; his origin, his growth, his hopes and fears, his loves and beliefs are but the outcome of accidental collocations of atoms.' Wherever he got his information, he seems to know much more about it than I do, or than any other man has ever known. To abandon religion for science is merely to fly from one region of faith to another, from one field of ignorance and conjecture to another. None the less many share his opinion. Unemotional, passionless necessity, nature, has given birth to passionate emotional man. All that we love, prize, admire is nothing. The soulless and inanimate has produced the living and loving soul. This unfeeling machine has somehow, we are assured, brought into existence the sensitive, trembling creature whose whole existence swings between misery and happiness, desiring one, hating the other. Man desires a parent but is parentless, desires God and is God-forsaken. So there is nothing for it but 'to gird on for fighting the sword that will not save', to substitute morality, its commands and restrictions, for the hopes and consolations of religion, to make the best of a bad business, to say 'Let us be humanitarians, let us hurt each other as little as possible, for to-morrow we die'.

And yet what a polished structure is this built for us by science, how admirably designed, how perfectly proportioned, the pride of its builders, and of all mankind. How admirable—and terrible. The worst is that the world, life, all things should be wholly senseless, without meaning, and the worst has happened. For if you ask, 'What is this power everywhere at work throughout the universe doing, this stupendous energy?' the answer is, 'It is doing nothing; it is a lunatic energy, making and breaking, building up and knocking down, endlessly and aimlessly.' What wonder, if this be all of which it is capable, we judge it a crazy performance, and snap our fingers at it? The universe has, by modern thought, been weighed in the balances and found wanting. Modern thought declares that we are but parts of a stupendous mechanism, a theatre of marionettes, in which all men speak their previously allotted parts, that every movement of our bodies and our minds is as strictly controlled as the wheeling of the planets and the swinging of the tides; that every hope springing up in the breast, every tear that falls from the eye, is a result not less rigidly determined than the tick of the

46

clock, or the movement of its hands upon the dial. We puppets within the gigantic grasp of necessity emit sighs like the doll pressed by the fingers of the child, the beats of our hearts were numbered from the beginning, and the pulses of our emotions already counted a million million years ago.

As regards ourselves, then, the teaching of modern knowledge is easily summarised. It proclaims our complete unimportance. And strangely enough the individual person, from his own point of view the most valuable of nature's achievements, has the shortest life. The law appears to be—the more worthless the object the more enduring, the more precious the more ephemeral. The stone outlives the flower, the oak of the forest the man. And the mind which observes and studies all the world contains, which makes the discoveries, which penetrates to nature's secret places, is the most transient entity in the whirling flux of things. It vanishes while the senseless objects of its study endure. The pavement on which we walk has a longer life than we, the buildings outlast their architects, the artist's brush the genius who used it. We perform miracles, but no room is left for the miracle worker. 'For myself everything, for the universe nothing.' Streamers of idly swaying sea-weed in the drift of its ocean tides, that is what we are, or the breathing of a melancholy tune, its notes in a falling fountain.

There is something peculiar in this self-depreciation, in the unanimity with which science and philosophy in our time combine to humiliate us. There is here, one thinks, more than is easily accounted for by the evidence for the thesis. We must remind ourselves that the concentration of modern enquiry into the nature of physical things inevitably exalts their interest and importance. 'A man may dwell so long upon a thought', said Halifax, 'that it may take him prisoner.' Do not forget that this priority is of our conferring, that it is we ourselves who have thus placed things upon the throne, we who have clothed the material world in the imperial purple of its present rank and dignity. The material universe, such is the modish view, has given rise to an infinitude of things, to all of which it is totally and equally indifferent, stars and systems, men and animals, morals, religions, philosophies, hopes, aspirations, ideals, aims, purposes, joys, sorrows, affections. The universe produces all these, and yet has no thought of any kind, no will, intention, design or interest.

47

It has no nobility in its own eyes, this wonder-working nature, no opinion of itself at all. It produces everything in utter absence of mind, and is wholly unaware that it has in fact produced anything. It does not even attain the dignity of feeble-mindedness. It is deaf, dumb, inane. Nor does it care whether it exists or ceases to exist. It is certainly remarkable, this cosmos, as described by modern science. Its indifference to itself and all its works and ways is amazing.

Or, shall we say that, perceiving—if nature may be supposed capable of perception—after the lapse of half an eternity, the futility of proceedings, however grandiose, without an audience, she decided to put some kind of sense into the proceedings? Man is a brilliant—or unfortunate—afterthought! Nature built the theatre and the stage for no particular purpose, and for inconceivable ages they were empty and worthless. Then came an inspiration—'A play's the thing!' In the opinion of some members of the cast a pretty dismal performance.

Be that as it may, in and for itself nature is manifestly nothing. Only in our eyes has it any significance. For us only does it contain any value; other valuators, apparently, there are none. The singularity lies here that man, the most trifling and ephemeral being, small dust in the scale, does what nature herself cannot do. He thinks. He admires, examines, reflects, and has even the audacity to criticise and disapprove. Nature, it seems, neither thinks nor aspires. Her activities are confined to everlasting, idiotic gyrations. Eliminate human history, the arts, sciences, civilisations, and what have you left? Remove man from the scene, and the vast machinery has no further point, the pageant is without spectators, and touches the zenith of magnificent absurdity. Man perishes while the ridiculous performance continues. It is exceedingly curious.

Agree or disagree as we may with these opinions, as King Canute could not by command restrain the rising sea, so no man can hold back the tide of knowledge. We must endure our destiny and accommodate our minds as best we can to a scale of things never dreamt of by our ancestors. If we desire to be, in Plato's phrase, 'spectators of all time and all being,' if we are to take measurements of the universe, we must endeavour to think in cosmic distances, in centuries and millenniums rather than in hours and months. Time was when our earth *was not*, though it may be three thousand million years of age. We must think of it not merely as it is to-day, but as it was in past ages, as it will be in ages to come. You cannot measure the universe with a yard of tape. Men desire things to remain as they know them, to be familiar and friendly. Nature will not have it so. She is implacable and restless, and countenances no calm, no stagnation throughout her whole vast estate. If we are to understand matters aright we must think in terms of convulsions which have made oceans where there were continents, and Himalayan ranges where there were seas, in terms of cyclical changes, of buried cities and forgotten civilisations, of races and peoples as they were in the Stone and Bronze Ages, yes, and far earlier. To get the scale of cosmic things we must perceive nature for what she is, as everlastingly and furiously dynamic, permitting nothing throughout her whole circumference to be at rest, not for so much as a moment.

Fate is a sea without shore, and the soul is a rock that abides,
But her ears are vexed with the roar, and her face with the foam of
the tides.

That all these upheavals and perturbations, of which science tells us, belong to the past and are at an end, or that they will be limited to the physical world, and need not be expected in human history, that the era of storms and revolutions is over, that nature and society have entered upon a static stage, that the peoples of to-day will remain the peoples of to-morrow, each inhabiting in peace its present territory, that we are about to leave the ocean for quiet river navigation, that our notions of the best life will remain those of all ages to come, is, I confess, a picture that refuses to form itself before my mind. 'A high-flown journalist named Rousseau', said Friedell, 'writes a couple of bizarre pamphlets, and for six years a highly gifted people tears itself to pieces. A stay-at-home scholar, named Marx, indifferent to and ignored by society, writes a few fat volumes of unintelligible philosophy, and a gigantic empire alters its whole condition of life from the base upward.' The disturbances of which I have spoken, in our outlook upon nature and human nature, have been matched by disturbances equally violent in the political arena. We have seen kingdoms 'moulting, sick, in the dreadful wind of change', three great empires dismembered and destroyed.

We have seen the collapse of ancient monarchies, the flight of kings. New Caesars have arisen. Democracy, everywhere praised in Europe fifty years ago, appears everywhere on the way to be abandoned. Parliamentary institutions in which we placed our trust seem to have no very brilliant future before them. Decaying in the West, by some strange paradox they raise their banner in the East; India places its hopes in the devices Europe has surrendered.

I am not prepared to believe that nature will never produce another Napoleon, who, like a whirlwind, indifferent to all moral judgments, will scatter peoples like chaff, or a Lenin, who will deal with our ethical codes as with the scythe of a reaper. In the heyday of the Roman empire its civilisation seemed founded upon a rock. It fell, and for five centuries Europe weltered in a sea of violence.

It may be that I am wrong. It may be that the world is on the way to become what it has never been, a home of rest for the gentle and the timid, a sequestered garden for those who hate the turmoil of the sea. I can well understand the religious fear, the humanitarian horror of its sullen skies, its mounting waves, and devouring storms, the disrelish for battle, murder and sudden death, the war in nature and the war in man. Life, as Christianity has always taught, as all clear-eyed observers have known, is a perilous adventure, and a perilous adventure for men and nations it will, I fear and believe, remain.

III

THE INSTRUMENT

She is a substance, and a reall thing,
    Which hath it selfe an actuall working might;
    Which neither from the Senses' power doth spring,
    Nor from the bodie's humors, tempred right.

For when she sorts things *present* with things *past*,
    And thereby things to *come* doth oft foresee;
    When she doth *doubt* at first, and *chuse* at last,
    These acts her owne, without her body bee.

When in th' effects she doth the causes know,
    And seeing the stream, thinks wher the spring doth rise;
    And seeing the branch, conceives the root below;
    These things she views without the bodie's eyes.

When she, without a *Pegasus*, doth flie
    Swifter then lightning's fire from *East* to *West*,
    About the *Center* and above the *skie*,
    She travels then, although the body rest.

When all her works she formeth first within,
    Proportions them, and sees their perfect end,
    Ere she in act does anie part begin;
    What instruments doth then the body lend?

When without hands she doth thus *castles* build,
    Sees without eyes, and without feet doth runne;
    When she digests the world, yet is not fil'd:
    By her owne power these miracles are done.

When she defines, argues, divides, compounds,
    Considers *vertue, vice*, and *generall things*,
    And marrying divers principles and grounds,
    Out of their match a true conclusion brings.

These actions in her closet all alone,
    (Retir'd within herselfe) she doth fulfill;
    Use of her bodie's organs she hath none,
    When she doth use the powers of Wit and Will.

For though our eyes can nought but colours see,
    Yet colours give them not their powre of sight;
    So, though these fruits of *Sense* her objects bee,
    Yet she discernes them by her proper light.

Then is the *Soule* a nature, which containes
    The powre of *Sense*, within a greater power
    Which doth imploy and use the *Senses*' paines,
    But sits and rules within her private bower.

If she were but the bodie's accident,
    And her sole *being* did in it subsist;
    As *white in snow*, she might her selfe absent,
    And in the bodie's substance not be mist.

But *it* on *her*, not *shee* on *it* depends;
    For *shee* the body doth sustaine and cherish;
    Such secret powers of life to it she lends,
    That when they faile, then doth the body perish.

Since then the *Soule works by her selfe alone,*
    Springs not from Sense, nor humors, well agreeing;
    Her nature is peculiar, and her owne;
    She is a *substance,* and a *perfect being.*

                                    Sir J. Davies

III

THE INSTRUMENT

The capacity of the vessel in which he proposes to embark should be the mariner's first consideration. Is it equal to the proposed voyage, of power likely to ensure success? One cannot hope to round Cape Horn in a skiff. Modern man requires as a basis for his life and activities some account of himself and his place in the scheme of things. He has intelligence, can it supply his needs? Our philosopher, Locke, with the sound sense characteristic of him, declared a survey of our own understanding, its origin, nature and extent, a necessary preliminary to any philosophical enquiry. That is to say, the human mind should first of all examine and estimate its own capacities. 'There is nothing either good or bad,' we read in Shakespere, 'but thinking makes it so.' It would appear to be the truth. There is nothing either good or bad, right or wrong, beautiful or ugly, save as thinking declares it to be. If then thought occupies so high a seat, wields a magisterial authority from which there is no appeal, must we not assume it equal to all undertakings, competent to determine all cases and terminate all disputes?

Certainly man's understanding is a noble faculty, of quality and fabric more divine that any other of nature's works. Mind is admittedly her greatest triumph, and much eloquence has been expended in the praise of this 'candle of the Lord'. 'All our dignity consists in thought', said Pascal. 'On earth there is nothing great but man, in man there is nothing great but mind,' wrote Sir William Hamilton. Epictetus went even further, so far as to describe reason as 'a fragment of God' (ἀπόσπασμα τοῦ θεοῦ). The higher the estimate our own age makes of man's mental powers the better, for it has entrusted everything without exception to their charge. It points out that truths obtained by revelation cannot be subjected to examination, and have no cogency, therefore, for any save the illuminated.

Yet when one looks back into the historical past, or even

53

around in the present, one wonders whether such praise is not overdone, a trifle excessive, whether in fact men can be said to think at all. We talk of reason, our rationalistic societies lay great store by it, but when did reason ever control human affairs, or does it now control them? As if arguments had ever prevailed when the emotions were deeply stirred, as if logic had been the guiding light of mankind. Revolutions which begin in the name of reason commonly end in wholesale slaughter. Men become weary of argument with the obtuse people who oppose them, and take to a quicker method of persuasion, throat-cutting. 'A whiff of grape-shot' is still the most cogent logic. William O'Brien, the Irish patriot, habitually divided his own countrymen into two classes—'loyal comrades' and 'loathsome ruffians'. These statements are as clear, definite and intelligible as you could wish. This is no doubt thinking of a kind. How shall we class it? Mr. de Valera remarked not long ago in the Dail (1934), 'Our attitude is that this money is not due. We are prepared to talk about it, we are prepared to send it to arbitration if necessary, but we are not going to pay it.' He knew his mind, but was he thinking?

Thought of a kind goes on all about us in the world, yet who believes, for example, that where there is universal suffrage there is universal intelligence, that where there is education there is good sense, that where there is representative government there is necessarily also justice? How great was James Mill's confidence in this *lumen naturale*, this unfailing lamp. 'Every man possessed of reason', he wrote, 'is accustomed to weigh evidence, and to be guided and determined by its predominance. When various conclusions are, with their evidence, presented with equal care and skill, though some few may be misguided, there is a moral certainty that the greatest number will judge aright.' He brings good news, but can we trust our eyesight when we read such deliverances? In what far distant planet had this philosopher spent his life? Some few, he thinks, may occasionally be misguided. I hasten to agree with him. I will even go further, and say that there have been some eminent thinkers who have troubled the waters of thought only to muddy them. Reason is an inexpugnable prejudice of the mind. Yes, but was Mahomet, let us say, rational, or Luther or Robespierre? They were leaders of human thought. Is Mustapha Kemal or Herr Hitler

54

rational, or the present regime in Russia? Opinions seem to differ. What bubbles we blow and call it thought! Human thinking, high and low, is worm-eaten with prejudices and fallacies.

Excursions into human history give us less encouragement than Mill. They show too convincingly for our comfort that even among civilised races, and the educated among those races, the power to weigh evidence, to judge of probabilities, to estimate character, to distinguish between sense and fustian, to discern quality in a picture, a poem, a statue, to discriminate between plausible and demonstrative statements, the relevant and irrelevant in discourse, to perceive the drift of an argument, to appreciate the difference between soap-box oratory and that of Demosthenes or Burke—that these powers are not very widely distributed. Speaking out of his wide public experience, Charles James Fox declared that the same reason dished out in ten different forms was as effective in debate as ten different reasons. 'The inconsistency of acting on two opposite principles',—Sir James Frazer is the authority I quote—'however it may vex the soul of the philosopher, rarely troubles the common man; indeed he is seldom even aware of it.' And he cites the following from a correspondent of *The Times*, who had lived long in the East and knew it well: 'The Oriental mind is free from the trammels of logic. It is a literal fact that the Oriental mind can accept and believe two opposite things at the same time. We find fully qualified and even learned Indian doctors practising Greek medicine, as well as English medicine, and enforcing sanitary restrictions to which their own houses and families are entirely strangers. We find astronomers who can predict eclipses, and yet who believe that eclipses are caused by a dragon swallowing the sun. We find holy men who are credited with miraculous powers, and with close communion with the Deity, who live in drunkenness and immorality, and who are capable of elaborate frauds on others. To the Oriental mind a thing must be incredible to command a ready belief.'

One sometimes thinks the less the majority of people reason for themselves the better.. 'What would become of the world', asks Burke, 'if the practice of all moral duties and the foundations of society rested upon having their reasons made clear to every individual?' Yes, indeed, what would become of it? 'When the people undertake to reason,' as Voltaire said, 'all is lost.'

55

Reason is to be our guide, say the rationalists. Have they ever told us 'whose reason'? Let them devote their days and nights to that interesting question. Possibly they take Goethe's view, that it does not reside in the common herd, but must always remain the possession of a few talented individuals. Let us go in search, then, of a subject upon which the high-stepping minds, the least clouded and most elevated, have spoken with unhesitating and harmonious voice. Pleasure, said Epictetus, is the chief good. It is the chiefest of evils, said Antisthenes. Men, declared Rousseau, are naturally good; they are naturally bad, said Machiavelli. It is on the same evidence that these distinguished people contradict each other. Virtue, proclaimed the Stoics, is sufficient for happiness. Without external goods it is not sufficient, said Aristotle. Virtue once achieved cannot be lost, say some; it can be lost, say others. Pity is a virtue, some thinkers have proclaimed: others that it is not a virtue. The world, many noble souls have taught, is a divine creation. It arose accidentally, declare other philosophers. The debate continues. Your kind, benevolent hearts propose to build upon earth a great temple of peace and concord. Show me where to lay the first stone, and I will build you one.

But perhaps it may be said, all this may be true, but how different if you embark upon a study of science. There you leave dubiety behind you. There you have something exact and positive, and ascertained beyond doubt. May I ask, 'Do you mean last century's science or this century's?' It is best to forget what science said yesterday if you are to believe what she says to-day. Science sheds its last year's conclusions as a snake its skin, or a crab its shell. Certainly if you confine your interest to practical matters, you may accumulate much useful, indeed invaluable information, as was done by the human race before the word science was invented. Study nature and you discover that air contains oxygen, that the magnetic needle points to the North. And if you enquire further you can add indefinitely to your store of such information, construct marvellous machinery, assuage many of your pains, work ten thousand wonders by your insight into nature's habits. But in respect of what we most wish to know, how far has science gone? To the question, 'What is philosophy?' Plotinus answers τὸ τιμιώτατον, 'what matters most.' There you have it. Has science anything to say on what matters most? Any information on the beginning or end of things? None. Has it anything convincing to tell us on the relations of the mind to the body? Nothing. About the destiny of the human race? About ethics or conduct? About systems of government? About international relations? Not a word. Anything solid and satisfactory about the human will, about love and hate, about justice and liberty? The oracle is surprisingly silent. Are these matters beneath her notice?

The appeal is always to reason, and to this court we must take all our questions and differences of opinion. And yet as Mons. Jaloux has said, 'It is in the name of Reason that St. Thomas and the disciples of the *Summa* accept the truth of the Church's teaching, and it is in the name of Reason that many refuse to believe in God. I think that the most reasonable thing is to avoid having too much confidence in Reason. Sometimes it seems to me the most capricious and elastic of all the forms of the imagination.'[1]

If the beginning and end of things, if speculations about God are too high for our intelligence, let us come nearer home. Can reason tell us anything about space, time, motion, energy, these familiar acquaintances, or the equally familiar remembering, feeling, thinking, with which we are on the easiest and the best of terms in everyday life? Can it tell us in any particular, any single particular, how we are what we are? I have not found it so. Does it *know* anything whatsoever? Has it discovered whether ours is the only inhabited star, whether there are other beings, like or unlike ourselves, in the universe? It appears to be very poorly endowed, this celebrated reason. Is it conceivable, can we credit it, that this majestic faculty may be at the mercy of so commonplace, so plebeian an assistant as information?

To ask reason to perform miracles for us is, perhaps, a little unfair. Let us set it simpler tasks. Let reason instruct us how to go about the writing of *Hamlet*, or teach us to paint like Velasquez, or carve the frieze of the Parthenon, or compose the Jupiter symphony. Its powers or its principles of knowledge do not extend even so far as these arts. I am not sure that I would intrust reason with the arrangement of a bowl of flowers. In respect of such things 'the sane man is nowhere at all compared with the madman'. Who says so? Plato, than whom no more resolute and uncompromising advocate of reason ever trod the earth.

[1] Quoted by Havelock Ellis in *Views and Reviews*, p. 155.

Possibly you are among those who distinguish between what men say and what things say, between knowledge and reasoning upon knowledge. Knowledge, you hold, comes to us through observation and speaks for itself. If you mean that an ounce of experience is worth a hundred tons of speculation, I agree with you. The sun shines and I am warmed. Water quenches thirst, and when thirsty I drink it—or something more palatable. The sharper the knife the better it cuts. If you assert that you cannot add to the strength of perception by arguments, you are right. I excuse anyone from proving to me the existence of rivers and mountains, men and cities. I have seen them. No further evidence on their behalf will deepen my conviction that they exist. It is already fixed and profound. Nor will any arguments induce me to doubt their existence. I perceive, I see and believe. But what is this seeing, this perception of which we hear so much? How far does it carry you below the surface, and into the true nature of things? You suppose that knowledge arises from the simple process of opening your eyes and keeping them open, that it filters in without any further activity on your part. It is given you, and there it is; its acquisition a passive process, exclusively an affair of sensation. Arguments, you think, may be met by opposing arguments, but there is a region where argument is silenced and ceases, the region of pure perception.

And how far then does perception take you? If anyone asks, 'How have you reached your conclusions about nature?—how has science arrived at her results?' you must not say 'by perception'. Dismiss such thoughts. We do not perceive the air around us, nor the growth of trees and animals, nor the relations existing between things. We cannot see the actual link between cause and effect anywhere, nor the vibrations which give light and heat, nor the electrons of which we are told matter consists, nor the genes out of which our bodies develop. Our perceptions give us none of this information. An innumerable series of judgments and concepts is involved in the conclusions you have reached. We belong to a world which requires elaborate interpretation.

Enquire of the philosophers, and they will tell you that this matter of perception is still more, indeed desperately complicated. They may even assure you that there is no such thing as pure perception, that it has no story of its own to tell, that it is a part, and a part only, of that active and energetic faculty we call thought, and that it involves memory and anticipation, fore-thought and afterthought. You place a rose before a mirror. The mirror reflects the rose, but has no knowledge of it, is not even aware of it. Well, the eye has no more knowledge, no more awareness, no more consciousness of the rose than has the mirror. In a word, to separate the seen from the seer is allowed to be finally and utterly impossible. We are, as Niels Bohr expressed it, 'both spectators and actors in the great drama of existence.' For we must not think of thought as passive, as arising out of perceptions, as steam rises from heated water, but as an activity, a doing, a going out towards, as grasping and mani-pulating the data of sense. It is this activity, or energy which is at once the characteristic of mind and its chief mystery. The senses, then, do not give us knowledge. An active, inner prin-ciple, wholly independent of the senses is essential to the process of obtaining it.

If you have not looked into this delicate affair of the relations between the mind and the external world, let me refer you to Professor Broad of Cambridge. There are exactly seventeen doctrines of these relations. You would not expect me to dis-pose of these seventeen doctrines with a wave of the hand. It will be wiser with the time at our disposal to look them resolutely in the face, and pass by on the other side. We may agree, it is on all hands agreed, that without knowledge, without informa-tion we are at a standstill. Without them reason is powerless, a pincer with one claw only. The strongest-winged bird cannot fly in a vacuum. The mill of reason must have grist. And in the attempt to understand nature and ourselves mere thinking sup-plies no grist. This grist we call experience. That heavy sub-stances fall to the ground more rapidly than light substances was believed by Aristotle. Logic told him so. How very natural and sensible a belief. But he was wrong. Galileo discovered the truth by experiments from the leaning tower of Pisa. A cer-tain King of Siam declared the Dutch ambassador mad when he asserted that in his own country during winter the water became so hard that men could walk upon it. The King was not pre-pared to believe so monstrous a falsehood. He, too, was mis-taken. Without experience logic wanders in the void.

Whatever else it may be, thought is at least an adjustment to its surroundings. A living organism cannot support itself by feeding upon itself, nor can thought exclusively feed upon itself. The mind, in Bacon's words; 'works upon stuff'. And in the end it turns out that science is nothing more than glorified common sense. It takes things as you and I take them, at their face values. It builds, as you and I build, upon the stuff of experience. And its method, the method of trial and error, is the time-honoured method by which mankind has always threaded its way through a puzzling world. Nature has curious devices, eccentric habits, and they have to be discovered. You cannot sit down in a dark room and reason out the habits of an electron. Nature must tell you its habits. Science is like a man who knows nothing of the machinery of a motor car save the effect of moving this or that lever. It is a study of surfaces, and can predict, as he can, the probable sequence of events from the observation of previous sequences. For the rest, to be exact, it knows precisely nothing. Science walks past with its head in the air if you ask it for its theory of knowledge. If you know of any work in which the scientific theory of knowledge is set forth, I should be extremely glad to hear of it. Science assumes, exactly as the soldier, the sailor or the busman assumes, the great unknowables beneath the surface of observed phenomena, space and time, motion and life and thought. And thus, though most men are unaware of the fact, it has nothing to say, or should have nothing to say, when the great fundamental issues, which involve all these, and much more, are in debate.

Look a little further into this very singular activity, this process of thinking. Hume, one of the clearest minds that ever pondered the mysteries, regarded belief, conviction, as a kind of firm, solid 'feeling'. Feeling is a very unwelcome visitor in rationalistic circles. 'The kernel of the scientific outlook', wrote Lord Russell, 'is the refusal to regard our desires, tastes and interests as affording a key to the understanding of the world.' This is the superb gesture with which we are familiar. Mention your feelings to those men of iron, our scientific friends, and you will be met with a cold stare and the acid enquiry, 'My dear sir, what have your feelings to do with the matter?'

Let us have, then, the true account of the activity we call 'thought' which makes it by contrast so trustworthy. It appears to have a local habitation. It resides, we are given to understand, or arises somewhere in the skull, and consists of or emerges

60

from a complicated series of neural changes, set in motion by various forms of stimulus from the outside world. It is finally and wholly reducible to the movements of material particles, and may be described, without any irreverence, as a kind of buzzing, which accompanies the movements, or a kind of noiseless activity to which the machinery gives rise; or, if you like, a sort of ghostly light which hovers over that internal motion. If thinking be the result of a physical process, it must be itself a physical process, and cannot give itself airs, or swagger it on some upper angelic plane.

How then can we suppose our thinking an infallible organ for the discovery of truth? In proportion as you lower the status of mind, the greater, one must conclude, should be your hesitation in accepting its deliverances. Come to any decision in the matter you please. Science has most certainly done nothing to strengthen the foundations of thought, the foundations upon which its stately fabric has been erected. It has, for example, demonstrated, if it has demonstrated anything, that we are the transient inhabitants of a microscopic speck of astral dust, in body and in mind evanescent electro-magnetic phenomena in a universe of formidable proportions, that we are the kinsfolk of the ape and the lizard, descendants of the lowliest organisms, and so has diminished our place and necessarily also the place of mind, in the scale of things almost to a vanishing point. How then can we regard our thoughts as of any validity or consequence whatever? Why should I waste my time listening to your arguments, if you yourself declare them tainted at the source?

That very honest and sagacious person, Darwin, caught sight of one aspect of this difficulty. 'But then', he wrote, 'the horrid doubt always arises whether the convictions of a man's mind, which has developed from the mind of the lower animals, are of any value, or at all trustworthy? Would anyone trust the convictions of a monkey's mind?' It is an awkward question, so awkward as to be generally avoided. I have never seen it discussed in the scientific journals. Who of us is prepared to take seriously the reflections of a dromedary or a baboon on the nature and constitution of the world? Why, then, take our own seriously? At what date, or during what century of human evolution, did our meditations become respectable and trustworthy? Was it yesterday or the day before? Monarchs with dubious titles to their crowns dislike enquiries into their claims. We need not ask, therefore, why the particular pattern of atoms called the brain has formed so high an opinion of itself, so admires itself and trusts itself. We may note merely that some philosophers, having done their best to cut off the branch upon which they are sitting, continue with superb confidence to sit upon it.

Suppose we put this question to our scientific friends—If the structure of the universe be reasonable or rational, how did this rationality enter into the world of particles in motion? If not reasonable or rational, how can you penetrate its structure, or account for its performances, by reason? Or again, if the world we know arose from a series of accidents, reason, you will allow, is itself an accident. Science proceeds on the assumption that the world is intelligible. If it be unintelligible or senseless, science falls into a heap of ruins. How charmingly simple to employ one form of motion in the skull to explain other forms of motion outside the skull, or one accident to explain other accidents.

Our troubles are not yet ended. Our philosophers seem unable to agree upon a cardinal point—What is, or what is not, to be regarded as rational? In what does rationality consist? What precisely is the satisfaction it affords? Let us suppose the whole system of things were discovered to be through and through intelligible, as a machine is intelligible, but at the same time satanically cruel, a devilish design: should we sleep in peace, and call it reasonable? 'I could not rest', said Mr. Bradley, the author of *Appearance and Reality*, 'in a truth if I were compelled to regard it as hateful.' This appears to be an admission of the utmost importance. Yet the metallic voice of science assures us that our desires are irrelevant, and we must therefore suppose that it would accept tranquilly a diabolical universe. Yet for some of us a diabolical world would remain an unintelligible world, wholly irrational.

Consider now another peculiarity, a malady, it should perhaps be called, of the human mind, from which it is a chronic sufferer. Every man fancies that what he now thinks he will continue to think. There is an air of finality about our present opinions. They seem secure and inevitable. And this in face of the most obvious and overwhelming evidence. For it will be universally admitted that knowledge is progressive, that we know to-day what was unknown yesterday. We are well aware, also, that this knowledge could not have been foreseen, or so much as guessed at in earlier times, like the discoveries of Clerk Maxwell and Faraday in electro-magnetics, or of Pasteur in the region of micro-organisms. We are aware that these discoveries have within a single generation profoundly affected our conceptions and outlook upon nature, and that nothing could be less probable than that they are the last or final discoveries. How slow, then, should we be to build upon them any positive creed. That similar revolutions of thought will never again take place, no man of sense will believe. Nevertheless, how hard it is to convince ourselves that we are not the sons of the morning, that the clue to the labyrinth may not after all be in our hands.

Men, we must bear in mind, have not always argued as they now argue. They have in some ages taken things for granted, as clear and obvious, that are now dismissed as nonsense, and attached importance to ideas or conceptions to which to-day no consideration is given. The mind has its seasonal prejudices. Of these inborn prejudices of the mind, difficult to dislodge, many examples might be given. For long it was thought self-evident that the heavenly bodies must move in circles, simply because the circle was looked upon as the perfect curve. Kepler proved that the planets moved round the sun in ellipses, an idea men of science found at first most painful, extremely disagreeable and difficult to entertain. Or take the idea of action at a distance, which Newton found so repugnant, indeed quite intolerable. In this repugnance we have the purest prejudice, unadulterated dogma, of which not a particle of proof has ever been given, a dogma to which no one in his senses would commit himself to-day. No one nowadays talks about the 'self-evident'; the 'self-evident' is under the gravest suspicion. We take it with a handful of salt. Knowing all this, knowing that opinion is always on the move, we cling none the less tenaciously to our present notions. And society is so sure of itself that it is deeply engaged in the effort to instruct the rising generation in the only true and proper way of seeing things—its own.

Does our way of looking at things, of seeing and thinking them, carry with it any guarantee of arriving at truth? In Professor Bergson's view the human intellect is an instrument created by nature for action, to see things in such a way as to work upon

63

them, and no doubt admirably adapted to serve our practical needs. Its application, however, beyond this field leads, he thinks, to a distortion of the object under examination. The comprehension of life, of its living flow is beyond conceptual thought, which, in the very effort to comprehend, arrests, divides and falsifies it. Life can be understood only by living. To understand any living thing you must, so to say, creep within, and feel the beating of its heart. Every creature knows at least enough about the world to support its own existence there. The intellect seems to stand in its own light, reducing all it contemplates to the shadowiness of its self-chosen concepts, and by its own confession we can know nothing more than these, its peculiar creation. Life lies too deep to be penetrated by them. It is an island fortress. You cannot march into it on your two feet of logic and mathematics. The Euclidean understanding, William James also believed, makes human experience not more but less intelligible. We are very easily misled. It is not the lofty sails but the unseen wind that moves the ship. A deceptive clearness accompanies the operations of the intelligence. The reason is not, as the rationalists so firmly believe, the most fundamental thing about us. The most fundamental thing is that we are living beings, and purposeful beings, and very complicated beings, of whom reason is an attribute, an instrument, but most obviously not the whole of us. Logic does not help you to appreciate York Minster, or Botticelli's *Primavera*, and mathematics give no useful hints for lovers. You can no more fit the activities and passions of men exclusively into intellectual categories than you can find room for the Atlantic Ocean in a gallon jar. 'I have fought sixty battles', said Napoleon, 'and I have learned nothing that I did not know at the beginning.'

This 'scepticism of the instrument'—and I desire to emphasise it—goes deeper still. It extends to language. Language must be acknowledged as the greatest of human achievements. To what a world it gives us entrance! What a thing is a dictionary! What a creature man, who makes and employs such a book! What reflections, theories, inventions are here represented! These myriads of words, all with meanings, references, distinctions. What a world of art, poetry, science, religion, philosophy, imagination and fancy here opens to our gaze. 'It is obvious,' remarks Hobbes, 'that truth and falsehood dwell only with those living creatures who have the use of speech.' And everyone knows that our thoughts are inextricably entangled in language. But there is a treacherous chasm between language and the reality of which it speaks. 'Words are the daughters of earth, but things are the sons of heaven.' Words are clearly not the things themselves. They are the counters we employ in the exchange of impressions and ideas, and no single one of them has precisely the same value, or connotation or boundaries in your mind and in mine. Their values approximate but are never identical.

Sobald man spricht beginnt man schon zu irren.

It is, besides, more than doubtful whether shades of thought which can be rendered, let us say in French, can be employed in Chinese. It may be that in the end no race fully understands another. 'We must get behind words', Berkeley counsels us, 'and consider the things themselves.' But how much more easily said than done. All our thinking is in terms of words, the universal medium of communication between ourselves and our neighbours. And this medium, speech, has been developed in the closest association with the world disclosed to us through our senses of touch, sight and hearing, more especially sight—the extended world with all its various sounds and appearances. To employ language beyond the bounds of sense is thus hazardous in the extreme. When we read for example, in scientific works, of attractions and repulsions, of electric and magnetic fields, we are immersed in a sea of metaphors. Nature gave us eyes and ears, but no senses for magnetic and electric currents, which lie as far beyond their range as the affections of the amoeba or the anxieties of the cuttle-fish.

If I were asked what has been the most powerful force in the making of history, you would probably adjudge me of unbalanced mind were I to answer, as I should have to answer, metaphor, figurative expression. It is by imagination that men have lived; imagination rules all our lives. The human mind is not, as philosophers would have you think, a debating hall, but a picture gallery. Around it hang our similes, our concepts. The tyranny of the concept, as, for example, that modern one, which pictures the universe as a machine, or that literary one, which thought of the critic as a magistrate administering the laws of the world of letters, the laws of the classical canon, laws like those of the

Medes and Persians, fixed and unchangeable—a concept which governed European literature for centuries—this tyranny of the concept is one from which the human mind never escapes. It hugs its self-imposed chains. Metaphor is the essence of religion and poetry. Take the similes, the figurative speech out of the world's poetry, and you reduce it to commonplace. Remove the metaphors from the Bible, and its living spirit vanishes, its power over the heart melts utterly away. The prophets, the poets, the leaders of men are all of them masters of imagery, and by imagery they capture the human soul. Nor does science escape from this entanglement. If language consists, as it does, of fossilised images, no wonder science finds it a treacherous medium. 'Our confidence in language', writes Lord Russell, 'is due to the fact that it consists of events in the physical world, and therefore shares the structure of that world, and can therefore express that structure. But if there be a world which is not physical, and not in space-time, it may have a structure which we can never hope to express or to know.'

But the difficulty goes even deeper, and we do not need to leave the material world to observe the havoc wrought in scientific thinking by the use of concepts borrowed from one science to explain matters in another, as when in biology the attempt is made to account for the purposeful movements of living creatures exclusively by the action and reaction of material particles, governed solely by the laws of dynamics.

To say that we are not to think anthropomorphically, as men think, will not help us, since it is no more than to say we are not to think at all. How else can I think than as I am constituted to think? How animals think, angels or archangels, I can form no conjecture. Our question is, Has the world any sense, meaning or purpose from our point of view, and not from the point of view of some other or imaginary being? By thinking, such is our embarrassing situation, we have not only to account, or attempt to account, for the world and ourselves, but to account also for our confidence in this queer process and to justify it. Thinking must cross-examine thinking as well as the witnesses on its behalf called into the court. Mind summons itself to the bar, and is at once pursuer, defendant and Chief Justice.

Who then will keep watch upon this watcher, or stand sponsor for his fidelity? In this predicament some ingenious people have

66

postulated a universal mind, 'consciousness in general', a kind of Lord Chancellor, with whom an appeal may be lodged. Here the difficulty is, where are you to find him? The only thinking with which we have any acquaintance is individual thinking, and of the various contributions from the various heads we make a common pool. In the multitude of these counsellors, unfortunately not all of one mind, is our only wisdom. Why are they not all of one mind? That question may be partly answered by asking another. When we say we are trying to explain something, what do we mean? Do we mean any more than that a certain state of affairs, a certain conclusion would be more agreeable to us than some other? What happens in our heads or hearts when we say, 'Yes, that is so'? What sets this final seal upon a process of thought? In daily life if a statement does not contradict itself, but tends to confirm a previous experience we incline to accept it. If we see, that is, we believe. If we do not see, we require evidence, and better evidence the less the statement accords with earlier experience; more, let us say, for ghosts than for a motor accident. But certain results seem to give satisfaction to some minds, and quite different results satisfaction to others. Certain types of explanation satisfy one age, appear to be truth itself, which to another seem irrelevant and even meaningless. Every historian is familiar with what are called 'climates of opinion'. Our minds may thus resemble the sea shell, which when placed to the ear sounds as if it echoed the murmuring of the waves, and yet the murmur is nothing but the murmur of our own blood, and reason may thus introduce us to

A world unreal as the shell-heard sea.

It was Hegel's view that the secret of the universe was penetrable by thought. Other philosophers have been very definitely of the contrary opinion, that human thought was radically inadequate, utterly incompetent to deal with the mystery of existence. To let loose our paltry fancies into the vast ocean of being with any expectation of success is, they insist, mere megalomania. Nature's secrets might conceivably be accessible to other and angelic minds, but not to ours. The key of our understandings will not fit this intricate lock. To nature's hieroglyphics we do not possess the clue. They remind us that even Socrates, the apostle of reason, had his 'daimon', which knew more than his intellect could tell him. They remind us, too, that Plato resorted to myth or poetry when its soundings failed him. By other thinkers it is said that the book of nature is unreadable for quite a different reason, not because it is in a foreign tongue, but because it consists of senseless scribblings, accidental and unmeaning scrawls. A document is clearly beyond interpretation in which the words contain no sense. The failure to find a meaning in life is readily understood, if there be none to find—to-day's fashionable solution of the great enigma. In that case

> Thinking is but an idle waste of thought,
> And nought is everything and everything is nought.

If the universe be unintelligible, manifestly we but waste our time. 'A lingering scruple', wrote Mr. F. H. Bradley, 'still forbids me to believe that reality can be purely rational.' If that be our conclusion, if the universe contains a surd, an irrational kernel, its secret must remain for ever impenetrable, impervious to thought. Reason bites only on reason, there is no comprehending the incomprehensible. We have reached the great barrier reefs beyond which no ship has sailed, or can ever sail. Thought dethrones thought, and reason abdicates.

Unwelcome though it be, however, even this conclusion does not leave us wholly destitute. Philosophers agree that our understandings are equal at least to our near and immediate needs. Somehow the world supports us, as it supports the tree or flower. We are somehow nourished, body and mind. In a measure we are at home in the universe. We are its offspring and its subjects; it is our native land. If the whole has not been revealed to us, enough has been revealed to enable us to live, move and have our being within it. To advance beyond this point Goethe and a host of thinkers have declared impossible. Of the universe, or modes of being within it, other than our own, we can form no more conception—he is reported to have said—'than the fish in the abyss of the deep (even supposing it endowed with reason) could emancipate itself from the influence of its conceptions, formed in that region of fins and scales, of which it is an inhabitant, or in its nether element create to itself a complete and accurate picture of the human form.'

On this view the mind has been developed as the hand has been developed, in adaptation to the requirements of our environment.

Thought is a deposit of human and racial experience in its prolonged contact with the world we inhabit, justified and consecrated by its success and services to mankind. By means of it we can steer our way through the world of the senses: beyond its rim or margin thought has no efficacy, no jurisdiction. 'Thought's the slave of life', said Hotspur, and in so saying lighted upon the innermost truth. If such be our plight we must accept our limitations, and, with the sceptics, 'suspend our judgments in all matters which do not refer to living and the preservation of life.'

Up to a point, indeed, we need have no misgivings. Our inexpugnable confidence in reason is abundantly justified in daily affairs, and fortified by the glorious successes of science in her own region of enquiry. Yet when all has been said against the human understanding that can be said, it still refuses surrender. Whatever be its disabilities the only grounds you have for your condemnation are those which itself supplies. To subdue reason you must employ reason. Arguments which set aside human reasoning on any grounds are themselves reasonings. Nor is there anything to take its place. It is all we have. More than that, the human mind is no mere excrescence upon nature, but a part of nature, and as a part of nature represents nature, an attribute as much at least as any other part of her innermost being. Yet again, the intellect grows with what it feeds on, expands with the information it gathers, and no limit can be assigned beforehand to its powers. You have no right at all to assume a static reason in an unchanging world.

Innumerable attempts have been made, in the interests of the spiritual life, to find a substitute for reason, to discover another than the intellectual path to the sanctuary, an inner way. Reason may, indeed, itself acknowledge that there are regions beyond its powers of exploration, veils it cannot lift,. and that knowledge may reach us by channels other than its own. The heart, as Pascal said, has reasons of its own. Yes, indeed, but every heart has its private and incommunicable secrets. There is no common ground. And here we perceive the intellect's grand prerogative and advantage. And remember its magnificent hospitality. Reason keeps an open house for all comers. It introduces us to a noble partnership. As men who speak the same language can communicate with each other, so in her domain mind answers to mind. Here we can come to an understanding with each other, exchange opinions, correct each other's errors, have our eyes opened. 'Cross-questioning', we read in Plato, 'is the greatest and most efficacious of all purifications.' Even when we have doubts, it is the mind that doubts. All criticism of the mind is done by the mind itself. Hume employed it to discover its own limitations. Kant employed it to find it unadapted to metaphysical and ontological enquiries; Bergson, to expose the pitfalls into which it may slip, the mazes in which it may lose its way. The reason is its own protector. Nor need we doubt that its present powers may expand, that they are prophetic of higher powers to come.

The universe slumbers in the soul, and we awake to it day by day. In proportion as we come to know it we come to know ourselves. Nothing is so much to be feared as any alliance with the μισόλογοι the despisers of reason; nothing so much to be desired as to follow whithersoever the argument leads. There is a line in Chaucer much to my liking, in his description of the King of Trace at the tournament. 'And like a griffon,' says the poet—

And like a griffon looked he about.

So does human reason look about him in the lists, like a lion, fearing no antagonist. On this broad and open way of the mind there are no concealments, no pretences, no hidden weapons. Your thoughts and mine cannot win success by lurking in the shadows, or striking at adversaries from behind their backs. They can be challenged, opposed, ridiculed, rejected in open discussion. Denounce the reason, attack it, despise it, you cannot do it to death. It will recover from every wound, and return to the encounter after every defeat. It opens the gates of the past and the future. Immortal reason, invincible, invulnerable, the glory of humanity, which goes from strength to strength, increasing rather than losing its vigour in the very turmoil of the contest itself.

We shall do very well in the company of reason until we try to account for reason itself. Then we are immediately at a loss, and plunged in the depths of the ocean. Meanwhile we must take as our motto the saying of Terence—'Nothing is so difficult as to be beyond the reach of investigation.' (Nil tam difficile est quin quaerendo investigari possit.) We are not to assume that what is now unknown is for ever unknowable. Reason till reason fail, till reason itself discover a power superior to its own—we must stand to that.

IV

THE HUMAN SITUATION

AN ANSWER

'In the sweat of thy face shalt thou eat bread.'

Since daybreak I have laboured until now,
Stretched on a shady bank and wipe my brow;
Enough bread garnered for myself and Eve.
God's punishment for sin, that I must leave
The paradisal groves of idleness,
Haunted by dreams of love and soft caress,
And with my body's sweat and patient toil
Ravish a harvest from the grudging soil.
'Tis hard, at times, in frost or burning sun,
Panting, to strive until the race be run;
Still, O most jealous and revengeful God,
I find in me to say, 'I kiss Thy rod,'
Not in submission, but in proud disdain,
My mind is not cast in so mean a plane
That all my joys should lie in slothful ease.
True, I would keep the shore in stormy seas,
No hero of romance, but, for its zest,
There must be some work done before my rest;
Labour may be a burden? so it may,
Yet better far than everlasting play,
If labour be the penalty of sin
I would transgress, the penalty to win.
    Perhaps, still smarting from that garden scene,
I challenge God with too severe a mien;
He may have failed His meaning to express,
And when He seemed to curse have meant to bless.

W. M. Gloag

IV

THE HUMAN SITUATION

Whatever height you reach in your philosophic flights you cannot do other than begin with the familiar world. From this planet you must take your departure, and to this planet return. And on this lowly and common ground you have no need to summon to your assistance the soaring minds, the pilots of the upper air. The values of existence, our joys and sorrows, are not calculated or determined for us by the philosophers, the theologians and the moralists. In respect of these values we can make our own estimates, and do very well without them. They are no better informed than we are. You and I are here their equals, and can judge for ourselves. Aristotle, Spinoza and the rest, let them for the moment keep their distance. No one, however sagacious or eminent, can argue us out of our personal experiences. Thought has its own domain and can reach upward to interpretations, but neither science nor philosophy has discovered the universe, nor the earth on which we dwell, nor the hopes and fears we find within our hearts. The familiar old earth supports us all, plain men and thinkers. What is all this talk about proof? Shall we go about to prove what we already know, that we are alive, and are aware of the surrounding elements and entities, or have souls to enjoy or grieve over our condition?

I am not wholly unacquainted with the books of the famous speculators. I delight in their society. Under their subtle and eloquent guidance, I have made many excursions into the empyrean of the Absolute. I have some little knowledge of the various metaphysical gambits, the opening moves, the Platonic, the Cartesian, the Kantian. Their proceedings remind me of the pretty battles between the professional *condottieri* of the Middle Ages, the manoeuvring for position, the checks and counterchecks. Like myself, many have found these campaigns excellent reading, the tourneys in which skill and dexterity the most admirable are

73

displayed, in which laurels are won, in which no wounds are fatal. As in the Gothic Elysium the warriors fight all day, slay or are slain, but spring to life and strength again to renew the joyous struggle on the morrow. On these bloodless fields the sharp, salt air of life's sea is scarcely felt; we are far inland in a sheltered and secluded vale.

But after the pageant return you must to the tedium of daily existence, to the never-varying, everlasting human situation. We may deny, for example, the reality of the world of the senses, but we must live in it. And of these aristocratic and remote encounters the plain man is hardly aware. How difficult would it be for him to believe that ingenious minds still busy themselves to disprove the existence of the soul or self, of which you and I are so poignantly conscious, resolving it into other and less reputable things, in order that it may be of small account when so resolved. Or, that still they go about with equal industry to dilute seas and mountains, continents and nebulae into atoms or electrons, and finally by still more determined analysis into undifferentiated Space-Time. For despite these Herculean labours things seem to remain much as they were, to impose upon us, to wear their well-known faces, and to work their old effects. The sun rises and sets, the tides rise and fall. Men eat and drink and take their pleasures as if nothing had happened. And when our souls and selves are dissolved away under the metaphysical scrutiny, we continue to be aware of ourselves, of the world around us, to hope, enjoy and suffer, and believe ourselves alive. How fascinating it all is!

Yet the plain man has in the end the best of it. He pays no attention, and everything drifts back to him. Nothing, for example, could be more unscientific than to assume the existence of mind before it is demonstrated. Let us proceed then without minds to the discussion. The plain man is in some fashion aware that you cannot. He is dimly conscious that the very questions that are asked, the form given to them, the logic employed, are his questions and his logic. Questions, he vaguely supposes, are asked only by minds, and logic not employed by the cleverest sticks or stones. So he remains indifferent and inattentive, knowing, without much pondering of the matter, that there is no alternative but to begin with his experiences here and now, and with this particular planet, his home. A secure habitation no one can call it. At any moment it may fail us. Yet, however precarious our tenancy, we are not trespassers in the world. It may be far from satisfying, nevertheless it somehow belongs to us and we to it. Some power not ourselves has been at work, and here we are.

The first and fundamental wonder is existence itself. That I should be alive, conscious, a person, a part of the whole, that I should have emerged out of nothingness, that the Void should have given birth not merely to things, but to me. Among the many millions who throughout the centuries have crossed the stage of time probably not more than a handful have looked about them with astonishment, or found their own presence within the visible scene in any way surprising. Our immediate impressions and requirements, the daily doings, comings and goings of others like ourselves absorb in the years of infancy all our attention. Life steals imperceptibly upon us, without any sudden shock or sense of strangeness. How quietly we accommodate ourselves to the situation! In our early years, when all is fresh and new, we take the miracle for granted, and find abundant occupation and endless variety of interest. We are busy looking about us, and grow accustomed to living, and nothing appears startling to which we are accustomed. Thus it is that in the existence of the world or ourselves there appears for most of us no cause for amazement. So far from asking with Coleridge the unanswerable question, 'Why should there be anything at all, any world at all?' we accept life without wonder and without curiosity. One might almost imagine that we were here on well-known ground, and but revisiting a country with which we had a previous acquaintance. Yet let the mind once awake—and distress of mind is the great awakener of mind—and this emergence from the womb of the immeasurable universe rises to its full significance, to tower above all other thoughts, the wonder of wonders, beyond digestion into speech. To find oneself a member of a particular family and society, among innumerable other families and societies, engaged in a round of activities, to feel, think, love, hate, to eat, drink, sleep, to be involved in all these multitudinous affairs, not knowing in the least why this state of things should be ours, how we came into possession of this peculiar nature, acquired these needs, powers and passions, how or why we were launched upon this most extraordinary adventure—once give way

75

to thoughts like these, and you are a prisoner for life, the prisoner of philosophy. But you will remain one of a negligible minority. And if it be a delusion to suppose that many human beings have been concerned with such musings, it is equally a delusion to suppose they have been spiritually minded, anxious about the state of their souls, eager for communion with God. All but the slenderest of minorities have been immersed in a struggle for existence, for material satisfactions, have sought the pleasures of the senses, or followed after power or wealth. Most have died, whatever their pursuits, in the full vigour of their sensuality, and all in the full tide of their ignorance. If there has been one God universally acknowledged, universally worshipped, in all ages and countries, it is money.

> What is here?
> 'Gold? yellow, precious, glittering gold?'

The inhabitants of Norwich in 1650 petitioned Parliament to grant them the land and other materials 'of that vast and altogether useless cathedral of Norwich' towards the building of a workhouse and repairing piers.

However it came about, here we find ourselves, and in many and most delicately balanced ways, adjusted to the business in hand. Had the adjustment been perfect, had the whole worked without friction, as the earth moves through the heavens without a disturbing ripple, our lives like those of the plants, without desire or pain, possibly a dim sense of happiness, a gentle, unruffled dream might have been ours. Nature appears to have begun, if she ever did begin, her great undertaking with insensate things, and it mattered not at all what she did with them. Whirling suns, seas, mountains, even plants, trees, flowers of all varieties might have come into and passed out of existence without disturbance of the great calm of eternity. But with the entrance upon the scene of that disturbing visitor, the soul, that singular entity which suffers and enjoys, with the coming of beings capable of sharp pains and acute desires, there arose a formidable situation. These entities sought satisfaction for their wishes and avoidance of suffering. They became struggling creatures, in possession of life, but not the life they desired. Every man goes about arm in arm with disappointment. They discovered a harsh limit to their power over things. They

76

found an enemy in the field, an evil thing, figured in all religions as the Adversary, the Opponent, the ἀντὶ θεόν, Ahriman in the Persian system, Lucifer or Satan in the Christian.

How unfortunate, some theologians tell us, that man gave way to mental curiosity, and so forfeited his happy lot in the Garden of Eden, rising to a level of intelligence above the lowlier, unaspiring animals, content with pasture, with the satisfactions of food and sex. They fared better, and ours, but for the great aboriginal catastrophe, would have been a like existence, without expectations or searchings of heart, without souls embittered by fruitless desires. The knowledge of good and evil was the fatal departure from the original design—Nature's error, or, as in the Christian view, the fault of man himself. The pursuit of wisdom brought misery, and to intelligence was attached a penalty.

There is a saying that nature does nothing in vain. Yet if she created automatic machines, and some thinkers like the behaviourists insist we are no more, why did she proceed to the blunder, for assuredly a blunder it was, of conferring upon them an unnecessary sensitivity to pain and pleasure? Without sensitivity machines work very well. How much better had she been content with insensate things. But we are not stones or trees, and in making sensitive beings nature went clean out of her way. Consciousness is an unpardonable blot upon her scheme, and for this philosophy an inexplicable enigma. So it is that, in the midst of nature, man appears not as her child, but as a changeling. Exiled from his native home of innocence, elevated to kingly rank in the creation, the bond between mother and son was snapped. She reared a disappointed and rebellious child, a critic of his parent, judging her morals detestable, counselling, as did Huxley, resistance to her rule and defiance of her authority. Cosmic nature, he declares, is 'no school of virtue', but the headquarters of its enemy.

That the world is not to their mind has never ceased to surprise, if not to exasperate the philosophers. Its pattern displeases them, and they would remould it nearer to their hearts' desire. Some religions think it past mending, but the passion for reforming the world and one's neighbours has afflicted all the schools of thought, nor has it yet been abandoned. Yet the patterns they would substitute have never been divulged. The most dissatisfied are chary of offering their alternative and superior worlds, nor does it appear that they know of any with which our own unfavourably compares. By some natural talent they perceive its deficiencies, but the plan of operations is kept a secret. Alfonso the Wise of Spain, indeed, remarked that 'he could have suggested improvements in the universe had the Creator consulted him'. Unfortunately at that moment a terrible thunderstorm burst over the Alcazar, and there is no record of his proposals, if he had any.

The world has been called *theatrum Dei*, God's theatre. And if we were merely players on the stage, repeating words put into our mouths, performing actions assigned to us, and like them really unconcerned, appearing to suffer and yet not suffering, the situation were beyond rebuke. It is unhappily quite otherwise. Feeling entered the world and let loose a torrent of ills—the sick heart, the ailing body, the distressed mind.

> All thoughts that rive the heart are here, and all are vain,
> Horror, and scorn, and hate, and fear, and indignation.

It is a curious speculation, yet not irrelevant to our present enquiry, how human lots are cast, so strangely varied they are. You are born, and no reasons given, a man or a woman, an Arab or an Andaman islander, an African pygmy or an Egyptian Pharaoh, a Chinese coolie or an English gentleman, a St. Thomas or an Ivan the Terrible. You are ushered into the world in the Stone Age, the fifth or fifteenth century, a vegetarian or a cannibal, of base or noble stock, the child of half-witted parents or of Viking breed, an imbecile or a fanatic. You inherit, according to the accident of your birth, a family blood-feud, a belief in Voodoo and a string of fantastic fetishes, or a Christian creed of love and charity. You are a warrior or a serf as Heaven decrees, are exposed as an infant born in ancient Sparta, die in middle life bitten by a poisonous snake in India, or live a respectable German merchant to a ripe old age. One of a million million possible lots is yours. Is it accidental, an act of God, or, as some have conjectured, a selection made by yourself in a previous state? How profound a mystery lies behind these so manifestly unequal conditions of human existence! And what justice is it, if one man languishes most of his life on a bed of sickness, and another enjoys health and happiness or sits upon an imperial throne?

78

Nature strews these inequalities of place, time, heredity, circumstances with a monstrous partiality. On what principles you are allotted good looks, a musical ear, a sunny temper, an affectionate disposition, a talent for figures, or denied these qualities does not appear. We are, the maxim runs, as God made us, and there the matter perforce must end.

Nor is it only our nature and disposition that we inherit, but the habits and traditions of some community, a Pagan, a Buddhistic or a Mohammedan creed, the *mos majorum*, the custom of our ancestors; and, with few exceptions, by these our lives are governed. These bodies of ours, as it would seem at haphazard distributed, are not negligible, or to be treated with cavalier indifference. From their tiresome demands and complaints there is no escape. They do very much as they please with us, often lame our best intentions and enforce our most sensual. To keep them in repair is a constant anxiety. What a despot is the stomach, whose caprices make us moody or cheerful, bland or irritable. Listen to the enormous laughter of Rabelais while he recounts the indignities to which the body subjects the mind, making indecency an intimate part of our lives. He mocks at nature, which delights in shaming us. Our pride revolts, we are nauseated by ourselves, as was Swift, or nervously and shamefacedly avert our eyes from the dishonours we must endure.

If nature gave us logic, she appears to be singularly lacking in what she bestows. For she herself drives no straight furrow, and exhibits an inconsistency which in a man would be accounted madness. Her habit is to turn upon herself, wound and afflict herself, undoing with her left hand what she has done with her right. What more inharmonious than that she should send hailstones to the destruction of her own blossoms and fruits, tempests upon the crops she has herself ripened to the harvest? The meteorite that, in 1908, fell in Siberia, about 100 tons in weight, destroyed the forest in which it fell for a radius of about forty miles. The lightning splits the tree, and sets the forest aflame. The sand of the desert or the encroaching sea turns fertile fields into barren wastes, and reduces whole populations to distress or starvation. It is her own features which nature thus rends and mangles. Wild beasts destroy 3000 persons every year in India, and 20,000 die of snake-bite. There are 700 million sufferers from malaria in the world.   Forty per cent. of the children born in Central China perish from cold or famine before they are a year old.

When people talk of nature, what do they mean?   Is it the immensity, the sublimity, the grandeur, or the indifference, the inhumanity she exhibits, of which they are thinking?   We know her wonders and splendours, we know also her disorders, her cataclysms, her tempests.   Nature is everything we admire and fear, everything we love, and everything we hate.   She is 'the sum of all phenomena'.   A perfectly ordered world, exact as a geometrical pattern, is the world desired by the logical mind. But how different the reality.   Before its irrationalities reason trembles.   The eruption of Krakatoa, in 1783, destroyed 40,000 human beings; the Quito, in 1797, also 40,000; the Lisbon earthquake, in 1755, twice that number.   Is human life a bubble? Within the present century, in 1908, and again, in 1920, similar disturbances in Sicily and China eliminated half a million lives in sixty seconds.   The eruption of Mount Pelé, in less than a quarter of an hour, laid the capital of Martinique in ruins, with the loss of 30,000 lives.   During the Yangtse floods in 1931 over a million perished by drowning.   Etna wakes and Messina perishes.   Islands are submerged with their human freights, like ships at sea.   In 1929 Ninaforu, in the Pacific, simply disappeared with all its inhabitants into the ocean depths.   Would these things be 'if the King of the universe were our friend'?   The larks are not always in the sky on an April morning.

Professor Bosanquet thought it exceedingly improbable that an earthquake would destroy London.   His reason for thinking so was not a geological one.   It would be, he believed, contrary to 'the world-wisdom'.   Such a preference by nature for London over Tokio or California is indeed very flattering to us as a nation, and very comforting.   But what are we to think of a philosopher who says such things?   You say nothing: you close his book.

Nature does not seem to know her own mind, or else she speaks an equivocal language.   Are her powers, perhaps, limited, and hers an imperium divided among satraps, or governors, not wholly in subordination to her central authority?   For if not, why should there be a discord between her animate and inanimate provinces?   The human mind looks for unity, yet everywhere in nature's realm contending powers are in conflict.   You

80

have the physical world indifferent to living things, unconcerned whether they exist or do not exist. In its turn, upon the insecure foundation of the body, the living organism, rises the mind, incapable, it would seem, of any independent existence. So that thought, love, hope, the soul and its affections, the whole intellectual structure of human life, are perilously poised in a trembling insecurity upon the material elements, themselves in continual flux.

Were nature constant in her intentions we might hope to understand them, but how at odds with herself this Lady Bountiful, mother of all living, when she counsels one species of her children to feed upon the bodies of others, not less her own creation, providing an armoury the most ingenious, claws and fangs and suckers, instruments of death, that one tribe of her offspring might the better murder the members of another, a device, to our poor uninstructed vision, neither lovely nor divine. Nature is no believer in disarmament. The bird preys upon the insect and the worm, the glow-worm feeds upon the snail, the ichneumon lays its eggs upon the caterpillar, which, when the grubs emerge, will serve as their food. There are animals which seem an incarnation of malice, like that dweller in darkness, the blood-sucking vampire bat. How difficult to think of the author of the Sermon on the Mount, how difficult to think of Christ as the son of the God of nature! Nature encourages internecine strife. Nor has she any favourites among her creatures, unless it be the insect tribe. There are not less than ten million varieties of them in existence. 'In India alone the loss of crops, of timber, and of animal products by insect damage is estimated at over 150 million pounds annually, and the death roll due to insect-borne diseases at over a million and a half lives.'[1]

Life is one throughout the universe, yet its parts are in conflict. Nature has her racks and thumbscrews. You cannot instruct her in any of the torturer's or executioner's arts. There is no kindness in the sea, no benevolence in the forest. If you complain that men are a cruel breed, you need not enquire whence they derived the propensity. It is inherited, and from the mother's side.

Perhaps these things should not be mentioned. Truth is a thorny rose. Sentimental writers do not dwell upon this theme. These star-gazers do not remind us of the *bellum omnium contra omnes*. How tiresome are the one-eyed philosophies. There

[1] *The World of Nature*, by H. C. Knapp-Fisher, p. 295.

will be brave men born after us who will not attempt to build up their spiritual lives on a diet of lies. All forms of life, all organisms in which it is manifested, are engaged in an unceasing struggle to maintain themselves against the disintegrating forces of nature. All are in conflict with each other for the means of life, clan against clan, individual against individual. Each exists at the expense of others, and keeps its foothold only by success over the rest. Here is a telegram from South Australia, dated Nov. 6, 1934. 'It is estimated that the farmers in Adelaide will lose at least three-quarters of their crops through the depredations of grass-hoppers, which are advancing in uncontrollable swarms on a front of 250 miles.' How deep it goes, this warfare, you may conjecture if you remind yourself that the very trees of the forest are battling with each other for the light of the sun, and that the plants have their defensive armour, the rose and thistle their thorns, the nettle its sting. Make your heart iron within you, when you remember that to live you must kill, either plants or animals. 'To live, my Lucilius, is to make war.' Hunger for food, hunger for life, of which war is merely the continuation, are the presiding issues.

It is no doubt necessary to think in terms of right and wrong, yet how much more convincing would be our moralists if they began at the beginning, if they could bring themselves to think first in terms of life and death. Who is ignorant that good and evil go everywhere hand in hand, in the closest, indeed inseparable, partnership? The misfortunes of one community make the fortunes of another. If England secures the world markets, they are lost to Germany. If oil becomes the necessary and universal fuel, the oil-producing districts flourish at the expense of those which have none. Among the competitors for a post, or the hand of a lady, one only can prove successful, and not invariably the most deserving. The magistrate and police depend for their livelihood on the swindler and the burglar, the physician upon the sick and disabled. Scarcity of food brings destitution to the poor and high prices to the farmer, and the higher a nation's standard of intellect and skill the worse for the incapable and unintelligent.

We are not sure of what best nourishes, or what damages, the delicate machinery of nerve and brain. We guess at the causes of our physical lassitude. Poisons circulate in our blood from origins unknown. We are surrounded by unseen foes. Nor are our souls less vulnerable than our bodies. Affections spring up in us only to be thwarted or forbidden, or we discover too late that they have been foolishly misplaced and are betrayed. Our very sympathies lead us astray. We are imposed upon by falsehoods and depressed by misunderstandings. The whole region of the emotions is subject to doubts, misgivings, confusion, and those who have shallow natures, feeling little, appear to be best suited for life. Instinct and desire point one way and mature reflection another. Duties conflict not merely with our wishes, but with opposing duties, so that we are in doubt where our loyalty is first due, which cause we should espouse, to which of the arguing voices we should give ear. And, do what we will, to live at all without inflicting injuries upon others is well-nigh, if not altogether impossible. 'A terrible thing is life', says Socrates in the *Gorgias* (δεινός ὁ βίος). He thought it a disease, and left with his friend, Crito, a commission to sacrifice a cock as a thank-offering for his deliverance.

Yet within this 'odious scene of violence and cruelty', as Mill, rising to a moral superiority over the universe, called it, there runs a counter current. So that in nature's speech there is an equivocation, an irony, an irony clearly discerned, with that unclouded vision of theirs, by the Greeks, and even by the simpler peoples of the earth. A recent traveller reports the philosophy of an African tribe: 'They said that although God is good, and wishes good for everybody, unfortunately he has a half-witted brother, who is always interfering with what he does. This half-witted brother keeps on obtruding himself, and does not give God a chance.' How kindly a view of Satan! And what is irony? It is a double-speaking, it is language which, since it is open to two interpretations, hides the speaker's meaning, in which a sense is wrapped other than the obvious sense, language which says one thing and yet means another. There is the irony, too, of circumstances, promising what they do not perform, or it may be performing what they do not promise, or by the event baffling confident expectation. For this ironical language nature has a fondness. Observe that this nature which wars upon herself is the nature which constructs the exquisite fabric of the living organism, and with a physician's arts ministers to the diseases she inflicts, produces in the body anti-toxins to defeat the toxins, administers anaesthetics, and exercises a *vis medicatrix* all her own. How difficult to recognise in the ferocities we see around us the subtle power which made the brain, which elaborated with consummate exactness the mechanism of the heart and lungs, all the devices by which the body maintains its existence! That nature should create a world full of difficulties and dangers, and thereupon proceed to place within it fabrics of an infinite delicacy and complexity to meet these very dangers and difficulties is a contradiction that baffles the understanding. With a cunning past all human thought she solves the problems she has, as it were, absent-mindedly set herself. The flood and the earthquake have no consideration for the plant or animal, yet nature which sends the flood and earthquake has provided, with foresight or in a dream, for the living things they destroy. She both smiles and frowns upon her own creation, and is at once friendly and unfriendly. Like a scarlet thread it runs through her dominion, this inconsistency. Side by side with the undeniable and admirable adjustment between things organic and inorganic, you have the hostility, the discordance. What wonder that men, bewildered by this inexplicable procedure, have supposed her governments distributed among a hierarchy of squabbling deities, persecuting or protecting this or that race of men— Zeus the Greeks, Jehovah the Jews? What wonder they supposed even the trees to be the better of protecting deities, the olive Athena, the vine Dionysus? Ah, nature! subtle beyond all human subtlety, enigmatic, profound, life-giver and life-destroyer, nourishing mother and assassin, inspirer of all that is best and most beautiful, of all that is most hideous and forbidding!

That the world is a unity the philosophers and men of science reiterate with a wearisome persistence. That it is united, they have the sense not to proclaim. How the world became disunited they have not told us. Yet in this procession of time and tears it is not so much the rivers of blood which flow through history, it is the broken hearts that appal us. What elicits human horror and indignation is not so much the suffering that the strong may with courage endure as the suffering at random inflicted upon the weak and innocent and defenceless. I read not long since of a child, who trustingly looked up the chimney to see the coming of Santa Claus. Her clothing took fire, and she was burnt to death. A painful world we might school ourselves to

84

combat, were it only rational, but the conjunction of pain and senselessness is hard to bear. Nor would the heroic race of men, 'toil-worn since being began', shrink from grief and wounds were it only assigned a noble task. But nature prescribes no tasks. She calls for no volunteers for a great essay. For the asking she might have millions. She points willing climbers to no Everest. The discovery of the goal—by far the most difficult task—she leaves to us. We are mountaineers by nature, but born blind, and must find for ourselves the Himalayan peak, if there be any peak, we are built to ascend, or else while away the time till the great axe falls, and the futilities are done with. Go where you will through nature, you find no directions for travellers. You choose your path, uncounselled and at your own peril, and the unlikely track may prove to be the best. To be clear-sighted is often to be short-sighted, as when the molluscs and crustaceans, protecting themselves with heavy defensive armour, entered with all their care and caution a blind alley, while naked, unaccommodated man, selecting the more dangerous path, advanced to the headship of living creatures.

Life is a unique experience. There is nothing with which to compare it, no measure of its value in terms of some other thing, and money will not purchase it. Yet with this pearl of price we know not what to do. Schopenhauer loves to dwell, in illustration of his pessimistic thesis upon the boredom of life, and cites card-playing, a kill-time device, as 'quite peculiarly an indication of the miserable side of humanity'. That mortals should desire immortality, and yet find difficulty in passing an afternoon —if you have a fancy for paradoxes, here is a pretty one. We contemplate eternity without horror, and find an hour of our own society intolerable. 'How dreary it is to be alive, gentlemen!' And how poverty-stricken is the human soul, which, even when armed with supernatural powers, can find no occupation for itself. Marlowe's Faustus, with Mephistopheles to gratify his every wish, can make nothing of his transcendent opportunity.

Tacitus draws a terrible picture of the *taedium vitae* which in imperial times descended upon the Roman aristocracy:

> In his cool hall, with haggard eyes,
> The Roman noble lay:
> He drove abroad, in furious guise,
> Along the Appian Way.

85

He made a feast, drank fierce and fast,
  And crown'd his head with flowers—
No easier nor no quicker pass'd
  The impracticable hours.

Or if, by good fortune, we inherit a nature abundant in resource, which finds every moment full of charm, and think the world a divine playground, another shadow darkens the windows of the soul.   As the child, enchanted with the fairy spectacle upon the stage, the joyous bustle and the glittering lights, whispered to its mother—'Mother, this is not going to end soon, is it?' we are startled to discover that

  in the very temple of delight
Veil'd melancholy has her sovran shrine.

To foresee the end of happiness poisons the springs of happiness. It will end, and soon.   We are permitted an hour at the pageant and the curtain falls.

It may be that, although appearances are against her, nature meant well by us, that her powers were limited.   She has done what she could, giving us a 'second best', since the best was beyond her.   It lay within her strength to confer life, but not to preserve it.   Yet one cannot refrain from asking, was it necessary that man's superiority should prove his bane, that his aspirations should end in the grave?   To create immortal longings in the ephemeral being of an hour, to implant in him passions never to be gratified, for knowledge never to be attained, for understanding never to be fulfilled, to give him imagination, a fatal dowry, since it enables him to contrast his true lot with a better, the poverty of his possessions with the abundance of his cravings— was this necessary?   It appears either a refinement of malicious irony, or a promise of fulfilment, but which?   The gods are silent.

Or is it that some Force, too wise, too strong,
Even for yourselves to conjure or beguile,
Sweeps earth, and heaven, and men, and gods along,
Like the broad volume of the insurgent Nile?
And the great powers we serve, themselves may be
Slaves of a tyrannous necessity? . . .

Oh, wherefore cheat our youth, if thus it be,
Of one short joy, one lust, one pleasant dream?
Stringing vain words of powers we cannot see,
Blind divinations of a will supreme;
Lost labour! when the circumambient gloom
But hides, if Gods, Gods careless of our doom?

There is, among her inconsistencies, another persuasive artifice of nature, for which, by any mechanical philosophy it is difficult, indeed, to account—the artifice by which she induced men to interest in a future they could not hope to see. She persuades them to self-sacrifice, to loss of life for their offspring, for their race, their country, to martyrdom for their faiths, for shadowy, intangible notions, less substantial than gossamer. By what arrangement of cranks, wheels and levers did she cozen this creature of a day to look beyond his own instant profit, his obvious gain? Why should hope have a place, heroism a place, renunciation a place in this automaton? Is cajolery among her talents? Manifestly the Spartans at Thermopylae were flattered to their ruin by a ridiculous pride of race.

View life as a whole, exert all your powers of fancy, take all history into your account, the embarrassing contradiction remains. On all sides it raises its sphinx-like, ironical countenance. Another and final illustration will suffice. At the heart of existence there lies an undeniable sweetness, which no philosophy has fathomed, and no railing accusation against life can dislodge. The complaints against it are legion. In all ages and societies goes up the bitter cry, 'Vanity of vanities, all is vanity.' 'All that exists', wrote Leopardi, 'is evil, that anything exists is an evil; everything exists only to achieve evil; existence itself is an evil, and destined to evil. There is no other good than non-existence.'

So much for life: not a pennyworth of value anywhere. Yet the doctrines and religions, and they are numerous, which condemn existence, offer no adequate explanation of the clinging attraction for a state they censure and profess to despise. From this so undesirable a possession their adherents are, for the most part, curiously unwilling to part. 'What sort of a pessimist is this', asks Nietzsche, 'who plays the flute?' The pessimists are not alone in vilifying life. They have the support of Christian preachers. 'The whole world', says Donne, 'is but a universal churchyard, but our common grave.' Christianity has little good to say of life, yet how reluctant the best Christians are to become angels. Like the worldlings they, too, are intoxicated with the pleasures of sense. They marry and are given in marriage. They succumb at times to song and laughter. Cheerfulness keeps lurking in odd corners of the horrid gloom. There is some magic at work here. Is it possible that something may be said for this vale of sorrows? Though not to be compared with the ineffable bliss we demand, yet as an alternative to nothing a case for existence can be stated. In fairness to nature you must enter this natural sweetness in the ledger of your account with her. The ecstasy of lovers, the joy in activity, the glow, the radiance, the sunlight, the perfume—omit these, and it is a caricature you have drawn, not the landscape. There is a music in the air.

> Riding adown the country lanes;
> The larks sang high—
> O heart, for all thy griefs and pains
> Thou shalt be loath to die.

Many philosophers have been defeatists. Diogenes and Zeno, Epictetus and Marcus Aurelius, Schopenhauer and Spinoza. Ἀπάθεια, ἀταραξία, nil admirari, indifference, impassivity, passionlessness, they are all one. Stoicism, Epicureanism, Taoism, how many creeds and doctrines are, in their essence, withdrawals from life? For them it is not an adventure but a weary pilgrimage. They take no pleasure in it. Sick of time, they take refuge in eternity. And we seem forced to the strange conclusion that Paganism suits world conditions better. Perhaps it should, indeed, be expected. For why should the haters of life be more at home in it than its lovers? The creed of the Northmen, for example, left room for activity and prowess, for skill and enterprise, for courage and adventure. They had a liking for the risks and dangers of existence, which gave a zest to living, and for a worthy antagonist, who put them on their mettle.

Life is like the sea, never at rest, untamed, moody, capricious, perilous. Many a man who knows the sea has sworn, and sworn again, that once on land he would never more embark upon so inclement, so treacherous, so hateful an element. And few who have so sworn have not heard with aching hearts her call, and longed for her bitter and incomparable society. Like life she lays a spell upon them, a spell not resident in her smiles, though smile she can, nor in her calm, though, like life, she, too, has her seasons of calm, her sheltered lagoons and quiet havens. Men are said to love flattery. The sea never flatters. They are said to love ease. She offers toil. Like life she deals in every form of danger, and many modes of death—famine, thirst, fire, cold, shipwreck. Like life she strips men of their pretensions and vanities, exposes the weakness of the weak and the folly of the fool. Wherein then lies the fascination, against which the soft Lydian airs cannot with men that are men prevail? It flings a challenge and human nature rises to a challenge. Men are by nature striving creatures, heroically stubborn, as is the mind itself.

> Still nursing the unconquerable hope,
> Still clutching the inviolable shade.

They love best what they do for themselves, for what they themselves make they have a great affection; what is given them out of charity they value less. The world seems somehow so made as to suit best the adventurous and courageous, the men who, like Nelson, wear all their stars, like Napoleon's marshals their most splendid uniforms, not that they may be less but more conspicuous and incur greater dangers than their fellows. Leonidas at Thermopylae, resolved to stand and die for his country's cause, wished to save two lads by sending them home with a message to Sparta. He was met by the answer, 'We are not here to carry messages, but to fight'. However it comes about, such men are more inspiring figures than the defeatists.

Matthew Arnold quotes with admiration Pope's rendering of the passage in Homer in which Sarpedon urges his friend Glaucus into the fight, the passage which in the original Lord Granville quoted on his death-bed.

> Could all our care elude the gloomy grave
> Which claims no less the fearful than the brave,
> For lust of fame I should not vainly dare
> In fighting fields, nor urge thy soul to war;
> But since, alas! ignoble age must come,
> Disease, and death's inexorable doom;
> The life which others pay, let us bestow,
> And give to fame what we to nature owe.

Cogito, ergo sum, said Descartes. 'I think, therefore I am.' He desired a platform, or rather an undeniable proposition as the foundation of his philosophic thought. His successors have not found it either undeniable or sufficient. They have rejected, too, such alternatives as 'I act, therefore I am'. 'I desire, therefore I am.' Let me suggest still another. No philosophers, or men of science, have so far had the hardihood, as far as I know, to deny us our pains. They relieve us of all else. They have taken from us our personality, our freedom, our souls, our very selves. They have, however, left us our sorrows. Let us take, then, as our foundation the proposition 'I suffer, therefore I am'. And let us add to it the converse and equally true statement, 'I am, therefore I suffer'. The privilege, if it be a privilege, of existence is ours, and we have paid the price required. We have discharged our debts. We have not had something for nothing. We have free minds, and can look around us with a smile. Nothing can any longer intimidate us.

V

THE HISTORICAL SCENE

Strange is the vigour in a brave man's soul.   The strength of his spirit and his irresistible power, the greatness of his heart and the height of his condition, his mighty confidence and contempt of dangers, his true security and repose in himself, his liberty to dare and do what he pleaseth, his alacrity in the midst of fears, his invincible temper, are advantages which make him master of fortune.   His courage fits him for all attempts, makes him serviceable to God and man, and makes him the bulwark and defence of his being and country.

Traherne

V

THE HISTORICAL SCENE

Where lies the main issue with which we are concerned?
Let us not lose sight of it. We desire, in Bacon's
words, 'to arrive at a true knowledge of the universe
in which we are.' Of this universe man is a part, from his own
standpoint, indeed, its absolute centre. What are we then,
what kind of a being is man? Theories of human nature are
plentiful, but theories elaborated in the study have no validity.
Men themselves must be our teachers, men as they go about the
world, and there reveal, naked and undisguised, the character of
their species, in its motions, manners and actions. If we are to
go to the root of things, it is not only the habits of nature we
must study, but the habits of men. Of what value is any attempt
to explain the world till you have faced the facts of the world?
And in history you have a faithful mirror, which reflects the features of humanity. In this field of enquiry surmise and speculation are ruled out. As in the doings of nature, so in the doings
of men you have an authentic document. There in their broad
outline the behaviour and beliefs, the acts and undertakings of
human beings are laid bare. We are not assailed by doubts, we
are not in the region of arguments. These things have been
believed, these things have indisputably been done. And when I
speak of history, I do not mean local, or partial or contemporary
history, but universal history. And looking over its scenes one is
tempted to ask, 'Is there anything ever new in it?' Was Marcus
Aurelius right when he said that a man of forty had seen all there
was to see, past or to come? Perhaps, if an intelligent man or an
emperor.

Before you sit down, then, surrounded by the books of the
idealists, to write your attractive essay on aesthetics, or spiritual
values, or Greek genius, it were well to walk abroad a little
through the centuries, and to accommodate your mind to the
bewildering variety the world exhibits, to a world, for example,

of which a part practises monogamy, another polyandry, in which peoples have practised human sacrifice without reproach, exposed their children to death without reproach, where these things were not merely familiar and accepted customs, but religiously upheld and commanded. If an understanding of the Cosmos be your aim nothing can be omitted from the vast account. It will be necessary to extend your reading beyond the lives of saints and poets, of English worthies and leaders of science. You cannot draw conclusions about the universe from the inspection of a six-acre field. It will be necessary to look into the biographies of Oriental despots and ambitious conquerors, to know something of Attila and Hyder Ali, as well as of Socrates and Savonarola, to ponder the practices of New Guinea as well as New York, the pastimes, pleasures and superstitions of the human race throughout the ages. There have been Neros and Borgias and Torquemadas, there have been men like Caracalla, who did to death twenty thousand innocent persons of both sexes. Among the civilised Romans the families frequently shared the fate of men who had incurred the resentment of rulers. Among Orientals the monarch succeeding to power not uncommonly thought it wiser to hand over all his relatives to the executioner. When Ivan the Terrible, who did much for the arts and commerce of his country, sat upon the throne of Russia in the sixteenth century, he murdered whole families to gratify his whims. In torture he took delight, and in one day consigned to slaughter 15,000 of his own subjects, with every species of malignant cruelty. During his reign friends, women, children, innocent of any kind of offence, were thrown into dungeons, poisoned, beheaded, burned. How came God or nature to invest this Satan with imperial power? His later career was a furious tempest of insensate bloodshed, in which ingenuity exhausted itself in the contrivance of mutilations and devices to inflict suffering. 'Beasts, misnamed men', assisted to carry out his orders, driving their fellow creatures into lakes, into boiling caldrons, flaying and tormenting, so that the heart faints at the human agony wrought by this one man.

A madman, no doubt. But a single custom, approved by a community, may from century to century work greater havoc than the enormities of a despot. How comes a race to adopt a practice like child marriage? In India, where nineteen thousand

94

children are born daily, rather more than a quarter die in infancy, more, that is, than 250 per thousand. In Paris it is 93 per thousand, in Berlin 88, in London 66. Of these Indian mothers, who become mothers before they have ceased to be children, three millions die annually in childbirth.

It is but a ripple on the mighty tide of life, which rolls remorselessly on. Do not let the armchair philosophers deceive you, nourished on 'solemn vision and bright silver dream', men who have been for the most part gentle and peace-loving persons, secluded from the tempestuous maelstrom of events, which constitute the story of humanity. 'This man imagines', said Cicero, on one occasion, 'that he is living in the Republic of Plato, instead of in the days of that of Romulus.' It was said of Pope that he mistook a coterie for mankind. And how easily all of us fall into the same error, thinking of the great world, past and present, as if it were a kind of enlarged copy of an English village. I do not commit myself with complete confidence to the philosophers when they expound to me the relations between the One and the Many; still less when they speak of human nature, not recognisable from their pictures of it. How pale their drawings appear beside the passions and intrigues, the hatreds and ambitions, the glitter, the pageantry and poverty of the vast panorama, 'the perpetual, immense and innumerable goings on of the visible world' (*ex visibilium aeterno, immenso et innumerabili effectu*) in Bruno's phrase.

Have they known and studied men who stop at nothing, men with boiling passions, so unlike their own mild preferences for tea over coffee, golf over cricket, or bridge over chess; men who have combined the finest taste and intelligence with utter ruthlessness, who were at once men of genius and without bowels? You prefer luke-warm emotions. The reformers have, indeed, a strong preference for tepid, anaemic folk. But do tepid emotions possess any driving force? To desire nothing at all was the Stoic prescription for the good life; to desire very little, and that half-heartedly, seems to be the panacea for the world's ills recommended by our modern doctors. As if nature would consent to this damping down of her eternal fires, as if the cessation of desire, so exalted by the sages, were not another name for death, the veiled and circuitous route to nothingness. Nature has something to say as well as the philosophers. Recall and ponder the past. Have the motives and aims of men and women ever resembled those of our study thinkers? Have these speculators, sitting above the clouds, at any time seen jealousy, envy, hatred and revenge at work—revenge, one of the most powerful motives that ever swayed the human heart, 'the sweetest morsel to the mouth', in the words of Walter Scott, 'that ever was cooked in hell'? Are these passions more than words to them? 'A man of mild manners', as said Hume, 'can form no idea of inveterate revenge or cruelty.' Have our philosophers, who deal in ethical theories, ever enquired into the souls of murderers and fanatics, of Mexicans and Peruvians, Aztecs and Polynesians, the thoughts of dancing dervishes, of Indian fakirs or Thibetan llamas, or tribesmen practising sorcery? Have they ever 'shuddered at the millions, and immensities and secrets of India'? It would be difficult to invent a story too outrageous to command belief, a doctrine for which it would be impossible to obtain support, a proposal too grotesque to be anywhere entertained. There appears to be a maggot in every human brain. There was no need, Goethe thought, to visit a madhouse to find lunatics. So numerous are the illusions, frenzies, hallucinations afloat in the world that some thinkers have been of opinion that our planet was the asylum of the universe for disordered minds. It is not merely the things men say, and they are fantastic enough, it is the proposals they seriously advocate, the proceedings in which they actually engage. Read the anthropologists for the evidence. The Nestinari, the dancers upon fire, of Bulgaria, walk for ten or fifteen minutes on red-hot embers, passing twice over them to make the sign of the cross, in the belief that by so doing they bring health and prosperity to their community.

The delusions from which men suffer are beyond computation, and the eye which ranges over the historical landscape blenches at the superstitions, cults and rituals which contain for our intelligences no grain of sanity, and seem an outrage upon all reason. Some beliefs, indeed, amuse us. According to the ancients, to dream of sheep is good for scholars, lecturers and teachers; to dream of asses is harmless, mules vary, oxen are good, but goats are bad. One wonders how they made these discoveries. Olaus Magnus, Archbishop of Upsala in the sixteenth century, declared he had been an eye-witness of a Norwegian sea-serpent's doings, which seized sheep as they browsed on a cliff a hundred feet above the sea, and swallowed ships, crews and all. Vossius, the Dutch scholar, advocated the execution of criminals in tragic plays to heighten the dramatic effect. In Russia at one time an attempt was made to put a stop to snuff-taking by slitting the nostrils of the rascals who practised it. There were Jacobins who wished to destroy the cathedral of Chartres, because it dominated too completely the republican town. Gandhi declared lately that 'an advocate of non-violence, like myself, would die before killing rats'. This saintly man, who has the secret for putting the world to rights, would permit the rat and the louse to carry typhus through the world like a prairie fire, to the misery and death of millions. And this is holiness.

It is not only individuals who can lose their senses, and yet continue to find devoted followers. Whole cities have frequently fallen into religious convulsions, entire populations given themselves over to frantic debaucheries. If the historians are to be believed, the Jews in Cyrene slaughtered two hundred and twenty thousand Greeks, in Cyprus two hundred and forty thousand. They devoured the flesh of their victims, 'licked up the blood and twisted their entrails like a girdle round their bodies.'

There is to-day much discussion of 'values' in the philosophical journals. But of whose values are these subtle disputants thinking? With values as estimated in Oxford, Valparaiso or Timbuctoo, as estimated by Indian widows flinging themselves upon the funeral pyres of their husbands, or frenzied mullahs, or Afridi snipers prowling round British encampments, or pilgrims on their way to Mecca, or Jews at the Wailing Wall in Jerusalem? Mankind has been much given to massacres, and, if recorded, the catalogue of them would fill a volume. When the Tartars burnt Moscow in 1570 it is estimated that half a million perished in the flames and accompanying slaughter within three hours. They carried with them into slavery on their retreat a hundred thousand women. A supply of women was a customary article, a portion of the tribute in the treaties between the Chinese and the Huns. A bird's-eye view of history does not present our species in a very favourable light. Wholesale butcheries, cities sacked and sown with salt, are among its commonplace occurrences. Lord Snowden recently described the Great War as the greatest act of human folly in history. He must have been reading *Stories for Little Arthur*.

Religion itself, Christianity itself, so far from presenting a picture of friendliness and charity in a fierce and warring world, introduces us to a narrative of jarring sects, furious controversies and revolting persecutions. During three centuries three hundred thousand persons were put to death for their religious opinions in Madrid alone. 'O Liberty,' exclaimed Madame Roland on the scaffold, 'what crimes have been committed in thy name!' Might she not with equal truth have said 'O Religion'? In the opinion of Chrysostom, Archbishop of Constantinople in the fifth century, the number of Christian bishops who would be saved bore a very small proportion to those who would be damned. Is it surprising that some have believed that a malignant demon sat by the cradle of the unhappy human race? 'Man', said Pascal, 'is an incomprehensible monster.' Byron is not more complimentary. He is 'a two-legged reptile, crafty and venomous.

You comfort yourself, no doubt, that these enormities are of ancient date, and now impossible. Not so. They are easily matched among Christian peoples within the lifetime of the youngest of us. I am not thinking of the daily murders in the centres of modern civilisation. There were 12,000 in the United States in 1930. I am not thinking of Turkey's record within the last twenty years. Come nearer home, and read, read for yourselves, the documented account of the doings of the German armies among the civilian population of Belgium. 'It contains a body of authentic and overwhelming evidence'—I quote from Mons. Maeterlinck—'upon the massacres at Ardenne, Dinant, Louvain and Aerschot, which enables history here and now to pronounce its verdict with even greater certainty than the most scrupulous jury of a criminal court.' The last fifty or sixty years have been as rich in assassinations of public men as any in the past. Fourteen kings and ruling princes, six presidents—of the United States, France and other countries—besides many viceroys, prime ministers and ministers.

Why do I recall circumstances so depressing? Merely because, in my judgment, indisputable matter has the priority over dialectical exchanges. It does not seem to me irrelevant, however strangely it sounds in the great debate on faith and morals, to remember, more especially when we are lecturing our neighbours after our national manner, that the Liverpool merchants, not so long ago, sold three hundred thousand slaves within ten or twelve years to the West Indies, for fifteen million pounds, or that Sir John Hawkins kidnapped natives in West Africa for the trade in negroes, in his ship, the *Jesus*. The effect of civilised man's intrusion into uncivilised lands, whether with selfish or unselfish intentions, has not been in the main to their benefit, but rather to their ruin. Assassination of rivals, a method of government hoary with age, and not ineffective, is still employed in countries which stand at the head of Western civilisation. 'Count Borgia', wrote a recent historian, Mr. F. S. Oliver, 'slew his thousands, the Terror its tens of thousands, Lenin his hundreds of thousands,' and adds the following note—'Strictly speaking, the statement should be "millions" instead of hundreds of thousands,' and cites from Sarolea's *Impressions of Soviet Russia*:

' "A Russian statistical investigation estimates that the Dictator killed 28 bishops, 1219 priests, 6000 professors and teachers, 9000 doctors, 54,000 officers, 260,000 soldiers, 70,000 policemen, 355,250 intellectuals and professional men, 193,000 workers, 815,000 peasants." ' That is about 1,750,000 were executed or massacred. In addition the same writer seems to be of the opinion that some 18 millions died of famine, a famine that Lenin had it in his power greatly to mitigate, if not altogether to prevent, but which he deliberately allowed to rage. The diminution of the Russian population during the period of his dictatorship would appear to have been about $12\frac{1}{4}$ per cent.[1] Is Lenin execrated? Not at all. He is revered as the saviour of his country, and his tomb is visited by multitudes of pilgrims, as if it were that of a saint.

This is the kind of material with which the historian provides you. Mark now the philosopher's way of thought. 'Evil', announces Spinoza in his *Ethics*, with much geometrical parade, 'Evil is nothing positive.' It is well to have it from so widely worshipped an authority, a leader in Israel. How blue and cloudless is his sky! What healing balm is here offered us! 'A little water', as Lady Macbeth remarked of the murder of Duncan, 'A little water clears us of this deed.' As the medieval exorcist scattered legions of devils with a sprinkling of holy water and a formula, so our philosopher puts to flight the agonies, the

[1] *The Endless Adventure*, p. 70.

99

inhumanities, the plagues and cruelties of the world with a single word—'Evil is nothing positive.' They vanish into the limbo of the negative, and our anxieties are at an end. For my part I prefer the old-fashioned Bishop Butler, who held the childlike opinion—'Everything is what it is, and not another thing.' When philosophers begin to substitute words for things one tires of their company. When we have enumerated the catastrophes by famine, flood and earthquake, from the spasms of the fevered earth, and they have not been few—in a single year half a million died of the ulcerous plague in North-Eastern Russia; and the victims of the Black Death are estimated to have numbered 37 millions in the East, and during one visitation over 3 millions in England alone, that is from one-third to a half of the entire population of that time—we have still to record Gibbon's opinion that 'man has much more to dread from the passions of his fellow creatures than from the convulsions of the elements'. Gibbon was very possibly a prejudiced witness. Whatever be the truth, you must ascribe responsibility for our earthly ills either to nature or to man. There appears to be no other alternative. And when we look

over wasted lands

Blight and famine, plague and earthquake, roaring deeps and fiery sands,
Clanging fights, and flaming towns, and sinking ships and praying hands,

the blame, if blame there be, should, on the face of it, be pretty equally distributed.

The pugnacity of the human species is in especial the target of the moralists. And certainly war has been its great industry. Napoleon invaded Russia with 600,000 men. Fifty thousand fell at Borodino, twenty thousand at the crossing of the Beresina. A thousand of the Old Guard returned. As Byron wrote of Acro-Corinth, which rises above the Isthmus to a height of nearly 2000 feet—

Or could the bones of all the slain
Who perished there, be piled again,
That rival pyramid would rise
More mountain-like through those clear skies
Than yon tower-capp'd Acropolis
Which seems the very clouds to kiss.

Abolish war, say our humanitarians, and you have abolished the worst feature among the rivalries of mankind. Reflect a moment, however, and you discover that you but drive these rivalries into another channel, in which the sufferings inflicted are, indeed, masked, but little diminished. Economic competition remains, waged with an easy conscience and no danger, a less noble form of war, yet as ruthless and merciless. Capture a people's markets, and you strike at its life. Where should we be if ours were captured? War is more dramatic and spectacular, but slow, grinding starvation wields no less deadly a sword. Between four and five millions perished from famine and attendant causes in Russia in 1933, and the world was quite unruffled, though no year of the great war had such a crop of victims.

It is the fecundity of nature against which our moralists should direct their indignation. Nature is the enemy. I have read that the bodies of over 30,000 infants are picked up every year in the streets of Shanghai. Until the reformers have found some means of restraining that fecundity, of reducing Nature's vast populations, these living creatures can hardly be expected to lay aside their weapons, whatever they are; they will continue to exert all their efforts to remain alive. And not men only. All living things multiply as long as they can find sustenance. The rabbit would overrun the earth if not checked. The progeny of a few musk rats, introduced from Alaska a few years since, have cost millions to destroy. If you dislike slaughter you must shut against animals, as against men, the portals of existence. Establish birth control universally among both, and your aim may be secured, but not till then.

And when this has been said, all has not yet been said. 'It is well that war is so terrible,' said General Lee, watching the great charge at Friedericksburg; 'we should grow too fond of it.' 'War', as De Quincey said, 'has a deeper and more ineffable relation to hidden grandeurs in man than has yet been deciphered.' And men may remain fond of it, as of all adventure with death in the balance. The romance of war may be dead. Its grim and ugly countenance has grown uglier still and grimmer. Yet when men rise in their stirrups, like Cromwell, on the dawn of a great encounter, will not their blood run faster? When mighty issues are at stake will they remain unmoved? Or are there never again to be any issues of consequence? There will, then, be no more nailing of colours to the mast. No colours will be worth nailing at the cost of human life. Never again will the cry be heard, 'Truth, freedom and justice though the heavens fall!'

I find it difficult to accept these propositions, nor should I care to belong to a society which accepted them. Certainly it would be a remarkable transformation. We should not know ourselves when it came about. We should not recognise human nature in the days of the great indifference to the old values held sacred through the centuries. I may, indeed, be wrong, but to me it seems that if there be anything at all, and many arguments have been advanced to prove that there is nothing at all, but if there be anything at all to distinguish man from the brutes, to lay the foundation for his superior dignity, it is his very singular faith in absolute and eternal values, against which he holds, or used to hold, nothing could be set, and nothing was of any weight, neither his own life nor that of others. Perhaps it was all a foolishness. But this foolishness had at least a regal manner, a style. It had an air, this creed of values above life's value. You could hardly refuse to admire the princely gait and presence of the folly, so high it carried its head among the cunning bargainers, hucksterers and investors, the astute and slippery profiteers of the world's markets and bazaars. Nor is life a great price to pay, so beset, as it is, with ills, and so fragile its crystal vase. Of creatures like ourselves earth has spawned millions upon millions. Of their passage across the stage they have left—the majority—no trace. A million die every month in China alone. Who misses them? Visit the valley of the Nile, that vast sepulchre, where for millenniums men have risen out of the dust, like blades of grass, to return again to dust. 'They were and are not,' their only epitaph.

Foreigners express astonishment at the insularity of English thought. I share it. We in these thrice fortunate isles, where a sum approaching five hundred millions is spent annually on social services, never so much as dreamt of in any other age or country, inhabit Paradise without being aware of it. Yet I find in myself a greater astonishment at the remoteness of philosophers from the world in which they live. One wishes they would thumb the leaves of the historical record before they constructed their admirable theories. They should, after the manner of the artists, have made some preliminary studies. They should have cultivated the acquaintance of plotters and revolutionaries, of angry souls in underground dwellings. They would write more convincingly if they had consorted, even in imagination, with cave-dwellers, and lake-dwellers, and tree-dwellers, talked with buffoons, and mountebanks, and charlatans, with sadists and pimps and procurers, as well as with priests, prophets and professors. They might have learnt something from the cynics as well as the logicians, from vikings as well as Christians, from corsairs and courtesans as well as from philanthropists, from berserker fighters, stark men, quicker with a blow than a word, whose joy was more in the argument of steel with steel than of sentence with sentence, who thought death in battle, 'with heroes' hot corpses high heaped for a pillow', the only form of death worthy of a man.

> A straw death, a cow death,
> Such death suits not me.

What have Hegel or Kant to say of such people, or the structure of their minds? It is well to keep the world as it was, and is, always in sight, with its conflicting aims and purposes, its roystering and carousing, as well as its church-going; its gambling and fiddling and cock-fighting, as well as ploughing and praying; its jesting and quarrelling and jobbery and money-lending and love-making, as well as its decencies and respectabilities.

If you ask, What have been the occupations and interests of men, the pursuits of their leisure?—you will learn something. Read for your instruction the ditties that are not to be found in the school anthologies.

> To keep game cocks,
> To hunt the fox,
> To drink in punch the Solway;
> With debts galore,
> But fun far more,
> Oh! that's the man for Galway!

If you wish to know your world, enquire into its luxuries and frivolities. Where the heart is, there the money goes. The extravagances of Oriental monarchs and Roman emperors are a proverb. 'The number of eunuchs in the palace of Constantius', relates Gibbon, 'could only be compared with the insects of a summer's day.' The Emperor Vitellius consumed in eating, we are told, six millions of money in seven months. Rome sent a million of money annually to the East for jewelry, perfumes and spices in Pliny's time. Large though it seems, a comparison of such expenditure with the present day might not be much to our advantage.

It was a source of sorrow to Prynne, the seventeenth-century Puritan—whose incessant and tiresome activities led Charles II to propose that he should be 'kept busy by letting him write against the Catholics and pore over the records of the Temple'—that Shakespere's plays were 'printed on the best crown paper, far better than most Bibles'. He was distressed to horror when told that in two years 40,000 play books were sold, they being more vendible 'than the choicest sermons'. In this year of grace he would, I fear, be sunk in still deeper dejection. The world has from the beginning been the despair of moralists, *rari nantes in gurgite vasto*, lost amid the prodigious variety of human beings, their motives, manners and pursuits, through the fifty centuries of which any record remains. To ask men to live contrary to their natures is to ask the shark to live in the forest, or the eagle under the water. It would be an enquiry of interest how far Kant's moral imperative has been the catechism of the race, of the two thousand million of our present fellow creatures, feverishly engaged in extracting from life whatever in the way of satisfaction it may afford. How far do his ethical principles govern society even in our advanced civilisation? 'As for us,' said Trotsky, 'we were never concerned about the Kantian, priestly, and vegetarian Quaker prattle about the sacredness of human life.' How jubilant would be our reformers if enthusiasm for the Kantian categorical imperative prevailed in the same degree as for sport in any of its forms, football, racing, motoring, golf. When the theorists set out to construct their Utopias one wonders where they will find the men and women willing to inhabit them. Are they all to be listless, docile folk, without passions, who read instructive books, and desire hidden and sheltered lives, who live, if they can be said to live at all, like plants, as pulseless and inoffensive an existence as the flowers of the field?

As in the atom the explosive energy of nature is locked up in a minute finite centre, so in the individual burns a flame kindled in her furnace. If by morals we mean—and how often it seems to mean little else—a reduction of nature's temperature, morality must fail, if virtue consists in desiring little, and that little without enthusiasm, if the acme of goodness is inactivity. If we hope to save the world by lowering its vitality, we have in nature a formidable antagonist, if we hope to build Jerusalem by drawing the hot blood from the veins of men. Nature is herself vitality. When your vitality fails, when life disappoints or proves too much for you, when you no longer care much for anything, or despair of obtaining what you wish, when you are ill, when you tire and weary of the struggle—then, indeed, you sum up against existence; seldom when the blood flows, when hopes are high and the heart beats strongly.

Human annals may make dismal reading, but their fascination remains. And in the end, say what you will, the pageant of human life has for the observer a great, if gloomy, magnificence. With no friends save his own indomitable spirit, man has made his way through the long centuries. Distressed, defeated, deceived, he continues to undertake his forlorn hopes and pursue his fantastic loyalties. Who would abate, wherever they lead, his resolution, his willingness to dare the wrath whether of gods or men, his refusal to count the cost?

Human sentiment has always honoured men cast in the heroic mould, the strong men of their hands, even when their careers, like those of Alexander and Caesar, the limits of whose fame are the stars, brought death to thousands, even when they waded through blood to the goal of their desires. How is this? It is strength we admire, strength which seems to reflect something of its splendour upon the whole human family. Men have always admired others whom no fears could terrify or distract from their purposes, no horrors tame, who accepted for themselves wounds and death rather than the relinquishment of their designs, who burned their boats, for whom retreat was more bitter than destruction. Great deeds are not done by desiring nothing.

To dwell upon man's destroying propensities, as if they constituted his whole history, were indeed an absurd falsification of the record, to think of him as wholly occupied in scattering firebrands and death. His inventive and architectural faculties are equally in evidence. If he has made wars he has also founded empires, laws and constitutions, the arts of government and peace. Like his Mother Nature he both makes and unmakes. He is, like her, Janus-headed. He is statesman and soldier, builder and destroyer, explorer and merchant, pirate, poet and artist.   He is composed of 'fleeting opposites', Don Quixote and Sancho Panza, idealist dreamer and practical planner in one. Think of his heart-breaking labours, astounding enterprise, fierce industry and indefatigable toil.   'The history of navigation', for example, it has been said, 'is a history of human martyrdom.' Think of the farming and building, the journeying and the voyaging, the caravans and trade routes through deserts and over mountains, of 'many an old captain hoisting out many an old barrel on to many an old slip'—all in the midst of perils, all at the cost of anxiety and hardship; and your wonder and admiration will drown your censures.   Who but men have crossed, sounded and charted the oceans, explored the Arctic and Antarctic poles, conquered sea and air, constructed great scientific and philosophical systems, built temples and cathedrals, written poems, dramas and romances, composed music, carved statues, painted pictures, constructed machinery, harnessed the unseen powers of nature, invented medicine and surgery?   And has all this been done by saints and ascetics?   Have the rough-riders, the vagabonds, the reckless ragamuffins not had a hand in it, and should it not be counted to them for righteousness?   These are questions to be pondered.

And still another.   Was it all, or was it not, worth doing, or would it have been better to live in the Garden of Eden cultivating roses for ever?   At least, through all the inclement weather of the world, arts and crafts have been invented, cultures established, nature explored.   Justice and sense have not perished out of the earth.   The voyage has had its interests and incidents. The ship of humanity has not foundered in the gales.

And science?   However you regard her attitude and aims, deplore her emphasis upon the body rather than the soul, you cannot deny the benefits she has conferred upon humanity. True it is that worldliness has under her regime superseded other-worldliness, that as one of her representatives, Professor Hogben, claims, 'our expectation of life has increased as we have learnt to worry less about the good life than about the good drain.'   Yet so impressive, so far-reaching are her achievements as not merely to silence all criticism but to arouse a noble enthusiasm, and enlist in the cause of humanity a legion of recruits, missionaries of her gospel.   Take modern medicine alone, the child of science, the most promising and brightest-eyed of her family.   If it has not mastered, it has so diminished as to rob bodily pain of its terrors. Plagues and pestilences have been stayed, a multitude of diseases—diphtheria, rabies, smallpox, typhus, yellow-fever, Maltese fever — to name only a few —almost exterminated. Great scourge-ridden tracts of the earth's surface rendered habitable, food values understood, vaccines and anti-toxins discovered, antiseptic surgery so established as to open up new fields of remedial agency, ailments of the mind as well as of the body controlled and relieved. This is a record, indeed, to which no previous age in history can produce a parallel. Within a century the expectation of life in all civilised countries has amazingly increased—in our own by sixteen years, in Denmark by seventeen, in parts of America by fifteen. Give to man and to his science their due. Who can be blind to such facts, or deaf to their eloquence?

That there have been accompanying disadvantages cannot be denied. All goods are associated with evils, and nature will not let us rest. A static world it is not, never was and never will be. There have been revolutions in the past, there will be revolutions hereafter, in the world of thought as in the world of events. We must expect the sudden and unpredictable. You may desire a stabilised system, an international agreement to keep things much as they are in respect of national boundaries, material advantages in wealth, coal, oil, trade facilities. It will not be given you. For all your entreaties the world will not cease to revolve. Nature is no friend of stagnation. Climates change, economic conditions change, birth rates rise and fall, labour is cheap here and dear there, a new invention, a new commodity is in demand, and cities spring up to meet it. Factories are built, uninhabited areas become crowded, peoples migrate, once populous districts are deserted. The seats of ancient empires are lost in the desert or the jungle.

> 'My name is Ozymandias, King of kings;
> Look on my works, ye mighty, and despair.'
> Nothing beside remains. Round the decay
> Of that colossal wreck, boundless and bare
> The lone and level sands stretch far away.

They will remain to haunt us, the mutability, the eternal flux, the ceaseless hostilities, the crooked ways of nature. The lovely has in her domain no priority over the vile, nor wisdom any advantage over folly in respect of its enduring date. Individuals, races, cultures, high or low, all obey the same law. They have their youth and age, flower and decay. Some perish in childhood, some are crippled by accident or disease, some attain power and place, confer benefits upon, or bring ruin to their neighbours. We can see no logic in it. There is no circumstance in the lives of individual men you will not find written large in the history of peoples and civilisations. And as no one can tell us why we grow old, stiffen and die, save that such is the rhythm of existence, so the rise and fall of nations and states is similarly mysterious. The words 'Destiny' and 'Fate', as rulers of mortal things, once so common, so continuously in the thoughts of reflective folk, like the Greeks or the Northmen, are seldom heard to-day. But their mighty power is not abated, they have not resigned from their imperial thrones.

In these circumstances, you may ask, Is anything worth undertaking in the world at all? Well, whether existence have meaning and value, or have none, here we certainly are, we living creatures. And the first and unescapable question for Christianity, as indeed for all men, is the simple question of acceptance or rejection of life, not as you would like it to be, but as it is, under the conditions which prevail, of life as universally experienced, as it has been lived from age to age. To hope for its alteration, for its acceptance of our pattern, the pattern of behaviour we prefer and prescribe, is a rainbow vision. Tell us, then, whether Christianity stands for living in the present world or against it, for participation or withdrawal, for action or quietism, for taking a share in the shaping of history, in its multifarious and dubious undertakings, a hand in the game, or refusing it. Throughout the history of the Church there has been a halting between two opinions, for co-operation and for withdrawal. It appears improbable that the future will permit the compromise. Denunciations are in vain, complaints against men and nations are in vain. And if the decision be to go down into the turbulent arena of human affairs, we may say, paraphrasing a famous passage of Lucan, that it will be with iron, and not with prayers we shall settle this war, and whether a man shall live or die. As for England and ourselves—

> Time, and the ocean, and some favouring star,
> In high cabal have made us what we are.

Our vigorous and valiant ancestors—perhaps they were too vigorous and valiant—had imperial dreams, and committed us to the rule of half the world, for which we have no longer any relish. Is it our duty to defend and maintain this heritage, or to relinquish it? And if we relinquish it, will it pass into cleaner hands, and mankind be better served? 'In every part of the world where British interests are at stake', said Dicey, 'I am in favour of advancing those interests even at the cost of war.' There is a refreshing decision about this declaration. Right or wrong, there at least spoke a man. To succeed in life you must believe in life. Horror and dismay are no helpmates in a battle. Empires like our own, which disseminate ideas, which impose themselves upon and influence the world, how could they accomplish what they have in fact accomplished without the will, the resolution and the power to do so? How can doubt, hesitation, absence of belief in your mission strengthen your hands, or how can soul sickness, hatred of life's conditions, disgust of the conflict enable you to play a leading part in the shaping of the future? If men and nations do not find life worth the living, or what it offers worth possessing, it is very certain nature will replace them by others who do. If an individual or a people ceases to believe in itself, its aims and ideals, others with firmer aims and beliefs will climb into the saddle. When a race or nation no longer desires place, power, position, influence, has no wish that its ways of thought should prevail, no desire to impress its seal upon future events, how can you suppose it will continue to stand in this hurly-burly world? Power in the world, the prizes of the world, must go to those who value them, and think them worth the effort to secure.

Civilisations arise, and continue to exist—and all history is the witness to the truth—when conditions are hard, only when they are continually threatened, only when they are determined to maintain and defend their rule. They decline and fall when the external pressure is removed, or the inner spirit decays. The surrender may disguise itself in many forms, of which humanitarian sentiment is one. 'If a country', wrote F. S. Oliver, 'will not stand up for its rights, it must surely lose them'. The spirit of giving in is the most fatal disease to which nations are subject, and it is apt to attack them, like a cancer, when they have arrived at the meridian.' You may, indeed, conclude that you will have neither part nor lot in the rivalry, you may wash your hands of responsibility for the madness and folly of mankind, you may renounce the contests, and refuse the challenges of ambitious competitors for your place and power, you may elect to leave its future to the bullies of the world. But it should be obvious that if the heart be set on nothing the earth contains or offers, nothing in the manner of the earth will be done there.

When England's day comes to an end the principles which have contributed to its coming, Christian, pacifist, or whatever they may be styled, will not thereby be strengthened. On the contrary, such is the irony which pervades things human, they will have brought about their own eclipse, their own dissolution, and the triumph of the opposing principles. The decline and fall of England, which will rejoice her enemies, will not be England's decline and fall only, but of all for which she stood, and not till then shall we know the extent of our miseries. I, at least, am not of the opinion that humanity, justice, freedom, no, nor Christianity, will be gainers in that fall.

VI

THE FAMILY TREE

O delight of the headlands and beaches!
   O desire of the wind on the wold,
More glad than a man's when it reaches
   That end which it sought from of old,
And the palm of possession is dreary
   To the sense that in search of it sinned;
But nor satisfied ever nor weary
      Is ever the wind.

The delight that he takes but in living
   Is more than of all things that live:
For this world that has all things for giving
   Has nothing so goodly to give:
But more than delight his desire is,
   For the goal where his pinions would be
Is immortal as air or as fire is,
      Immense as the sea.

Though hence comes the moan that he borrows
   From darkness and depth of the night,
Though hence be the spring of his sorrows,
   Hence too is the joy of his might;
The delight that his doom is for ever
   To seek and desire and rejoice,
And the sense that eternity never
      Shall silence his voice.

                              Swinburne

VI

THE FAMILY TREE

Addison desired his readers 'to consider the world in its most agreeable aspects'. Times have changed. Not so, our modern teachers. They trample upon human pride and show no mercy to human pretensions. And this very disregard of our feelings seems to confer merit upon their verdicts, and to invest them with the mantle of truth. Yet the pleasant is not necessarily false, nor the unpleasant always true. Nevertheless, to many men, whether they are right or not in so interpreting modern knowledge, it has brought disillusion. It bears the stamp of honesty, and so much the more chills their hearts, and gives the lie to their most cherished hopes and aspirations. We are assured indeed by some of our spiritual comforters that nothing of importance has occurred, nothing to shake the foundations of religion and morals. But the world has not been deceived. It is conscious that an earthquake has taken place, that the veil of the old temple has been rent in twain, from the top to the bottom. It is not merely that the universe has expanded to terrifying proportions, that human beings have become ridiculous Lilliputians, hardly discernible in the stupendous expanse. It has dawned upon men that there is no escape from the conclusion that they are simply animals, one species among thousands, and with no claim to any royal or divine prerogative: lords of creation, if you will, but certainly not heirs of heaven.

I cannot accept the view of some theologians that man's animal ancestry may be set aside without anxiety as of no serious import, that their predecessors of the last century had no cause for alarm when Darwinism received the *imprimatur* of science, and that they needlessly exaggerated its bearing upon faith and doctrine. If man could be proved a separate and unique being, how eased were the situation for theologians. The old belief in the human species as a special creation, altogether peculiar and outstanding, laid a firm foundation for the great cathedral of religious thought.

Regard man as a creature among other creatures, of the same lineage, and you are involved in a very delicate and difficult operation. You are immediately driven to the question: How then is he to be distinguished from the rest? You cannot make light of the query: it is crucial for religion and ethics. No doubt he has by virtue of superior intelligence placed all the other tribes under his feet. The distinction is not sufficient. Too much hangs in the balance. Is this difference one of kind, or merely of degree? Such a difference as anyone can see between the octopus and the camel, the caterpillar and the eagle, or something far deeper? The churches have built high upon the difference, whatever it be, but have they built on quicksand or the eternal granite?

It has been the habit of theologians and moralists to overlook the lower creation. These unpretentious beings were left out of account as spiritually and ethically negligible. They have had their revenge. To treat the whole animal kingdom, as most religions have done, with calm disdain, is no longer possible. Personally I am not at ease with a theology which has forgotten them, as Christianity appears to have done. And when you are now asked, 'Where yawns the impassable gulf between us and them?' when you are requested to produce the title-deeds for man's unique status, you must make some answer. A supreme dignity and a grave responsibility attach to the rank you claim for him. You base upon it the assertion that he stands in a peculiar relation to God, has need of religion, and is responsible for his actions. To these matters the other creatures appear to be indifferent, and to do without them well enough. What need have we of religion, if they have none, or of morals, if they have none? 'They do not lie awake in the dark, and weep for their sins,' as Whitman wrote. 'They do not make me sick discussing their duty to God.' They are not expected to display virtuous habits, exercise self-discipline, or respond to the calls of conscience. They adapt themselves to nature with the most perfect composure, appear, indeed, to know all about it, and without much thinking, and with far less hubbub and noise seemingly manage their affairs rather better than we, with all our elaborate machinery of talk and thought. I have a great respect for them. To conclude curtly with Bacon that 'men are not animals erect, but immortal gods', however agreeable a proposition, and turn your attention elsewhere, will no longer serve.

You may say that theories, such as those of Lamarck or Darwin, are no doubt of great interest, yet they add little of consequence to what everyone knows. True enough. What do we all know without their assistance? No exhausting enquiry is needed to instruct us that the inhabitants of the earth form one family. The similarities between all animals, even between plants and animals, are obvious to any observer. Their protoplasmic basis, their cellular and bodily structure, their respiratory and digestive processes, their capacity for growth and reproduction, and if we like to go further, the presence, for example, of the same blood groups in men and anthropoid apes—a great multitude of such resemblances almost leaps to the eye, and quite apart from Darwinism, or any other theory, proclaims the solidarity of living things.

Moreover, if we reflect, we see that they are inevitable. The various forms of life accommodated themselves to the situation here on earth as they found it, and similar methods and structures were necessary to fulfil the conditions. Similarity of anatomical structure, of physiological processes, therefore, proves very little. All forms of life, if life were to establish itself upon this planet, necessarily made use of the materials available, the oxygen, hydrogen and carbon, by similar devices. If you have no other materials with which to build your house but clay, or wood, or stone, you must use wood, or clay, or stone, and your design will be governed by the substance you employ. There is no need to labour the point of physical resemblances, or to make much of them. Animals are very much like ourselves in a hundred ways. We all know that, and there are many men who feel that the affectionate relations between a dog and his master go further to establish the unity of living creatures than all the scientific doctrines. Life is one. And we may add consciousness in some form is to be found where life is to be found, dreaming as in plants, half-awake as in animals, or wide awake as in ourselves.

That living things form a single community, then, is no new thought. How could it be? All animals, including man, Archelaus taught two thousand years ago, were generated out of mud, and had the same manner of life. Many ancient sages had like thoughts. The Indian doctrine of reincarnation recognised the links between the various species. Buddha himself allowed that he had been in previous lives an animal. 'Before this', said

Empedocles, 'I was born once a boy, and a maiden, a plant, and a bird, and a darting fish in the sea.' Leibniz held strongly by the law of continuity, and believed that 'all the orders of natural beings necessarily form one chain', that they were, so to say, parts of one and the same curve, that plants were in some sense imperfect animals, and that there could not be 'separation between the different orders of beings which together fill the universe'. Berkeley was of the same opinion. 'There is no chasm in nature, but a chain or scale of beings.'

Allow all this. Nevertheless the publication of Darwin's books came as a shock. It clinched the matter, and brought it a little too near for comfort, out of the realm of airy speculation into that of knowledge. And the vexatious question recurs: Can any distinction, keeping in mind the immense weight of the theological structure it must bear, can any distinction capable of supporting it be drawn? What is to be said?

Of course men are animals, it may be answered, but how much more. Leave aside for the moment man's ethical and spiritual instincts, his ideals and aspirations. Consider only his obvious characteristics. The first witness to his astonishing ascendancy is his erect posture, his lifted gaze, contrasted with the hanging head of the quadruped. The second that he alone invented speech, the magic-working instrument, beside which all other inventions are childish toys. 'The *differentia* of man,' wrote that eminent anthropologist, Dr. Marett, 'the quality that marks him off from the other animals, is undoubtedly his power of articulate speech. If language is ultimately the creation of the intellect, yet hardly less fundamentally is the intellect a creation of language.' How the ages meet! Homer knew it long ago. He spoke of μέροπες ἄνθρωποι, beings endowed with, or dividing the voice, articulately speaking men.

A third witness to man's unique status, upon which the philosophers have laid the greatest emphasis, lies in his singular talent to frame ideas with which nothing in nature corresponds, images and thoughts which outrange and transcend the visible world and all that it contains, which deal in meanings and values utterly remote from our material surroundings. Socrates in the *Phaedrus* makes of this the final criterion. Man is the only reasoning being, and reason, as Schopenhauer phrased it, is 'the faculty of forming concepts', that is, of framing ideas, as of justice, beauty, truth, imperceptible to sense.   These are conceptions without physical counterparts, and have no substantial existence in space. Search earth and the heavens, and you will find no trace of them. Nature never heard of such things.   They are of man's own making, the exclusive property of the human soul.   If nature has done what man has never done, and cannot do, he also is a creative agent, and has done many things of which she never dreamt.   He is a being with double vision.   'Sagacious of his quarry from afar', he looks before and after, recalls the past in memory, and builds the future in imagination, the cities and palaces of his spacious dreams, patterns of his own, never planned by nature, built in the empyrean, and beyond even her regal powers. Show me, for example, her sonatas and her symphonies.   Thus it is that he has made his escape from the prison of material things, thus emerged into the open air of mental and spiritual freedom. Have any animals looked round the world and evolved religions, or wondered at the stars and constructed astronomies?   Have they invented music or mathematics?   What have the lizards and the apes done for geometry?   Or what have they to say about the gods?   They do not ask 'Why was I born?' 'Why am I cold, hungry, miserable?' 'Who made me thus?'   There is no speculation in their eyes, and for them the wildernesses of space hold no secrets, the starry labyrinths no symbols of a high romance.

How did man come to evolve abstract thought, to discover general principles?   Does his anatomy account for it, or his breathing system, or digestive or glandular?   In the realm of thought if not elsewhere he has achieved an element of freedom. He can at least think what he pleases, view the world in which he finds himself as good or bad, treat it with disdain, contempt or approval, accept or reject it in his heart.   The prospect widens, infinity opens to his gaze—

Hills peep o'er hills, and Alps on Alps arise.

In many, if not in all respects man resembles the ape.   Place the bones and structure of apes and men alongside each other and there is not much to distinguish them.   The skeleton of Newton did not differ so greatly from that of a chimpanzee.   At an early stage in their respective careers there was nothing to choose between them.   Emphasise the resemblances by all means, but the more you emphasise these resemblances the more troublesome it becomes to account for the *Principia*, for the imperial mind,

Voyaging through strange seas of thought alone.

One begins to suspect chat, despite the likeness, in some fashion man differs from the animals. You will not, however, discover it from reading the books of the biologists. They never mention anything save his animal characteristics. The discovery that he transcends them biology leaves to you. You must go elsewhere for this information. The origin and bodily structure of the human species may not greatly instruct and may even mislead us. Nevertheless let us hear what has been said.

Life took possession of its estate, we are told, five hundred or a thousand million years ago. The exact figures have not been issued. It has blossomed into all the forms we see around us, from the daffodil to the dromedary, from the amoeba to man. The origins of life are still shrouded in mystery, but there is a formidable array of arguments from embryology, palaeontology, genetics, or experimental breeding, to suggest that all the different species, plants and animals alike, have a common ancestry. The eternal quest of the human mind for unity will have it so. Nothing can shake its determination to derive the many from the one. How, then, has it come to pass? And here the magic word is Evolution, which to use is, indeed, a sad affliction, since it has lost all meaning, but a word which is unavoidable, which our age is persuaded opens all the locks. Ask yourselves this question—'Does evolution mean improvement, progress?' Or, more simply, 'Is it better to be a monkey than a tadpole, a tiger than a crab, a man than a gorilla?' Our scientific friends, having nothing to do with matters of 'better' or 'worse', cannot tell you. Does evolution, that is to say, mean merely that as time goes on things are altered—we have first one species and then another, perpetual changes—is that all it means, or are we getting somewhere? Upon this point science preserves a rigid silence. Evolution is its favourite word, but what exactly evolution is, or what it means, I have personally been unable to discover. What a boon it would be if the Royal Society would only define it for us. But they know better than to try.

The publication of Darwin's world-shaking books, *The Origin of Species* in 1859, and *The Descent of Man*, twelve years later, opens a fascinating chapter in the history of human thought. Huxley, his champion, 'Darwin's bull-dog', tells us how the theory was received; on the part of men of science with immediate and delighted acceptance, on the part of the theologians with horror and passionate opposition. What is of equal interest with the doctrine is the light it throws upon human nature, human reasoning and human motives. How profoundly we are affected by our secret wishes, our instinctive preferences and prejudices. It is vital to distinguish, though the plain man takes little interest in the distinction, between 'the fact of evolution and the manner of it', in the phrase of Romanes. Darwin's singularly modest programme was not in fact an evolution theory at all, nor does he use the word, subsequently popularised by Herbert Spencer. He confined himself to a single issue, the origin of species. Given the existing variety of living things, must we regard each variety as immutable, each now as it was from the first? Is it not more probable, is it not the truth, that new species originate from the selective action of the environment upon the chance variations among the individual members of each family? Darwin's was in no sense a philosophic doctrine. It refrained from speculations upon the origin of life. It passed over without mention the metaphysical problems associated with substance, change, growth, causation. However powerful, for example, as a method, evolution possesses no originating impulse. It is not a form of energy, a force or a power; 'it cannot create the conditions of its own possibility.' It operates, if it can be said to operate, within a situation already present. Evolution doubtless may be supposed capable of much, but how did the conditions necessary to evolution arise? Is evolution a god, which created these conditions as well as itself?

The supreme attraction of Darwinism lay in its exclusion of special creation and the idea of purpose. That was its peculiar charm. For that reason it was exultantly received and proclaimed as the final truth. 'It is very absurd', remarks Kant, 'to expect enlightenment from reason, and yet to dictate to her in advance upon which side she must necessarily determine.' None the less it was agreed that the doctrine must be true, and there followed a sustained effort to prove it true. Never has there been greater zeal and industry displayed in search of corroborative evidence. We see it to-day in the search for fossil remains of early man or man's immediate predecessors, the interest in the human or sub-human types found in Java, Pekin, Piltdown, Heidelberg, Neanderthal and Rhodesia. Here you have a faith, which so seized upon the mind, such was the devotion it inspired, as to energise thought to find the grounds upon which it might be firmly established—a belief, that is to say, which preceded the evidence. And why? Because the thought that it might not be true was utterly hateful and intolerable. With the utmost frankness Huxley himself gives us the clue to the jubilation with which Darwinism was received, and espoused before it was demonstrated. The doctrine, he tells us, did men of science the immense service of freeing them from the dilemma, 'Refuse to accept the Creation hypothesis, and what have you to put in its place?' Expressed succinctly, we may say, the theory was a God-send to the disbelievers in God. It postponed at least, though it could not finally expunge, the alternative of God as the cause of all things. For the moment the unwelcome concept of a creator sinks below the horizon of thought, and so ceases from troubling. Mysteries, indeed, are not disposed of, they are merely shelved by removing them into the far distance. They become, however, less vexatious, as someone we dislike may be forgotten in his absence, much less exasperating than his presence. Thus God died away into the infinite beyond, and freed of his immediate company many philosophers and men of science breathed more freely. The theory eased the mind, and offered leisure to develop further the thesis of naturalism as against supernaturalism. Let us be just, too, and bear in mind that there was no alternative within sight. Evolution theory must be true, because otherwise we should not know what to believe, a humiliating and monstrous situation. It was this or nothing, or rather it was this or a choice between God and blank amazement, a most disagreeable dilemma.

Could any history be more interesting or instructive? Let us recommend it for study to the psychologists.

To return to the origin of species. 'In dim outline', wrote that eminent biologist, Bateson, 'evolution is evident enough. From the facts it is a conclusion which inevitably follows. But that particular bit of the theory which is concerned with the origin and nature of species remains utterly mysterious.' No one will deny the grandeur of the evolution conception. The picture makes a powerful appeal to the imagination. The prospect is vast and pleasing. We have a magnificent bird's-eye view, as from a mountain-top, of the whole history of life unrolled before our wondering eyes. The panorama is spread out there before us. We are enchanted, and need no further evidence that here is the explanation of all things.

Descend, however, from your mountain height, look a little closer and what do you find? Everywhere a pertinacious discontinuity, everywhere gaps and barriers, separation, a great diversity of disconnected species. Examine into the matter, condescend to particulars, to details, and you come to a dead stop. Throughout the whole scene you are at a loss to show exactly how a single species has given birth to another. You rub your eyes. How is this possible? Since evolution is a certainty, why should the petty particulars prove so troublesome? 'Ideas', said Bateson, 'which in the abstract are apprehended and accepted with facility, fade away before the concrete case. It is easy to imagine how man was evolved from the Amoeba, but we cannot form a plausible guess as to how *Veronica agrestis* and *Veronica polita* were evolved, either one from the other, or both from a common form.'

All then is not easy sailing. Lamarck, to whom is due the first likely theory which attempted to account for new species otherwise than by the separate creation of each, believed that they were differentiated from each other by the influence exerted upon living things by their surroundings. In response to the environment they changed their habits. These new habits produced changes in the organism, which were inherited by succeeding generations from their parents, who first acquired them. The offspring of the giraffe, for instance, inherited the long neck, which the habits of its ancestors, stretching for food on the higher branches of trees, had produced. The inheritance of acquired habits was thus the pivot of Lamarck's theory, and the chief agent at work the environment.

Darwin took a different view. Reading, he tells us, Malthus' *Theory of Population* in 1838, he was struck by the struggle for existence present in nature, and concluded that, as a result of this struggle, favourable variations among individual members of a species would tend to their preservation, and the preservation of their equally fortunate progeny, by whom these natural variations, as distinct from those acquired by habit, would be inherited.

Variations certainly occur in every family; no two children are ever exactly alike. Offering no explanation of these variations—a different and difficult problem—he concluded that natural selection, that is, the selection by the struggle for existence, of the more vigorous individuals, or those better adapted to the prevailing conditions, would lead to their survival, and thus to the emergence of the different species.

Darwin, then, trusted to the inheritance of slight, random variations of a kind favouring survival. Take a look over the whole scene. Some forms of life remained stationary, satisfied; worms, for example, sharks and crabs. The limpet has remained unaltered for three hundred million years. How unenterprising! Was it placidity of temperament or sheer indolence? Others, like the dinosaur family, are extinct. A vaulting ambition for majestic dimensions worked their ruin. Throughout the whole dramatic story you may read of success and failure, advance or degeneration. And, throughout, two factors, and only two, as far as we can tell, have been at work—the organism and its surroundings, the germ and its environment—the germ with all its hidden talents, its secret powers, the environment with all its potencies, the influences it brought to bear upon the germ—light, heat, nutrition, climate—whose several and combined effects upon plant and animal we can but dimly guess. To which of these factors are we to assign the leading part, to the internal or to the external factor? On this issue no agreement has been reached. Somehow they are interwoven. Then we have the third unknown, heredity itself. What does the living creature transmit to its posterity? What does it not transmit? Does it bequeath acquired habits? Can it be shown that somatic modifications, as they are called, are in fact inherited? Some biologists answer 'Yes', others 'No'. If they can be inherited, are they permanent? Again no agreement among the experts.

Who shall decide when doctors disagree?

Once more. Variations occur: what causes them? Neither for the small, nor for the great, called mutations, has any satisfactory reason been assigned. They must, we are informed, be looked for deep down in the obscure region of the invisible genes, conjectured entities, like the electrons. And it is as much a question why a child resembles its parents, as why it differs from them.

Each school of thought, and there are many, has its own difficulties to meet. There is no disputing that the organism responds to the influence of its surroundings. In the same environment, however, a limit to change is quickly reached, as has been shown by artificial breeding. A species is 'an interbreeding community', and when adjoining species are mated, their descendants are usually sterile hybrids. And how in the world could a variation in a single individual of a species consisting of millions give rise to a new and different type? Again the fossils indisputably exhibit the extinct species, but the intermediate forms, the half-way animals, the links between the species, where are they? Evolution is a Becoming, a chain in which we must believe, but it appears to be a chain which consists chiefly of missing links. There is a curious absence of the immediate parents of the existing species, and where in plants are these transitional forms to be found?

For a layman it is all very confusing. I have been unable to discover any accepted view of the origin of species. There are Darwinians and Neo-Darwinians and Neo-Lamarckians. Agreed they are that evolution must have taken place, but how? Transformism remains a dark secret. You would think that if the Darwinians believed in the doctrine for the right reasons, the Lamarckians believed in it for the wrong, yet both are staunch believers. But any reasons are good enough for a foregone conclusion.

We must leave a good deal to the future, and to the experts to put the finishing touches to the picture, to bridge the awkward interval between the reptile and the bird, to provide a well-accredited ancestor for the vertebrates, the back-boned animals, still orphans. We must also leave it to them to decide the part, if any, played by sexual selection, of which Darwin wrote so interestingly, and how in especial it applies to plants. As for natural selection, it is now clearly seen to explain nothing, and for the reason that it is a negative, not a positive factor, which can eliminate but not create characters. The evidence from embryology which at one time seemed so convincing, the idea that the development of the individual, ontogeny, repeated the development of the branch to which it belonged, phylogeny, the theory of recapitulation, has encountered unexpected obstacles, and is already rather tarnished. Again the rising of the sap in spring, how it climbs the tree, seems a simple matter. If you can show how it comes about you will earn great praise from the biologists. And lastly the miracles of mimicry, they also have to be accounted for: butterflies which look like leaves, beetles which resemble moss, and insects which can imitate anything, twigs or stones. If you are searching for artists, do not visit the National Gallery, if for miracles there is no need to turn to the pages of the Bible. For both, go to nature.

As for ourselves, and how we came to be what we are, there are some points still to be settled. Do not tell us that man has progressed owing to his superior brain. We can see that for ourselves. Tell us rather how he secured the brain. There are ten thousand generations between us and our simian ancestors. Was the human brain the result of a series of happy marriages? Biologists are unanimous that our progenitors became men at least a hundred thousand years ago. Some give us a more ancient lineage, and believe the human species has been in existence for half a million; others that it has undergone practically no change for two or three million years. With these speculators time counts for nothing. As some experts give us a longer, others provide us with a more aristocratic descent. It is said that our progenitors were arboreal animals. It is also said that they never passed through the monkey stage, but descended, or ascended, from a creature of the Tarsius type, a nocturnal mammal. Others are convinced that our forefathers branched off the tree of life at a much earlier stage than either of these animals. You are at liberty, within limits, to choose your own pedigree. The difficulty is that you cannot recall past conditions, or say what did, or did not happen a million years ago. Experiment, that is, nature speaking here and now, is the only voice before which science bows its head.

Man's ancestry then is not so simple and blunt a matter as it was in Darwin's or Haeckel's day, and the tree of life tends in the pictures rather to resemble an open long-handled fan, or a pollarded willow, whose many branches spring direct from the main trunk. So stern is now the task of the evolutionist that some thinkers have been forced back to the conclusion that not only does no theory so far presented fit the facts, but that evolution means nothing more than a gradual unfolding of what was present from the first, the unrolling of a scroll, or a picture, of which the parts appear as they are successively illuminated. If that were so, then evolution would be so diluted as to differ little from creation. A factor essential to the solution of the problem appears to be missing, or it may be that a wholly new conception is needed to unify our knowledge and illumine our darkness, a conception the future may supply. When I remember how in physics the old firmly established views on gravitation and causality have gone by the board, I pause, I reflect, I withhold my decision.

Evolution theory is a grand, even an inspired conjecture, yet wears an unfinished air. And behind all this play of arguments and counter arguments stand the great unknowables, time, space, substance, change, causation, smiling ironically down upon the to-and-fro excursions of our troubled minds. With a great show of wisdom we are telling ourselves little, with profound learning exploring fathomless depths, where all soundings fail. Not at one stride, *non uno itinere*, as we fondly fancy, shall we reach the truth.

We know what we knew at the beginning, that in respect of his physical structure man is part of the animal kingdom. Detach or disentangle ourselves from the rest of the organic world we cannot. It seems probable, indeed, that the human race is immeasurably older than we were originally told, and that before us were sub-men, not monkeys. It seems probable, too, that in bygone ages there were not only many races, but several varieties of men, to whom the different types in the modern world, red men and yellow, black men and white, owe their respective origins. If we seek for ourselves an incommensurable rank, matchless, incomparable, if we claim a standing all our own, it must be looked for in the region of mind, associated, we know not how, with an animal organism, the body,

> Which has so many rare and curious pieces
> Of mathematical motion.

The origin of species, the history of life, is one thing, but what is life itself, the breath of existence, in which all are sharers? What is this palpitating principle, this awareness of ours, without which there is in effect nothing, since without it nothing can be known, and before which the mind itself, possessing it, recoils with stupefaction? And the scientific answer is, something recent, something, as far as our vision extends, altogether new, utterly unlike anything that had previously existed, and that need never have been. There is no apparent reason why life should ever have appeared. The star galaxies were not in need of living things. The universe could have done very well without them. If we are to believe what we are told, it got along for incalculable ages quite comfortably without our society, without any form of life or mind, and the greater part of its stupendous bulk does not now contain a trace of this mysterious essence. How this information has been obtained I am ignorant. Life, it seems, is a new comer, a thing of yesterday, a late arrival out of the void, which stepped upon the stage, and made its first bow to the universe only a thousand million years ago. Before that, through all past eternity, the Cosmos did not contain a living thing, or living soul. This is what you are asked to think. This current, this indefinable energy, life, emerged apparently from nowhere, and for no ascertainable cause. When it appeared, however, it exhibited the most startling and fantastic abilities. This chance arrival proved a perfect genius. You would suppose it would instantly have been swept away by the torrent of flying matter, the furious cascade of whirling atoms. But no! the interesting stranger declined to leave. He had, perhaps, no other home. The quarters provided were not too promising, draughty and comfortless, shaken by earthquakes and electric storms, yet he decided to make the best of them. Undiscouraged, the new and enterprising arrival, life or consciousness, resisting and overcoming the force of gravity, took hold upon matter, and proceeded to work up against the tide—the ebbing tide of energy, to make use of its loss or dissipation, the increase of entropy, which the passage of material nature ordains. By this ingenious device it made headway. So far from drifting with the stream, it made use in all manner of surprising ways of the flowing current, borrowing in fact from the failing bank of cosmic resources.

Thus on the river of time life appears as an eddy, a movement running counter to the main current, to the direction of inanimate nature. Deriving strength from a source not its own, it proceeded to adapt itself to the conditions, to filter into crevices, to grow, to reproduce itself, a very clever trick, and gave rise to innumerable forms, patterns and novelties unknown in the pre-

126

vious history of the universe. One is lost in admiration of this novice's performances. Its inherent powers of adaptation are extraordinary. That simplest of creatures, the single-celled amoeba, can by degrees accommodate itself to life either in fresh or salt water. Animals can become habituated to deadly poisons, men, as we know, to breathing at altitudes they could not at first endure and live.

At no point in the remarkable history could a human observer, had he been present, have foreseen a single step in the journey to come. Ere the planets were born, the story of the solar system, or our earth, could not by such an observer have been so much as guessed at. Nor when the planet was a molten mass, 'a fiery clod', when continents were taking shape, could any spectator have foretold this strange new power which was to reverse the flow of things, and mount as it were the cataract, employing the force of Niagara to climb it as it fell. In that far time it would have needed more than archangelic intelligence to predict the plant and animal, the surging life to come of air and sea and forest. Nor when it appeared, or the predecessors of man appeared, could human history have been imagined—the emergence of mind, of the dynasties and religions, the pomp and splendour of the great empires, the achievements of man in the arts and sciences. Nature, whatever she is, guards her secrets well, and what her next undertaking may be, what now

the prophetic soul
Of the wide world, dreaming of things to come,

broods in the deep recesses of her imagination no prophet can foretell. Life appears the result of the back-wash of the tide of energy which produced the solar system; but some inscrutable agency is here at work, behind and within and throughout all things, after which our puny minds toil in vain, unable to decipher its character, aims or purposes, or even to determine whether these words, coinages of the mortal brain, have any meaning when applied to this supreme, immeasurable power.

Life, then, appeared as an uninvited guest in the material world. It was not there, and behold, it was there. We can add nothing to this meagre information. Its assault upon inorganic matter, its storming of the citadel, has all the appearance of an essay against mighty odds, like a battle between David and

Goliath. The material elements do not appear to have offered it a kindly welcome, or rushed to its assistance. Life has no salamander qualities, and as far as we can tell is not very comfortable save within the narrowest limits of temperature, those of ice and boiling water. Who could have believed that this frail flesh, this delicate system of equilibriums, so easily shattered, could, even when a foothold had been obtained, have successfully contended with the unruly elements, the stormy energies, 'the tumult and confusion all embroiled', of the wild original abyss. Yet somehow it prevailed. And by tactics all its own.

Life seems to have gained its famous victory over matter by the use of weapons new and unknown in the universe, as the Carthaginians secured their early triumphs by the use of elephants. Suddenly appearing as if out of some other dimension, employing devices and resources of a surprising kind, instinct or intelligence, call them by what name best pleases you, turning the flank of awkward obstacles by a sort of stealth or peaceful penetration, it took possession of the whole realm. For life to make its home upon a burnt-out star, looks like the result of a forlorn hope, promising no success. Yet look what it has accomplished. The waste spaces covered with verdure, forests with trees of a hundred thousand varieties, sea, air and land swarming with living things of all conceivable shapes and forms, sunning themselves in the satisfaction of existence. If you have room left for further wonder read the recent discoveries of the marine biologists. In the ocean depths, where a great darkness reigns, there are fish which carry with them their own lanterns, of many and amazing designs, hung on bracket-like filaments, or disposed in different portions of their bodies, so dexterously contrived, that beside these tiny lights the stars themselves appear poor and commonplace.

If life had a battle to fight for a standing on the earth, the advantage once gained was rapidly consolidated. Myriads of creatures established themselves on the narrow ledge they had won. And now arose a desperate struggle, a spectacle from which our timid natures recoil with horror, a struggle among these creatures to maintain their hold upon the icy and treacherous slope. How numerous were the competitors for a place, for so doubtful and ephemeral a benefit as life! The rule appears to have been 'Anything to keep alive'. There are fish which shelter in the gastric cavities of sea anemones, within the shells of molluscs or crabs, animals like the remora, which attaches itself by suction to the skin of the shark, partaking of such fragments of its patron's diet as come its way. There are beetles which board themselves upon ants, and companionships within the same burrow between certain birds and reptiles. The puffin keeps house with the rabbit, and the owl with the snake, a risky and often fatal dwelling for the former's brood. The louse has adapted itself to life, a relatively harmless life, we are told, on the human species, but is to be pitied when typhus invades the body of its host. It is infected and doomed to die. Life scatters its seed like dust. Its fecundity is its mainstay, and the accompanying waste appalling. The herring produces forty thousand eggs a year, the tape-worm a hundred million. The plain truth is there is not room upon the earth for a tithe of the creatures which desire to possess it, and but for the most drastic destruction the world could not contain the living things it engenders. Famine, drought, pestilence, and especially the war of species upon species preserve the balance. The infant mortality of the human race, prodigious as it has been, could not of itself suffice to check its increase beyond all bounds. Primitive peoples commonly sacrificed their children that the tribe might survive. We think this expedient inhuman and prefer to prevent their coming to birth. One thing is beyond debate. Only by interference with nature can you hope to provide room or sustenance for the multitudes which would otherwise cover the earth as the waters cover the sea. It is to that problem that the League of Nations should direct its anxious attention—that above all.

What is the origin, one asks oneself, of this so urgent, so invincible an impulse to exist even for a passing hour, or what is the attraction of being over not being, of life in the crowded and warring world, which makes it worth the turmoil and the hardship, the anxiety and ceaseless strife? In what consists the satisfaction of an ant's existence, of a worm's or a crocodile's, we can form no conception. To account for our own passionate attachment to living is not easy. Their minds, if they have minds, are a *terra incognita*.

The power or energy which operates throughout nature, animate and inanimate, by which her whole system is sustained, manifests itself, modern science teaches, not in a continuous, unbroken current, but is discontinuous, that is, periodic, rhythmical. The flow exhibits phases of activity followed by phases of repose, and of repose by activity. Matter itself, physics assures us, is granular, and as Quantum theory demonstrates, all energy displays itself in spurts, or gusts, in units or particles, described as ergs. When the electron swings from one orbit to another it gives rise to a unit of radiation, of energy equivalent to that lost by the atom. Whether we think in terms of waves or particles, adopt the vibration or the corpuscular theory of light, or combine them under some new conception, like wavicles, the principle remains unaltered. Energy invariably shows itself disconnectedly, in *quanta*, in packets or gushes. Pause precedes action and action is succeeded by pause. Throughout the whole realm of nature it is the same. The very crust of the earth rises and falls in long and stately rhythms. Spring, a phase of activity, is followed by winter, a phase of repose. We see it in the mating impulse among living creatures. We see it in the processes of reproduction and growth. We observe it in the eleven year cycles of sunspots, in the alternations of sleeping and waking, in the action of the lungs and heart, even in the pulse of mental attention. 'There is no such thing', says William James, 'as voluntary attention sustained for more than a few seconds at a time.' We attend, that is, to any subject not continuously but by fits and starts, in waves. The principle may be seen at work everywhere and in everything. Our diseases exhibit the same discontinuity. Fevers have their rhythms, returning in strength on the third or fourth day, and in certain types of mental disorder there is a similar recurrence. Language, too, is essentially rhythmical. We make our accents strong or weak. In all words which consist of more than one syllable there is always an accented and an unaccented syllable. Go deeper, and study the phonographic record of a single word, and you find it consists of a series of minute vibrations. The word 'Constantinople', on such a record, shows five or six hundred. The greater rhythms of the world are reproduced in the lesser. And the human organism contains in itself innumerable rhythmical processes, which preserve it in an environment, itself a system of undulations. To crown all, we may be sure—I am at least myself convinced— consciousness, too, which lies at the very centre of our being, has its pulse, shares in the rhythmic beat of the cosmic measures.

We may agree, then, that the efforts of nature in every region may best be described as intermittent and recurrent. Evolution theory cannot overlook, though, as far as my knowledge extends, its exponents have taken little note of this pertinent fact. To these periodic bursts of nature's energy, then, in my judgment, are due the varieties of species the world contains. That they have resulted merely from a series of random variations, and by insensible gradations, appears in the highest degree improbable. It appears much more likely that, as the unpredictable leap of an electron, for which no cause can be assigned, gives birth to a photon, a unit of radiation, so in the organic world sudden and equally unpredictable changes, gushes of nature's pulsing and eternal fire, produced the multiform variety of living things. It is by way of a staircase, and not a slope, that man has mounted the eminence on which he stands.

Whatever be the truth, the term evolution is but a mask for our ignorance. No cause can be assigned for nature's rhythms, her spurts of activity and repose, save that it is her way, the essential character of her operations from everlasting to everlasting. And had we vision we should foresee summers of the mind, and winters yet to come, cycles without end. Nature has, like ourselves, her days, and nights, and months and years, her seasons of rising sap and flowery spring, of autumnal withdrawals and slumber before another dawn. Man is a microcosm of the macrocosm. We have not found the measure of nature's cycles, and can fix no dates for her recurrences. They are too vast for our scale. Death will overtake her, say our modern instructors, and doubtless they are right. But her death will be a sleep. Refreshed, she will shake her hyacinthine locks, and rising get to her task again.

VII

THE ANCESTRAL ESTATE

Sometimes I should soar above the stars, and enquire how the Heavens ended, and what was beyond them? Concerning which I could by no means obtain satisfaction. Sometimes my thoughts would carry me to the Creation, for I had heard now that the world which at first I had thought was Eternal had a beginning: how therefore that beginning was, and why it was; why it was no sooner, and what was before, I mightily desired to know.

Traherne

VII

THE ANCESTRAL ESTATE

The fashion of thought no longer permits us to separate things from their surroundings.

> All are but parts of one stupendous whole,
> Whose body Nature is, and God the soul.

So wrote Pope two hundred years ago, and with the omission of the last clause, the same verdict is given to-day. All things are patterns within a larger pattern, parts of a vast process, which is the process and the passage of nature. The essence of modern science, Sir James Jeans tells us, is that 'man no longer sees nature as something distinct from himself'. Nineteenth-century men of science thought of nature as something quite apart from and outside themselves; there for ages past and to be, there for ages to come.

For convenience sake, let us, however, keep to the familiar division, and continue to say, where we have life we have of necessity two factors. As the organism needs an environment, the environment, if there is to be life, needs an organism. Where resides the virtue by which the germ develops into the mature animal—within itself, or within its surroundings? Where life is present they are never found apart. They belong to each other and work together. They are, indeed, manifestly one. There is an understanding between them.

If we take first the germ, we note that its genius, for it assuredly possesses some kind of genius, is inherited. Life in our experience arises only from previous life. *Omne vivum ex vivo.* Inheritance is thus, perhaps, the greatest, as it is the most obvious fact taught by observation. What then do we inherit? Or rather, what do we not inherit? From our ancestors we inherit the country to which we belong, its laws and customs, its institutions and social regime. We inherit from them our bodies, our sex, the fashion of our features, the colour of our

135

skin and eyes, our hair, our very dimples. His finger-prints, if closely examined, reveal the race or community to which a man belongs. Does anyone suppose that we made any of these things, or have any responsibility for them? We are composite creatures, to whom our forbears have contributed each his share, parents a half-share, each of them a quarter, grandparents a sixteenth each, and so on in the grand chain. Our temper and talents, our graces and disfigurements, our tendencies to glaucoma or haemophilia, are inherited. We inherit the blood group to which we belong. In a word we inherit the genes, upon whose combination and distribution everything depends. In our genes lies our destiny. And what, then, are these dictatorial genes, which order, seemingly, our whole existence? Where shall we shelter ourselves from their despotic control? Can we hide from ourselves, or run away from ourselves? We are bound hand and foot. There is nothing of private ownership left to us. I had forgotten. One thing is left to us, our duty, obedience to the moral law, to the codes and conventions of our race and country. Society insists upon this duty, the moralists insist upon it. We are not responsible for our features, but only for our characters.

This burden of responsibility is, apparently, all that is truly our own. We are not accountable for anything in our surroundings or equipment, and are yet accountable for all that we do or think. A singular situation, and a disquieting prospect. You may argue that it is preposterous and unjust. You may say, 'Very well, then, suppose I disclaim responsibility, what then becomes of human society, of the ethical and legal systems, which are its cement, and preserve it from total disruption? Individual responsibility is the pivot of society. Deny it, and the whole elaborate structure crumbles into immediate and irreparable ruin. Only if we suppose, as mankind has always supposed, that amid all that we patently do inherit there is in each of us something personal and ungiven, over which we have indisputable control, only on this assumption can human existence be preserved from a vast inconsequence, or regarded as more than an interminable inane procession of lay figures, on a "long fool's errand to the grave" '.

Take this line of argument, and you will be answered that, as far as society is concerned, society can very well look after itself, and has ways and means of compelling obedience, willing or unwilling, to its demands. Society takes a firm grip of the situation, and stands no nonsense. Science, too, is equally unruffled and indifferent. Science presents you with the facts to deal with as you please. Your conclusions are not her affair; if you become tiresome about the matter, she will probably refer you to the moralists. They cannot so easily and with nonchalance look the other way. Seeing that the case is serious, they make strenuous efforts to save the situation. If the plain man argues in this fashion, as he appears to have fair reason for arguing, their anger knows no bounds, they are virtuously and mightily indignant. They employ against him an elaborate and crushing dialectic. Whether you are a bundle of inherited qualities or not, whether you have free will or not, you are none the less most certainly responsible. They go so far as to assert that men are responsible for their behaviour only if their actions are throughout causally determined, and could not be responsible if they were not so determined. I can understand their exasperation, but I have a great difficulty in following their arguments. Doubtless they are excellent arguments, but their very subtlety gives me an uneasy sense of insecurity. So important a proposition as this of responsibility should, one thinks, speak for itself, be altogether beyond dispute, need no supporting walls and buttresses, and stand up like a mountain in the sight of all men. Fortunately for most men it does. They never doubt or disclaim responsibility. Perhaps I am wrong, but of one thing I feel sure. Had man not already believed in his freedom of choice, had a conviction of free will not been cunningly implanted in him by nature, had the arguments for its reality really been needed, the arguments of all the moralists, even had he understood them, would have failed to persuade him. Fortunately for them and for us they force an open door.

And now, what are these all-powerful genes of which I have spoken? Are they real or imaginary entities? The genes are the units of the characters upon which heredity depends. They are, you might say, the atoms of the organic world. They cannot be seen, and cannot be counted, so their number in a germ cell is unknown. But within this germ cell there is a nucleus, which consists of chromosomes, visible through the microscope, and within these chromosomes lie their constituents, the invisible ultra-microscopic entities, the conjectured genes, which are supposed to carry all the heritable qualities that are, or can be passed on from one generation to the next. Is each individual, are you or I, more than a bundle of inherited characteristics? Since extracts from the thyroid and pituitary glands have power to dislocate or to restore personality, our bodily life seems to be very much a matter of chemistry.

Were I a physiologist I could introduce you to a multitude of impressive and significant facts in respect of our physical structure. Physiology tells us, for example, of the hormones, like adrenalin and insulin, extracts from the pancreas; adrenalin which can arouse the emotion of fear, insulin, which alleviates diabetes. It tells us of the various vitamines, necessary constituents of a healthy diet, too much, or too little, of which may lead to beri-beri, to rickets or to scurvy. It tells us of the ductless glands: of the pituitary, the master gland, the most important of human organs, because of its intimate contact with the brain, and its action upon the other ductless glands; and because, also, it regulates growth and reproduction, and is the seat, if there be any, of personality. Physiology tells us how this gland, if stimulated, will produce a giant, if starved a dwarf. It tells us how a deficiency in the thyroid causes myxoedema, an excess exophthalmic goitre. It has been found that tadpoles if fed on thyroid gland become frogs hardly larger than flies, if fed on the thymus grow into large tadpoles, and never become frogs at all. Extracts from this gland work miracles, accelerate growth and prolong life. Certain aquatic newts, Mexican salamanders, become on thyroid diet a larger and terrestrial variety. So far from being intellectually or morally above our environment, we appear to be its slaves. We become angry or agreeable, reasonable or unreasonable, as it dictates. So susceptible are we to drugs and extracts at the disposal of the chemist that it seems as if Anatole France's Doctor Socrates was right, and we could keep in bottles substances capable of altering our characters, making us virtuous or vicious, cheerful or despondent. The phials ranged on his shelves contained fluids which could transform or abolish the will of fifty thousand men. 'These substances', he claimed, 'were not essentially laboratory products,' but were 'scattered throughout nature.' 'In their free state they envelop and penetrate us, they determine our will; they condition our free choice.' What can we conclude but that in fact they are our creators?

Physiology has much more of interest to say. It tells us of the incidence of certain characteristics among first-born children, that left-handedness is more often found among criminals than normal persons, and is associated with disabilities like dumbness, that some feeble-minded types occur more frequently at the end of a family, that colour-blind men are much commoner than colour-blind women, that from some diseases, like haemophilia, women are exempt.

Many men of science like to think that the genes are physico-chemical structures, and that life arose in a chemical ferment in the first, or protogene, through the action upon it of cosmic rays, an interesting hypothesis, not less probable, indeed, than that it was the work of an angel. In the absence of evidence all speculations are of approximately equal value, and you can take your choice.

When we approach the boundaries of life the organisms become progressively smaller and more numerous. Bacteria, whose habits can be studied under the microscope, are as the sands of the seashore in multitude, some harmful, some bene-ficial. But smaller still, so small as to be invisible, are the so-called 'filter-passers', the viruses, known to produce many among the deadliest diseases—distemper, foot-and-mouth dis-ease, smallpox and influenza are examples. Whether the viruses can be described as living creatures is not known.

Next above the bacteria come the single-celled animals. Each living thing begins as a single cell, which by absorbing water and food grows and divides, and again divides, till in the various animals from the Amoeba, a single-celled creature, to man, the number of cells rises to millions and billions. If in this remarkable and immortal animal nothing hindered the sub-divisions, its descendants would in a week equal the earth itself in size. And yet of this most primitive thing it has been said by Jennings: 'If Amoeba were the size of a dog, instead of being microscopic, no one would deny to its actions the name of intelligence.'

When our biologists talk of cells they employ an appalling arithmetic which reminds us of the astronomers and the stars. The nerve cells in the cortex of the human brain number, it is computed, about nine billions within a single inch. Our bodies, like those of the various plants and animals, are composed of

139

cells. We are one and all constellations, cellular communities. There are within these communities brain cells, and liver cells, and stomach cells, each variety engaged upon its own separate task, yet all working in harmony to keep the body healthy and alive.

You may ask, 'Of what are these cells composed?' The individual cell, which can by modern methods be immensely magnified, and its picture thrown upon the screen, is there seen to be a veritable vortex of an incredible complexity, a world in itself of filaments, globules, vesicles, each with its own peculiar function, and all in perpetual agitation. It is a whirlpool of snake-like gliding and darting movements, in the most intimate and interlocked associations. You must remember that these unceasing activities and gyrations within the cell are super-imposed upon the far deeper, unseen vibrations of the inorganic electrons which compose the ultra-microscopic and atomic foundations of the whole physical system, the system whose relations with space and time are unique and unascertainable. Living matter is said to consist of protoplasm, a mere word which like so many others is employed as a cloak for our ignorance. Nor will it help you here. For not a trace of it can be found either in the nucleus or the body of the cell. If, however, you like to use such words, you will be pleased to hear that it is a singular living substance, of different composition in different species of creatures, but ultimately analysable into chemical constituents. This substance, therefore, hides the secret of secrets, the mystery of life. But as you already know all about it, that it contains nothing but chemicals, the story has come to an end.

It is difficult to see how anything more is to be said. Life is the result of a chemical ferment, and we may leave it to the experts to work out at their leisure the history of the world, of life and mind in all their ramifications, in terms of chemistry. When that has been done, we shall return again to the beginning, and ask the physicists, 'What are carbon, oxygen and hydrogen?' And, after consultation with the mathematicians, they will answer—'They are configurations of space-time.' 'The formation of celestial bodies,' said Kant, 'the causes of their movements, and in short, the origin of the entire Cosmos, will be explained sooner than the mechanism of a plant or a caterpillar.'

I have spoken of the germ cell. Within it is a nucleus, and within the nucleus are the chromosomes, and within these again the famous genes. The chromosomes, so called because they can be stained with colour, are of a definite and constant number for each species, 16 in the germ of the guinea-pig, 24 in the mouse, 48 in the hedge-hog as also in the human being. The body in the higher animals, like ourselves, develops from the union of two cells, the sperm and the ovum, contributed respectively by the father and mother, so that out of the 48, each parent contributes 24; but with a certain difference in one pair of the male chromosomes, called x and y. No two germ cells are alike, and the conjunction of a single sperm and ovum may give rise to an immense variety of patterns. We are partakers in a gigantic lottery. From a single marriage any one of innumerable, differently equipped, variously endowed individuals may come into existence. We are not, indeed, to imagine that the chromosomes, or their constituent genes, provide us with ready-made characters. Rather they provide the tendencies, the capacities, the idiosyncrasies, that is, the raw material out of which the character as a whole, under the stimulus of its surroundings, its upbringing and education, may be built. Yet if some men are born with a silver spoon in their mouths, others enter the world with a millstone round their necks.

In the end there remains something for which physiology is not yet prepared to give an account—our personalities. Where among these combinations of genes and chromosomes are we to suppose the self to be seated, the unique self, of which each one of us is vividly aware, as the centre of his whole existence? I do not forget that there are hard-hearted thinkers who deny the existence of the self. Let us postpone that question. At least they do not deny the existence of consciousness. That would be difficult, since here we are, you and I, manifestly self-conscious beings. And we must believe that our parents might have had many other and quite different children, wholly unlike us, each child possessed of, each endowed with, peculiarities of its own, and with this same sense of personality. So also their parents before them might have had quite other children, as might their forbears from the birth of time. The day and the hour of the marriage were the ministers of fate. Think of the fortuitous matings in the ages that are gone, tens of thousands and thousands of thousands.   Thoughts like these bear us away with them into infinity.

> Born into life, man grows
> Forth from his parents' stem,
> And blends their blood, as those
> Of theirs are blent in them.
> So each new man strikes root into that far fore-time.

In each family a few, a very few, out of legions of possible human beings came into existence.   They are, shall we say, among the favoured few?   Why were they, like ourselves, so singled out?   And at what moment did this self of ours, so precious to us, this 'I', this individual person attach itself to the chromosomes from which our bodies have sprung?   And are there somewhere souls awaiting their opportunity to be born?   'I stand terrified and amazed', wrote Pascal, 'to see myself here rather than elsewhere, for there is not the slightest reason for the here rather than for the elsewhere, or for the now rather than for some other time.'   And we may add, 'for any time at all', no reason why your 'I' or mine should ever have entered into the world or life.

You might very naturally suppose—it was for long supposed—that within the living cell were parts corresponding to the different portions or organs of the body to be.   That, as Leibniz taught, the original cell or egg was already the animal to come on a microscopic scale, that is, in miniature.   Nothing so simple. That is not nature's way.   The germ cell is a unity and does not become specialised for the production of the heart or lungs, or any other part of the body till it has attained a certain maturity. If at an early stage it be divided or subjected to pressure, or even if a portion be removed, the germ retains all its powers.   It possesses the astonishing faculty of providing any necessary organ out of any part of itself.   Utterly unlike any machine, the cells, too, in living things can act for each other, and work together for a common purpose.   This co-operation of parts is everywhere present in natural organisms.   What governs the procedure? Who or what presides over the organisation?   Where dwells the wisdom in the germ capable of detecting deficiencies in itself when they arise, where the intelligence, for it certainly simulates intelligence, which can transfer to the remaining parts duties previously performed by others?   You would think a germ

142

would hardly be aware that it had lost a portion of itself, and would work blindly on, quite unconscious of any injury or defect it had sustained. This pin-point of matter, which the physicists, taking up the tale where the biologists lay it down, analyse for you, as they do all substances, into spinning charges of electric energy, this speck of life, which is a whirlwind of billions of electrons, revolving in their orbits about 7000 million times in the millionth of a second—contains within itself the power of becoming a human being, with all its organs complete, brain, heart and lungs. It contains within itself the power to develop the eye, the ear, the will, the emotions, the thoughts that make a man. It contains within itself the power of reproducing its kind, of recalling the features, the smile, the complexion, the trick of speech, the grace of carriage that characterise the parent stock. This speck of matter contains within itself these note-worthy powers.

Take the eye alone. The germ contains the ability, among other odds and ends, to produce a retinal surface sensitive to light, which can distinguish between vibrations of 450 million millions a second, which give the sensation red, and 750 million millions a second, which give the sensation of violet. How did it come about that the eye responds exactly to a certain series of wave lengths among an immense series, picks out these waves from a multitude of others? You might be inclined to say these things were miracles, but the age of miracles is past. Miracles do not happen. Still if you can satisfy yourself that these accomplishments, these endless varieties of behaviour to meet unforeseen contingencies arose out of haphazard collocations of atoms in a white-hot gas, at a temperature of a million degrees, out of an incandescent maelstrom of darting electric flashes, if you are satisfied that any evolution theory can on this basis, juggling with genes, account for life and mind, I quit the field in your favour. I allow your superior penetration. For my part I am struck dumb. The spider mocks the mind, and the caterpillar or the cockroach terrify the imagination.

Aristotle thought there was nothing in the end that was not in a measure in the beginning. The beginning was prophetic, it foretold what was yet to come. In the view of Kant also, it was impossible to avoid the question, 'To what end, or for what purpose was this organ, the eye or any other, developed?' You may ask what caused it, but the answer to that question does not explain the organ, whose use or object cannot be brushed cavalierly aside. Do not, I pray you, confuse causes with reasons. You are, let us say, present at a naval battle. You hear the salvos and see the destruction of a vessel. You describe, and rightly describe, the shell fire as *the cause* of its destruction. , But *the reason* of the firing is quite another thing—a quarrel between' nations. If you propose to account for the eye, for example, the need for it, its value must be considered. To suppose it an accidental variation is sheer absurdity. For it appeared not in one line of evolution alone. As Bergson pointed out, the cuttle-fish and the vertebrates, creatures not related to each other, both developed eyes on their own account in wholly different ways, and from different parts of the organism. Each was its own architect; each had the same end in view, but they took different routes to that end. Some fish provided themselves with a bi-focal arrangement, for sight not only in water, but in air. The eye of the bird is adapted both to near and far vision. The butterfly's eye contains five thousand lenses and fifty thousand nerves. These various eyes were means to certain definite ends, the very obvious end in each case that the creature might have the advantage of vision, and that advantage of a kind specially suited to its own way of life. Except by reference to the purpose or use of these eyes you can say nothing sensible or intelligible about them. There are folk who tell you that these are fortuitous occurrences, that nature's bow was drawn at a venture, and that all her millions of arrows struck each the centre of the target by sheer accident; they were aimed at nothing in particular. Were a painter without eyesight to produce Da Vinci's *Last Supper*, Raphael's *Dresden Madonna*, Titian's *Sacred and Profane Love*, all by sprinkling canvases at random with a brush dipped in unseen and unselected colours, should we not crown such an artist with admiring and bewildered praise, and cry 'This only a god could do'?

I am well aware that the doctrine of design is suspect, that it can be riddled with destructive criticism, yet how this 'immanent end', this internal teleology is to be got rid of, I cannot tell you. I recall Swift's comment upon epic poetry. Easy it is to produce, said he, if one has the genius, but the skill lies in dispensing with genius, with any kind of talent. So with nature. Remarkable, indeed, had been her works had she possessed mind, purpose and foresight, but how much more remarkable, how admirably skilful to produce these interesting things without a particle either of intention or sense! Perhaps intelligence, perhaps brains, are a mistake. How much better we might have got on without them!

Organisms, it is by all observers allowed, behave as if they had an end in view. They aim at self-preservation, their actions have a purpose. At times they appear unconscious of the purpose, yet conscious or not, they strain after it, they desire to attain it. An animal is interested in its environment, and continually attends to and adapts itself to the changing scene, according to its inherited and its own individual experiences. How can you ascribe interest to a blind mechanical process? Animals watch, listen, appear to ask themselves 'What is that noise?' 'What is that moving object?' You see the dog all alive, attentive, with lifted paw. 'Is that a stranger', he asks himself, 'or only that stupid domestic cat of ours?' The famous experiments of Pavlov, on 'conditioned and unconditioned reflexes', are beside the point. They do not prove, and cannot prove, as they claimed to prove, that behaviour on the part of living creatures is mechanically or automatically determined. The dog's intelligence grasps, or attempts to grasp, the whole situation. His consciousness is all the time at work, for without it the gong he hears, the light he sees were without any meaning for him, and if uninterpreted could have no bearing of any kind upon his behaviour or the ends in view.

The activity of an organism is not a motiveless activity. Nor do we find biologists of any school, vitalist or mechanistic, who ignore final causes. They ask and ask continually, 'What end does this organ, the eye or ear, the heart or muscle, serve in the animal economy?' If it serves no end why is it there? They will tell you that an organ that serves no end degenerates and disappears. We judge organs as contrivances, by their uses and functions. How else could we judge them? They are there for some reason, and every creature may be described as the embodiment of its desires. The body is the outcome of its wants, adapted to strive after and to secure them.

We must conclude, then, that 'a growing thing is known by what it grows to', and that its body fulfils the needs of the animal.

If you say the body creates the needs, you have to provide a reason for the body's existence. There appears, as we have seen, no conceivable reason why animal bodies should ever have arisen. Space and time, the sun and stars, did not pine for their society. They were not restless in their solitude, unhappy because they were lonely, and wanted someone to talk to. Living creatures were quite superfluous and unnecessary additions to the universe; they bring no obvious profit to the sum of things. Why then are they there? Once more, if the atoms or particles, the oxygen, hydrogen and carbon, built up in combination the many million varieties of living organisms which support themselves and reproduce their kind, I should be obliged if you would inform me further whence and how these particles obtained their singular power of co-operating, constructing and organising, of combining together into a unity.

The unity of the organism, the co-ordination of its parts, there you have the supreme enigma. The organism involves some principle of integration, some ability certainly not present in the original atoms of carbon or oxygen taken by themselves. Whence did it come and where reside? Unless you first answer this question you can proceed no further. This first step includes all the rest. You have reached the foot of an inaccessible precipice. It towers high above all efforts to explain life, and ends in the clouds. The peak of this mountain is out of human sight.

We arrive then at the integrity of the organism. In living things there is an agency at work beyond the detective power of the microscope to trace. Leibniz defined an organism as anything that had a 'soul', or principle of unity. It was, he thought, rather in the nature of a force than of a substance or quantity. Well, matter or substance is now defined as energy at a certain velocity. Aristotle in his *De Anima* speaks of the ἐντελέχεια, the actual being of the body, its absoluteness, that which makes it what it is. This integrity or absoluteness belongs to the whole, and is, as it were, its mentor or adviser, though without spatial or measurable relations to the parts. None the less it directs their operations. It governs the activities of the organism, teaching it to undertake new and unaccustomed duties, to adapt means to ends, to respond to novel situations. Whatever it be, the inner being of the organism exhibits all the marks by which we recognise intelligence in ourselves.

We have not exhausted the hidden talents of the germ; whole libraries would be needed to record them. It is time, however, to turn to the second factor—the surrounding world, its environment. When life appears, it appears in a world which somehow supports it. Life in all its forms depends upon nutrition, and cannot get along upon its own resources. Moreover, on its arrival upon the scene the living creature anticipates without a particle of previous experience, yet with perfect confidence, that it will receive the necessary assistance. The baby is extremely annoyed if its food be not forthcoming. The chick, when it emerges from the egg, immediately begins to peck about, as if it had been in the world before, and knew all about the arrangements. It expects to be provided for, or to find what it requires. Nor, despite this tremendous assumption, is it usually disappointed. Animals are already experts, the moment they are born, in their several ways of life. The bee is an adept in the making and storing of honey, the beaver an engineer, and the spider a professor of web-spinning.

These curious circumstances suggest not only personal talents, they suggest a harmony between living things and their surroundings. It has occurred to many thinkers, Schopenhauer among the rest, that the world is just as suited to be the home of living creatures as they to make it their home. Our planet might have been, like most of the heavenly bodies, incapable of supporting any form of life known to us. We cannot, indeed, affirm that life in other conditions than ours is impossible. It might have been built upon other materials than the compounds of carbon. Perhaps elsewhere it has been. It might have developed a different type of metabolism. Life's resources are quite unknown to us. Yet the fitness of the environment here and now is a matter of interest, and demands consideration.

There are certainly some remarkable features in this planet of ours which suggest that it was designed as a grand theatre for the performance to be later enacted, as if the coming of life had been somehow anticipated. Nature at least so arranged matters here as to provide the sea on which the ship could float. I do not overlook the fact that had things happened otherwise we had not been here to discuss them. They happened as they did happen. The very peculiar qualities of oxygen, hydrogen and carbon made possible a habitable world. The absence of these properties might have forbidden life's entrance upon the stage, or turned it aside into quite different channels. And at first sight, as we have seen, the conditions looked far from promising. Yet there are notable peculiarities in the situation. There is an interweaving and interlocking so close and intimate that the absence of a single factor—for example, that the greatest density of water is at a temperature of 4 degrees Centigrade, a most singular feature in the economy of nature, of which no explanation of any kind is forthcoming—would alter the entire situation or render it wholly impossible.

Observe this also. Though local changes are continually taking place, through millions of years the climate of the world has remained astonishingly uniform—a notable fact when we remember how narrow are the limits of temperature within which life can exist, how slight a frost ruins crops, how drought destroys vegetation. There is, too, the curious inclination of the earth's axis on its journey round the sun, a tilt of 23½ degrees, which itself completes a rotation once in every 25,868 years, and gives us the precession of the equinoxes.

Much was needed to fit the earth for human habitation— chemical and physical preparations of its surface, the breaking down of rocks into soil, upon which the plants could take root and grow, and so provide food for the earliest animals. Even volcanoes assisted in the process, by raising to the surface and scattering in dust the deep-lying strata, rich in lime and phosphorus, to form fertile plains. Rain-water is filtered and purified as it sinks down below the surface soil, and emerges in fresh springs. There appears to be 'a general harmony between organic and inorganic matter, a something that seems to show that nature is nature for a purpose.' This purpose, too, is suggested by her care for the continuation of the species, if not for its individual members, the impulse to mating, for which, as far as I know, biology offers no explanation. What emphasis has been placed upon sex, and if nature is destitute of aims, how are we to give any rational account of it?

Last in our reflections upon the environment we come to climate. Wide as is the world, looked upon as a dwelling-place for mankind it is far from spacious, and might, indeed, be regarded as chiefly scenery, so narrow are the limits of habitable land. The oceans occupy three-fifths of the earth's surface, and

148

the Pacific alone rocks in a cradle of 70 million square miles. Add the mountain ranges, the Alps and Himalayas and the snow-capped Poles, add the lakes, rivers, deserts and forests, and how little is left. Nor are the resources of what we possess by any means inexhaustible. Soil erosion, as in China, where 400 millions have daily to be fed, is continuous and unrepaired. The march of the interminable and hungry generations treads out its fruitfulness. Grazing lands are stripped bare, forests cut down, dusty plains replace once fertile fields. In Northern Europe, with its regular rainfall and cool winds, the land recovers. But in America, not to speak of the swarming Orient, calamity is near at hand, so near, indeed, that farmers are already migrating from the exhausted territories, and in less than a century, the prophets foretell, a crisis will be reached, and economic ruin stare a great people in the face.

Civilisations are bought at a price, and great populations lay a heavy toll upon the countries they inhabit, reducing to penury for all her riches their mother earth. We but nurse delusions when we think the human race approaches the millennium. Vast migrations of peoples will take place in the future as they have taken place in the past. Men increase while the fertile lands are shrinking, and the hunger for them will not diminish.

It was illness, he tells us, that made Nietzsche a philosopher. It was for the sake of improving his delicate health that Nelson was sent to sea. Perhaps, then, philosophy and England owe something to poor health, a condition we all desire to avoid. Good health has always been prized as the first and greatest of blessings. Yet perfect health is not common. Out of 20 million school children in the United States 14 million were, after examination, reported to suffer from some defect. The proportion is high, and would probably be higher rather than lower, were the whole world made the basis of enquiry. That bad health lies at the root of a great proportion of human suffering and misery is beyond dispute. From this cause spring a legion of ills, ranging from bad temper to theft, from drugging and drunkenness to suicide and murder. Health is the high road to earthly happiness. So strangely blended, nevertheless, is human life that sickness and disease have at times played a beneficent part in the history of men and nations. Both health and illness are in part a matter of inheritance, yet hardly, if indeed at all, less a matter of cli-

149

mate. It has been demonstrated by Dr. Ellsworth Huntington that a high level of physical vigour and mental energy can be reached and maintained only in certain types of climate, and these are sparsely distributed, only to be found in very limited areas of the earth's surface. Climate, too, is a factor of high economic importance. We speak of good times and bad times, but these appear to be closely related to good and bad seasons: when from drought or floods crops fail to ripen, the barometer of health falls, privation and unemployment, nervous disorders and diseases increase, the curve of a community's prosperity takes a downward turn, and the death-rate rises. We in these islands are the most fortunate, the most favoured of nature's children since we enjoy admittedly the healthiest climate in the world—a variable and stimulating temperature, which though continually changing rarely rises, and then only for a few days at a time, above 70 degrees, or falls much below 30; a region not too moist or too dry, and ventilated by storms, fresh currents of air. These are the conditions in which mankind is at its best both physically and intellectually—the best conditions for both closely correspond. They are also the conditions in which, if we accept Dr. Huntington's findings, the great civilisations of the past have arisen.

There have been great climatic fluctuations in historic time, and geologists have proved that even greater fluctuations have taken place in the remoter past. These pulsations of climate, great and small, follow each other in a rhythmical series. The ice cap crept south at certain periods in our planet's history to within thirty degrees of the equator, at others tropical or semitropical conditions prevailed as far north as Greenland. Where water was long ago plentiful there is now aridity, where the water level in lakes is at present high, it formerly was low, where forests stood there is little vegetation, and lands once tilled and fertile are to-day desert. What do we in these islands know of the sun's power? 'The heat of Arabia', wrote Lawrence, 'came out like a drawn sword, and struck us speechless.'

Whether we think of ourselves and our private lives, or of mankind in general, we perceive how closely human destiny is associated with the pulsing energies of nature, of which we are for the most part utterly unconscious. Continents float like rafts upon the earth's surface. Greenland, for example, is drifting to the west. From the depths of space, from the furthest stars, influences pour down upon us, as in cosmic radiation, from sources at which we can but dimly guess. How significant is the cycle of sun-spots, some so large that all the planets might find room in one of them. Do they attract even our idle wonder? Yet they, like all things, have their pulse, and are more numerous, Sir James Jeans tells us, at intervals of about eleven years, as they were in 1928, and will be again in 1939. You suppose them unimportant. Yet they hold the fates of men in the hollow of their mighty hands. Our terrestrial weather follows their swinging rhythm and—as has been proved by the ring growths of aged trees—changes from cold and wet to warm and dry, in response to their periodic activity. The more sun-spots the wetter the summer, and the thicker the ring of that year's growth. The water levels in Victoria Nyanza repeat and corroborate the arboreal tale: the highest levels are reached after the sun-spots have been most numerous and brought the wettest years.

We can well believe that a certain type of climate favours and accompanies civilisation, and is, indeed, one of its necessary conditions. That civilisations belong to moderate, not torrid zones, history provides indisputable evidence. Man is not at his best in the tropics, where the heat undermines will power and makes sustained effort, intellectual and physical alike, difficult. The tropics, it is well known, induce inertia and enfeeble purpose. The spirit may be willing but the flesh is weak. In too stimulating climates, on the other hand, the struggle to keep alive is exhausting. They produce nervous disorders, and exhibit a high rate of suicides. Whether religions tend to conform to zones of climate is an interesting study, not yet undertaken. Yet why not, since we know some climes are more favourable to intelligence and industry, and some more friendly to moral qualities than others?

Whatever nature has in mind, manifestly it is not that we should exist as mere pensioners on her bounty. Perhaps she desired to harden us, body and soul, for some project in the distance, for whose attainment still firmer resolution and endurance are needed. Perhaps sterner battles than the world has ever known have yet to be fought.

And at last, when all is said that can be said, what do we discover? When we have enquired of all the sciences and gathered all obtainable human knowledge, gathered by telescope and microscope and all the rest of the apparatus, we discover that we are still confined to the sensible world, to the clear bright world of which our touch and sight and hearing tell us. And we suppose that when they have handed in their report the whole tale is told. Yet in truth we are their prisoners, and how innocently infantile to suppose that touch, sight and hearing can introduce us to all the aspects and all the secrets of the universe. Curtain after curtain might lift, and yet leave us far from the reality. The truth is we are so 'cabin'd, cribbed, confined' as never to see beyond our noses. Nor is that all. If we could enlarge our minds so far as to remember that a scene is not an act, nor an act the play, that even a national drama is no more than a 'three hours' traffic of the stage' in unending time, then the long vista of things, the magnitude of the affair in which we are in-volved, might come home to us, then we might realise that, in De Quincey's phrase, 'some greater interest was at stake, some mightier cause than ever yet the sword had pleaded or trumpet had proclaimed', in which all human history is a mere episode. The sum of things is too great for our imagination, and our present life seems a term of imprisonment. In a measure it is so. Here is man:

> Man whom Fate, his victor, magnanimous, clement in triumph,
> Holds as a captive king, mewed in a palace divine;
> Wide its leagues of pleasance and ample of purview its windows;
> Airily falls in its courts, laughter of fountains at play;
> Nought when the harpers are harping, untimely reminds him of
>   durance;
> None, as he sits at the feast, whispers Captivity's name;
> But, would he parley with Silence, withdraw for a while unattended,
> Forth to the beckoning world 'scape for an hour and be free,
> Lo, his adventurous fancy coercing at once and provoking,
> Rise the unscalable walls, built with a word at the prime ;
> Lo, in unslumbering watch, with pitiless faces of iron,
> Armed at each obstinate gate, stand the impassable guards.

Who are these mighty and angelic guards? Their names here, among mortals, are Time and Space, whose flaming swords turn every way, and keep the gates of reality and the talismans of God.

VIII

THE WIDE WORLD

How can we know?   How can we understand?

   .   .   .   .   .

How can we know, who know our truth is based
On finite facts by infinity effaced,
By parallels that meet in space behind,
On matter that is force, unconscious, blind?
How can we know whose knowledge is so small?

   .   .   .   .

How did the Chaos burgeon into life?
Did it imagine, when the toil begun,
'Twould blossom into star, and moon, and sun,
Rolling to rhythmic music?   Toil seemed vain.
Mistily, vaguely, dizzily it spun
Racked with strange pain,
In fiery rain,
Through black abysses, while the cosmic power
Compelled it into bird and beast and flower. . . .

 .   .   .   .

Truth is eternities away,
And we but climb
In the dark of Time,
To the dawn of day.

Macfie

VIII

THE WIDE WORLD

In the great arch of night above our heads about five thousand stars may be seen by the naked eye. In their marchings and counter-marchings they make a brave show, yet are in fact scarcely so much as a swarm of bees in all Asia, a spray of blossom in the limitless abyss, where 'a hundred thousand million stars make one galaxy, and a hundred thousand million galaxies the universe'. The stars we see are but a handful, and their removal would not disturb by as much as a decimal the calculations of the Angel of their courses. We may be sure that for every human being in the world there is not one star apiece—there are ten thousand. Viewed from the bodily angle, no comparisons can express the insignificance of man among the cosmic magnitudes upon which our astronomers exhaust their eloquence. Theirs is a terrifying artillery. Under the bombardment of their dimensions and distances the spirit shrivels. We are afraid, and the marrow of our bones is dried up With time and space as their allies they diminish us to pitiable atomies. The earth is a mote of dust, and the sun itself a diminutive fire-fly. We inhabit the puny satellite of an inferior orb. There are millions of stars so immense that room could be found for millions of our petty sun in one of them.

If you are not already dizzied by magnitude and number in these expanses, you may proceed to ponder the multiplicity of motions, the comings and goings of these celestial armies, beginning with the diurnal and annual circlings of our own planet, the wandering of its poles, the journey with its companions towards the constellation of Hercules at the rate of two million miles a day, and concluding with the grand revolution of the starry system to which it belongs, completed once in two hundred and fifty million years.

The physicists and physiologists emulate the astronomers and paralyse our faculties with a like arithmetic. There is an inner deep to match the outer. A drop of water confounds us. It contains millions upon millions of molecules, and you may say galaxies of electrons. Each liver cell in our bodies is composed of three hundred billion atoms. Light, you think, is a rapid messenger, since it can travel seven times round the earth in a single second. Yet it brings late news of cosmic events. A great flare in the heavens, observed in 1901, the result probably of some stellar collision, took place, it is calculated, in 1551, when Edward the Sixth was king, and what the telescope reveals to-day in the nebula of Andromeda is a very old story of happenings a million years ago, so long has it taken that lightning flash to reach us across the stupendous gulf. And where were we, and what the human race, when that beam shot forth on its journey? And how in a universe so wide can we creatures of a day continue to strut, and pose and bluster, or look upon ourselves without contempt?

Yet it needs not to muster battalions of facts like these to reduce us to a proper humility. How slight a thing is man amid the works of man himself! The pyramids belittle the Pharaohs who built them, and men are humiliated by their own monuments. Caesar in his capital, amid the temples and palaces of Rome, presents but a poor appearance. The bishop beneath the soaring towers of his cathedral, the captain on the bridge of his battleship, a fabric of vast and intricate design, hurling thunderbolts, is no considerable object. They are barely visible, these men, amid their magnificent surroundings.

What then are we to conclude, and what moral draw? Are we to accept a timid inferiority, abase ourselves before the work of our own hands, rank the sculptor lower than his image, the architect of St. Peter's less than his creation, estimate Socrates or St. Paul by their stature, and fall on our knees before the Milky Way? This were, indeed, a grotesque transvaluation of all values. I am unable to accept the philosophy either of the telescope or the microscope. Kant reverenced the starry heavens, and no doubt did well to do so. Hegel despised them. For all their luminous splendour these majestic constellations are for the most part mere balloons, spaces filled with gas. Disdain or reverence them as you please, to be overpowered by mere magnitude is preposterous. 'This,' said Malebranche, when he first saw a microscope, 'This is the end of size'—a sane and penetrating judgment. 'Large' and 'small', what is the meaning of these words? None, save the meaning we give them. And what is the unit of these measurements? The unit we assign. Size is a matter of comparison, as is heat. The degree of heat on a scale of temperature is without meaning when applied to a single particle. There is no such thing as an absolute standard in the physical world. These estimates are of our own devising, governed by the scale of our bodies, and their adaptation to the surrounding phenomena.

Nor between size and quality is there any calculable relation. No one can measure for you the length and breadth of beauty or desire, and none is so foolish as to judge a canvas of Da Vinci's by its extent, or apply a footrule to the Dialogues of Plato. How insignificant a trifle, if you care to pursue such comparisons, is the eye itself. Here are no imposing dimensions, yet it is a signal triumph of nature, possessing powers the lordly constellations appear to lack. There are in the optic nerve half a million fibres, and some millions of cells in the retina. They work in concert. Perhaps the eye should be to us a source of deeper wonder than the stars. Perhaps the material perspective, which assigns the nobility to the scenery rather than the play, is the most distorting and the cheapest of all our many illusions, overlooking, as it does, the mind, 'which measures every wandering planet's course,' knows more about the stars than ever they knew, matters of which they are wholly ignorant, and will be, for all their superb proportions, till their dying day. St. Augustine declared the human soul, even the animal soul, of greater dignity than the entire inanimate creation.

Natural it is, and indeed inevitable, that visible things should in daily affairs take precedence over the invisible. Reasons are at hand. The eye is a compelling and persuasive witness. 'It cannot choose but see.' It has its office, and performs admirably the functions of its office. And to unreflective minds the external world appears the sole and enduring reality. By comparison how pale are our thoughts, those bloodless, flitting shadows; what a misty twilight realm the mind's. From this illusion no doubt nature intended us to suffer, an illusion similar to that which assures us that the earth is flat and motionless, though the contrary is the truth, that it is a sphere and its motions many.

The world includes this trifling object, man, as it includes the primrose and the cloud. Yet, by a curious paradox, in its comprehension this puny object goes beyond and includes the world within which it is found. Man is at once contained within, and ·himself contains the world in his thought. Thus, if his outer and physical vision minimises his importance, his inner and intellectual restores and enhances his estate. The shining systems hung in the heavens, like the great prehistoric monsters of earth's earlier days, have nothing but their bulk, their hugeness, with which to astonish us. They have neither theology nor mathematics. They neither feel nor understand. Nature, 'the lonely, with her sightless eyes', what value or significance, without us, or other similarly endowed beings, has her existence at all? A universe without spectators! Ponder that idea. Indeed it is a question whether we have here an intelligible proposition. Certainly in that solitude, if it be imaginable, in a scene without spectators of the scene, it matters not at all what happens, if anything can be said to happen, where nothing is anywhere, at any time, by anyone seen, heard or known. A universe sunk in the abyss of everlasting neglect, from which it might as well never have emerged, since no word of it, no thought of it, has ever been whispered, can it be described as in any intelligible sense existing? Remove thought from the scene, and all the worlds vanish, they are lost in the darkness of primeval night.

This is not a matter to be lightly passed over. Say what you will, in us nature comes to life, and before this rising from the dead we are speechless. Do you ask me to believe that nature overstepped herself, making she knew not what, and what she need not have made? Do you tell me that consciousness,

> The eye with which the universe
> Beholds itself, and knows itself divine,

is simply a thing among other things, to be placed alongside the river or the stone? I shall not be easily persuaded—you strain my credulity, gentlemen. You are of the opinion that the arrival of the audience in nature's theatre was an irrelevant accident. See now how minds differ. It would be for me too apropos and brilliant an accident, too startlingly relevant an irrelevance. You have not crossed the *Pons asinorum* of philosophy until you have perceived the necessity of mind, that upon its operations, its recognitions and appreciations all hinges, that in thought you have the end, and aim, and justification of nature. I conceive that we miserable atomies have some business to be where we are, a function, and no inconsiderable one, a place in the procession, since there is no view without the viewer, no measurement without the measurer, no knowledge without the knower, in effect no universe without an intelligence to be aware of it.

It appears to me she knew very well what she was about, this lady nature, that she foresaw more and provided for more than we imagine—in a word, is not so empty-headed as we suppose. She took pains at least not to be a wall-flower, passed by without notice. She had a fancy for an audience, for admirers. Can we imagine Being, as Plato asked, to be devoid of life and mind, and to remain, in awful meaninglessness, an everlasting unseen empty picture? Let us say for the present that life, consciousness, mind have not strayed accidentally into the universe. There never was a cosmos without life, consciousness, mind. They are among its attributes, constituents of its innermost being.

You cannot, indeed, lay violent hands upon thought, yet ideas, whatever they are, exercise a wide jurisdiction. Why is a scientific theory accepted or rejected? Because reason lays down its law. What is this pallid ghost, reason, that it dares to intrude into the proud and glittering assembly of substantial things, this insolent pretender to authority, which goes about to question the testimony of the senses, this self-appointed magistrate over the heavens and earth? What is this ridiculous shadow, which in the majestic presence of sun, moon and stars should be treated with imperial scorn? The world lying there before us, just there, despite of us, stern and irremovable, clear, sharply outlined, wholly independent of us, and all that we do and think—that world surely brooks no denial, and needs no supporting arguments. Nature as she truly is, this is the nature of which science desires knowledge, virgin nature, apart from its perception by any human eye or living thing, unaffected by any contemplating mind, nature as she was before the eye was fashioned or the mind was born, a nature without spectators. Surely a most desirable knowledge. By all means let us have it. The chief aim of science throughout its history has been to avoid the confusing and exasperating intrusion of the observer, to elude his presence, to suppose him not there, on a journey, or attending to his private affairs, or gossiping with his neighbours. But how are you to get along without him? There's the everlasting rub! How are we to cut his acquaintance, or give him notice to quit?

The Greeks were accustomed to speak of the *peripeteia*, the change or reversal in fortune or circumstances which marked the turning-point in a drama. Such a *peripeteia* took place about the beginning of the present century, a reversal, a crisis, which, though many workers are hardly even now aware of the convulsion, shook the citadel of scientific thought to its foundations, and as a philosophy, left it in ruins. Science stumbled upon the vital mysteries, and awoke to the true situation. Of this revolution Relativity theory and Quantum theory were merely the heralds. It displays itself, and is, in fact, the discovery by men of science of the metaphysical assumptions in all their reasoning, the least expected and by far the most momentous of their many and brilliant discoveries. In their eagerness, in their triumphal progress, they had accepted without enquiry the plain man's view of the world, assumed, like him, space, time, motion, causality and all the rest, at their face values, and suddenly found themselves immersed in 'the great Serbonian bog, where armies whole have sunk'. Without exception the sciences involve these, and a dozen similar concepts, and all had been taken for granted, all employed as if in no need of scrutiny.

The crisis came when the structures of science were seen to be, like the child's buildings on its nursery floor, constructed out of obliging blocks, and doors and windows, all supplied, already adapted to meet the necessary requirements of the young architect's design. But space, time, motion, causality are not things, they are not objects, they are concepts of the mind, and the moment you mention them the thinker is at your elbow. In daily life we are not concerned with an interpretation of the sum of things. We may take matters as we find them, without anxious enquiry into their nature—the sights and sounds, the motions and the causes. But begin to philosophise, to speak of the ultimate reality, of things as they really are, and all this must cease.

The crisis arose with the recognition by men of science that to the external world of their investigations there is only one door, the door of human consciousness. Before you can examine things you must first become aware of them. More than that, in all your observations you carry with you the prepossessions of the observing mind itself, its powers and prejudices. That is to say, the observer is a part of his observations. But since the Renaissance science had taken the mind for granted, and as having no hand in the game; it supposed itself dealing with virgin nature, pure and undefiled, uncontaminated, in no way affected by human thought. And lo, looking over his shoulder, or rather in the very recesses of his observations, the man of science found the companion he most desired to avoid. Do what he would, he could not rid himself of the society of his own mind. Like the old man of the sea on Sindbad's shoulders, it clung to him, and could not be shaken off. With what result? That the concepts of the mind, all its prepossessions, entered into, became a portion of, and affected his findings. He had regarded thought as 'a mere pensioner of outward forms'. Now into the broad sunlight emerged the menacing, incontrovertible truth that in the picture he drew of nature he was invariably himself present, and that his presence gave to the picture features which virgin nature never had, nor could have. In a word, science discovered philosophy, in which it had steadfastly refused to believe, and had supposed a negligible flibbertigibbet.

A cloud, the size of a man's hand, first showed itself on the horizon—the affair of the so-called 'secondary qualities'. Of what colour is an electron? The light from a receding star, say the astronomers, becomes redder, from an approaching star violet, and base calculations upon the colours exhibited. But what if this redness is neither in the star nor in the garden rose, any more than the pain is in the knife that gives you pain, or the pleasure in the flower that gives you pleasure? At first it was supposed that the observer merely touched up the original canvas of nature a trifle by adding the secondary qualities, like colour, smell, taste; but, upon further analysis, the primary qualities, so-called, like resistance and extension, went the same way. They, too, were seen to involve a subjective judgment. Things or objects vanished, they became, in Professor Whitehead's phrase, 'nothing but an average stability of certain events in a set of agitations'.

Presently out of the cupboard emerged all the metaphysical skeletons, the everlasting unsolved enigmas. No account of the world, to put the matter in a single sentence, scientific or any other, can go beyond this point, that it is the world as experienced, and experienced by an observing being, who brings with him the mysterious faculty of experiencing. Nature apart from ourselves, and the mind in ourselves, we simply cannot know, and must not pretend to know. Outside ourselves we cannot travel by any gymnastics. To sketch the landscape as it appears to no one, while it remains unseen, to think in the absence of any thinker, are difficult operations. Do not mistake me. By most philosophers it is agreed that over against the thinker there certainly exists a universe not of his making, a world 'common to all', as Kant expressed it. To its true character, nevertheless, no one has found the way. Some link there is between them. We cannot believe that the observer and the world encountered each other by accident one fine day in the vasty fields of space. But how are they connected? All we can say is, no observer without a world, and yet no world without an observer. Or again, in Kantian language, perception without conception is blind, conception without perception empty. We can come to no other conclusion than that the marriage of things and thought is indissoluble. What God has joined no man can put asunder. Nature intended mind, desired to complete herself, to make an entry into society. It has the look of a clearly defined undertaking.

How, then, you will ask, does science live and flourish? Not by its theory of knowledge, for it has none, nor by its philosophy, if it can be said to have any, but by its technique, its methodology, by the brilliant success of its practical achievements, which have conferred innumerable benefits upon mankind, and won for its pioneers their immortal and deserved renown. How weak is science in explanation, but how mighty, how impressive in action! Mind is the veritable throne of science, and all lovers of knowledge bow before it. Yet betrayed by some inexplicable perversity, or some mad ambition, many of her disciples keep company with a proletarian metaphysic, declaring at one moment that consciousness is an irrelevance, an empty shadow, an *epiphenomenon*, at another that it is a mode of energy, like heat or electricity, and by either route plunge at length into a vortex of perplexities, and make sorry work of their own conclusions.

Yet how is an exit to be found? If we are to be fair, we must allow that science is in a dilemma, revolving in a closed circle, and by her own choice left without an alternative. When I speak of science I mean materialistic science. There is no other. Possibly the statement surprises you. Yet surely it is obvious that science and materialism are one, and cannot live apart.

They condescend to recognise no world save that which can be seen, touched, handled and measured. On sense experience, analysed, probed, expanded, and on sense experience alone, the whole structure of both is founded. What can you do? Matter talks matter, and science knows no other language. To admit any dimension or order other than the physical would be to abandon the ground on which she stands, to sell the pass. Suppose another order to exist, suppose an independent world of thought, science has no means for its exploration. There is no scale in physics for determining, let us say, the value of a poem, or the aspirations of a saint, no instruments for the measurement of Milton's imagination, or Rembrandt's soul. What follows? If you speak of such things at all she is willy nilly driven to declare that these also, in the final account, belong to the material system, and are in the end composed of electric charges. Of what else can she say they are composed? To admit a world beyond her powers of inspection would be to sign her own death warrant. Worst of all, it would open again the door, which at the Renaissance was slammed and barred against the myths and superstitions in which men had so long and fondly believed, the chaotic fancies, unchecked and uncontrolled by experience and experiment. Leave the plain world of the senses, and what foothold have you, what security? You enter a region where anything may be asserted, and anything believed.

Europe at the Renaissance submitted itself to a new discipline, and substituted nature's textbook of observable facts for the book of poetry. It was a momentous decision, a crossing of the Rubicon. The die was cast. So it came about that life, mind, consciousness came to be declared the resultant of physical processes, and to prove them so became the goal of scientific endeavour. 'The aim of modern physiology', says Höffding, 'is to conceive all organic processes as physical or chemical.' If this key will not fit the lock, science does not look around her for another. She admits no other, for she has no other. She files and oils the old key, and clings resolutely to the hope that some day it will be found to turn the wards.

The verdict to be reached is determined before the evidence is taken, the conclusion that the whole history of life and mind, the music of the poets, and the thoughts of the thinkers, the religions and policies, all loves and tears and laughter, fears, despairs,

163

hopes and ideals, can be unequivocally explained in physico-chemical terms, that the study of man, no less than that of nature, is simply the study of what the senses reveal and in the end of physical chemistry, to which without remainder they can be reduced.

By the thinkers among men of science this vaulting programme has now been tacitly abandoned. The day of reckoning has dawned, or if you will, the day of sanity. How has it come about? So complicated is the story that only a genius could present it. Bear in mind that physics cannot outsoar or transcend physics, a physical enquiry can only end in a physical explanation. Bear in mind also that all the sciences follow in its wake. If all things are built, and we are assured they are built, of unsubstantial, flying swarms of electrons, biologists must remember that all organisms consist of them; physiologists must not forget when they speak of thought, of will, of passion, that they are speaking of the subtly-woven products of this spider's web of spinning charges, however absurd it appears. To this its unassailable sovereignty, physics owes the breathless attention with which we follow its thrilling career, its exhilarating pursuit of the ultimate reality, the fundamental constitution of things.

What, then, is the latest news? Two bodies of explorers are at work, one company upon the large-scale phenomena in the telescopic heavens, the structure and motions of the starry systems; the other upon the small-scale, the microscopic or sub-atomic phenomena, and in both regions the Olympian mathematicians preside over all the deliberations. The latest news that has reached us, as everyone knows, may be summed up in four words —Relativity theory and Quantum theory. Four words! Or if we add Radio-activity—five words. But how startling, how revolutionary their message. Yet it is not one message but two, for these theories conflict. The small and great phenomena are not on friendly terms. Quantum theory has not been assimilated by Relativity theory, and it would not be too much to say that bewilderment reigns in both camps.

Consider the situation. Matter, a substantial something underlying and supporting its various qualities or appearances— colour, hardness, weight—is an ancient and time-honoured conception. It has had a long and successful life, but senility has overtaken it. By degrees its powers began to fail; its mass was found to vary with its velocity, a strange thing: then energy and mass were found to be identical, and matter finally became another name for energy. We must now, it seems, define matter as 'a complex of gravitational, kinetic and chemical energies which are found to cling together in the same space'. We think of gold, for example, as a solid body, but it is chiefly empty space. We scarcely recognise our old friend, matter, for which physics has no further use. A kind of visible motion, without substance, has taken its vacant place. There are no static things or objects, located in fixed positions. All is process, movements, events, some slow on our scale, like the drift of continents, some fast, like radiation. There is nothing either permanent or indestructible.

Stranger still, the new view declares that matter, whatever it be, and however it be described, is utterly inert, and without initiative, a do-nothing, an incorrigible idler. Pushed and pulled here and there, it is in truth merely the evidence, or index to our senses, that a power not its own is at work in the neighbourhood. Do not fancy—it is a very common error—that electrons and protons are material particles, carrying electric charges. They are not substantial things at all, they are not incarnations of energy, they are simply atoms of electricity.

The scene has changed, and with a vengeance. The new view maintains that it is not in matter that the energies of nature reside, but in what seem to us the empty intervals, the vacant spaces between objects—it is there that all the activities of nature have their unseen habitation. They reside in the electric, magnetic and gravitational fields, of which we have no perception at all, of which our senses tell us nothing, and of which till yesterday the very existence was unknown. Tangible and visible things are but the poles, or terminations of these fields of unperceived energy. Matter, if it exists at all in any sense, is a sleeping partner in the firm of nature. Space has taken over the concern, and does the business in the back premises. All that happens, happens in the void or vacuum, to which we give the name of space.

What, then, is this industrious space, which we had imagined to be pure, idle emptiness? That concept, too, has a curious history. For ages thought of as 'a universal container', as doing nothing and simply there, a kind of listless, unoccupied Absolute, we must now think of it as a factory of unseen humming batteries. With Faraday and Clerk Maxwell came the notion of space as filled with an active ether, a hypothetical medium, which served as the vehicle for electro-magnetic phenomena, like those of light and heat. Some medium had to be found, and yet no trace of the indispensable vehicle could, despite the bravest efforts, be discovered. How was this difficulty overcome? Most simply and ingeniously. True, it was said, we cannot find ether anywhere, but here is space: let it undertake the necessary duties. So ether was summarily deposed, and space crowned in its stead. Finally, as you are aware, on a suggestion of Minkovsky's, time, previously regarded as a separate entity or concept, was united to space and a joint monarchy proclaimed.

Such, in brief, is the romantic story. This Space-Time, you are to remember, has now been endowed with physical as well as geometrical properties. It has become a substance which behaves differently in different places. There is radiation in space-time, many types of it besides light. It is a hive of prodigious, of furious activity. Beyond the visible spectrum there are electro-magnetic, infra-red, ultra-violet rays. There are X-rays and γ-rays, all differing from light only in respect of their wave-lengths. There are alpha-rays, which radium discharges with the velocity of ten thousand miles a second, and there are the recently discovered cosmic rays, of penetrating power two hundred times greater than any of the rest, and more powerful by day than by night, whose source no one knows.

Viewed through Relativity theory and Quantum theory, as through a pair of binoculars, the universe presents a bizarre appearance. The first, Professor Einstein's dazzling conjecture, is not indeed universally accepted, yet is none the less a masterpiece of human wit. It declares that you desert meaning when you speak of simultaneity, a common time throughout the universe. Each moving system has its own. Each of us carries a local time about with him, his private watch. It declares that there is no sense in speaking of distances or durations save within a selected frame of reference, or in talking of matter, which is a misleading name for energy at a certain velocity. Further, among various possible geometries, Professor Einstein adapted from Riemann a geometry which differs from Euclid's,[1] which

[1]In Euclid's geometry two straight lines cannot enclose a space, and the sum of the three angles of a triangle is equal to two right angles. In Riemann's geometry two straight lines can enclose a space, and the three angles are greater than two right angles.

accounts for gravitation in a wholly different manner from Newton, as the result of space-time properties; and so dispensed with the old notion of a pull or attraction between bodies at a distance from each other—a mysterious force implied, but unaccounted for, in the Newtonian scheme. It substitutes, however, one mystery for another, since not so much as the glimmer of an explanation is offered why the presence of a large body should curve or distort the space in its vicinity, or why space should be so described at all.

In these regions you and I are manifestly not entitled to any vote. This only can be said, that a strong body of dissentients rejects the Einsteinian doctrine. For the ascription of physical properties to space, for the assumption of warps and creases in that medium, there is, they contend, neither need nor warrant. The geometry is an arbitrary choice, selected to provide the desired results, and the facts may be explained without the abandonment of the Euclidean system. Space and time, moreover, it is argued, are not homologous, or structurally alike. Time has a past and future of which space knows nothing. Geometry takes no note of time, and is independent of time, and to talk of motion as if it were a thing, as in itself curved, or possessing velocity, is to plunge into a swamp of nonsense. Time, too, of which we have an inner consciousness, is more comprehensive, more fundamental, than space, and of deeper metaphysical significance. So the malcontents conclude that the Minkovsky hybrid, Space-Time, is an arbitrary and untenable construction. Professor Milne, for example, employs the idea of a non-physical space, constructed out of temporal experience, regarding length and distance as combinations of time measures, which alone are taken as fundamental. Space-Time as an objective entity he thinks the purest fancy, and Relativity is for him merely 'the comparison of the experiences of different observers who can communicate with each other'.

From any standpoint the devastation wrought in all our previous ideas is shocking. Gravitation—well, it seems that in certain parts of space, repulsion and not attraction may be at work. The velocity of light may not after all be a constant, for in a gravitational field it follows a curved path. Causality, the granite foundation, without which, it was supposed, no scientific progress could at all be made, is in many quarters more than suspect, and on the way to be abandoned.   For Lord Russell it is 'a relic of a bygone age'.   'An Indeterminacy principle', or 'waves of probability' are installed in its room.   Atomic phenomena are not predictable.   A rift has appeared in the causal sequence. For all we can tell, these phenomena may even be controlled by a power external to physical nature, an angel or a God.   From the same state of things, from a given initial condition, not one determined result only, but various results may follow.   An atom of radium may for no ascertainable reason disintegrate to-day or next week, or last a thousand years.   Our familiar friend, light, presents an insoluble conundrum.   No one can tell you what it is.   Certain of its aspects can be accounted for if you suppose it a wave motion, others if you regard it as a beam of travelling photons or particles.   If you adopt the first opinion diffraction remains an enigma, if the second, the photo-electric effect disputes your passage.   Stars, hills and seas, the furniture of earth and heaven, fade away into a mathematical residuum, into equations.   Space-Time alone survives, a strange monster, with a physical head and a metaphysical tail, unheard of in any previous history.   We are left with Space-Time and its configurations, that is, with configurations of we know not what.

A year or two ago Professor Einstein calculated the size of the universe.   It was finite, and its diameter was 216 million light-years.   It now appears that his calculations may have gone astray. It may, after all, be infinite.   One is not greatly surprised.   Any-one of us can tell, even you and I, that it is one or the other.   Yet if infinite it is not curved, for infinity has neither shape nor boundary.

Do not, I pray you, fancy even for a moment that I take pleasure in the perplexities of these brilliant pioneers.   I have much too deep a respect for talents far outranging my own.   I desire to claim their feats for that divine investigator in man we call the mind.   From any angle I cannot bring myself to think it secondary or derivative, to describe it, with Hobbes, as 'nothing but local motion in the organic parts of man's body'.   Motion enquiring into the character of motion, matter looking into this little affair of its own construction!   How interesting are such ideas.   Can matter come to think?   It will be time enough to consider the question when we have been told what matter is.   Science, the science of molecules and atoms, of protons and electrons, of measurements and the calculations of energy, stands across the path of its own philosophy with a drawn sword. Energy is translated into energy. The motions of the atoms of the brain must therefore pass into other motions. There is no end or exit from this closed circle. If consciousness emerges, if hopes and fears emerge, if sympathies and affections, science should tell us 'Into what other physical motions do they pass?' What movements do they in their turn set up in the world of atoms? You must not tell us they do nothing, or are mere witnesses of the unending performance. We must be told what in the physical system do they move. This gulf remains unbridged.

For myself I am of the contrary party, which holds, with Cudworth, that mind is 'senior to the world, and the architect thereof.' Thought is at least an indisputable factor in the scheme of nature, and by thought alone can it be studied. The vast and imposing array of scientific facts, observations and measurements, what are they but findings of the mind, and how can they be reached without the organisation provided by the mind? How else are they arrived at? The primacy of thought consists simply in this, that everything is submitted to its judgment and valuation. There is nothing anywhere more secure upon which it can rest, and the intelligibility of nature we assume has no other assurance. The confusion of our times appears to me the inevitable consequence of an unphilosophical physics, which endeavours to explore the abyss of being, as does Professor Einstein, with material apparatus, with rigid rods and synchronous clocks—God save the mark!—which is based upon physical observations alone, which looks upon space and time as amenable to measurement by laboratory instruments.

I read recently that Professor Einstein has a new theory in mind, towards the formulation of which he has had the aid of some startling new 'pictures of space'—I quote from *The Times*— 'photographed with the mathematical "lenses" of a "cosmic camera". These "photographs" indicate that 'space is not one thing, but two identical sheets joined by many new bridges.' These are wonderful thoughts, indeed, and wonderful proceedings. When I read of them I am convinced that I have eaten of 'the insane root that takes the reason prisoner'.

Quantum theory, which has to do with small-scale, subatomic phenomena, has gone far deeper and nearer the centre than the more sensational Relativity theory. No one disputes its

conclusions.   We are in the vestibule of the *mysterium tremendum*.
Listen to this.   'In Atomic Physics'—I quote Professor Dingle,
'neither space nor time separately, nor space-time has any significance.'   What a thunderbolt!   'The appropriate substitutes',
he continues, 'are not yet known.'   No, they are not known,
and we may even conjecture that they will be hard to find.   A
hundred matters of sublime interest confront us.   We have, for
instance, the theory of the expanding universe, which asserts
that the spiral nebulae are receding from us at fantastic speeds,
150,000 miles a second, that the very character of space is changing before our eyes, and that the day will dawn when our successors in this galactic system will say 'good-bye' to the rest of
the universe, which will vanish from their sight.   More harrow-
ing still, we encounter Entropy, the famous Second Law of thermodynamics, Carnot's principle, which tells us of the one direc-
tional movement of nature.   'Time's arrow', as Professor
Eddington calls it, points remorselessly one way, towards the
degradation of energy, which, in a state of temperature everywhere the same, is paralysed, and unavailable for any rebuilding
of the burnt-out Cosmos.   The final state of things will be a
ghastly lethargy, nothing for evermore will again take place.   On
this way to death, this descending staircase into extinction, it was
that life climbed, against the stream, and put forth all the miracles
of living creatures, of mind and all the miracles of mind.   So the
universe, unable to keep itself alive, is subject to the same dark
destiny as its children.   It, too, must die, and darkness be left to
bury the dead.   Well, perhaps, and perhaps not.   Physics may not
have the last word in cosmic history.   The universe has not always
been what now it is, and may yet, indeed certainly will, undergo
transformations as unpredictable as it has undergone in the past.

Space is thought's, and the wonders thereof and the secret of space;
Is thought not more than the thunders and lightnings—shall thought
        give place?

In the age-long encounter between mind and matter, thought
and thing, it is not matter which has in our time gained upon its
adversary.   The standard of mind it is that has gone forward, and
is planted on the captured heights.   Our successors may look
back, I believe they will look back, upon us as belonging to an
age in which was fought the greatest and most momentous among
the decisive battles of the world.

IX

THE ONE AND THE MANY

Did all the world in one fair flame appear,
And were that flame a real infinite,
'Twould yield no profit, splendour nor delight.

. . . . .

One star made infinite would all exclude,
An earth made infinite could ne'er be viewed.
But one being fashioned for the other's sake,
He bounding all, did all most useful make:
And which is best, in profit and delight,
Tho' not in bulk, they all are infinite.

Traherne

I like in France the chivalry,
The Catalonian lass for me,
The Genoese for working well
But for a Court commend Castile.
For song no country to Provence
And Treves must carry't for a dance.
The finest shapes in Arragon,
In Juliers they speak in tune.
The English for a head or face,
For boys, troth, Tuscany's the place.

THE ONE AND THE MANY

'Be sure to study the great diversity of human nature,' said Kant. Wise counsel. The most troublesome thing in the world is the individual man. If anything is in evidence he is in evidence, and the varieties of this creature are without end. Many are the races and many the temperaments. Who will enumerate them? There are vehement and hot-headed men, selfless and conciliatory men. There are sybarites and ascetics, dreamers and bustling active men of affairs, clever and stupid, worldly and religious, mockers and mystics, pugnacious, loyal, cunning, treacherous, cheerful and melancholy men. There are eagles among them, tigers, doves and serpents. They display, varying as they do in appearance, talents, behaviour, every type of unpredictable reaction to their surroundings. 'He was a comedian on the stage,' said the wife of a celebrated 'funny' man, 'but a tragedian in the home.' History is, in consequence, the despair of philosophy. The mighty Hegel, who twirled the universe round his finger, found history much more difficult to handle, for it consists of the doings of innumerable, unique, obstinate individuals. They decline to submit to any common measure, or to be marshalled under any unifying principle. Their proceedings are incalculable. The essence of individuality lies precisely here—its wilfulness. You cannot predict what it may do.

If individual persons are the despair of philosophy, single instances, unique events, are equally the despair of science, utterly refractory and clean beyond her range. History consists of separate, unique events—the battle of Salamis, the capture of Constantinople, the sailing of the Pilgrim Fathers. The affections of science are set upon docile things and events, susceptible of classification, and assignable to laws—laws which govern many cases, and preferably all cases. If each individual goes his own way, if electrons set up for themselves, there is an end to prediction. Then science, which glories in prediction, which desires to obliterate differences, has no option but to fall back upon a calculation of averages. In the world of men, however, averages soon fail you. If a Napoleon or a Lenin chance to be born, philosophy and science avert their horrified gaze. No one can tell what may happen. A single person, anatomically similar to the rest, proceeds to turn the world upside down. To plot the curve of Cleopatra's career is beyond the mathematicians. 'Had her nose been shorter', as Pascal said, 'the whole course of the world would have been altered.' And, fortunately or unfortunately, nature pours out these interesting, unique beings in extravagant profusion. She never repeats her patterns, not so much as in the making of a single leaf. She appears to have as her chief end the multiplication and intensification of their peculiarities, and to rejoice in them. The human mind, as represented in philosophy and science, nourishes a devouring passion for unification. To our discomfiture nature displays an equal passion for novelty and unexpectedness.

What can be made of this heterogeneous mob of individuals, this riotous confusion of events we call history? Logic demands the universal, and nature supplies nothing but the particular. The world, we know, has no exclusiveness. It contains everything, provides for everything, welcomes the ugly and the beautiful, the high and the low, the good and the bad. We human beings are not so broad-minded. We discriminate, we approve and disapprove. Nature exhibits no discrimination, neither likes nor dislikes. How are we to explain this incongruity, and how are we to account for the age-long, sustained effort of science and philosophy to submerge the particular in the universal, to be rid at all costs of the unique individual and the unique event? The answer is not far to seek. There can be no philosophy or science of unique individuals or events. They have simply to be accepted. They are irrationals. Reason cannot deal with them. For what do we mean by rational? We mean that which is reducible to a principle, a rule or order; an entity which refuses submission to any law or principle is irrational, and lies altogether outside the province of our poor, groping understandings. In brief, such an entity is just itself and a law to itself. Each man's self, for example, is such an entity. So it is that science and philosophy cry out for a unity, or postulate a unity. They have no choice, their very existence is at stake. The world, they insist, is one, for if it be not one, the game is up, and reason quits the field.

Take a look at the matter from another angle. Needless to say, we are not the architects of the world, we have not made nature. It is spread out there before us, a picturesque collection of heterogeneous, wholly dissimilar objects, here seas, there mountains or deserts, plants or animals. Nature revels in their various shapes and colours. That is what we see, the picture as it hangs before our sight. Faced with this variegated scene, this multiplicity of things, the eye is very well pleased, the artist entranced. The inquisitive intellect is, however, on the contrary, extremely ill at ease, confused, restless. As a picture this world of ours is no doubt satisfactory enough, these green fields, rushing rivers, grazing cattle, flying birds. You might even go so far in enthusiastic moments as to call it charming or sublime. But all these forms and colours, these endless differences, cannot by the enquiring mind be simply taken for granted. They have to be accounted for. How have they arisen?

In the endeavour to understand how they came about the human intellect is struck by a brilliant idea. How much easier, it tells itself, would be the comprehension of these endless diverse things if they could be shown as in the end identical, arising out of one thing, substance or state—if, for example, as Tyndall claimed in his famous Belfast address in 1874, in matter was to be found 'the promise and potency of every form and quality of life', of all the world contained. By this captivating idea not Tyndall's alone, but many great intellects have been spell-bound. For this identity, or unity, they have hungered with an inappeasable appetite. This has been the aim of their strivings, their shining ideal. 'Most cosmogonies have taken as their starting-point', writes Sir James Jeans, 'the supposition that the universe started as a chaotic mass of gas.' With some more subtle philosophers it is Space-Time. You heave a sigh of relief, your enquiry has reached its goal, at last you understand. All that is, was or ever shall be, originated from Space-Time or Gas. In one or other you have 'the promise and the potency of every form and quality of life'. You have now discovered that all things, the stone and the river, the star and the butterfly, the rose, the eagle and the banknote are, despite their superficial differences, one and the same, forms of the identical underlying substance. And to this list you will add also all existing minds; all thoughts that men have had were once present, in some fashion, in a flaming mass of incandescent gas. Reason itself, which enquires into the matter was necessarily, of course, also somehow present in the promise and potency of this original substance. To begin with there was nothing else. For this unity you may coin any name which suits your fancy. Call it God, and you will satisfy the theologians, Energy, and the man of science will be content, the Absolute, and you will secure the votes of the philosophers.

The formula has one weakness, its moment of success is also the moment of failure. It is as if having observed that all books consisted of words, you proceeded to the conclusion that they were all in the same language and finally indistinguishable. Shakespere and Marie Corelli are exactly alike. The awkward thing is that when differences disappear, the world disappears. The peculiarity of the world is this very multiplicity and heterogeneity, the fact that it is infinitely and unsubduably varied. Not only do the differences remain when you have disposed of them, but if, indeed, you did succeed *per impossibile* in disposing of them, existence, which is variety, is precipitated into an undifferentiated unity, which is, in effect, whatever you elect to call it, blank nothing.

Where now is the evidence for this pious opinion? There is none, save the mind's prejudice in its favour. 'Academic philosophers ever since the time of Parmenides', says Lord Russell, 'have believed the world is a unity. The most fundamental of my beliefs is that this is rubbish.' Yet, with few exceptions the great system-builders are against him. For the most part they stand resolutely on the side of the One. If, however, we look around us, and ask for the evidence, it appears to support and support impressively, overwhelmingly, the case for the Many, the multitudinous variety of existing things, from clouds and trees to thoughts and emotions. The attachment of the mind to the One seems to arise from some kind of aesthetic satisfaction the idea offers. It provides a support for the mind. As the bird, blown out to sea, seeks rest in the rigging of a ship from the surrounding waste of waters, so the mind, wearied by the ceaseless tempest of its multifarious impressions, seeks a refuge from the

eternal flux of transitory things, and is driven to declare the vexatious, unmanageable Many an illusion, a passing show.   The
Whole, or One, has somehow fallen into plurality, but the true
supreme or ultimate reality remains, none the less, unques-
tionably in the One.   For reality, if you enquire of the philosophers or the men of science, invariably resides where you least
expect it.   It is at once everywhere and nowhere, and eludes the
most painstaking search.   It conceals itself in the Absolute, as
we have seen, or in Space-Time.

You have thus in philosophy a distressing situation, to which
the new-comer has difficulty in accustoming himself, the tiresome and perplexing situation that the appearance is never in any
circumstances the reality, and the reality never puts in an appearance.   You and I, for example, since we are undeniably appearances, must pay the penalty.   'The purely individualist self, or
mere individual', General Smuts tells us, 'is a figment of abstraction.'   He talks the language of the philosophers, by which the
plain man is dumbfounded.   No doubt, we must all agree that the
solitary hermit is rarely to be met with.   Robinson Crusoes
do not abound.   No doubt the scene of operations for most of us
is the community to which we belong.   We are all children of
earth and are supported by the surrounding universe.   Yet it
may be pertinently asked, 'Is it not this very separateness that
makes the individual what he is?   Is it not his essential quality?'
The single person may even go so far as to place himself in strenuous opposition to the society in which he finds himself, *Athanasius
contra mundum.*   'Those who speak of men in general, speak of
nobody,' said Stilpo.   However much of an abstraction he may
be, the religious and legal systems place upon the individual the
burden of responsibility for his own character and conduct.   It is
the individual, for example, who has to make the best of his lack
of ways and means.   It is the individual who knows where the
shoe pinches.   It is he, the figment of abstraction, who is
hungry and thirsty, who thinks, wills and feels, and it is he who
bears the burden of his soul's anxieties, upon whom all the demands are laid, who is blamed or praised, rewarded or punished.
It is this unfortunate who suffers and dies.   In answer to the
incessant requirements of the other figments of abstraction, as
for example the tax-collector, he is never permitted to plead that
he is a mere appearance.   In contrast to the noble reality, which

despite its ubiquity, or by reason of it, has 'neither a body to be kicked nor a soul to be damned', the individual, having both, is in a sorry plight, the most miserable of entities. He is continually in the firing line and receives all the wounds. According to this logic the army is real, but the soldiers have no true existence. Yet this body that can be kicked and this soul that can be damned confer upon their unhappy owner no sort of compensation, no dignity, no privileges. Properly speaking, it seems, he does not exist at all. Alas, for our poor selves! The pessimists have something to say for themselves when they declare that the separation of the One into the Many was a lamentable error.

If now we turn from the metaphysicians to the ethical idealists, the men with a mission, who propose to improve matters, we meet once more the same famous problem of the One and the Many. They, indeed, like the rest of us, are sadly conscious that, in respect of human beings at least, the world is emphatically not a unity. If it were, they would be out of employment. Finding, as do the metaphysicians, that the diversity is intolerable, they determine that a unity it must be made. If men, as is only too evident, are not of one mind, they conceive it their business to see to it that they become of one mind, agreeing together, animated by the same principles and the same aims. The idea is, we may concede, fascinating. Yet over against them, as over against the philosophers, stands nature as before, in determined opposition. While all these thinkers are busily engaged in their favourite task of unification, nature perversely pursues the opposite path of diversification. She is, as we have seen, the great separater. She separates element from element, plants from animals, one species from another species, and erects barriers between them. Look at the creatures of the sea and land, every variety of insect, bird, fish, walking, flying, and creeping thing. Nor does it end there. Different patterns of life and culture prevail over all the inhabited lands. The castes in India are not numbered by hundreds, but by thousands. The fishermen who make their nets in one way will neither associate nor marry with those who make them in another. Intoxication forms a part of the religious rites among American Indians, war is unknown among the Eskimos. The ancient Mexicans practised self-torture, as the Indian fakirs do to-day. One man's reason is to another damnably unreasonable. Death is preferable to 'loss of face' with the Chinese. It was at one time their custom to erect statues to dishonour traitors and politicians who had brought evil to their country; we do so to those who have brought it benefits.

To the disgust of the reformers, the world is a tower of Babel, a confusion of tongues. And not merely a confusion of tongues, but a confusion of desires and purposes. For it is not races and languages which separate men so sharply as the varieties of their nature and disposition. What seems wisdom in the West seems folly in the East. What delights one disgusts another. The adventurer is at a loss to understand the satisfaction to be derived from committees and conferences. The lover of sport is amazed at the scholar's milk and water tastes. The artist looks upon the moralist as a fanatic, and the moralist returns the compliment by thinking the artist a libertine. The lover of power obtains no happiness from the visions of the mystic, the lover of pleasure sees only folly in the mortifications of the saint. They incline to regard each other as degraded or perverted. Every being pursues the ends dictated by his own nature or needs. The hater of war cannot conceive why Marlborough or Hannibal should not have been willing to spend their lives growing cabbages. The Chinese regard the soldier as the most debased type of human being, the Japanese look upon him as the noblest. The humanitarian Godwin was of opinion that 'monogamy is the most odious of all monopolies', and the Christian bishop regards bigamy with horror.

Human life seethes with dissensions and disapprovals. When men no longer fight with rifles, they fight with economic weapons, and universally with their tongues. We disapprove, and that heartily, of our neighbour's opinions, of his habits, of his tastes. Even when they have no effect upon our own fortunes, we cannot bear with this or that characteristic of other men, their horrid manners or ridiculous accents. Disapproval occupies the greater part of our conversation. And if nothing were left of which to disapprove, the salt of life would lose its savour. Nothing, we think, our world-planners think, could be more desirable than a unanimity of opinion, which would solve all our problems. Men should certainly think alike, feel alike, love and hate the same things, have, in short, a common standard of values. Best of all, if they accepted without demur our preferences, our sympathies and antipathies. They unhappily do not, and we have to accept the exasperating situation. 'Nothing is good for everyone', as the Greek sceptics pointed out, 'as snow is cold for everyone, for the same thing is judged good by one and evil by another.'

Moreover, if we desire to hold to our own convictions, how can we expect our neighbours to yield upon theirs? Upon what do we base our own superiority? 'Show me the man', said Plato, 'able to see both the One and the Many in nature, and I will follow in his footsteps as though he were a god.'

This ancient problem of the One and the Many, then, has two sides, the metaphysical and the practical. Both have exercised the minds of men throughout the ages. If the reality is one, as the philosophers maintain, how did it become so amazingly diversified? How did the original One come to develop these antagonistic forces, these discontinuous parts? How did the particularities arise?

Linus, a Theban, was, the historians inform us, the first man who taught that all things originated in one thing, and when dissolved, returned to the same thing. And, as we have seen, the great calamity, many have argued, the cause of all our woe, was the tragic disruption of the One into the Many. In their view, therefore, our hopes should be centred upon the return of the Many into the all-embracing Whole, from whose bosom they should never have emerged. That is, when the thought has been stripped of all its philosophical wrappings, how much better had there been no world at all. Nor is the thought very complimentary to the original One, which is credited with a vast absurdity, the preposterous folly of letting loose a legion of ills for no purpose. The One, had it possessed any wisdom would have remained the One, at rest throughout eternity. Why produce all this discomfort, why all this doing merely in order to undo? To this question no coherent answer has been given. The attempts to build a metaphysical bridge between the One and the Many, the whole and its parts, are countless, and not an arch has ever yet been completed.

And the practical problem, the chief concern of the moralists and reformers, has proved no less intractable. Not all, indeed, yet a number of our troubles arise from the fact that there are a good many people in the world, about two thousand millions.

They do not think alike, nor desire the same things or the same type of life.

> For no three of us will agree
> Where or what churches there should be.

If we assume that not more than one in twenty have opinions, we have still a hundred million opinions. Men do not agree upon what God would have them do, even when they believe in His existence. They do not agree how life should be lived. They are not in agreement upon the best means of obtaining felicity, either in this world or the next. How then is co-operation among them to be brought about? How are the varieties among men and their desires to be eliminated? How is the required harmony to be attained? Not, I think, by 'addressing eloquent insults to the human race'. The majority must rule, you think. But the rule of the majority is not, as Burke saw, a law of nature, and there will be recalcitrant minorities. How are they to be dealt with? By ruling them justly? What you call justice they regard as monstrous tyranny.

The idealist aims at a grand consensus of opinion. We cannot blame him. He has to meet, however, 'the huge army of the world's desires.' 'Men cannot work together', said Confucius, very wisely, 'until they have similar principles.' Precisely; whose principles, then, are to be selected for the laurel crown? Whose ideals are to be accepted as the universal ideals, to which all others, perhaps yours and mine, are to be sacrificed? That the world-wide diversity of aims, interests, opinions leads to quarrels, conflicts and war needs no demonstration. Not till the interests of men coincide can you expect their wills to coincide. These interests, however, are in everlasting collision.

The question is not simply how men are to be persuaded

> To seek another's profit
> And work another's gain.

There remains the task of selecting among the competing principles those most worthy above all others to enlist the combined and sustained support needed to establish them. Let us suppose a parliament of man—upon which some rest their hopes for the future—to be established for the determination of these guiding principles. How awkward would it be, indeed how unpleasant, if it chanced that our peculiar national traditions and ideals found no favour there, if others distasteful and even abhorrent to us were preferred, and our sympathy and support were required for customs, laws, institutions, or even a religion alien to all our cherished ways of thought and profoundest convictions. You think the idea preposterous. I am not so sure—far from it. We suppose that our religion and our principles must commend themselves to all the peoples of the world, now and in the future, as the best, as destined to prevail, to be accepted, and to endure till the end of time. Yet what reason have we to dream such dreams? Look at the facts. We are a people of some fifty millions. And our birth-rate, like the birth-rate of some of our immediate neighbours, is falling fast, so fast that, if the present decline continues, in a hundred years our population will be below ten millions, and in some European countries no children would be born at all. Over against this Europe, of which we are but a fragment, is an Asia, not to speak of Africa, with a population of over a thousand millions. During the last century the population of the world has doubled. Asia is 'an ant-heap of men'. The population of Russia alone outnumbers the whole of the rest of Europe. The population of Japan has doubled within the last sixty years, and is now increasing at the rate of a million annually. India's population rises by ten millions annually. Does it appear very probable that, within a century or two, it will be our descendants, and not the children of these teeming races who will possess the earth? With our very limited population, our falling birth-rate, our practice and advocacy of birth-control, is it not much more probable, is it not certain, that our trade and institutions will suffer hardship, that we may even be dispossessed of our present territories?

There is a further question. Would these prolific peoples not have a moral claim to be our successors? Have we any divine right to the best things of the world in perpetuity? Of course, we may shrug our shoulders, and not think of these things, but the avoidance of thought will not retard their arrival. The immediate prospect has an exceedingly dreary look. 'I confess', writes Dean Inge, 'I have been amazed and appalled by the total and almost unresisted destruction of liberty in one European country after another. I could not have believed twenty years ago that such a thing was possible.' The Dean appears to have read history to little purpose if he looked forward to a static world. There are ages still to come, and imagination dizzies at the flight of past and coming time.

A recent very learned student of history, Mr. A. J. Toynbee, tells us that there have been twenty-one civilisations in all so far, of which fourteen are wholly extinct. Before half the time the physicists predict our planet is likely to last, if civilisations follow each other at the same rate in years to come, we may look forward to a million and a half civilisations of varied style and pattern, before the chequered story of humanity ends in the final destruction foretold by the law of entropy. And some of them will be, one conjectures, extremely unlike our own. The primacy of Europe, which we thought everlasting, her exploitation of the East, has gone. Her monopoly in trade, in manufactures, in the management of the backward countries is fast vanishing.

It will not be claimed that the prospects even of the Christian religion are at the moment very promising. Two thousand years have passed since the birth of Christ, and the Christians in the world are still outnumbered by two to one. Christian values are not everywhere, nor have they been during its history at all times, acceptable. Had the Northmen succeeded, as they came near doing, in establishing their culture upon Europe by force of arms, we should to-day have been living under a wholly different standard of social and moral values. Instead of meekness and self-abnegation, the Christian virtues, we should have admired self-reliance and personal honour. Dignity would have been prized above purity, and self-confidence above self-effacement. And not without some advantages to the community. In a society like theirs men are known for what they are; their prowess in battle and wisdom in affairs are open, recognisable qualities. There are no shelters available for the coward or the knave. In the dense thicket of present-day civilisation men may flourish without a single virtue. Every form of deceit, flattery, cunning, hypocrisy masquerades in the assembly, 'the caterpillars of the commonwealth' wax to great proportions, when in a viking society they would have been the thralls they should be. Who can assure us that Christianity will win all hearts? The world is not throughout animated by Christian principles, but by very different principles. It will prove a considerable undertaking to convert it. The Christians are outnumbered by many millions. In India under our government there are more Mahommedans than there are people in Great Britain. A great European country, Russia, has openly and officially rejected its ancient faith and espoused atheism. Our creed is there ridiculed in theatres and picture-houses. Mottoes are everywhere displayed which declare religion of any kind not merely absurd, but the chief enemy of human welfare and progress. 'Give up fearing God, Brothers,' 'Religion is the opium of the people.' The Chinese, a people of four hundred millions, are, and have always been, their historians tell us, atheists. The old pagan gods have risen from their graves, and are looking around them again in the world to-day. No, despite the idealists, who, in the interests of world unity, desire to submit our institutions to the jurisdiction of a League of Nations, or a Parliament of Man, I should myself be extremely reluctant to do so. I think we might be out-voted. And how distressing it would be if, in the sacred cause of world unity, we were requested to become Mahommedans, atheists or Hindus.

Even in countries where Christianity is still the nominal creed, it seems to be of a different brand from ours. 'In Mexico you may see the parish priest coming out of church, after saying Mass, with a fighting cock under his arm, all ready for the fray.' In some countries Christianity has acquired a distinctively Teutonic flavour. A German lady, writing to an American friend, after the events of June 30, 1934, exclaims, 'Hitler has killed his friends for the sake of Germany. Isn't he wonderful?'[1] Wonderful perhaps, but government by assassination suggests a different variety of Christianity from that favoured in England. We are told by the same author of a German boy, whose prayer, on making his first communion, was 'that he might die with a French bullet in his heart'. I fear he harboured some unChristian sentiments, this lad. The differences among races will require a good deal of eradication. So passionate is the devotion in Spain to the bull-ring that Spanish writers have described the arena as 'the sands of God'. Belmonte, its greatest matador, 'stands', we are told, 'in this age for Spain, among the supreme tragic artists of his country.' 'Cervantes, Goya, Belmonte', that is the company in which he is placed.

Do you disapprove? Then you do what that very great and

[1]*European Journey*, by Philip Gibbs.

very good man, Edmund Burke, declined to do. You draw up an indictment not against a single person, but against a whole people. Your moral sense is very properly outraged. I congratulate you on your moral superiority over a Christian nation of twenty millions. One thinks there must be more in it than you suppose, something not to be so summarily dismissed.

This matter of morals and moral indignation is of great interest. War, for example, arouses our sternest disapprobation, and we are clear that it should be abolished. But what about motor traffic? I submit that it, too, might be abolished. Motors are a very recent invention, and you cannot assert them a necessity of civilised life. Till a few years ago the world did very well without them. Wars are usually waged in some one's interest, and for some sort of reason. Motors slay and wound on our streets and roads for no reason and in no one's interest, not men only, but women and children in tens, in hundreds of thousands. This is 'killing no murder', war without declaration of war, this slaughter of our own kith and kin, 7000 done to death yearly and 230,000 maimed and injured. In seven years about 50,000 have been slain, and over a million and a quarter wounded in this country alone. It is all quite open and unabashed 'carnage. With what shuddering horror and indignation would this slaughter have been received as the result of an air raid! How are we to account for the marvellous placidity of our humanitarians? They never murmur. How easy, how desirable—a matter, indeed, of the utmost simplicity—to end by a single act of Parliament this hideous massacre. Have they ever advocated it? We have anti-war leagues and resolutions in plenty. I have not heard of any for the suppression of motors. How is this? Will some one be good enough to tell me why the one kind of killing is condoned, the other condemned? Is it because the pleasure and the profit of the one exceeds that of the other? Is it that moral sense must give way to convenience? Is it that the slaughter is not yet so excessive as in the late war? After all, there have only been over 15,000 children killed since the war, and only between 500 and 600 children killed so far this year. Will some one explain to me the absence of moral indignation in this matter? Will some one tell me why our merciful hearts are so hardened that this wholesale murdering of the innocents distresses them not at all, while the thought of war so afflicts them? I suggest the enquiry into the subject as an instructive occupation for the mind. If you undertake it, you will incidentally gain some insight into humbug and hypocrisy, into the dark region of human motives, of thought and conduct. Satan will be amused when you try to explain exactly why this state of things is tolerable and war intolerable. You will also learn how things which seem the easiest and the simplest to do, may yet be pretty difficult.

The doctrine of the perfectibility of the world is old. It is not, however, Christian doctrine, rather, as Schopenhauer perceived, it is radically irreligious. Men cannot get along without religion. If one is abandoned another is adopted. And all our humanitarianism, all our philanthropy and welfare work are efforts to fill the great spiritual void left by the decay of faith, drab substitutes for the older creed. The spirit of man craves a friendly God, and you give him economics. He asks for immortality, and you say, 'Be content, here is beer and bacon.' Since there is nothing beyond the present to be hoped for, let us make the only lives men will ever know less pitiably wretched. As the tide of religion has receded, the tide of this creed, the only alternative, it seems, has correspondingly risen. Miracles, once the province of the Church, will now be performed by the State, which will provide a heaven on earth, here and now. I am not to be understood as decrying humanity, kindness, philanthropy. These are no new things. They were not discovered yesterday. It is the gospel that is new. These things have always existed, and will continue to exist. There was plenty of kindness in the world, before it was set above the Olympian gods, above truth, and freedom and justice, before emotionalism was placed upon the throne of Zeus and took the wheel of the universe. In the new Garden of Eden, when we enter it, there will be good roads and water supply, unlimited picture houses, unstinted soft drinks, excellent sanitation, and humane slaughtering, the best of schools and wireless installations for everyone, free concerts and lectures for all. There will be no far horizons and invincible hopes. We shall cease to think of birth and death, of the infinite, of God, and the sublime secrets of the universe.

I am not much in love with these sixpenny Utopias. Men have other thoughts than these—thoughts that wander through eternity, and projects unattainable in time. How childish to think that the world's griefs are all of economic origin. Our world planners have great designs for the filling of empty stomachs. Let them ponder the more intricate problem—the filling of empty hearts. The troubles of the world have by the brilliant diagnosticians, like Robespierre or Marx, been assigned to a great variety of causes. Landor thought the best initial step towards the amelioration of its sufferings would be 'to strangle the last king with the entrails of the last priest', or vice-versa. The giant or dragon to be slain is differently pictured in different generations. In one age monarchs are declared the public enemy, in another the aristocrats, in another the bourgeois class, or the capitalists, the bankers or the Jews. The millennium is not yet, however, in sight.

And under whose leadership are we to advance towards it? There is never any lack of seedy reformers, 'the Projectors and Schematists', for whom Swift had such contempt, who suppose themselves entrusted with a divine mission for the betterment of the human lot, 'sky-blue idealists', as Carlyle called them, kind hearts and muddy understandings, 'potato' philosophers, who see their way to provide beef and beer, or preferably beef without beer, for everyone from East to West; the grass-green enthusiasts, who in their mind's eye see men over all the earth sitting for ever at their cottage doors, festooned with ivy and honeysuckle; who are persuaded that if wars should cease, gambling be put down and love-making rendered respectable, if men in their more energetic moments were given a ball to play with, a harmless woolly ball, God would be better pleased.

> The oyster-women locked their fish up
> And trudged away to cry 'no Bishop'.

Even morals become a nightmare when we reflect upon its self-appointed representatives. What sort of world would it be in which Wesleyanism or Anglicanism ruled the scene? in which throughout its breadth and length not a soul ever kicked over the social traces, in which there were no idlers, or spendthrifts, or jesters or Sir Fopling Flutters? Does anyone in his senses really wish for an undiluted respectability throughout eternity? A perfectly ordered world is not, though it may be to yours, to everyone's mind. Some would prefer a disorderly as vastly more interesting, and a risky life as better worth living and infinitely more attractive. Must we look forward to wholly conventional lives, all alike, on the model of a colony of ants, in standardised buildings, with hot water provided, lifts and electric light, where all men think the same thoughts and pursue similar ends? If this be what is promised us, then indeed the life of all our blood

> Is touched corruptibly, and the pure brain,
> Which some suppose the soul's frail dwelling-house,
> Doth by the idle comments that it makes
> Foretell the ending of mortality.

Science has worked wonders in our time, and may be confidently expected to work still greater wonders. The Utopian architects, as might have been anticipated, have turned to her genius for assistance and encouragement. If science be permitted to take matters in hand no bounds can be set, Professor Haldane assures us, to human progress. Diseases will, of course, be banished. Men, he predicts, 'will be able to think like Newton, to write like Racine, to paint like the Van Eyks, to compose like Bach. They will be as incapable of hatred as St. Francis.' Man's life will probably be measured by thousands of years, 'and every moment of his life will be lived with the passion of a lover or discoverer.' One can see it will all be very wonderful. Professor Haldane is a man of science, the grand manner of the prophets sits well upon him, and I have no kind of claim to challenge his forecast of what science can perform. It may be that the Professor Haldanes of the future will be able to manufacture any kind of men to order, cynics or saints, chess-players or engineers, poets epic or lyrical, or any brand of humorist, philosopher, Adonis, or Admirable Crichton to suit the requirements of society. And what more could you want? Well, shall we say, for one thing, justice, a small matter which this programme does not include? Would you in possession of this heaven upon earth be content to forget the past sufferings of human kind? Would a happy lot for men and women to be some day born obliterate or compensate for all that the previous generations have endured? Do not these humanitarian schemes overlook, with a singular inhumanity, the millions who have perished without even a glimpse of the glories to come? They are of no account. Yet what have the new-comers done to deserve the felicity denied their predecessors, and will they be of any greater account when their day, too, has come?

> Oh dreadful thought, if all our sires and we
> Are but foundations of a race to be,—
> Stones which one thrusts in earth, and builds thereon
> A white delight, a Parian Parthenon,
> And thither, long thereafter, youth and maid
> Seek with glad brows the alabaster shade,
>
> .   .   .   .   .   .
>
> Not caring that those mighty columns rest
> Each on the ruin of a human breast,—
> That to the shrine the victor's chariot rolls
> Across the anguish of ten thousand souls!

The thoughts of our well-meaning reformers appear to be directed to one end only, the cessation of strife, and the consequent cessation of effort, for which there will no longer be any need. But how false it is to suppose that human beings desire unending ease, unthreatened safety, that their *summum bonum* is cushioned comfort, a folding of the hands to sleep. That way madness lies. What then is left to occupy their interest and attention? They desire rather difficulties, such is their nature, difficulties to elicit their powers, to keep them alert and wakeful. They wish to be alive. In the absence of resistance to desires, desires decay, and an intolerable, an appalling tedium invades the soul. Whose lives do we read with interest and admiration? The lives of men lapped in comfort from the cradle to the grave? Or of those who in the face of odds have accomplished their ends, good or bad? When the soul of man rises to its full stature, with what disdain does it regard the sweetmeats and the confectionery. In their anxiety for human welfare, in their collectivist schemes, the sentimentalists have overlooked the individual man. They submerge him in the sea of their universal benevolence? But who desires to live in the pauperdom of their charity? Every man desires to be his own architect, and the creator of his own design, the sentimentalist himself among the rest. And the last and greatest insult you can offer to the human race is to regard it as a herd of cattle to be driven to your selected pasture. You deprive the individual of his last rag of self-respect, the most precious of his possessions, himself. If you treat him as a thing, an inanimate object, which can be pushed hither and thither, if you treat him as one of a drove of oxen, you take away his birth-right, and for this loss nothing can compensate him, not all the soothing syrups and honeys of the world.

To its eternal honour Christianity has stood steadfastly for the sanctity of the individual. To imprison the human spirit is the unpardonable sin, the attempt to make men automata, to force them into the same mould. No means will ever be found to induce human beings finally to surrender themselves, either body or soul, to a dictated felicity, to satisfactions chosen for them, whatever vulgar Caesars rule the world. And upon this rock all forms of regimentation, of standardised existence will eventually shipwreck. Every type of compulsion is hateful, always has been, and always will be hateful, as long as men are men. Was this freedom about which the poets have raved since the world began, for which men have died in millions, worth the bones of a single soldier? Have you ever asked yourself why men have fought for liberty? Not for amusement. Freedom they must have, whether they know or not what to do with it, freedom to choose cause or party, order or disorder, the good or the bad, to steer each his own vessel to the port of his desire. Take away his choice, and you make of him, for all your benevolent inten-tions, a chattel or a slave. There is a rebel in every man; men will revolt and demand again their freedom. As Dostoievsky expressed it, when everything is smooth and ordered and per-fect, 'in the midst of this universal reason there will appear all of a sudden and unexpectedly some common-faced, or rather cynical and sneering gentleman, who with his arms akimbo will say to us, "Now then, you fellows, what about smashing all this reason to bits, sending their logarithms to the devil, and living according to our own silly will?"' And he will have followers in their thousands. Men desire the strangest and, in their neigh-bours' eyes, the most incomprehensible, the most irrational, the most preposterous things.

The astonishing thing about the human being is not so much his intellect and bodily structure, profoundly mysterious as they are. The astonishing and least comprehensible thing about him is his range of vision; his gaze into the infinite distance; his lonely pas-sion for ideas and ideals, far removed from his material surround-ings and animal activities, and in no way suggested by them, yet for which, such is his affection, he is willing to endure toils and privations, to sacrifice pleasures, to disdain griefs and frustrations, for which, rating them in value above his own life, he will stand till he dies, the profound conviction he entertains that if nothing be worth dying for nothing is worth living for.

The inner truth is that every man is himself a creator, by birth and nature, an artist, an architect and fashioner of worlds. If this be madness—and if the universe be the machine some think it, a very ecstasy of madness it most manifestly is—none the less it is the lunacy in which consists the romance of life, in which lies our chief glory and our only hope.

X

THE MIGHTY OPPOSITES

Though the bleak wings of Fear oppress my sky,
Though sharp her talons vex my shrinking flesh,
   I would not bid her fly.
While Fear remains my Hope can yet abide,
My heart still beat, my senses comprehend,
   The gods be satisfied.
But should Fear pass on some wild panic night,
What if I saw in the calm, certain dawn
   My Hope had fled the light?

T. A. COLLINS.

X

THE MIGHTY OPPOSITES

To all our queries nature answers never a word. 'God makes nothing but riddles', says a character in one of Dostoievsky's novels, and like all travellers before us we have found it so. What disturbs the philosophers, what perplexes the moralists, what, in brief, calls for explanation is, in Nietzsche's phrase, 'the antagonism at the heart of the world.' These excellent men cry out for a harmony between their surroundings and themselves, and to their distress encounter a disharmony. Through the whole realm of creation it runs, the inner and manifest contradiction, which puts them out of countenance. How is this? they enquire. The work of God, the Almighty, should be—who can deny?—without a flaw, 'one entire and perfect chrysolite'. Unhappily it presents itself to their eyes, and to ours, as imperfect, darkened, not by an occasional and passing cloud, but by a canopy of gloom, infected by manifold confusions and disorders. The evidence for a divine and stable government of the world is far to seek, and they wring their hands. A profound and inexpugnable discord appears to pervade, to be, indeed, a part of the structure, an ineradicable constituent in the very nature and constitution of things. The universe is undeniably at war with itself, and ruled, if by any powers, by rival powers. Faced with so deep-seated a disorder, for what can the poor mortals, its inhabitants, hope?

> The troubles of our proud and angry dust
> Are from eternity, and shall not fail.

It has been borne in upon the simplest souls in all ages, as clearly as upon philosophers, that if a creative and beneficent principle is at work in the world, a destructive and apparently maleficent principle is also at work, equal in power, equal in the extent of its dominion. Save to the eye of faith the universe

195

displays a dual personality, kindly and cruel, philanthropic and inhuman. If God is in evidence, Satan is also in evidence. Ormuz and Ahriman are in array against each other, the powers of light and darkness, of organisation and disorganisation, construction and destruction, health and disease, life and death. Who has not heard in the rhythm of nature the threatening note, the deep, disquieting roll of her thunder? There is terror in the world as well as beauty, horrors are mingled with its sublimities. It both captivates and alarms. Within the swirling vortex, the endless coming and going of events, within the circumference of the greater motions, the convulsions in the heavens and upheavals in the fevered earth, there are on the human level corresponding upheavals and convulsions, alarms and excursions, everlasting changes and perturbations.

> So between the starry dome
> And the floor of plains and seas,
> I have never felt at home,
> Never wholly been at ease.

Such is the world as we know it, and such the conditions of existence: nor can the most soaring imagination provide us with an alternative model, or even assure us of its possibility. Things as they are wear the countenance of fate, the unbending brow of necessity, and who are we to quarrel with the gods?

It has occurred to few philosophers that the discords may be a factor in the scheme, that the situation may have its advantages, a brighter side, and may be even a necessary condition of existence. They have seldom reflected that this clash of opposites may have brought it about that we have a universe at all, and that we ourselves, its offspring, are in being, that from this dark soil of conflict creation sprang. So far we may advance with assurance, the disharmony has at least banished an otherwise incurable and intolerable monotony. But for these oppositions in nature and human life, 'the world-wide warfare of the eternal Two', nothing had taken place, all were still, sunk in a motiveless, motionless stagnation. The busy scene of events had been a desert of idleness. Movement implies resistance, high implies low, and light, darkness. If there be no East there is no West, if there be no North there can be no South Pole. There are good kind souls who suppose it possible to have good without evil. But liking involves disliking, and approval disapproval. The antithesis is everlasting and unavoidable. From the clash of opposites has arisen the world with all its varieties, its infinite diversity of creatures. They are our fathers and mothers, these Twain,

> . . . out of which Earth and Heaven were born.
> And from their mingling thence are poured abroad
> The multitudinous birth of mortal things,
> Knit in all forms, and wonderful to see.

In the tension of the opposites is the mainspring of the Cosmos, manifested in organic nature, as in all the circumstances and interests dispersed through the wide ways of men. Out of their great debate arise politics, art and philosophy, for the same duality is present in the central keep of the mind itself, where there is always 'a pro and a con', in the conflicting thoughts, the bright and dark angels that sway the course of history. You meet the cut and thrust of these duellists in the collision of wills, the quarrels and animosities, the exchanges and repartees, the sinner-hoods and sainthoods. *Idem semper sentire, nihil sentire.* To feel always the same is to feel nothing. If all things were alike, all men alike, all thoughts alike, what pleasure, what interest, what anything could there be? As the harmonies of the painter or musician arise out of the blending of the colours and the notes, so the mixing and mingling of its elements give to the world its values. 'All beings have souls,' said the Italian mathematician, Cardan, 'even in plants the passions of Love and Hate are at work.' 'Could differences be abolished sweet love were slain', as the Greek poet expressed it. And our own Blake put the matter also in a sentence. 'Without Contraries is no progression. Attraction and Repulsion, Reason and Energy, Love and Hate are necessary to human existence.'

The poets have little to learn from the philosophers. Yet philosophers there have been who had sight of, and made no wry faces over the truth, who accepted human destiny with a high tranquillity of soul, and even went so far as to proclaim conflict a boon to mortals. Hesiod long ago spoke of Ἔρις, strife, as a blessing to men, ἀγαθὴ βροτοῖσι. 'The spice of life', said R. L. Stevenson, 'is battle.' But let us turn to that most penetrating of thinkers, whose every word bears the stamp of genius, the sage of Ephesus, who, five hundred years before Christ, made that thought his own.

Heraclitus, the 'dark' or 'difficult', was by birth an aristocrat and hereditary ruler of his native city. But this great original was in temper a solitary, a lover of the hills and woods, rather than of the agora, devoted his life to philosophy in preference to politics, and ended his days in the society of nature. To his sombre message he added a biting tongue, to his searching intellect a disdain of the multitude. This man had, nevertheless, the esteem of Socrates himself, to whom, it is said, Euripides gave a book by Heraclitus, and afterwards asked him what he thought of it. 'What I have understood', replied Socrates, 'is good; and so, I think, is also what I have not understood; only the book requires a Delian diver to get at the meaning of it.' The profound mind of Heraclitus foresaw from afar many concepts of modern science. He perceived the subjective factor in perception, insisted, as does the most recent physics, that all objects are in perpetual motion, though their movements are beyond our range of vision, and that if you look for truth, you should expect the unexpected. The contradictoriness, the turbulence, the centrifugal and centripetal forces, the multifarious variety and clashing currents of things, these he declared both necessary and good. Its vicissitudes and frictions are at once the essence and the salt of life. In the great arena of human enterprise men were served by antagonisms, which developed their powers and proved their mettle. There quality could be discerned, there the slave could be distinguished from the freeman. To him it seemed the human race needed the spur. That spur was resistance, opposition. In conflict men discovered their own souls, encountered obstacles, called upon all their potential strength to overcome them, and so took the mountain path to greater strength, to fame, and to godhead itself. Effortless existence was for him a term without meaning, a condition not to be found in nature. The doctrine of Heraclitus is patrician doctrine. He would not have men avoid issues, flee encounters, seek cradled felicity, or burrow in shelters. Like Nietzsche he desired them to become supermen. Of his winged sentences here are a few.

'Homer was wrong in saying *Would that strife might perish from among gods and men!* He did not see that he was praying for the destruction of the universe; for if his prayer were heard, everything would come to an end.'

'We must know that war is universal and strife is right, and that through strife all things arise and pass away.'

'But for the injustices men would not know the meaning of justice.'

'Men do not know how what is at variance agrees with itself. It is an attunement of opposite tensions, like that of the bow and the lyre.'

What now is the sum of this philosophy? The law of polarity was for Heraclitus, the λόγος, the inner thought, or supreme principle of the Cosmos. All energies had their contraries, and from the strain their opposition engendered the world had arisen. In a word, no oppositions, no world. These rival forces were, in fact, the two inseparable halves of the same thing, as are the concave and convex sides of a curve, they were contrary yet complementary activities, which by their union in disunion produce an attunement, a hidden harmony, better than an open and evident. For that which strives against another in reality supports itself. As heat implies cold, justice implies injustice. Sickness it is which makes health desirable, fatigue gives sweetness to rest, evil is the buttress of good. We may go further and say things produce their opposites, good sets up a counter-current of evil and evils give rise to good.

The ruling idea of Heraclitus takes us straight to the heart of modern science. It teaches that in the absence of resistance energy has no power, and vanishes. Without two levels or states of differing potential a current of energy cannot show itself at work, or be at work. The famous law of entropy depends upon this principle. If all the particles in the physical universe reached the same degree of heat, no power could anywhere be exerted by one upon another, and nothing could ever again take place. We are reminded, too, of Newton's saying—'I am induced by many reasons to suspect that they' (the phenomena of nature) 'may all depend upon certain forces by which the particles of bodies, by some causes hitherto unknown, are either mutually impelled towards each other, or are repelled and recede from each other; which forces being unknown, philosophers have hitherto attempted the search of nature in vain.' The conflicting energies, though at variance, are nevertheless, Heraclitus taught, in their essence one, and the contests, to which their opposition gives rise, are necessary, just and right. Their thrust and counter-thrust uphold the keystone of the great arch of existence. Think of the children's game of see-saw. When one end of the beam is exalted, the other is depressed, yet it is the same beam.

Heraclitus held—a crucial point in philosophy—and here Plato is our witness, that the ultimate Reality is at the same time One and Many, the Many constituting the One, which it may be said is 'both willing and unwilling to be called Zeus', or God, since it transcends in all its aspects and attributes the parochial language of men.

For our sentimental times this doctrine has an unpalatable, even a disgusting flavour. Strife as the corner-stone of the universe, what thought could be less tolerable? Strife anywhere, at any time is for us the arch enemy, the idea of its necessity hateful, and the praise of it an abomination, a blasphemy. When Heraclitus declared strife the keystone of existence, he spoke, or did not speak the truth. Possibly you disagree with him. Do not then squander your energies in denouncing his doctrine. There is a better way of employing your time—disprove it. If you fail, there is still another resource open to you, to which I have already referred, the avenue of retreat. You may take the path recommended by the gentle, the strife-hating sages, the sufferers from a 'spiritual agoraphobia'. You may withdraw yourself, abandon action, forsake the arena, insure your peace and salvation; you may, like Achilles, sulk in your tent, and leave the world to its fate. 'We must release ourselves from the prison of affairs and politics,' said Epicurus. You may become one of those beings, who, in Bishop Creighton's pleasant phrase, are 'as good as gold and fit for heaven, but of no earthly use'.

To retire in disgust or displeasure from the monstrous mellay of life has often been described as 'the celestial way'. Yet, it may be asked, what is there celestial about it? Needless, I think, to remind you that a conception similar to that of Heraclitus, the sense of a rift, or fissure or dualism in nature, unconsciously felt by many men, meets us full-front in Indian philosophy. But with a difference. Thought is there concentrated on retreat, and the way of retreat proclaimed as the way of salvation. The love of life is the root of all evil. Destroy it, and your foot is on the heavenly path. Escape from the contending opposites is the

wise man's goal, to be attained, as with the Stoics, by desireless-
ness, a passionless impassivity, disdain alike of pleasure and of
pain.   Through this indifference, apatheia, ataraxia—the recipe
is always the same—the emancipated soul enters into Brahma,
where concern for life's petty perturbations, its joys and sorrows,
passes utterly away, and all struggles cease.   'I will take my
lodging', says the Indian sage, 'at the root of a tree, surrendering
all things, loved as well as unloved, tasting neither grief nor
pleasure, neither cherishing hope nor offering respect, free from
the opposites, with neither fortune nor belongings.'
   Do not disturb the saint by asking him how this state is to be
distinguished from non-existence.   He will not condescend to
answer.   The horror of life must be strong upon you when you
desire to exchange it for utter nothingness.   You pronounce the
final condemnation of life, and of God, its architect, when you
thus sentence it to death.   'Men who love nothing in the world'
—it is Buddha's saying—'are rich in joy and free from pain.'
This is a strange richness: it dispenses with love.   And the old
question for theology emerges again.   What sort of God is that
who creates a world from which men require to be saved?   He
is to save us, it seems, from Himself.
   There are mystics who claim that the world is perfect, a proposition troublesome to establish.   We must judge by the wits we
have, and not by those we have not, with the knowledge we
possess, and not with the knowledge we cannot obtain, from the
evidence at our disposal, and not from that which is not supplied.
There are also mystics who hate the world, but how this detestation of His creation is consistent with the love of its Creator
presents an intricate knot difficult to unravel.   The flight to God
from the works of God has an ironical flavour.   What kind of
welcome in the courts of Heaven can such fugitives expect?
They do not hope, one fancies, to enter the Presence, but expect
rather to be somehow lost in the throng, and cease to be any
more themselves.
   While India fixes her gaze upon release from life's burden by
escape into the invisible and spiritual from the material present,
China looks steadily at things as now they are.   Indian philosophers are metaphysicians, for ever talking of the One and
Supreme Reality.   The Many they despise.   All that we see
around us is mere illusion, Maya, deception.   Chinese thinkers,

on the other hand, like Confucius, for centuries China's guiding star, are realists, in whose eyes the concerns of the present have an importance. Earthly life and the ordering of its daily affairs are the paramount issues. Something, they hold, can be done to mitigate our inevitable afflictions. Think first, they counsel, of to-day, and how it may best be spent. Much is possible. Good manners, for example, are not to be despised, nor good temper. How greatly they assist to remove the asperities and frictions incident to human intercourse! And who can deny the charm of elegance, of style, the pleasure to be derived from music or verse, or a shapely vase from the hands of a cunning workman? The Chinese are connoisseurs, in delicate flavours, in rare and evanescent perfumes. A lovely flower, an exquisite profile, a choice tea, a touch of quality, wherever found, has for them its value.

Here also, in this realistic land, where the mind has taken a practical turn, and addressed itself to the urgent and immediate demands of the present moment, the needs above all other needs, if we are to live at all, of food and shelter, of some form of social organisation—here also has arisen a philosophy, which, if it does not actually echo Heraclitus, strikingly resembles and recalls his favourite thesis. To the twin opposing forces in nature the Chinese give the names of Yang and Yin. Emanating from 'the Grand Extreme', the Absolute or God, the indescribable and unapproachable ground of all existence, they are, we may say, its ministers or instruments, from whose contention, which is also co-operation, the world was born. Yang is the positive process, Yin the negative. You may call them also the masculine and the feminine, the active and passive, the advancing and retreating principles. Yang is the south, the sunny side, Yin the dark or shadowed. Yang is brightness and heat, Yin darkness and cold. Alternately they manifest themselves, as in the ebb and flow of the sap in vegetation. With Yang spring and summer are in the ascendent, with Yin autumn and winter. Each is, in a manner, rooted in the other, and all things partake in their partnership. The rose unfolds in the sunlight, but its roots seek the darkness of the soil. They are counterparts, neither can exist by itself alone. Together, losing or gaining in turn, they create the rhythm of events in nature. Theirs is the throbbing pulse of her heart, theirs the pendulum swing, which marks the ticking of the cosmic

clock. Now the stress or accent of Yang is felt, now that of Yin.
Within the human sphere of thought and action Yang is growth,
joy, profit, honour, fame. Yin is decay, loss, distress, misery,
ignominy. Age succeeds youth, and sleep alternates with waking. In the world's contrapuntal music note is sustained
against note, and we have a ligatured or syncopated rhythm,
whose accents fall where by the ear they are least to be anticipated.

The Absolute or God, certain philosophers say, includes and
harmonises the adversaries, which in the field of time are at everlasting odds. 'The upper link of nature's chain', as Bacon
expressed it, 'is fastened to Jupiter's throne.' In the final
summing up existence is to be identified with good, merged in
the great Original of light or darkness, for they know not which
to call it. We must wish it so, and believe it so. But this is
faith. The harmony, if harmony there be, is hidden from mortal
sight. The nexus between existence and good, though sought with
passionate tears and prayers, has never been found, nor yet a
nexus between existence and evil. The optimists and the pessimists alike have failed. Unhappily the logical bond, which
should unite what is with what ought to be, in our way of thinking, is absent. We, argue as you please, are manifestly tossed
upon the stormy surface of the opposing tides. Within us and
without us are many witnesses that we like nature are under the
rule of the contraries.

Psychology has come upon the truth that, within the soul of
man, the same pair of opposites, which are at work in the great
rhythms of the universe, are at work here also. It tells us, for
example, that they determine our philosophies. 'The monistic
tendency belongs to the introverted attitude, the pluralistic to
the extraverted.' You find them exemplified in the L'Allegro and
Il Penseroso of Milton. The spiritual problems which Shakespere
has set forth in Hamlet, Macbeth, Othello, exhibit phases of the
inner conflict, as history displays them in the wide theatre of the
world. At the crises in human life the protagonists enter, and
the scene is set for their encounter.

> The genius and the mortal instruments
> Are then in council; and the state of man,
> Like to a little kingdom, suffers then
> The nature of an insurrection.

The conflict may take innumerable forms, and the opposites emerge in every region of human thought and character, in all the political, theological, social controversies throughout the generations. We are, for example, not less creatures of appetite than followers of reason. We are both egoists and altruists. 'There is a constant quarrel', the Spaniards say, 'between Beauty and Chastity.' Look around you and see in society and the individual the antagonistic forces ceaselessly in action. Instances crowd upon us; in some natures the internal struggle reaches the intensity of civil war, and, as in the souls of St. Paul and Luther, though waged within a single breast, it may pass on its decision, with formidable and revolutionary results into the world of public events, and alter the destinies of mankind.[1] On the one side you have each man's natural devotion to himself, his own personality and identity, displayed in his love of life and self-preserving instincts, in the pursuit of private aims, and in the fear of death, which puts an end to them—impulses the moralist, for all his efforts, can never uproot. On the other side a deep desire for a firmer support than, in the roaring flux of things, his own powers provide, a longing for a refuge, for a merging of his frail, separate individuality in a corporate whole, for a firm foundation in the changeless, for the strong arms of the everlasting: the longing of the spirit, which is the essence of all religions, to return after its *Wanderjahre*, and become a partaker in God's peace. The love of life and the hatred of life are the two great moods of the human soul. Between these poles life swings, between the desire for personal activity amid the shining things of time, and the desire for the calm of eternity, the desire to be on the journey, to be up and doing, and the desire to be at the journey's end. Not in individuals only; you will see whole races of men on the great highway, going and returning, outward bound or homeward bound. You will find them consumed with the passion for enterprise, intent upon life, its bustle, animation, novelties, encounters. And you will find them weary, desiring only absorption in some harmonious unity, the battle over. And throughout it all we have the good souls who direct their anger against God that He made such a world, and

[1]Creative conflict is very frequently apparent in the work of genius, where two contrary emotional states set up a tension. Genius indeed is commonly the result of a racial mixture.

the other good souls incensed against their fellow men that they pursue their private ends, and will not unite to regain Paradise.

In these moods of acceptance and rejection you hear the beat of nature's heart. The endless dialogue of which life consists, the likings and dislikings, meetings and partings, loves and hates, correspond to something in the universe itself. Look where you will, the contraries, the antinomies confront you—the animate and the inanimate, heat and cold, summer and winter, day and night, body and spirit, man and woman, thought and the thing, appearance and reality, the conscious and the unconscious, the limited and the boundless, continuity and discontinuity, time and eternity. From the contention of the opposites comedy is born as well as tragedy, the preposterous and ludicrous, the absurdities and humours, the fantastic topsy-turviness of things, not less than the calamities and catastrophes. The sweet and bitter waters are from the same spring. I submit to you that life is a greater thing than the moralists have perceived, and that the poets see it in its true dimensions. When in *Henry V* we hear of Mistress Quickly's death, and Pistol's disgrace, when we hear that Nym and Bardolph have been hanged, how many of us are so much in love with virtue as to rejoice? 'I believe', said Dr. Johnson, sturdy moralist though he was, 'that every reader regrets their departure.' And who is so besotted as not to agree with him? Would you rid the world of their kind? 'A life rich in dereliction, the life of beggars, drunkards, idiots, tramps, tinkers, cripples, a merry, cunning, ribald, unprotesting life of despair, mirth and waste'—God's tolerance for these superfluous persons· disgusts you. You would contract His spacious universe into a tidy garden of saints. Yet there are lovable scamps, of whom the world is full, who astonish us by doing magnificent things of which their virtuous neighbours are quite incapable, exhibiting a self-sacrifice or a cheerfulness in adversity, or in face of death, which saints might envy. So baffling are the aspects of life when a sudden illumination comes from the heart of darkness.

In his *Laws* that hot-gospeller, Plato, becomes very stern with his fellow creatures. In the state he pictures, a Fascist state, there is no liberty of opinion, no toleration of disbelief, or interference with the established order. And the penalty is death, as it was the penalty of heresy in the early Church. The wise folk who know what is best for the world are to be congratulated.

To know that you are a prophet of the Lord is a great thing—to have no doubts. It is a great thing to be so deep in His counsels that you can speak *ex cathedra*, and hand over delinquents and dissentients to the executioner.

The passion for reforming one's neighbours out of existence, or at least out of the existence they prefer—and the two are often found together—afflicts even more grievously those who have lost their faith in God than those who believe in Him. The seceders to the church of the ethical idealists, having dispossessed God of His authority, are at no loss to replace Him. They mount the vacant throne, deify their own consciences, would have men bow and worship their ideals, and proceed to establish a tyranny more irksome than that of their ecclesiastical predecessors,

> More haughty and severe in place
> Than Gregory or Boniface.

'Be my brother, or I will slay you.' *Sois mon frère ou je te tue.* Who conferred upon them this astounding magistracy? What, one wonders, do our reformers propose to do with men in whom the opposites are in startling evidence, with a man, let us say, like Charles James Fox, who made his great speeches in the Commons on nights between those he spent in gambling and drinking? 'The most brilliant debater', said Burke, 'the world ever saw'— 'all fire and simplicity and sweet temper', in Creevey's words, 'perfectly exempt', in Gibbon's, 'from any taint of malevolence or vanity or falsehood.' This man spent a quarter of a million on cards and wine before he was twenty-five, and fiercely resented any interference with his personal habits. He would lose £16,000 on Tuesday night, speak in the House on Thursday on the *Thirty-Nine Articles*, sit up drinking the remainder of the day at White's, and win £6000 before leaving for Newmarket on Friday. This was also the man who fought all his life for every liberal principle, for toleration and Catholic emancipation, and who during office abolished the slave trade. What do you propose to do with such a human volcano? Would you replace him by some bloodless respectability? Perhaps our reformers cherish the secret hope that nature has ceased to produce such men. Let us hope, they pray, that God or nature will refrain from making these upsetting people; another Napoleon, for example, the most splendid genius, Acton thought, who ever trod the earth, who yet had few scruples, sacrificed two million lives, had none the less legions of devoted followers, and built himself a pyramid of remembrance which will crumble only with human memory, who in his own words, wanted the empire of the world, and the world invited him to take it. The reformers will no doubt see to it that budding Napoleons may be early discovered and strangled in their cradles.

'Never, no, never', exclaimed Burke, 'did nature say one thing and wisdom say another.' I suggest that some hesitation would be to our intellectual credit before we condemned her outright, and set ourselves in opposition to her mighty scheme. Despite all that may be said and said truly of her divisions, her cruelty and inhumanity, or if you prefer it, indifference to our pains, I cannot reconcile myself to the lofty and unqualified disapproval, the off-hand condemnation of the universe. I cannot take kindly to the open defiance of its ways. Mill spoke of 'the odious scheme of nature'. 'Let us understand', cried Huxley in a moment of rhetorical exuberance, 'that the ethical progress of society depends, not in imitating the cosmic process, still less in running away from it, but in combating it.' Ajax defies the lightning. Nature, then, is wrong and we right, she vicious and we virtuous. Our rationalists are very sure of themselves, our ethical idealists throw a bold challenge indeed to the divine mother that brought them to birth. Is the mannikin in his senses when he postures before high heaven?

I can find no warrant in the human intellect for a defamatory verdict on so vast, so immeasurable a thing as the sum of all existence. To take to ourselves a larger wisdom than the Cosmos has a whimsical, not to say insolent, look. By her own methods nature has brought us into being, raised us above the inorganic world, and conferred upon us a primacy in the organic. By her own methods she has elevated us to intellectual heights whence at least other heights can be discerned. Is this nothing? Are human skill, strength, dexterity, judgment, vision, genius, 'the hero's heart, the lover's lute' nothing? Is it nothing to have witnessed the astounding pageant, to have had a share in the shaping of events, to have known human friendships and associations? How tiresome are the fault-finders!

'The sage', said Confucius, 'demands nothing from others. He does not murmur against God, or complain about mankind.'

Others with deeper knowledge and brighter minds may deem themselves qualified to judge nature's case. I cannot. I prefer to think that our knowledge or our reason may be at fault. The choice, as Nietzsche saw so clearly, lies between a 'yea-saying and a nay-saying' to life. Men of sense will, I am persuaded, continue to accept rather than refuse. To spend life in denying life—what a programme! And nature will see to it that the 'yea-sayers' will prove the stronger party in the end. From them she will select her recruits, and commit to them the course of future events. That they will fall into line, however, at the bidding of our sentimental reformers, I should be slow to believe. Presently when the whole earth is explored, and mapped, and intersected with roads, there may be difficulty in meeting the needs of the active and adventurous, the Caesars and Napoleons, the fierce men and the fighting peoples. They will look around for action, for something to do, and will be troublesome. Will you set them to make daisy chains? Will tea and skittles satisfy them? These occupations may not suit their fancy. Our good friends, who would forbid gambling and alcohol, and much more, who would have all men at home and in bed by ten o'clock at nights, are they aware that they propose to suppress the very springs of vitality, that if they drive the energies of nature underground, these energies will gather strength and blow them at the moon? They have not reckoned with the creative and destructive agencies of the nature they would put in irons. They are men sitting on a Vesuvius, whose blast will presently make cinders of their schemes. They are afraid of life, and have excellent reasons to be afraid. Looking over the world is like looking down into the fiery crater of a volcano. Nature is violent, and has not exhibited any marked preference for anaemic folk, for those who despised life, or turned their backs upon it.

The alternatives between which we have to decide are plain enough. The stage is ours. Here we are, thinking beings, evolved somehow through inconceivable periods of time. Either nature clean overshot her mark, adding to the creatures on this planet an unnecessary species, ill content with its lot, and sighing after impossible Utopias, or the appearance of such a being is an index to some deep withdrawn idea in nature herself, prophetic of issues not yet reached in him, or even in his furthest reaching thought, of which, as in all her previous doings, she has given no more than hints in the intellectual and spiritual strivings of man-kind. So far men are the crown of nature's efforts. Can she go further? Will she permit them to fall back into the void, and bring the sorry effort to an end? Should they, as some say, seek the void, or entrusting themselves to the vessel which, though storm-tossed, has yet escaped shipwreck, continue the voyage with good heart?

If I have not made matters clear, let me try again. That the world came to its present state from the hand of God or nature, as easily as your will moves your hand, that Not-Being passed smoothly into Being, is no certain truth. That it emerged from the womb of nothingness at a word, who can tell us this? What reason have we for thinking that it was an easy thing to call into existence a universe of conscious and interacting intelligences, to harmonise their desires, to attain perfection in such an enterprise in a moment of time? It may well be that to attain to man's mind and soul a great circle was required, like the great circle sailed by mariners. So hard a thing it may have been to found the state of man.

Tantae molis erat Romanam condere gentem.

Life involves suffering, so far the pessimists are right. I am well aware that it may even be suffering past endurance. Many have judged death a blessing. There were in 1931 in Great Britain alone 5000 suicides; there are, it is said, 70,000 annually in Europe, double that number in the United States.

Here I and sorrows sit,
Here is my throne, bid kings come bow to it.

Nevertheless, Leibniz was also right when he described ours as 'the best of all possible worlds'. What an absurdity, you say, when pain is the universal language of the race, the only language everywhere and at all times understood. But you have forgotten the opposites, upon which creation rests. 'Evil', as a writer on Plotinus has written, 'is a necessity, if there is to be among the degrees of reality a world like ours, and our world, such as it is, is in so far a manifestation of goodness and beauty that its existence is preferable to its non-existence. For we have to remember that the question is not whether men and animals should be what they are, but whether they should be what they are, or not at all.'[1]

[1]Thomas Whittaker, *Priests, Philosophers and Prophets*, p. 68.

What is it, then, the fugitives from the 'splendid misery' of existence desire to avoid? It would appear themselves, not this life, but any life. They desire everlasting and unbroken felicity. But existence is built upon the opposites, which stand and fall together. The desire to escape them is ever present with us, but escape them we cannot. Expel the evil and with it vanishes also the good. The capacity for pleasure in conscious and sentient beings like ourselves rests upon the same foundation as our capacity for pain. If you can feel the one you can feel the other. In proportion as our natures are sensitive to joy they are sensitive to sorrow. As you can experience happiness, in like proportion you are exposed to the experience of suffering. Thus it is that men judge of existence as they themselves experience it, some approving, some disapproving, according as it provides a surplus of satisfaction or dissatisfaction, of pleasure or of pain.

Viewing life as a whole, Plato was of opinion that the existing universe was better than none. It is this, the world of the opposites, or nothing. Was he, perhaps, wrong? Were it within your powers, would you, since its ills are irremediable, destroy it with a word? Since existence is a unique experience, there is nothing with which we can compare it, no measure of its value open to us in terms of some other thing. We may think of it, and judge of it as we please. And the verdicts upon the value of life, as we might expect, are singularly varied. We are all 'exiles from our dream', but what in fact do men desire? I should be obliged if some one told me. Is it to sit with folded hands throughout eternity before the Beatific vision? Is it the life of Hume in Paris, where, he tells us, 'he ate nothing but ambrosia, drank nothing but nectar, breathed nothing but incense, and trod on nothing but flowers'?

Heraclitus taught, as we have seen, that men were wrong who praised and sought the easy path, the putting off of burdens, escape from effort and anxiety, from hardships, even from war itself. They were wrong, since, though they knew it not, they asked for the end of the world. And to this foolishness they added a pusillanimous desire for idleness, for wages they had not earned, a cheque for everlasting enjoyment. Men cry out for a felicity they have done nothing to deserve, a felicity, moreover, under lock and key, safe for ever. But, whatever it may have been, it was manifestly not nature's design to establish a pauper colony of idlers on her dole. She provided, in the phrase of Keats, 'a vale of soul-making'. Variety, even violent variety, is the breath of being. Through the contraries, and in no other way, is thought encouraged, intelligence heightened, consciousness intensified. In their antagonism is our salvation. They are 'the hounds of heaven', hunting us, that we may develop all our powers. 'He that wrestles with us', said Burke, 'strengthens our nerves, and sharpens our skill. Our antagonist is our helper.' Satan, if we understand matters aright, is the ally rather than the enemy of Michael, and both God's servants. Between them, between 'His Darkness and His Brightness', there is exchanged, despite their contrary rôles, 'a mutual glance of great politeness.' But for their partnership in contention nothing could ever take place. Without them were neither ups nor downs, neither projects nor endeavours, neither undertakings nor accomplishments. The fire and life and movement, the colour and music and mystery of the world are of their making. For to end all quarrels and conflicts would be to end all energies and splendours and graces, since it is in passion and action they display themselves, and not in either peace or indifference. 'If I am very, very good in heaven,' asked the little girl, 'shall I sometimes be allowed to have a little devil up to tea?' Her wisdom exceeded that of the philosophers.

'Nothing great in the world', as said Hegel, 'is accomplished without passion.' The intellect does nothing without interest, and the soul is the prime mover. This philosophy has the advantage over others that it reflects, and alone accurately reflects, the human situation. It begs no questions, and makes no complaints. It accords with universal experience. It accounts for the comedies as well as the tragedies. It does more, it maintains the necessity of things as they are, since the opposites are the twin pillars of existence. A perfect world, without any need of our assistance, where everything is to be had for the asking, who wants it? Who, even were it possible, could bear with it? Without successes or failures, without tears or laughter, without passions or interests? Action and endeavour are in the marrow of our bones. We cannot, indeed, be sure at any time, or in any cause, that we are right, our opponents wrong, or that the good for which we strive will be unmixed with evil. If you wait for such a certainty, you will sit in your armchair for ever. 'If one were to do nothing except for a cer-

tainty, one would do nothing for religion, for it is not certain.'
It is Pascal who says so—Pascal! We are none of us wise, we
are all of us on the way to wisdom. Stand then to your principles,
whatever they are, take this side or that. Follow your star till
you see a brighter. 'Let us think no more about them,' said
Virgil to Dante, in the *Divine Comedy*, of the luke-warm neutrals,
'but look once and pass on.' Whatever else you are, says nature
to us, be a man. 'Enter these enchanted woods, you who dare.'
Let each man cast his spear, and leave the issue to the immortal
gods.

PART II

XI

THE WILL TO LIVE

For giving me desire,
An eager thirst, a burning ardent fire,
    A virgin infant flame,
A love with which into the world I came,
    An inward hidden heavenly love,
    Which in my soul doth work and move,
        And ever ever me inflame
With restless longing, heavenly avarice,
    That never could be satisfied,
That did incessantly a Paradise
Unknown suggest, and something undescried
    Discern, and bear me to it; be
    Thy Name for ever praised by me.

Traherne

IX

THE WILL TO LIVE

The first step in philosophy is not a step; the first step in philosophy is to open your eyes. Not until he has looked round him, and with more than a little astonishment, in the actual world, not until he has in some measure become 'a spectator of all time and all existence', has any man a standing in the realm of thought. The majority of us are rustics, whose daily perambulations round the village pump mark the limits of our travel. 'The winds of the world', in Walter Page's phrase, 'have not ventilated our brains.' I do not except the learned doctors,

> profoundly skilled in analytic,
> Who can distinguish and divide
> A hair 'twixt south and south-west side—

who know, it may be, the language of the brain but not of the soul, who know what algebra is but not adversity, comfort, but not dismay, sobriety, but not savagery, what respectability is, but not fury, madness, despair, who are strangers to nature and the passions in the raw, in their wide, untamed expanses. There is another way of thinking than theirs, more fundamental than logic, and another language than it speaks, God's thinking and God's logic, the universal, invincible, terrible logic and language of facts.

Of this logic and language we have already endeavoured in some measure to remind ourselves, to recall the magnitude of the universe, which is our dwelling, the vast scale of its spatial and temporal dimensions, the violence and inconsistency of nature in her walks and ways, the singular character of human life, its vicissitudes, varieties, afflictions, its startling contrarieties and discordances, the contending currents, 'the light and sound and darkness' of the broad sea of circumstances to which we give the name of history. We stand now upon the verge of a still more perplexing region. To the question, 'What does human experience tell us?' is added another, 'How came this strange experience to be ours?'

215

And again, 'What is its purpose or meaning, if it have any?' In brief, 'What is to be made of it?' Clearly, in putting such a question, we have more than enough on our hands, in a word—the impossible.

So far we have travelled, we may say, through occupied territory. All of us have lived, looked round us a little, seen a little, heard a little, known a little, but there lies now before us range upon range of peaks unscaled by any climber, a

> wall of eagle-baffling mountain,
> Black, wintry, dead, unmeasured.

For of what are we supposed to attempt an account? Of everything, of all existence. Not merely of our immediate surroundings, of human activities and undertakings, but of ourselves, and our powers, such as they are, of accounting for anything, of that unspeakable enigma, consciousness, of the faculty of knowing anything, feeling anything, of our interest in anything. We are to account for, or attempt to account for, will and desire, love and hate, for philosophy, art, music, poetry, science, religion, for stars and systems, good and evil, Newton's *Principia* and Shakespere's plays.

To account for all these, since all are included in existence, is the philosopher's programme, not lacking, we may agree, whatever else it lacks, in ambition. And so far with what results? The results, it may also be allowed, and as might be expected, are disappointingly sketchy. Among them a few bold drawings, by great masters of technique, from Plato's sweeping hand, or Hegel's, have attracted attention; the majority of efforts have been as water spilt upon the ground. And, indeed, no one can be so bereft of intelligence as to enter light-heartedly upon such an undertaking, to suppose it within the compass of any man to solve the overwhelming riddle of Being, or to fancy that the best of minds can do more than perceive the profundity of the abyss. The mind is certainly a part of reality, but the part is not the equal of the whole. There will remain throughout time and beyond time the final unaccountableness. That man can do so much as set about an enquiry into his own origins is sufficiently astonishing, and his chief claim to dignity. That he should succeed is a fantastic notion, never on this side of sanity to be entertained. Enough that he has had the audacious fancy to spread his

216

wings for such a flight. 'He who knows that he does not know', says the proverb, 'is never a fool.' Reality is not to be caught in the meshes of our human concepts and categories. The net we fling contains no water when it returns to us, only a few drops cling to it. As Athanasius confessed that the more he pondered the central mystery of Deity, 'the more he thought, the less he comprehended,' so with all of us. For the understanding in which we put our trust appears to recede with the increase of knowledge. We journey and never arrive.

On the wall of a stanza in the Vatican may be seen one of Raphael's masterpieces—*The School of Athens*, a famous picture with fifty-two figures. There are depicted Pythagoras and Diogenes, Empedocles and Archimedes. There you may see Ptolemy with his celestial globe, and Socrates conversing with his pupils. There in the centre are Aristotle pointing to Earth and Plato to Heaven. Let us suppose the sala inhabited by a colony of flies, to whom the picture is a familiar object. They have many times crossed and recrossed it. They perceive the irregularities of its surface. They may be aware of the varieties in the patches of colour, and possibly of the odour of the pigments employed by the artist. Knowledge of the picture they may be said to have, but how much? They have experience of some of its features, and scientific flies may have analysed, from a fly's standpoint, its ingredients. Yet of why it is there, or why these colours take these particular patterns they know, and can know nothing. They see, indeed, all that is to be seen. There is no obstacle, no barrier between them and its wealth of artistry, of beauty and meaning. None the less some magic intervenes, so that of the scenes in the picture, the Greek history and Renaissance thought of which it speaks, of Plato's philosophy and Raphael's dream, they are and must remain for ever ignorant. For them all this is eternally remote though near, and impenetrable though unguarded. The fault is not in the picture, but in themselves; nor in a thousand, nor in ten thousand lives can they cross its invisible and inviolable threshold. Even for the human observer, unless he be already in its secrets, it has no voice, and analysis of its physical features avails nothing. The deeper the analysis goes the further it wanders from the true path of understanding, even from entrance through its open gate to the labyrinthine corridors of past and present time.

So with us and the universe. The obstacle to our comprehension of its nature and structure is nowhere else than in us; the disability is ours. The banquet is spread, and nothing is denied us that we can take for ourselves. All that we need is to overcome our own infirmity; and here at hand is our instrument, philosophy, neither greatly triumphant nor much in demand. The plain man, as we have already noted, eschews and disdains it. 'A plague', he cries, 'upon these acrobatics, this eternal and inconclusive debate, where the disputants exercise their wits by refuting each other. Philosophy is but a child's hobby-horse, on which men rock themselves to and fro without advancing. The best that can be said for these thinkers, who have had all the time there is for their researches, and continue to disagree so heartily, is that they have saved us much labour. They have at least explored for us a *cul de sac*.'

If, then, philosophy has failed, what profit to pursue the phantom quest? It is written in the book of fate that we should do so. We question things that we may fulfil our destiny, satisfy the inward craving, pick up, as Newton said, a few pebbles on the shore of the great ocean, avoid absurdities, estimate probabilities, and the better provide for our necessities here and now, in our present state. The intellect is man's burden, but not less his pride. With the emergence of mind in us living creatures rose up immediately the cosmic problems, those staring spectres, and the human soul is like the terrified magician, who had learnt the formula which conjured up the spirits from the vasty deep, but not the spells which quelled or bound them. Before the advent of the enquiring intelligence there was peace. No questions were asked by the early inhabitants of the earth, by the dreaming mosses or the plants, nor among the happy-go-lucky lower animals. Thinking it was that upon its arrival became entangled in a maze of its own construction. It discovered the perplexities of the world, and propounded the problems only to find that it must itself supply the answers. Thus it was that, as Shelley vividly expresses it, man

> fled astray
> With feeble steps o'er the world's wilderness,
> And his own thoughts, along that rugged way,
> Pursued like raging hounds their father and their prey.

Perhaps—who knows?—we might have been happier, happy as

children are happy, had the intellect never awakened in us to propound its troublesome questions. As it is, however, we have now no choice, and must turn to our religion or philosophy to answer them, to explain to us this our human situation.

And it is the life we know, and as we know it, earthly life, bodily life, life as universally experienced, that we must first look in the face; begin, that is, with our eating, drinking, talking, commonplace selves. How came this kind of existence about? If, for example, we are, as many have held, and as may be true, embodied souls, it remains to be understood why they are embodied. Presumably for some reason. Presumably if nature produced bodies they serve some end; something of importance, or some necessity is there represented. Certain mystics, like Plotinus, in their spiritual fervour, despised this material framework of ours. They waved it aside as an encumbrance. How they proposed to get along without it I cannot tell. For centuries, too, with many Christians the human body was under grave suspicion. They had little to say in praise of it. It has been beyond measure abused. One would suppose it a kind of monster, a sink of iniquity. How much better we should have been without an unruly member, like the tongue, for example. St. Francis, you may recall, in the kindliness of his heart, spoke of 'Brother Body, the Ass'—for a medieval saint an extremely generous estimate. But its vices, if we are to believe the Fathers, are legion. It harbours fleshly lusts which war against the soul. Why then, in the name of all the gods at once, was it thrust upon us, and if either worthless or an enemy, by what unkind fate, what unfriendly agency are we so afflicted? It is a suspicious circumstance that bodily wishes, affections, hopes have so much more interest, so much more apparent naturalness than the so-called spiritual. Arguments 'taken from real life and the actual condition of the world', as Sydney Smith said, 'brought among the shadowy discussions of ecclesiastics always occasion terror and dismay; it is like Aeneas stepping into Charon's boat, which carried only ghosts and spirits.'

Any system of thought which sets forth by flouting facts, which leaves this flesh and blood, this earthly lot of ours—whether you disapprove or approve of it—unaccounted for, or condemns it out of hand, leads to a swamp of contradictions, and can have no future. Of all such systems time works the ruin. They 'go down the wind, and darkness takes them home'. And for the simplest of reasons—they quarrel with the fundamental nature of things. They assume that the world is not what it should be, and that human nature should be utterly different from what in fact it is. These are very violent assumptions. Certainly a higher and more widely distributed intelligence would have done no harm, but then to have been created angels at the beginning would have been better still, and saved many human misadventures. Things must be taken as they are and explained as they are, or not at all.

And we have seen reason to think that the world is what it is of necessity, if a world there was to be. It has a structure, to which, as to the structure of our bodies, we must willy-nilly submit. And to go no further, this material system of tubes and wires, of pipes and cisterns, leaves us in no doubt where we stand. How evident it is that we cannot do what we like with them, or go where we please! They impose upon us the sharpest limitations and restrictions. We cannot breathe under water or fly to the moon. They implant in us a number of ineradicable appetites and desires, which to resist may be painful or perilous, or altogether impossible. In a word, we cannot have it all our own way either with the world or with ourselves. They do not permit of anything or everything.

> The stars and seas, for good or ill,
> Have made me subject to their will.

We meet with resistances, life is a tension, and thus early among our experiences we make the acquaintance of disappointment. The world doubtless has a certain plasticity, we can work upon it and effect certain changes in it, yet there is a rigidity in its structure not of our making, and if existence in the world is to be accepted you must accept it with its necessary and accompanying conditions. To have a regard for what is possible is, therefore, the beginning of wisdom. If such be the case, then clearly a perfect and everlasting happiness in the world, even if desirable, is clean out of the question. Worship perfection by all means, but do not ask for it or expect it.

We conclude, then, at the outset that the conditions of our present lives simply do not permit of the unbroken felicity we crave, and can never permit of it—a matter strangely overlooked by theologians and Utopian dreamers alike, the theologians who talk of lost paradises, once enjoyed, now forfeited by disobedience to the commands of God, and the dreamers who build on foundations the earth does not provide—that is, castles in the air. It is their false premises which betray these good souls, their misconception of the nature of things and the human situation. They have misread the map, and are for ever lost in the mountains of No-man's land.

So, too, if you speak of the body as an irrelevance, a tiresome burden, you are precipitated into a swamp of confusion. An odour of sanctity attaches in our vocabulary to the word 'spirit'. When, however, we speak of 'things of the spirit', of men as 'spiritually minded', or the reverse, it were well to ask ourselves what exactly do we mean. The word 'spirit' is in our language and thoughts set over against matter, and heavenly things opposed to terrestrial things. Yet this dichotomy is full of perils. On what grounds are terrestrial things so maligned? And how do we know them, or distinguish them from the superior things? If I have, let us say, a liking for poetry or painting, am I spiritually minded? Am I then on a higher moral plane than if my taste lies elsewhere, in travel, or mountaineering, or military history, or medicine, or machinery, or law? Is mathematics a more spiritual exercise than flute-playing, or does social study give me a better chance of heaven than athletics? Am I less spiritually minded if I prefer an out-of-doors life, and am interested in plants and animals, than if I have a fancy for church music or high ritual? Am I nearer God if I reflect on the mysteries of life and death than if I am immersed in civic and political activities? Is the 'interior' meditative man a higher type of being than the busy 'exterior' man, the man who lives more in solitude with his own thoughts than he who is active and about with his neighbours? Things are by no means as simple as we are told

We know nothing of any life save life in the body, and to denounce the senses is mere madness. We hear sometimes of holiness. Is it something other than unselfishness, sweetness of disposition, kindliness? Is it better than these, and with what acts is it associated that are not associated with an altruistic disposition? Does it consist in a capacity for awe and reverence, some kind of cosmic emotion, and if so how does it qualify for eternal happiness? Questions like these are worth asking ourselves. Our bodies, I fear, however great an encumbrance to the spiritual life, will remain with us to the end. How are we to get rid of them?

Let us assume as little as possible, and begin with things as we find them. How, then, do we find them? Well, as we have seen, not greatly to our minds. As a place of residence this planet is not highly recommended. Nor, in their turn, are its inhabitants described in enthusiastic terms by the divines and moralists. 'What can you tell me about Winchester?' said the traveller on the coach to its driver. 'Debauched, sir,' was the answer, 'like all cathedral cities.' If the saving of the soul should be our main concern in this world, one can see that it is a matter attended with the greatest difficulties.

Yet, whatever its drawbacks, in this undesirable neighbour-hood, where you would least expect to find it, you meet with the will-to-live, a very noteworthy principle, not easily overlooked on your travels. The will-to-live is ubiquitous, universal, insistent. Nature advertises it, all existence manifests it, life in every creature gives it the clearest utterance, and well we know it in ourselves. There the hounds of this desire to be alive and remain alive are in full cry. So profound and pervasive is the instigation of this instinct, upon which all else appears to rest, that we might well conclude with Schopenhauer that it is more fundamental than thought or mind, and gave birth to the whole creation. For we cannot dig deeper to find a surer foundation. Speculate you may on the origin of things, but this imperative principle is not, like the Absolute of the philosophers, beyond mortal sight or imagining—

Pinnacled dim in the intense inane.

It is at every moment, and everywhere, in frank and open evidence. And moreover it is clean beyond logic, nor can reason offer any explanation, the most meagre, of this corner-stone of our being. For the intellect is the servant of the will-to-live. It holds aloft the lamp by which the will may the better see its way, perceive and make use of its opportunities. But one thing there is upon which it can shed no light, the will itself, which is beyond logic and understanding. Of its origin or nature the intellect can tell us nothing. And, however discouraged it may be by the pessim-ists, this inscrutable principle, this mysterious prompting to con-tinue living, to remain in the world, is by common consent well-nigh invulnerable, and of all our instincts the most difficult to dis-lodge or subdue. Achilles in Homer, you may remember, had no hesitation in declaring his preference for any earthly lot, were it even that of the serf or drudge, to the shadowy existence of the underworld, the abode of the dead in Hades.   Observe this also. The will-to-live cannot be ascribed to a source in the surroundings of our present home, which are far from salubrious or attractive. The world is no cornucopia of undiluted delights, no Elysium, in which you have only to ask and it is given you.   On the contrary, the will-to-live meets here—what need to repeat the story?— with all kinds of discouragement, with frustrations, oppositions, vexations beyond number.   They are rife, they have not to be diligently sought for, as Diogenes is said to have sought for an honest man in broad daylight with a lantern.   Yet somehow, and here is the riddle, the most convinced pessimists are in no haste to die.   Like the philosophers who disbelieve in reason yet continue to employ it, the pessimists, having proved life intolerable, continue to tolerate it.   The will-to-live holds its own manfully even against the well-to-do professors of misery.   Your easy chair is your great breeder of melancholia, yet luxury itself cannot prevail against this inward imperative, this clinging to life, whatever its conditions.

> No churchyard is so handsome anywhere
> As will straight move one to be buried there.

Some other ground must therefore be sought for the will-to-live than the satisfactions existence offers or provides.   You must look for its genesis, its roots, elsewhere than in the world of experience, which thwarts, denies, and gives the lie to this illogical passion, that in academic theory has not a leg to stand on.   If you enquire whence is derived this resolution at all costs to remain in life, you will get no answer.   Physics knows nothing of the matter.   Biology, physiology, psychology alike are silent.   The will-to-live submits to science no title-deeds for examination.   It offers neither justification nor defence.   It is an autocrat, and the intellect and passions bow before it.   This imperial instinct derives, then, from the invisible and unknown; it is, that is to say, in its nature and essence throughout metaphysical, and possibly for that reason worthy of respect.   Reflect a little, and you perceive that whatever its source, the desire for life accompanies each creature on its entry upon the visible scene, and no account of its previous history can be rendered, or of the fountain whence it sprang. There are, as Pascal said, certain principles, of which our knowledge is as certain as any given by reason. We find them, as it were, in our cradles. No reasoning can make them more sure or more intelligible than they already are from the first. Without assuming these principles—for example, space, time, matter, motion—without taking them for granted, reason is unable to take a single step. Upon them logic erects its propositions, and from the starting-point they provide proceeds upon its way. So also with the will-to-live. In every living thing we observe a turning towards the expansion or fulfilment of its being, together with a corresponding aversion from the denial or frustration of that being in any form or degree. Good is for all living creatures alike and without distinction whatever enriches, evil whatever impairs or diminishes their contentment and repose. And never till the birth of man, never throughout the whole creation, did any doubts of life's value raise their heads. The will-to-live has no doubts. It is fundamental, instinctive, unthinking. No animal questions it. For all living creatures save ourselves life is sufficient, and, as Aristotle thought, though no good should go with it, itself a good. Here then is a mystery deeper than most—the quarrel of life with the conditions of life, the revolt of mankind. The intellect arrives, and with its arrival, strange to tell, contentment fades. It brings tempest on its wings.

If the source or origin of the will-to-live is hidden from us, at least we know its habitat. It is, as far as we can see, invariably lodged in separate, individual organisms. They are its embodiments. And hence arises the famous or infamous struggle for existence. The will to existence leads directly and inevitably to strife. For the unreflecting individual entity, of which the will is the mainspring, sacrifices, thoughtlessly and without compunction, all other existences to its own ends. They form its environment, and are subjected to its private purposes. To sustain their needs the plants make use of the material elements, and in their turn are consumed by the animals, and they by others stronger than they, including man, the master of them all. And so it goes till the level of the conscious intelligence is reached in the human race, in *homo sapiens*. With the dawn of the intelligence, and not till then, arose the dark suspicions of the worth of life, and the formidable problems of religion and ethics took their

224

present shape. With these problems our fellow-creatures, the lower animals, are placidly unconcerned. A lowering day it was, an ugly day it must have been, when the first man stood face to face with the idea of the worthlessness and absurdity of life, when it dawned upon him that the grapes were sour. On that day a chasm opened at his feet—the chasm of the unintelligible. Or not so much the unintelligible, which might after all be borne when the sun was warm, the air pleasant and food abundant. Not so much the unintelligible as the irrational, a deep uneasiness that the gods or nature had played him false, that the cup of life but sparkled at the brim, the discovery that his wishes were forever to be met by hostile looks from nature, by angry opposition from his neighbours, by projects incompatible with his own. How deep and natural is the instinct that all our desires should be at once fulfilled! Even the child in its cradle weeps at the oppositions offered to its every wish.

So, early in human history the will-to-live was challenged, and there followed 'all the cursed, everlasting questions', as Dostoievsky called them. How to justify, men began to ask, their own seizure of the best, or how the conflicting purposes, their own with all the others, were to be harmonised, strife evaded, hatreds avoided, wars ended, unbroken happiness attained. They have not been answered, they are with us still, the exasperating questions. How in the face of this universal conflict is the individual to secure his own ends, how exist, expand, realise his innermost, his profoundest needs, without interference with lives and purposes no less justifiable than his own, without injury to them, without the destruction or subjugation of the rest, the vast concourse of other living creatures? Each and all, you and I, have their moral rights to what existence offers. Every man has his case and his claims as undeniable as those of his neighbours. They have not been answered, these questions, not one of them. They have gathered in strength with the passage of time and history. 'Gathered in strength' did I say? To-day with us as a people, peculiarly susceptible in this respect, they force themselves upon our attention as never before, cling to it with unrelaxing tenacity, and the great debate, whose issue no man can foretell, nears its forthcoming and fateful height. To them is due the gloom, even desperation, of our time, and no one can foretell—for who knows?—whether we shall not, in our turn, go the way of the East, pray for deliverance from the wheel of existence, and turn our backs upon the ambitions and pursuits of the contending nations, whether our Christian religion will not melt imperceptibly into a world-despising creed, and declare power, wealth, influence and empire the merest breath-blown bubbles, with which childish toys the wise man and the good man will have nothing to do. This once proud people, grown conscience-stricken, may choose to relinquish its privileges and liberty, resigning to others the control of its affairs and destiny. Strange things have happened in the past, and strange things are still to come. It goes back, as we count time, a long way, the revolt against living at all in so preposterous and hostile a world. The Greeks had a story of a Phrygian king who sought for long to capture the satyr Silenus, wise, it was said, with supernatural knowledge. At length in the king's gardens in Macedonia, where grew the most fragrant roses in all the world, the satyr was taken, and brought before the monarch, who put to him the question of questions—'What is best and most desirable for men?' For long Silenus was silent. At last, to obtain his release, with bitter laughter he replied—'Oh wretched race of a day, children of chance and misery, why do ye compel me to say to you what it were most expedient for you not to hear? What is best for all is for ever beyond your reach: not to be born, not to be, to be nothing. The second best for you, however, is soon to die.' *Optimum non nasci, aut cito mori*.

If I were asked, 'What in your opinion is the most marked change which has come about in this country during your own lifetime?' I should answer, 'Beyond doubt the rapid growth and extension of humanitarianism.' As religion has declined, the gospel of humanitarianism has *pari passu* gained in strength and support. It is our new religion. And the change is the more surprising since science, which dominates modern thought, as religion previously dominated it, provides no platform for the doctrine of sympathy with the weak and help for the incompetent. Pity is nevertheless the note of our times, the virtue of virtues which has gone near to swallowing all the rest. Strange, is it not? for the Stoics and many other philosophers thought it a vice. This spread of tender-heartedness has led to all the social services, the innumerable charitable organisations, societies for the prevention of cruelty to children and to animals, societies for the abolition of violence, of capital punishment, for the preservation of peace and the outlawry of war. We have come to dislike sports which involve the hunting of hares, foxes or deer. So great is our sensitiveness that the mouse or rabbit in a trap makes us miserable, and the sight of a butcher's shop nauseates us. The habits of the cat in pursuit of birds, the ferret sucking the blood of its prey, the serpent fascinating it, the spider or the plant which ensnares its living victims we view with shuddering aversion. We would convert these fierce creatures to vegetarian habits. So far has this sympathy carried us that it extends to assassins and murderers under sentence of death, whose approaching end afflicts us more than the deaths of their forgotten victims. Above all life must on no account be taken or sacrificed. If we exalt the sacredness of life into a religious principle, as many have done, where are we to end save in Buddhism, which not only refuses a diet of animal flesh, or to brush away an insect, but in its stricter sect commands you to wear a veil over your mouth lest you unwittingly swallow a fly? Does this teaching enjoin us to relinquish the world and leave the insects in possession? There are over a hundred thousand varieties in Africa alone.

Contraries—such, you remember, has been our contention—are implicit, as Heraclitus held, in the world's structure, and without them world there would be none. They are ultimate and irreducible. In their tension is its life. 'Excesses, defects and contrary qualities', as Bishop Berkeley said, 'conspire to the beauty and harmony of the world.' The contraries are the dancers, whose advancing and retreating steps, whose turns and counter-turns create the vital rhythms, and to them is due not life simply, but life in all the exuberant, the magnificent variety of its patterns. They produce and preserve its savours, they provide its never-ending multiplicity of interests. The loves and hates, the order and disorder, the wisdom and the folly, all deeds, events, circumstances are of their making. And among them are the irreconcilable ideals of men. Men see things from their own angles in time and place, in conformity with their circumstances and their own individualities. How else could they see them? Everyone sees through his own and not another's eyes; and if all came to see alike, the scroll of history would be rolled up for ever. Everything that has been said, or can be said of the world by those who have lived, arises out of their souls' experiences, the lonely vision of each. They differ, these visions, as night from day, as light from darkness; the vision of those who hate and those who love existence; of those who in horror of its interminable warfare take the path of resignation and retreat, and of those who in their joy of living choose the path of acceptance. Between these, its extreme poles, swings the thought of humanity throughout the centuries, it may be unexpressed or half unconscious. It is the same world, the same landscape, which amazes, horrifies or delights its inhabitants, so varied its aspects, so multiform their reactions, so dissimilar their hearts and minds. Religion fears the world, its indestructible and powerful attractions, and urges the higher claims of the eternal values. But time, too, has its competing claims, not easily rejected by the lovers of life. And behind and above the storm and confusion, above the hurryings to and fro, the advances and retreats, the alarms and despairs, the preachings and protestations and proclamations sits, enthroned in silence, the inscrutable and mysterious will-to-live.

What room for cheerfulness is here? What hope of any exit from our troubles? If you fail to find an exit it will not be for want of guides. There is the programme of the naturalists, which commends itself to many, perhaps to most minds. Why should we try to escape, or transcend life as we find it? It is there to be flavoured and enjoyed. Be content with what you have, the colour and fragrance of the rose, the bouquet of the wine, the conversation of your friends, the lively gossip, the ebb and flow of events. Why regard this life as insufficient, as the ante-chamber to another, or a forerunner of some Utopia? Why spend yourself in labour for successors who will render you no thanks, or strive after a heaven of which you have no information? Take things as they are, without forward or side-long glances at some other and imagined state.

Or if this does not please you, there is the guidance offered by other thinkers. You may elect to tread, with more fastidious spirits, the mountain path. There is, for example, the thesis recently and eloquently argued by Dr. Schweitzer. As the will-to-live in ourselves advances to a higher insight it turns away from the hideous and intolerable conflict. It perceives that far from its iniquities and cruelties an inner independence may be attained, a happiness secured without the aid of external circumstances.

The soul rises above them, as with the Stoics, to a higher height. 'He who in the present state', says an ancient writer, 'vanquishes as much as possible a corporeal life, through the cathartic virtues, passes in reality into the Fortunate Isles of the soul.' Follow this counsel, resign the glittering goods of the outer and passing world, and the resignation brings peace.

The solution here offered of the teasing riddle by the denial and abandonment of earthly things and their futile values is not, indeed, new—it is the well-worn path of the ascetics. It is the gospel which long ago, like a mounting tidal wave, swept the East, and submerged its vital activities. _ In one or other of its many forms, mystical or ethical, the refusal or denial of the will-to-live has in the human story played no small part. In the days of Laotze, the Chinese philosopher, 500 years before Christ, the sensitive hearts, the peace-lovers fled away from the violence of the times into the hills and deserts, as in the European Middle Ages they took refuge in monastic seclusion. At one time in Europe there were no less than 37,000 religious houses of the Benedictine order alone, not to speak of many thousands belonging to other brotherhoods. It has a siren voice, this summons to fold our tents, and slip away from the world's coarse prize-fights, the senseless clatter of its merry-go-rounds. Yet how difficult it is to distinguish its accents from those of terror and despair. The intellect—the proud instrument evolved by the will-to-live for its own ends, the furtherance and fulfilment of our desires—appears now to turn traitor, to desert to the enemy, and declare the struggle vain. It proclaims the virtue of retreat. The advice has the ugly look of a betrayal, of defeatism. Like Enobarbus in Shakespere's play, when he forsakes Anthony to join his foes, the mind might well, one feels, be seized with remorse, and cry out upon itself as

A master-leaver and a fugitive.

Nor can we believe that this proposal will prove universally acceptable. Distrust of life, aversion from life, fear of life—a sparkling trio of friends these to accompany one upon any expedition. 'I'm not prepared', says a character in one of Mr. Somerset Maugham's novels, 'to be made a fool of. If life won't fulfil the demands I make on it, then I have no more use for it. It's a dull and stupid play, and it's only waste of time to sit it out. I

229

want life to be fair. I want life to be brave and honest. I want men to be decent and things to come right in the end. That's not asking too much, is it? . . . Resignation? That's the refuge of the beaten. Keep your resignation. I don't want it. I'm not willing to accept evil and injustice and ugliness. I'm not willing to stand by while the good are punished and the wicked go scot free. If life means that virtue is trampled on, and honesty is mocked, and beauty is fouled, then to hell with life.'[1]

One can sympathise with this malcontent. He wants things to come right in the end. Well, so do we all. He is not willing to stand aloof with his hands in his pockets while injustice is done and beauty fouled. Well, who will blame him? He is not willing to let the world go by, and as a conscientious objector, secure his own salvation and survey in serenity from his lofty moral elevation the shipwreck of the world. Certainly this proposal of resignation asks a good deal from the brave and generous and ardent souls, whose blood boils at the sight of wrongs. Will you tell them not to draw their swords for the innocent and afflicted? Will they be content to raise their hands to heaven in pious horror and do nothing, in full view of the outrages and the inhumanities? How numerous are the world's voices, how varied the instruments, how divergent their tones. In one quarter of the compass you hear the note of passivity and surrender, in another of indignation and revolt; in one age of delighted interest and activity, in another of distaste and withdrawal; in one race of ambition and expansion, in another of quietism and mystic meditation. There were no conscientious objectors among the Spartans, no sentimentalists among the Red Indians, no saints among the vikings. One hears of no pacifists among the Japanese, no hermits in Greenland, no world-despisers in Mexico or the Argentine. Who will number the responses to their environment that human beings have displayed? Life, which has summoned many men to heroic endeavour, has driven many also to despair and self-destruction, and made others again half mad for the love of God. The angel who appeared to Saint Teresa thrust through her heart with a spear of gold tipped with flame, not once but many times, and left her all on fire with the love of God; and so exceedingly sweet it was, despite the terrible pain she would not have fore-

[1]*The Narrow Corner*, pp. 272-274.

230

gone it. Is it possible, you ask yourself, that Saint Teresa or John of the Cross lived in the same world as our own poet?

> We for a certainty are not the first
> Have sat in taverns, while the tempest hurled
> Their hopeful plans to emptiness, and cursed
> Whatever brute and blackguard made the world.
>
> It is in truth iniquity on high
> To cheat our sentenced souls of aught they crave,
> And mar the merriment as you and I
> Fare on our long fool's errand to the grave.

Or again when you read the words of George Fox—'When I came near to Lichfield I saw three steeples, and they struck at my life:' there is a man of religion, you say. Yes, and here are the words of another man of religion, the founder of a faith which numbers over two hundred millions in the world to-day—Mohammed: 'Three things have been specially dear to me in this world. I have loved women and pleasant odours, but the chief solace of my heart has been prayer.'

Or compare medieval Europe, Christian Europe, with China, whose civilisation maintained itself for centuries on Confucianism —till recent days the philosophy, the religion and the ethical system of three hundred millions of human beings. What was this powerful teaching? Secularism. The creed of good manners, of gentlemanly behaviour. It had nothing to say of God, of a supernatural world, or a future existence. Or contrast the middle centuries, that unique period in our European annals, with the centuries following upon the Renaissance. How different their respective views of the world, how opposed their systems of belief! Yet in each the doctrines universally held are felt as inevitable, as unassailable. Each age thinks itself in possession of the true and only view possible for sensible men. Among individuals you find similar and violent contrasts, determined by their temperaments. How many prophets and moralists have seen human life as a nest of vipers, and on the other hand how many have seen it as an enormous jest, like Aristophanes, whose thunderous laughter still reverberates round our intellectual horizon, or like Rabelais, holding both his sides in his colossal mirth. To suppose it possible to reduce to unity the innumerable responses and reactions of human nature to existence is an opium-eater's dream. Yet is it all so dreadful if, as we have concluded to be beyond doubt the case, these very contradictions and collisions have given us a world to live in, if to them we owe our very existence?

'To be, or not to be, that is the question'—and one of considerable importance. It will be part of our business to consider the answers that have been given to it. Meanwhile we may perhaps agree that life has for most men at least its moments, that if absolute perfection be unattainable, there are persons and actions that approach it, graces and beauties worth the seeing, and days on which it was a happiness to be alive. Yet it is not upon these bright points of light the argument hinges. Nor yet upon the truth that the contraries constitute the web and woof of things. It turns in the end upon your decision whether the command of the will-to-live be the command of a god or devil.

Yet, that for the moment aside, we might ask ourselves whether, despite their forbidding faces, the contraries, the mighty opposites, have not, since they keep us alive, something to say for themselves. What were Hercules without the lion, or St. George without the dragon? Where philosophers without their problems, or saints in the absence of sinners? To our preposterous race obstacles are the breath of life. It turns wearily and dejectedly away from the easy and obvious, and delights in its exertions and its pains. If you would make human beings happy, give them a task and a cause, and the harder the better. They rise to their full stature only when challenged. Startle the soul into admiration, ask of it the impossible, to join the forlorn hope, and it is endowed with angelic strength. Ask nothing of it, and the soul retires. Enters in its place the captious, querulous, resisting, arguing, quarrelsome intellect.

It is when the gods call them that men rise to the crest of their powers. Then they become themselves gods and hasten to join the Olympian society. Their greatness lies in their dreams, and in a heaven of idleness they would suffer the torments of hell. 'Tis beyond the wit of angels or archangels, not to say philosophers, to comprehend us, the most mysterious and perplexing of creatures, who look round us for dangerous undertakings and invent miseries for our delectation. When Everest and Kinchinjunga have been climbed, men will look back regretfully upon the past happy days of bitter cold and aching limbs, of vile discomfort and appalling danger. They will weep like Alexander because there are no more worlds to conquer, and will presently project journeys to the Moon or Mars, devising undertakings with which joyfully to connive at their own destruction. They will never cease to attempt the impossible and assault the impregnable. The negations, laws, regulations, suppressions are without avail; there is in them no inspiration, they have no summoning power. Deny human beings their liberty and they are in continual revolt. Awaken their souls, and you can do with them what you please. They walk erect and become heroes and demi-gods. To all appearance we are actors in a moving scene, where nothing is at stay. Why should we be reluctant to allow it, and to say that life is 'a becoming'? If we could permit ourselves to think that we have neither come from nothing nor return to nothing, that time has wide margins, that the gods have other thoughts than ours and their eyes are fixed upon a far distant goal; if we could postpone our condemnation of nature and of man, of nature which explores in every species the possibilities of existence for the greatest variety of living things, and of man a being hardly yet awake— if we could think these thoughts, and I can find no reason for supposing them unwarrantable, we might keep our souls alive, and need not end in blank despair.

Three things at least have not been proved, and may be regarded as exceedingly improbable. The first that nature has exhausted herself in producing what she has produced, that she has come to the end of her tether, and that nothing more need be expected of her. The second that all existence, all modes of being, lie open to the inspection of our physical senses, that their vision exhausts nature's whole domain. The third that the human mind has reached the zenith of its powers, that its capacities have all been fathomed, and no surprises need be looked for in its future history. For myself I disbelieve all these. Who has determined the limits of the mind or set bounds to its journeying? Who has proved it a finished article, as Kant and others have in effect assumed? 'To conceive a mind as initially perfect, or to conceive it as becoming finally perfect,' as Gentile said, 'is to conceive it as no longer a mind.' It may well in virtue of its own nature have an infinite capacity for expansion. The justification of life consists not in the increasing felicity we fondly fancy it should here and now provide, but in the infinity of its possibilities, the endless variety and succession of its individual figures, the happiness it offers despite its pains, and in the inextinguishable hope, as invincible as its sadness, which, like the light of heaven, bathes the whole creation throughout its vast circumference in a mysterious radiance.

XII

TO BE OR NOT TO BE

O Lord, the children of my people are Thy peculiar treasures,
Make them mine, O God, even while I have them,
My lovely companions, like Eve in Eden!
So much my treasure that all other wealth is without them
    But dross and poverty.
Do they not adorn and beautifie the World,
  And gratify my Soul which hateth solitude?
Thou, Lord, hast made Thy servant a sociable creature, for which I
    praise Thy name,
A lover of company, a delighter in equals;
  Replenish the inclinations which Thyself hath implanted,
And give me eyes
To see the beauty of that life and comfort
Wherewith Thou by their actions
    Inspire the nations.
Their Markets, Tillage, Courts of Judicature,
  Marriages, Feasts and Assemblies, Navys, Armies,
Priests and Sabbaths, Trade and Business, the voice of the Bridegroom,
    Musical Instruments, the light of Candles, and the grinding of
    Mills
Are comfortable, O Lord, let them not cease.

Traherne

XII

TO BE OR NOT TO BE '

Among a good many other things, the universe has produced mind, mind in man. How it has come about no one knows, but—strange to relate—in this mind has arisen a critic, which has some insolent comments to make upon its creator, if a creator there be—a somewhat singular state of affairs. The dog barks at its master. Or you may say the child—a thankless child—rebukes its parent. The being to which it has given birth turns upon the world, and declares the whole design, of which it is itself a part, a bungled business.

> Ah Love! Could thou and I with Fate conspire
> To grasp this sorry scheme of things entire,
> Would we not shatter it to bits, and then
> Remould it nearer to the heart's desire?

Whence did human thought derive its right to mount the seat of judgment, whence obtain its superior wisdom? With what other worlds are we acquainted, with which this of ours can be compared to its disadvantage? By human thought the universe has been judged, and by human thought condemned. Has this self-elected censor, our intelligence, this product of the whole, any private or privileged information wherewith to assess the value of the whole? Is any god speaking through the human mind when it rejects the world, and if so, what god other than its maker? The creator cannot well be supposed to reprobate his own creation, so it must be some other god.

Our position was, you remember, that existence and perfection were incompatible. They exclude each other. Existence and imperfection are twins, children of the same parents, the mighty opposites, the father and mother of things. Existence without contrasts, without inner differences and divisions, is a word without meaning, or rather such an existence is, we may say, indistinguishable from nothing. And we reached the con-

237

clusion, disappointing though it may be, that this was the best possible, since it was the only possible world. Unfortunately the best possible does not satisfy human nature. The world should be better, in fact perfect. Some philosophers go about saying that the Absolute, that is, the whole taken together, is perfect, and all within it, therefore, if we had eyes to see, also perfect. The theologians, too, assert that God, the world's maker, is perfect. Who or what is then to blame? God, who made it, or man, who somehow destroyed its original perfection, or some unfortunate accident? Our position is that the imperfections are inherent in its necessary and unavoidable structure. The philosophers of the Absolute, on the other hand, declare that we are mistaken, that the imperfections have no real existence, they are mere human, short-sighted illusions; and the theologians, who, on the contrary, admit their reality, ascribe them to sinful man. However you account for them, the imperfections seem at least to exist, or why do we so rack our brains to put matters right? Occasionally even the 'perfection' philosophers are to be found, rather illogically, advocating changes, and most observers are agreed that something urgently needs to be done.

On all sides it is pretty generally allowed that the world falls woefully short of humanity's requirements, more especially of its moral requirements. In some respects possibly it might pass muster. The view from a distance might, for example, with some trifling re-arrangements, even be approved. 'Men must know', remarks Bacon, 'that in the theatre of human life it is reserved for gods and angels to be lookers on.' To imagine ourselves angels, not to say gods, is a little difficult, but let us indulge the fancy that we are superior spectators of the world drama, in the stalls and not on the stage, casually interested in the performance, but otherwise unconcerned. What should we think of the play? We should, I conjecture, find it entertaining. We should praise the theatre as an imposing edifice, and declare the scenery excellent, the plot intriguing and full of incident, the characters numerous and charmingly varied, the acting wonderfully realistic and convincing. To disapprove of the world as a spectacle would, we may agree, be hypercritical. As a passing show it leaves little to be desired, and is probably as well worth seeing as any other staged in the universe. Anaxagoras and Nietzsche both thought this planet worth a flying visit. Conrad had a somewhat similar opinion. 'I have come to suspect', he wrote, 'that the aim of creation cannot be ethical at all. I would fain believe its object is spectacular, a spectacle for awe, love, admiration, or hate, if you will, but in this view—and in this view alone—never for despair.' But a spectacle for whom? This detached view of existence is for us fantastically remote. After all we are doers and sufferers, and much too deeply implicated in the events and circumstances to take them in a purely aesthetic or Pickwickian sense. To live in the world and to be, as we are, subject to all its accidents, is a somewhat different thing from looking at it through an opera-glass.

To know, then, where we stand is a matter of vital consequence. And, in the attempt to explain or account for things as we see them, we are like to lose our wits. For to the human intellect the world is a veritable delirium, a smoking whirlpool, where there is small standing room for logic, and for reason not an inch of foothold. In the presence of this boiling cataract, this turmoil of passions and events in their bewildering commotion, our mortal minds are aghast. And, worse still than incomprehensible, it is for gentler natures, and in particular for the divines and moralists, a hateful scene of vice and violence. Human thought, indeed, in its attempt to deal with such a scene, discovers in itself a conspicuous disability, an inherent weakness. When it meets with movement, change, with many separated things, it is utterly defeated. Unless they can be pigeon-holed, ticketed or classified, they cannot firmly be laid hold of, and are in consequence abhorrent. Rest and changelessness seem, to our way of thinking, the proper and natural state of affairs, of things as they should be. Being, as the philosophers call it, needs, we feel, less explanation, while multiplicity, motion, or Becoming, on the other hand, are in their essence abnormal and distressingly unintelligible. The human intellect appears to have two bugbears, and two heart's idols. Its bugbears are change and manyness, its heart's idols permanence and unity. Like the bird by the snake, it is fascinated by identity, by sameness. The unchanging is for ever the object of its search throughout the whole scheme of things, precisely, indeed, what cannot be discovered there, and what is only to be found or imagined to exist in the primal immutable one, the whole of Being.

So it comes about that there is one matter upon which philosophers, theologians and moralists are in agreement. They stand shoulder to shoulder in their antipathy towards, or their recoil from, changing things, separated things, and in their demand for the stationary and the immutable. To understand the world, so the philosophers think, its flux, or flow, its dizzying movement must be arrested. If it were frozen into fixity, brought to a standstill, we might go some way towards understanding it. The moralists, for their part, demand that men should abandon their individual and selfish purposes; they must unite, come to think alike and agree together. The Many must be reduced to One. So also the theologians. The separation between God and His creation must somehow be broken down. God must be all in all. Whether we desire to understand the world with the philosophers, or to overcome it with the moralists, or to escape from it with the men of religion, the unity of the whole must in some way be attained.

Reflect a moment and you perceive that, without exception, they are asking for a vision the world does not provide, which it emphatically declines to provide, since it presents a very different vision,—disunion, separateness, multiplicity, incessant change—in short, a stupefying chaos. For throughout the universe everything appears to be at odds, in collision with some other thing; one energy is opposed by another energy, growth strives against decay, life battles with death. Men, too, are in antagonism with other men. Nowhere in this den of antipathies is to be found a semblance of the order, the permanence, the harmony or union of forces, hearts and ideals so deeply, we think, to be desired.

> Man is hurled
> From change to change unceasingly,
> His soul's wing never furled.

Apart from the business of keeping alive, and the purse with which to do it, 'that money affair, that Bill-pestilence', what a trial even at the best of times we are to each other! For my neighbours I may have a liking, and even school myself to tolerate their absurd and cantankerous prejudices. But how easily their tastes solidify into practices which interfere with my ways and habits, into restrictions on my most innocent undertakings. If my neighbour neglects his garden, weeds grow up, and the impartial winds scatter their seeds in mine. If his cocks crow or his dog barks, my slumbers are disturbed. If he adds a wing to his house my view suffers, and my property is reduced in value. If he throws out an additional window, he overlooks my summer-house, and pries upon my cherished privacy.

And all the while a perfect world exists. Where? you ask. Not only in the mind's eye, but in fact, a world untroubled by the contraries, where discord, change, disunity are unknown. No serpent enters, no conflict disturbs that garden of repose. All quarrels are ended, all clamour stilled. Sin and pain alike are banished, and

> No sound of human sorrow mounts to mar
> The sacred everlasting calm.

It is the country of blessed union with the serene and immutable One. To enter it you have little to do—you have only to die.

> No man can ever know perfect felicity
> Till Otherness be swallowed up in Unity.

And some have said that all men, unconsciously it may be, nourish in their hearts a secret desire for nothingness, a desire to have done with the storm-swept world, in which they feel themselves strangers and aliens, and to be again at home in the only perfect country in the wide universe, the land of dreamless sleep. Matthew Arnold has a poem in which he contrasts the life of man with the better life of the sea and the stars, since

> With joy the stars perform their shining,
> And the sea its long moon-silvered roll;
> For self-poised they live, nor pine with noting
> All the fever of some differing soul.

The moon and stars are not, however, really happy, whatever the poet may say, and do not in fact shine brightly save for us; and save for us, or some other beings like us, might as well not be there. Nature, one is given to understand, has no private satisfaction of any kind in her everlasting and indefatigable toil. Why she ever undertook it, Heaven knows. No one seems pleased. And what has religion to say? It has been argued that religion, too, is nothing more than a concealed desire to escape from the mad confusion of life, the cruel injustices, the feverish strife, and that the thoughts of peace, eternity and God are merely a veiled longing for death, the consoling vision of the fugitives from existence, the familiar preference of the mystics for the perfection of eternity to the known imperfections of time—

> rejoicing secretly
> In the divine perfections of the grave.

However this may be, here for the present we are, and though they will not long distress us, we dream and plan to improve our temporary surroundings.   Those, indeed, who find life as it is, and the world as it is, pleasantly attractive, have no need of dreams.   At rare moments, here and there in human history, in men and times of abounding vitality, so brightly shone the sun that the golden hour sufficed.   Existence seemed beyond a doubt desirable, better than non-existence—as in the palmy days of Greece or England.   In Shakespere's English histories you breathe a summer air.   The energy and full-bloodedness, the spring and buoyancy of their spirit ring in the very language of his characters.   In Falstaff's, for instance, a man full of zest, enjoying life and every moment of life, overflowing with exuberance, welcoming all company and every undertaking with huge delight.   These are not tired or disillusioned souls, whose days are 'sicklied o'er with the pale cast of thought', overwhelmed with 'the heavy and the weary weight Of all this unintelligible world'.   Their language is the language of sanguine men—read for evidence the speeches of Hotspur—who push their fortunes, love the world and its opportunities, rejoice in its adventures and hazards, are prepared to take risks, are never afraid, who meet danger halfway, and are happier in the prospect of combat than of rest and security.   What vigour, briskness and vivacity they display; with what crisp conviction they converse and act.

Nerve never fails them.   They have none of the wounded animal's desire to seek the darkness of retreat.   It was by such audacious, and not, we must allow, over-scrupulous men, that England's greatness was built, with their trading, and privateering and warring—

> Westward Ho! for Trinidad and Eastward Ho! for Spain,
> And 'Ship-ahoy' a hundred times a day.

In those days England's pulse, to use Emerson's phrase, was 'like

242

a cannon'. Her sons were then neither humanitarians nor sentimentalists, but 'human, all too human'. They took their advantages and thanked God for them, struck down their adversaries without hesitation, thanked God once more, loved themselves and their country, and made death proud to take them. 'Sire,' said Sir Walter Hungerford to Henry V, at Agincourt, 'I would that we had here ten thousand more good archers, who would gladly be with us this day.' 'Thou speakest as a fool,' cried Henry. 'By the God of Heaven, on whose grace I lean, I would not have one more even if I could.'

But the world has known far other men and other moods. 'Fools and foolery', they cry, the disillusioned sages, 'what devilry is here? What in the end were all these brutal triumphs worth?' This barren activity, this insensate strife, this savage slaughter, they will have none of it. And if you are of the company of the heaven-born as against the earth-born, you will call these sages the illuminated souls, wiser far, spiritual natures, sweet, sensitive, profound. To them was vouchsafed a sight of better things than these gigantic follies, these insane ambitions, which make of life a 'hideous storm of terror'. Go where you will, then, you find the opposites, the contending currents in the world without, as in the world of thought within.

This famous doctrine, the great refusal, the gospel of renunciation, fostered by the horror of life's agitated sea, had its birth in the East, as had the mystery religions, which overran the Roman empire in the days of Augustus. Passivity is its keynote, withdrawal from the traffic in external things—'the prison', as, you remember, Epicurus called it, 'of affairs and politics'—into the inner sanctuary of the self. In turbulent times when life is insecure, injustice rife, when tyranny and violence rule the mundane scene, there is for meek natures no refuge save in flight or submission. When the race is to the swift and the battle to the strong, the weaker must go to the wall. 'You must kiss', says the Oriental proverb, 'the hand you cannot bite.' In such times this gospel offers a peace within when there is none without. It invades dispirited or conquered races and civilisations past their prime, when the sap of youth no longer floods their veins, when desire fails and the grasshopper becomes a burden, when the glitter and the glamour fade, when the bustle of the assemblies and activities has lost its charm.

Lux ex Oriente. From the East it came, its spiritual home, this promise of an inward calm and felicity, rarer and far more precious than the world's blood-stained rubies. And in Greece, Greece itself, where the tree of life had its golden season, its *annus mirabilis*, its unparalleled vintage year, where it burgeoned into leaf and flower and fruit as never before or since, in the soil even of Greece itself the dark cypress of negation took root. And there its name was Stoicism. The earliest Stoics, though Greeks, were men of Eastern birth or extraction; but in the Hellenic climate, as was most natural, a spiritual mood became a firm and reasoned creed, an up-standing, four-square philosophy of life. Over outward things, so runs the Stoic thought, we have, it is evident, no power at all, over the material elements or seasons, over chance or change, over decay and death. They are too strong for us, and there is no logic in their proceedings. Nature is irrational; the just suffer no less than the unjust, the young die as well as the old. Nature, too, is immoral, and has for goodness no more respect than the earthquake for its victims. But man, man is rational, and his mind is an independent kingdom, over which material things, over which nature herself, for all her brutal strength, has no sovereignty. From its impregnable fortress the free soul may look down upon, and defy, all her embattled powers. What matter her atrocities? What matter any miseries the wicked may inflict upon the good? Withdraw into the citadel of the self, and you can disdain these Satanic forces. Your contempt for them disarms them. You are their over-lord and master. Nay, more, you become a god. 'My mind to me a kingdom is', where I am the unchallengable ruler.

The virtuous man has thus supreme control over his own actions. Things beyond his power are no concern of his, and towards them he maintains an attitude of calm indifference. 'Give me', says Epictetus, 'what you please, and I will turn it into a good. Bring me illness, poverty, suffering, condemnation to death—all this shall be turned to profit.' If the condition of your own soul be sound, and if—here is the hard matter—you care not whether you are well or ill, in prison or on the rack, whether your friends and children suffer and die, your country perishes, whether you yourself live or die, if you can view all such things as unconcernedly as you observe the flight of a bird or the falling of a leaf, you may, indeed, claim divinity. 'The spiritual man', writes Santa-

244

yana, 'resigns existence as gladly as he accepts it, or even more gladly; because the emphasis which action and passion lend to the passing moment seem to him arbitrary and violent.' So delicate and fastidious is his taste that a misplaced accent ruins his life.

Of all the world-rejecting creeds Stoicism has the proudest and the grandest air. It substitutes, it is true, ethics for theology. Whether there be gods or not, man is sufficient to himself, and has no need to call for heavenly aid. 'You bear', it proclaims, 'a god about with you.' And in this claim to self-sufficiency by a finite creature Christianity discerns, and cannot but discern, a blasphemy, a monstrous and diabolical pride. Yet the early Christians approved the Stoic emphasis on virtue and its contempt for earthly things, and from the pagan armoury drew weapons for their own. Stoicism, indeed, so permeated European thought as to leave its stamp upon all the subsequent philosophies and creeds. It meets and defies the world. The Stoics were no runaways; they were aristocrats and stood their ground. None the less theirs was in essence a world-denying creed, however high it holds its head above the others, the openly defeatist counsels and exhortations. What were the last words of Tolstoy as he lay upon his death-bed? 'To escape, to escape', he whispered. To escape from what? From the City of Destruction, from which Christian, you remember, fled, as Bunyan so vividly describes in his *Pilgrim's Progress*: 'So I saw in my Dream that the man began to run; now he had not run far from his own door, but his wife and children perceiving it, began to cry after him to return: but the man put his Fingers in his Ears, and ran on, crying, Life, Life, Eternal Life.'

Or was it death he was really seeking? Is 'eternal life' only a soothing name for the perfect life, in other words the life of the grave, or the celestial life of the stars?—A question of some moment, yet to be considered. Tolstoy, like Christian, was in search of a refuge. Like him he fled from the City of Destruction, even from his wife and family. So too the early Christians fled from the world's Vanity Fair. It was in the very hey-day of the Roman empire that the submissive East conquered the aggressive West, conquered Rome itself, the centre, the capital of the world's glory, where the lust of the eye and the pride of life had its stronghold, its proudest and mightiest keep. Here is how Arnold describes it:

The brooding East with awe beheld
  Her impious younger world,
The Roman tempest swell'd and swell'd,
  And on her head was hurl'd.

The East bow'd low before the blast
  In patient, deep disdain;
She let the legions thunder past
  And plunged in thought again.

.   .   .   .

'Poor world,' she cried, 'so deep accurst,
  That runn'st from pole to pole
To seek a dream to slake thy thirst,
  Go seek it in thy soul!'

She heard it, the victorious West,
  In crown and sword array'd!
She felt the void which mined her breast,
  She shiver'd and obey'd.

She veil'd her eagles, snapp'd her sword,
  And laid her sceptre down;
Her stately purple she abhorr'd,
  And her imperial crown.

She broke her flutes, she stopp'd her sports,
  Her artists could not please;
She tore her books, she shut her courts,
  She fled her palaces;

Lust of the eye and pride of life,
  She left it all behind,
And hurried, torn with inward strife,
  The wilderness to find.

And one asks oneself, were these fugitives from life on the path
of wisdom? Does the Power which produced them require of its
creatures, during their brief years on earth, the sacrifice of all
natural joys and affections upon the altar of negation? It is a stiff
doctrine. Yet it has been accepted. And I suppose few of us
can at times withhold our astonished admiration from the un-
flinching courage with which men have followed their guiding
stars, whatever these stars may have been. At other times we
ask whether religion and morals, like other guiding lights, have
not also had their fanatics, their desperadoes, who will stop at

nothing. I do not speak of the injuries men have inflicted upon others, but the fury they have let loose upon themselves. What wild, astounding dreams have they not harboured, what lunacies have they not devised? They have in times past exiled themselves from society in deserts and among mountains. They have, like Tolstoy, fled from their wives and families. Their self-inflicted penances and punishments, their fastings and flagellations pass belief, and are enough, in our softer times, to fright the devil. In their search for virtue they have imposed upon themselves vows of eternal silence, have starved themselves and denied themselves sleep, have gone naked and in chains. Some have thought it a sin to enjoy their daily bread, to use pillows, to shave their faces, to taste any kind of pleasure in music or poetry, to indulge in laughter or wear a cheerful countenance. They have associated filth with sanctity, and confused rude manners with goodness, despised learning and the arts, and made of life the hell they endeavoured to escape. Men have been terribly deceived by their religions, more terribly than by any philosophies; read for evidence the history of Hinduism and its greater horrors extending over centuries. 'What a mystery', as Sydney Smith said, 'is the folly and stupidity of the good.'

Or were they, perhaps, in the right? One and all, these schemes of salvation declare war upon the will-to-live, as the supreme enemy of mankind. It must be resisted to the uttermost. Tread natural desires under your feet. Reject the body and its sensual appetites. Practise a sexless virtue. Fly from the follies and temptations of the world. The recipe is always the same, negation, 'Nay-saying', as Nietzsche called it—becoming, as it were, a ghost while yet alive.

What are we to make of this repugnance to life so conspicuous in Eastern religion and morals? Do not tell me it is extinct, and no longer anywhere to be found. I will give you an illustrious example from the present day. Describing himself, his own tastes and convictions, our famous contemporary, Professor Einstein, in painting, so to speak, his own portrait, paints to perfection the portrait of a hater of existence, a world-despiser. It is a drawing to the life, the very man himself. In the affairs and activities of his fellow creatures he takes no interest. 'I have never', he writes, 'belonged to my country, my home, my friends, or even to my immediate family with a whole heart.' There you

247

have it. He depicts himself as a man never at home in the world. Existence nauseates him. He looks, so he tells us, upon 'individual existence as a sort of prison' and 'longs to escape from personal life', echoing Plato's old and famous phrase, τὸ μὲν σῶμα ἐστιν ἡμῖν σῆμα, 'the body is the tomb of the soul.' He disbelieves in human freedom and has no desire for any future life. 'An individual who should survive his physical death is', he says, 'beyond my comprehension, nor do I wish it otherwise; such notions are for the fears or absurd egoisms of feeble souls.' He 'abhors the military system, the worst outcrop of the herd nature', and war is for him 'a mean, contemptible thing'. 'Religious truth', he tells us, 'conveys to me nothing clear at all.' He 'cannot entertain for a moment the idea of a being who interferes in the course of events'. 'I see the watch, but I cannot see the watchmaker.' 'There is', he thinks, 'nothing divine about morality; it is a purely human affair.' Yet, observe, he has a sense of social justice, of social responsibility, and speaks of 'the solidarity of human things'. And well he may. For when he looks round the world terror takes hold of him. Morals, you see, do not lose their importance with the departure of God. Far from it. On the contrary, they are invoked with the greater passion to occupy the vacant throne of the universe. When God has been deposed ethics is crowned in His stead. It is then the ethical idealists hasten feverishly to erect their humanitarian temples, and call upon their new god to save them. It is then the weak look anxiously round for some other helper against the world, 'With dreadful faces thronged and fiery arms.' They cannot help themselves, and are in desperate plight.

How clearly the Orient speaks in this great man, in his Pantheism and Internationalism, in his yearning for tranquillity and social union, in his horror of multiplicity, his desire for the end of all separateness, for death and the calm of eternity. He is without hope in the world of the Many, his hopes are centred in the perfect One, the Absolute, the immutable Whole. Of course all this has nothing to do with logic. It is an emotional revolt against the conditions of existence. The compass points are reversed, South is North and North South. Here race and temperament speak, as they spoke with Spinoza, in their clearest accents, in the language of the world-renouncing East, which, in its extremity, made of its fears a religion, and of repugnance a system of morality. In its view, as in Professor Einstein's, the curse of existence is disunity, and the oppositions it engenders are anguish to his soul. Disunity and existence, multiplicity and existence are, indeed, one and the same. The many minds of many men inevitably make of the world a seething caldron of dissension, of restless rivalries. And the revolt from the society of your fellows is nothing else than a revolt from life itself, from time and its perturbations, the only refuge from which is eternity. For such men the incessant frictions, the contending wills, the demands made upon them by others, even their cheerful animation, become obnoxious and insupportable. Devouring their souls and avoiding the ways of men they become hermits, go apart from the throng into the woods and hills, to find in solitude, in communion with nature and eternal things a foretaste of celestial calm, a relief, a felicity which the tumultuous arena, the treacherous and flying flux cannot give.

The praises of solitude have often been sung. There, even while an earth-dweller, you are told, you enter Nirvana, and its heavenly silence, as in the grave, where you will never more be disturbed. Dr. Johnson, indeed, thought solitude 'dangerous to reason without being favourable to virtue'. That, however, is another question, and we must not suppose it is the saints only who have felt its seductive charm. 'For more than a month', says a recent writer, 'I had been living with the desert and the sea in absolute freedom, and it was very disagreeable to have the spell broken by the presence of my fellow creatures. . . . Alone in these solitudes I had felt myself in the midst of the vast universe, in which some mysterious instinct urged me to lose myself. Woe to the man who has once experienced the bliss of this divine communion with nature; every time he is compelled to return to the herd he will suffer from an awful solitude.' Who is the speaker? You would suppose him a poet or a mystic. But these are the words of a Frenchman, De Monfried, a smuggler of hashish. Where the 'extravert', as he is sometimes called, finds his chief delight in society, in the cheerful stir and animation, in family relationships, in the sound of human voices, the convivial meetings, the hum, the bustle, the banter and debate, the introvert seeks his pleasure in retirement, in the loneliness where all discords die away, all babblings cease. While life lasts he is a sufferer, and craves for peace, peace, it may be, at any price, for which he will sacrifice anything and everything, if needs be even his honour, or what men call his honour, his freedom and his country. In this mood of the human soul, obligations and loyalties may wholly vanish and egoism win the day. The man who dies for a cause or country has made out his case, but what has that man to say for himself who has a care only for his own salvation? He has one resource. He can wholly and altogether deny the value of existence. The will-to-live may be accused, placed on trial, found guilty of all human misery and sentenced to death. 'Dead is the world's delight!' And since in the justice of that sentence millions have acquiesced, since the worthlessness of life is a conclusion distilled not by a few disgruntled malcontents only, but from the experience of multitudes, you are brought to a halt, and may not pass it negligently by. Indeed you cannot, for upon this mood has been erected a formidable philosophy, the philosophy of Pessimism.

We have contended that this, though far from perfect world has certain claims on our respect. It was the only possible world. If, however, the pessimists be right, no world at all would have been better, or at least a universe, if such could be, without consciousness, a universe of insensate things. Arguments cannot determine this issue. Merchants of gloom and traders in despair will always find customers. 'Tis easy to employ a paper currency, destitute of human value, as do the philosophers, whether of the East or West, who spurn time and reserve their commendations for eternity as the soul's true haven. These dark-robed worshippers of oblivion but express in windy circumlocutions their abhorrence of the world, and their conviction that the spirit of evil presides in undisputed sovereignty over all sentient existence.

It turns, then, the issue, in the last resort, upon the individual bias, the personal equation. As in days of political upheaval men become Puritans or Cavaliers, so in religion and philosophy they are swept by natural and unfathomable sympathies, by birth or destiny, into opposing camps. No, arguments cannot settle this issue. Yet something may be said. It may be said that the charge of utter senselessness against the sum of things, against God or nature, demands a strong case and a stout advocate. To convict either God or nature of inferiority, whether in wisdom or in any other respect, to ourselves, the creatures of a day, who see no more than the fringe of things, will need, one cannot but think, some pleading. And, however good the case appears, invectives against living carry in the end little conviction. To be in order not to be is scarcely an alluring proposition. Nor does it seem probable that men will either be cajoled or intimidated into the wearing of a hair shirt all their life long. The world will remain worldly, if for no other reason than that the fugitives, the disbelievers in life—such is nature's supernatural cunning—leave few descendants and their race perishes.

The adversaries of nature have never proved themselves her match. She made fish to swim and birds to fly, and did not build the human soul for retreat. It will fight on. Nature does not, however deficient in sense, stultify herself. She took pains to keep things going. To tell human beings that they are already at birth dead men, as if they had not enough to put up with, that they were ushered into being in order to turn and rend themselves, is a doctrine the majority are not likely to accept. It will seem to them what it is, a doctrine of the tongue and not of the heart, a playing of the fool for pastime. There is here some concealed madness. Life itself never fails to discomfit the philosophies of ideas, which fly before it 'like ghosts from an enchanter fleeing'. And if you ask yourself of what type were the peoples who have made history, who have placed their stamp upon the events of time, there can be but one answer. They have not been the world-forsakers, who

Saw life a dream in Death's eternal sleep.

To reduce life to a minimum, to be humble and submissive, to save your soul alive by solitary prayer and meditation—that counsel has been given by many good and talented men, of whom, perhaps, you may think the world was not worthy, whose lives and teaching form a part, and not the poorest part, of our human heritage. Yet remember when you listen to their message that the cause for which none will fight is a lost cause, the cause or country for which none will adventure their lives will go down before the cause or country men place above their lives. Such is the law of nature. Nothing has ever been accomplished by resignation, the willingness to put up with anything, to submit to anything. All that has been done has been achieved by the ' no surrender ' principle. And if you hold empires, and states, civilisations, arts and sciences worth the building, it is well to recollect that more is needed, much more, than the saving of the individual soul by communion with eternal things. 'In nations', wrote a recent historian (F. S. Oliver), 'meekness is not a virtue, but a contemptible and very dangerous vice.' No doubt the men who gave little thought to eternity and did the work of time, who had ambition, who were aggressive, who loved the world, were often, too often, sadly mistaken, and let loose upon their fellows a flood of troubles; yet for some reason they have been held in honour above the dwellers in the deserts or the anchorites upon their pillars. *Dum vivimus vivamus.* While we live let us live. While we see about us the starry systems, the colours and shapes and varieties of so many living creatures, while this stupendous panorama is spread out before us, a vision, one would think, not merely for mortals but for the immortals to look upon, a sulky and sullen humour it surely is which cries out upon it all, 'Get thee behind me, Satan!'

'He who spits against Heaven', say the Spaniards, 'spits in his own face.' The world, talk as you please, is God's will or nature's, to which the will-to-live in ourselves is the undying, the incorruptible witness. There is, as Shelley said, something within man 'at enmity with nothingness and dissolution'. Why or whence comes this never-countermanded order to every living thing to fulfil its being, to remain in existence? I am not acquainted with any answer to this question, scientific or philosophical. Nor do I anticipate any. Certainly from the systems that view the world as an eternal stationary whole you need hope for no relief from your troubles. If it be not a Becoming, if nothing is in fact happening, or if the cage in which we are imprisoned is merely revolving in the self-same everlasting cycles, then they are right who have thrown down the gauntlet of defiance to the insane whirligig we call the Cosmos. But the will-to-live points beyond the present. We are not, indeed, in nature's confidence, and may be likened to sleep-walkers, mysteriously upheld by some secret influence. In us some project is at work, some end foreshadowed.

You recall the δαίμων of Socrates, his mentor or angel, which possessed a wisdom beyond that of the philosopher himself, although he had been pronounced by the oracle of Delphi the wisest of men. His δαίμων knew more than Socrates. The human race, too, has its δαίμων, its mentor, better informed than its wisest representatives, the acutest philosophers. Like the guardian of Socrates, it knows what is yet to come. When I hear the voices counselling surrender I place myself on guard. I tell myself the will-to-live, which contemplates the world's outcries and commotions with Olympian calm, is more to be trusted than the logic of the kings of thought, the champions of the academic schools, and demands more than a measure of respectful consideration.

This race of ours has emerged from the womb of the immeasurable universe, and no one has told us how. Man has emerged from dark unconsciousness, and is in some degree an independent being—how far we need not now discuss. He has become a person, a separate self within the whole. Can we at this stage reasonably conclude that his selfhood is to be deplored, and what he has already gained a worthless vanity? Have we sufficient evidence at this point of time to count the human adventure a nightmare only, an evil dream? Does wisdom now dictate that what has been already gained should be abandoned, and that we should sink thankfully back into union with the whole, from which we should never, save for some appalling blunder, some catastrophic folly, have emerged?

· It is the will-to-live which has given birth to human love and human art, the soul's ideals and its hope of immortality. Why turn away from the simple and evident truth? If then you despise and reject life, you necessarily despise and reject with it beauty, the affections and the society of your fellow creatures. To have friends and lovers, a share in time's activities, to exchange and compare experiences and thoughts with your companions, to be a part of the great scene, to recall the histories, the adventures of the preceding generations, of the others who have made the journey before us—all this you declare a negligible nothing or an intolerable misery. You see only tragedy in the triumphs of the human spirit. Shrouded though it be in mystery, the will-to-live speaks out of the depths, and is less concerned with what is than with what is to be. It keeps good company. It consorts with the powers of nature, with her thrones and principalities, with thoughts that have not yet found their way into the clear light of human consciousness, with the cosmic principles that rule the spheres. Under its guidance the race has been wiser than its instructors, has declined to sit with them in ashes, and has continued to say to life, 'Good morrow, you are welcome.'

In the opinion of Plato there were three sorts of philanthropy, that of a courteous, cheerful and hearty disposition, which put strangers at their ease; another which displayed itself in acts of kindness; and a third, which consisted in being good and pleasant companions, adding to the gaiety of social occasions. To which of these types do the despisers of life, daring neither to live nor to die, belong? Can they be said to belong to any? Of these types of valuable men the moralists, busy with their denunciations, have had too little to say. For my part I would fain capture the cavalier temper, with its touch of fine free carelessness, not going much in fear of either life or death, not much, indeed, in fear of anything, the temper of men battle-worthy and exalted above their present station. You must make your choice, you cannot be all men at once, or capture all varieties of perfection. Many varieties of men there have been, to any one of which, had our fates been in our power, we might gladly have belonged—poets, saints, heroes. We could ill spare any of them. There is one, I think, not greatly esteemed, of which our country has had many representatives. Let me call him the gallant blade. He thinks seldom and little about the learning, the problems or the prizes of the world. Light-hearted, unaffected, this Mercutio-like person is without aggravated solemnity or portentous gloom. He has his faults. His days and nights are not devoted to meditations upon virtue, to theories either of living or of art. He is destitute of metaphysical gifts. He has no talent for reforming his neighbours. Rather he rejoices in their society, and himself radiates good humour and cheerfulness, making this his contribution, and no negligible one, to the welfare of society. He carries with him a gusto for the present hour, which even moralists might envy and saints forbear to chide. And when adventure offers he tosses his sword in the air to catch it by the hilt. He is hope incarnate, a child of 'the virgin, the ever-living, the lovely to-day'.

'To impose one ideal upon all men', as Professor Read said, 'is an intolerable torture, that never has been, and ought not to be submitted to.' We may be at ease in the matter. It never has been and never will be while the world lasts.

Sir James Frazer speaks somewhere of 'the masked wizard of history' who, by ways to us astonishing and unsearchable, has yet led, as it seems, the human race by the hand on the rocky path of its destiny, to the point at which it stands. Whether you look back or forward, the view combines, certainly, terror with sublimity. And for all we can tell, nature's way may have been the only way, and hers no forthright path, but an undertaking of supreme, unimaginable difficulty. It may well be that to found the great commonwealth of living creatures required a long circuit, tedious essays, false starts and unprofitable explorations. All kinds of universe cannot exist together, and there must be some sufficient reason for the universe that is. If a world without the opposites there could not be, who can tell us that in such a world to make a home for the human race was a short and easy task? And who can be sure that refusal to play a part in it may not be a fatal decision, running counter to a great essay?

If history have any meaning, we are upon a voyage hardly yet begun. We do well, I submit, when we put our trust in 'the masked wizard' behind the scene—when we look back, we know not why, with instinctive fascination upon all the historical movements, refusing to sacrifice any one of them, the ethereal radiance of Greece, the majesty of Rome, all facets of the human spirit represented in the ancient cultures and civilisations, the accumulated wisdom, the capitalised experience of the generations that have gone before us. If they have made errors, they have amid their tribulations also worked wonders. I can find no better knowledge than in their affirmations.

The plain man, not too fastidious to live with his fellows, is the ideal spectator of the troubled scene. For his simple wisdom, his untutored soul, his shy, inexpressive intelligence, unperplexed by dialectic, unsubdued by failure, I confess an affectionate regard. I embrace the philosophy of the vulgar. This plain man has been at his best 'when walking towards the gods', in the phrase of Pythagoras, when his loyalties were aroused, his affections engaged, his courage kindled. How comes it that he is at his zenith in adversity? How came the race into possession of hope, that mysterious sustainer of all effort, the most constant and enduring of our life's companions, our friend of friends?

In these two instincts, the will-to-live emanating from the darkness whence we came, and hope, a shining light in advance of us, nature speaks from the depths of her heart. Here if anywhere you have her testament signed and sealed. So deep is the fountain whence they sprang that against all the evidence they even carry us in thought beyond the grave. Have the psychologists begun to account for them? If you can discover for them any naturalistic interpretation, the pessimists have it, and I yield the case. For if they lie to us it is the universe that lies, and to what end I cannot fathom. Unless, indeed, you suppose these two, the love of life and hope in life are a trickery of nature, whereby before she slay us she may the longer torment us.

While we live then let us continue to live. But what next? Is it to live for eternity, as some would have us do, or, as others, for time? I answer that for us there is no choice. There is no living for eternity, save in time, in its dreams and activities; nor can there be supported without the heroic heart, the resolution

To strive, to seek, to find and not to yield,

the heart and resolution of the English admiral, who on the dawn of an engagement remarked, 'I have taken the depth of the water, and when my vessel sinks my flag will still fly.' And for those in doubt, in alarm, either for themselves or the ship of humanity, there are the words of St. Paul to the trembling gaoler—'Do thyself no harm, for we are all here.'

XIII

THE GREAT DIVIDE

Columbus, who, by using subjective assumptions, a false hypothesis, and a route abandoned by modern navigation, nevertheless discovered America.

Jung

XIII

THE GREAT DIVIDE

With the will-to-live in human beings neither religion nor ethics are on good terms. It causes them infinite misgiving and vexation, and they incline to see in it the enemy both of God and of society. For on what principle do all living creatures consistently act? On the principle, as we have seen, of doing the best for themselves always and everywhere. But this principle brings them necessarily into conflict with the others animated by the same principle. The will-to-live, by the very law of its being, searches diligently in each and all of its embodiments for more and fuller life. Each is, in a word, the incarnation of selfishness. And religion and ethics are thus brought into collision with the many individual wills, deplore their egoism, and for the greater good of the common weal, for social ends and purposes, would have them abandon the pursuit of their private goods and separate desires. They stand, that is, for unanimity and peace, for law and order, against the 'who-knows-what-next?' apprehensiveness we all dread, against the capricious self-willed person, that incalculable quantity, doing what he pleases, when he pleases and as he pleases. Unless he be curbed, or converted from his self-seeking habits, how can society be saved from endless alarms, dangers and disturbances? How else can we sleep in security and comfort?

The surface of the great ocean of existence, over which religion and ethics look with such anxiety, is in continuous unrest and agitation. It should be, they appear to hold, calm and motionless, reflecting, as in a placid mirror, the peace of God. What is the cause of its agitations? No other, they assure us, than the opposing minds and aims of self-intoxicated men. Alas!—though upon this distressing truth they do not care to dwell—in the will-to-live we have simply nature herself speaking, that majestic, creative and sovereign nature, which contains all things and is all things, whose unsubduable, quivering activities are but the symptoms of her life, the throbbing pulses of her mighty heart.

But if, indeed, it be this omnipotent power against which religion and ethics are in arms, the situation is nothing short of desperate; so desperate and inexplicable that they face it with extreme reluctance. Of the delinquencies of men they are very ready to speak, and have much to tell us, but of the delinquencies of the universe, of which the will-to-live in ourselves is a manifest product, they rarely complain. They may even praise its beauty and sublimity. Human beings they boldly and unhesitatingly call to account for their doings, but to call nature to account, which brought them into being and made them what they are, that is a different matter. For in the first place, to pass an adverse judgment on nature goes perilously near passing an adverse judgment upon God, and in the second place, they perceive that to attempt to combat nature would be to attempt the impossible. As well try to resist an avalanche.

You are acquainted—who is not acquainted?—with this awkward hiatus, or rather with this frowning theological precipice no mountaineer has ever scaled. 'In knowing more about the world', wrote the late Bishop Gore, 'I am learning more about God.' Well, he was learning many and terrible things of which he never spoke, upon which men of religion are for excellent reasons unwilling to discourse or dilate. If nature's ways are the ways of God, its Creator, they certainly do not recommend themselves for adoption in human society. If the voice of God is to be heard, as religion asserts, in our ideals of goodness and kindness, He speaks in a very different voice in the world at large, in a voice there of power but not of friendliness.

> The earth is full of anger,
> And the seas are full of wrath.

We are surrounded, as everyone knows, by devouring and pitiless forces. How merciless is nature's demeanour, and how terrible at times her visitations. How many tender and loving hearts she has broken, how many innocents massacred! That she also produced them, that her victims are her own children, is the flaming paradox. Who has resolved it for us? Not Plato, not Kant, not Mohammed nor Christ. They have thrown no glimmer of light upon our situation, nor revealed to us the cause of our sufferings.

It is here that religion and ethics conspicuously fail us. For the pains of life they offer, indeed, remedies; but when we ask for their causes, when we ask why we are required to endure them, they are silent and provide no explanation. So perceiving that with nature nothing can be done, nothing with her torrid heat and polar cold, her earthquakes, fevers, tempests, sharks and tigers, that she is beyond talking to, heeds no remonstrances, and must be allowed to go her own unpleasant way, the preachers and the prophets leave her in peace, and devote their attention to human beings, with whom there appears to be more hope of dealing. We are ourselves, they tell us, chiefly responsible for our own sufferings, for the dissensions, wars and tumults, for example, by which the world is vexed.

Yet when we look about us we are not so sure that malice, hatred and uncharitableness are the sole causes of our tribulation. Though religion and ethics are slow to charge nature with iniquity, she cannot be altogether acquitted. Nature cannot be left out of the account, and is seen to be in some measure to blame for our distress. To take a simple and single instance. The world adds fifty thousand souls a day to its population, and has increased its inhabitants within the last fifteen years by some three hundred millions. This cascade of new life, these millions, desire food, warmth, comfort like the rest of us. Three-quarters of the present dwellers on the earth are already upon the very brink of famine and destitution. Where then for the new-comers are habitable land and means of living to be obtained? Or are they to be blamed for desiring them, or for the struggle to obtain them? The will-to-live, that is, nature herself, is at work in them, a force when lives are at stake, neither to be gainsaid nor condemned.

What, in such a case, then, do religion and ethics propose, what practical proposition? Here is an example of the bewildering predicament in which mankind finds itself. We would substitute, if we could, our moral order for nature's order, yet, so far from stretching out a hand to help us, she adds to our difficulties, and accumulates our perplexities. Who does not see, if the purpose of God be represented in nature—and what other means have we of discovering it except in His works?—who does not see in the dislocation, the cleavage, between nature, the life-giver, and our religion and ethics, an impassable crevasse? Of nothing in the wide universe are we the creators. The will-to-live is given us, like all else, and is not of our making. And observe how assured it is, and without hesitations. It knows, or supposes itself to know, quite well, what is both good and bad. The good is what ministers to the free activity, expansion and contentment, the bad is what frustrates, diminishes or denies the aims and desires of the living creature. 'When I steal my enemy's wife', said the negro chief, 'it is good, but when he steals mine it is bad.' What could be simpler? But now upon the scene arrive religion and ethics, proposing to substitute for these simple values quite other values. And addressing the will-to-live, nature's deputy in us, they advance the astonishing statement, 'You do not know your own needs. You are utterly and miserably mistaken. Nature has deceived you. What you think good is bad, and what you think bad is good.'

In so saying religion and ethics find themselves in very strange and suspicious company, not only in opposition to nature, but arrayed, to all seeming, among the adversaries of life, the world-despisers and world-deserters, in the company of thinkers like Santayana, whose 'moral philosophy', he tells us, 'is the philosophy of abstention and distaste for life', among the pessimists, like Schopenhauer, who cry out against separate, individual existence, the world-order, as the root of all human misery, and declare that the sooner it comes to an end the better. Personal life is essentially sinful, and must be abandoned. So the will-to-live is invited to deny its nature and go out of existence. And the thought, no comfortable one, immediately invades the mind, 'Is it possible that ethical codes are merely a subtle device on the part of the weak majority to disarm, or circumvent the strong minority, to cajole them out of their advantages, and is religion, perhaps, in its essence a flight from the world, from the undertakings and activities to which nature prompts us, not so much an encouragement to live as an invitation to die, aiming at a value which puts an end to all values, a proposal arising less out of a love of God than out of a detestation of the inevitable conditions of existence? Is its true message, however cloaked with eloquent phrases, that the less we have to do with life in the world the wiser and the nobler we shall be?'

A stamp of the foot will not resolve this knot, nor call angelic armies to your aid. Looking back through history we can see how slight, indeed, has been the success of religion and ethics, at the best a very partial success, and that only secured by the assistance they have received from a secret ally in the human soul. For here, as everywhere, we are entangled in the opposites, the contending eagles 'with ages in their plumes'. The will-to-live is at work in us, a force not to be easily set aside nor destroyed, but there is also at work in us the will-to-love, an influence which is represented by our ideals of perfection, a passion as undeniable as that which resides in the will-to-live, for truth, goodness and beauty, which need no bush, to which religion and ethics make their appeal. Their source is hidden from us, as the source of the will-to-live is hidden from us, yet they, too, speak with authority and persuasiveness.

Throughout its history mankind has been haunted by a dilemma —at whose door shall its troubles be laid? That we ourselves, the men and women now in the world, are in any way responsible for its distractions is a proposition too preposterous for any save the fanatics to entertain. No one any longer believes it. Honesty forbids. 'We cannot find by experience', said the sagacious Bishop Butler, 'that all our sufferings are owing to our own follies.' Some mysterious agency has been at work, whose doings we cannot fathom, and from which we are estranged. Yet we desire, and desire ardently, to think well of that mighty agency, for its might, whatever we may think of its morals, cannot be questioned. We desire to believe in its good intentions towards us, and even to worship it. 'The Romans', said Polybius, 'were more religious than the gods themselves.' Surely, we think, the gods cannot be our enemies. Men cherish the idea that the powers above look upon the human race with a friendly eye. They have not, however, at all times been of that opinion. 'If we were as rich as you', said a Hindu poet, addressing the gods, 'we should not allow our worshippers to beg their bread.' A great mass of forbidding evidence raises itself up against the thesis that the gods are kind. In the eyes of early man the case against them looked black. It was in past times very generally feared that they regarded mankind either with jealousy and disfavour or with complete indifference. Or, if they concerned themselves at all with mortal affairs, they bestowed their scant and capricious favours upon this or that tribe or community for reasons hard to determine. Never till the advent of Christianity was the doctrine anywhere widely disseminated of a loving God, a benefactor of all mankind. Fear of the gods, yes, and an uneasy suspicion of them, much of that, indeed, there was; but affection, a happy trust and confidence in them, no!

Poets and thinkers since the dawn of reason have not seldom been driven to think of human life as cruelly unreasonable, and of man as a wild animal caught in a trap. Turn to the *Prometheus* of Æschylus, or to *The Book of Job*, in our own Bible, and you may read eloquent descriptions of the human lot;—its desolation ascribed not to men, but to the Governor of the Universe Himself. When Job's friends, in conformity with Jewish religion, contend that it is his own sin which has brought upon him the divine displeasure, he breaks out upon them in scornful indignation. He refuses to listen to such sophistries. The sense that he has done his utmost to serve God and do righteousness, and none the less been betrayed and abandoned, is strong upon him. The outbursts of the most modern pessimists are matched in his fierce utterances:

> I will not restrain my mouth,
> I will speak in the heaviness of my spirit,
> I will complain in the bitterness of my soul.

> Were I to call, and he answered
> I would not believe that he heard my voice.

> He mocks at the despair of the guiltless.

Job submits because he must, but is not persuaded either of the benevolence or of the justice of God. With what scornful irony he answers his critics.

> No doubt ye are the people,
> And wisdom will die with you.
> But I have a head as well as you;
> I am not inferior to yourselves:
> Yea, who knoweth not such things as these?

What things? That evils befall the righteous as well as the unrighteous, that virtue is no shield against the misfortunes and miseries of humanity.

And this very thought of an indifferent God, which accounts so simply and easily for our human state, appears in the meditations of many great masters of life and of speculation. It prevails to-day. 'We stand at all times', wrote Herbert Spencer, 'in the presence of an infinite and eternal energy from which all things proceed.' The attributes of this power do not include either friendliness or benevolence. Human beings do not come within the range of its vision, if it can be said to have any. Gazing at the prodigious massif of that great Himalayan peak, Nanga Parbat, clad in its eternal mantle of snow, General Bruce describes his emotions. 'It gave one a feeling of impossibility; it gave one also a feeling that one wasn't there, and it gave one a feeling that if one wasn't there, it didn't matter. In fact it was a liberal education in itself.' So God appears to many minds in these present times. 'I may say,' writes the author of *Thirty Years in the Frozen North*,[1] 'I may say that I am myself a Catholic. But I have not been in church for the last forty-five years, and for all that time I have never said my prayers. I have no religion, because it was no use to me up North. When I am living up there in that far-off corner of the world, and see how terrible nature is at close quarters, I come to the conclusion that we all originate from earth and water. Even the Eskimo, who is stupid, and has never been to school, points to the icy rocks around him, and says, "That is your God, who created you".'

Go to Spinoza, the 'god-intoxicated' philosopher, who has much to say of God and the love of God, and you will learn that God's thoughts have no more likeness to man's than the Dog-star has to the dog, the barking animal. How shattering a hammer stroke! Or go to the poet Blake, infected with the Gnostic heresy that the Demiurge, the world-builder, was the adversary of the true God, and you will hear that in his opinion 'the Creator of this world is a very cruel being'.

Through the myths and fables of many races it runs, this theme of the indifference or tyranny of the cosmic powers. And with it the accompanying theme that mankind has had its champions, who met that tyranny with determined opposition, like Prometheus in the Greek myth—

With courage never to submit or yield.

They were semi-divine beings, these comforters of persecuted humanity, who conferred upon it benefits, denied by the grudging gods. They procured for men fire from heaven, fire to which a peculiar sanctity and value were in early times attached. They were also light-bearers, bringing to them knowledge, which

[1] Jan Welzl.

265

smoothed the rugged path of human destiny. They suffered, these benefactors of the race, at the hands of the jealous deities for their friendliness to mankind and were thus worthy—so said the poets—of the gratitude and honour they received. 'The reason Milton wrote in fetters when he wrote of God and angels,' declared Blake, 'and at liberty when he wrote of devils and hell, is because he was a true poet, and of the devil's party without knowing it.'

Interpret these early stories as you prefer, at least their critical attitude towards the celestial powers is sufficient evidence of the profound discordance felt in all ages and among all peoples between human beings and their surroundings, the inexplicable disharmony between their desires and dreams, the resistances they everywhere encounter.

Disappointment with life in some form or other lies at the root, too, of all religion. Had life contented us, had it been all that we could wish, we should be already in heaven, and in no need to seek happiness here or elsewhere. And to persuade men that the Creator was a God of love, and their misfortunes of their own contriving, has proved an embarrassing and not too successful undertaking.

Do not let us be told that the will-to-believe was absent. The desire for a protecting Providence is writ large in human history. And man could not but marvel that the infinite and majestic Whole of Being, call it by what name you choose, the One or Absolute, should be blind, deaf and heartless. Human logic and human emotion both revolt from the conception of the grand procession of nature, the sum of all creation, as

a tale
Told by an idiot, full of sound and fury,
Signifying nothing.

Our minds cannot take kindly to such a juxtaposition of ideas, to magnificence unrelated to wisdom, and grandeur divorced from soul. If you have reached the conclusion that the universe is an iron-bound mechanism, you may close your churches and put away your books of devotion. To worship a machine, however vast, is no less an idolatry than to do obeisance before a graven image. Humanity will have it that omnipotence and benevolence should somehow be in alliance. It is Plato's thought, and none more natural. Deny, however, that Heaven can be to blame for our

266

condition, for 'the giant agony of the world', and what alternative offers itself, and where are we to look for its explanation?

Let me recall to your memory a famous passage in Cardinal Newman's *Apologia*, in which he describes the dismay which overcame him, when he looked out upon the human scene and saw it as the prophet's scroll 'full of lamentation and mourning and woe'. 'To consider the world',[1] he wrote, 'in its length and breadth, its various history, the many races of men, their starts, their fortunes, their mutual alienation, their conflicts; and then their ways, habits, governments, forms of worship; their enterprises, their aimless courses, their random achievements and acquirements, the impotent conclusion of long-standing facts, the tokens so faint and broken of a superintending design, the blind evolution of what turn out to be great powers or truths, the progress of things, as if from unreasoning elements, not towards final causes, the greatness and littleness of man, his far-reaching aims, his short duration, the curtain hung over his futurity, the disappointments of life, the defeat of good, the success of evil, physical pain, mental anguish, the prevalence and intensity of sin, the pervading idolatries, the corruptions, the dreary hopeless irreligion, that condition of the whole race, so fearfully yet exactly described in the Apostle's words, 'having no hope and without God in the world'—all this is a vision to dizzy and appal; and inflicts upon the mind the sense of a profound mystery, which is absolutely beyond human solution. What shall be said to this heart-piercing, reason-bewildering fact? I can only answer, that either there is no Creator, or this living society of men is in a true sense discarded from His presence.'

Newman did not stay to ask himself whether any other world than that of the contraries was possible. He assumes its possibility. He assumes also, apparently, that such a perfect world had at one time actually existed. He assumed, certainly, that there might have been quite another and better world, in which other ways of life, other types of enterprise, other forms of government, would have been found, a world whose inhabitants would have been good and happy, sinless and deathless as the angels in Paradise. A perfect universe seemed to him the only natural universe, whereas our part of it, the actually existing world, was unnatural and utterly incomprehensible. Why he

[1] *Apologia pro Vita Sua*, chap. v.

267

should have thought so, or assumed it should be so, we need not now consider. We can see that in this indictment a pious and beautiful soul is speaking. His feelings overflow, and they are not those of our bright optimists, who with a few coats of humanitarian paint will turn earth for you into heaven. His eyes are open. The author of this passage is a man in spiritual extremity, who in his straits was driven into the dilemma, from which, as we have seen, the exit is hard to find. Either there was no Creator, or 'the human race was implicated in some terrible aboriginal calamity'.

The dilemma left Newman no choice. Since he could not accept the conclusion of a world without a Creator, the human creature must himself be held responsible for the situation. It must be that through revolt and disobedience he had fallen from God's grace. 'Man had rebelled against his Maker.' 'The unaided reason', Newman tells us, 'when correctly exercised, leads to a belief in God.' He found, moreover, the conviction of God's existence in the depths of his own being, no less certain than the conviction of his own existence. He was thus irresistibly impelled to the view that the human race had been its own evil genius, its own destroyer—to the view known to us all as the Fall of Man.

While some, then, of the great speculators have ascribed the sorrows of the world to God, others have with equal confidence attributed them to God's creatures, to sinful mortals. And there is something exceedingly remarkable in the persistence and vitality of this Eastern conception, which ascribes the sad estate of mankind to the transgression of some divine ordinance.

What possible interpretation can be given, what justification offered of this conception, of which biology and history know nothing? Of man's rise both have much to tell us, of his fall they never speak. When did he fall, and where? Clearly, indeed, in this conception we have an allegory, and not less clearly it corresponds to some mysterious intuition, echoing from the depths of the human soul.

What then was the original sin, the *damnosa hereditas*? Metaphysically interpreted, it was the revolt of the Many against the One, whose transgression it was to become the Many, to prefer a personal independent existence in time to a life hidden with God in eternity. Somehow it became possible for human souls to embark upon separate lives, to enter each upon individual existence, to exchange a blessed unity for the pursuit of private aims—in a word, to choose Becoming on their own account to Being, remaining with the One; to prefer a progressive to a static state. Thus the sacred calm, the motionless perfection of Heaven, was shattered, and behold the world of separated selves, each seeking a false felicity, the unattainable end of personal happiness. Of necessity it followed that for this fault, the flight from God, remedy there could be none save in repentance, liberation from the burden of selfhood, and the long and toilsome journey home to the undivided whole of Being, the perfect and immutable Unity. The essence of religion appears to be the recognition of the One. Forget not in your individualism the One. What doth the Lord require of thee? To remember the One.

Needless to ask at what point in man's history did the separation, the dire event, take place—when came man to take so momentous a decision. These are unanswerable questions. Let us ask instead, how in the light of this conception of the Fall of Man is Christianity to be interpreted? It was claimed by Schopenhauer—a remarkable claim—that he was Christianity's best, indeed its true, interpreter, who expressed its innermost thought, that of deliverance from the self, from the tyranny of the will-to-live. Jesus Christ, he declared, 'ought always to be conceived as the symbol or personification of the denial of the will-to-live.' Schopenhauer contended that the later readings of Christ's message had forgotten or overlooked its true significance, and degenerated into dull optimism. 'To turn against the will-to-live, to deny it, is', he wrote, 'the only absolute good, the *summum bonum*, the only radical cure for the disease of life.' And again, 'Certainly the doctrine of original sin—the assertion of the will—and of salvation—the denial of the will—is a great truth, which constitutes the essence of Christianity.' The less man is entangled in any human activity, national, social or domestic, the less associated with other men, the Many, his fellow sinners, the nearer he approaches the primal state of unity and blessedness.

This self-styled apostle of Christianity made one or two attempts to meet the powerful objection to his creed that a revolt against the will-to-live, should it prove successful, must lead to the extinction of all life, to final nothingness. In the end, however, he accepts the inevitable conclusion, accepts nothingness, more attractively expressed in theological terminology as union

269

with God, as the final and desirable state. He turns his back
upon time, and declares for eternity, in which all distinctions
vanish, and

> The dewdrop slips into the shining sea.

The secret, then, is out. Life is a huge mistake. The best is
never to have been born, the second best to die.

Was Schopenhauer's interpretation of Christianity correct? It
must, I think, be acknowledged that to the Eastern ideal of ascetic-
ism, or world-refusal, our religion inclined in the early centuries
a ready ear. If Christ's teaching be not a rejection of the social,
political, intellectual and artistic interests that life offers, we
can scarcely refuse to admit that it has been widely so interpreted.
We have only to think of the ascetics and their austerities, their
suspicion of all the bodily appetites, their aversion from worldly
activities, their dread of sex and exaltation of chastity. Christianity, by its acceptance of the Eastern conception of man's fall,
is committed to a world view, a complete philosophy, to a condemnation of the present world, to the belief that it was preceded
by a better, a Paradise that man has forfeited, from which, by his
revolt from God, he is exiled. It is committed to the conclusion
that in deliverance from our earthly lot, and return to our former
state, lies our only hope.

This interpretation of existence is in essence the creed and
philosophy of India. Is it also the creed of the Christian churches
to-day? Or, if not, is Christianity anything more than an ethical
gospel, the religion of philanthropy? How difficult it is for the
plain man to know where he stands!

And to resolve the knot one question above all others should
first be faced and answered, upon which even in theological circles
you may observe in these times much hesitation. What are we to
understand by this ambiguous and equivocal term, eternal life, of
which philosophy and religion speak? Heaven, eternity, union
with God—are these phrases synonyms for the extinction of
individual existence? In this matter falsehoods and hypocrisies
abound. Ask the philosophers or the divines and you plunge
them into deep discomfort. How many of them beat a retreat,
like the gods and goddesses of Homer, into a protecting cloud,
into a smoke screen of monstrous verbiage! This eternal life of
higher values and ideals is by no means to be confused, we are

told, with everlastingness. It can be enjoyed here and now. And one asks oneself whether it can anywhere else be experienced save now, and only now, in time, the negligible time with which we were accustomed to contrast it, whether, indeed, it be not—a curious paradox—the life of time and no other, lived on some higher and more spiritual plane, without promise of any continuation beyond our few and troubled years. There is much talk of the unreality of time, but this eternity, so important while we are yet in time, ceases apparently to have any further significance for us at our death in time. How lucid and fascinating are the conceptions of the philosophers! It is well, if this be so, to bear in mind that this eternal life will not restore to you your lost friends. It will not reunite lovers parted by death, nor provide any compensation for the cruelties and injustices men have endured. Did Spinoza believe in any future for the individual man, or even desire it? Or did Hegel? Or do any of our advanced theologians? Is theirs not the poetic immortality which in *Adonais* Shelley assigned to Keats, that he had become 'a portion of the loveliness that once he made more lovely'?

> He is made one with Nature: there is heard
> His voice in all her music, from the moan
> Of thunder, to the song of night's sweet bird;
> He is a presence to be felt and known
> In darkness and in light, from herb and stone,
> Spreading itself where'er that Power may move
> Which has withdrawn his Being to its own:
> Which wields the world with never-wearied love,
> Sustains it from beneath, and kindles it above.

What could be more beautiful? He provides certainly for the dead man a magnificent cemetery. Yet of all this the poet himself after his brief career has ceased to be conscious. He is no longer aware of the loveliness of which he is now a part. It has for him no longer any interest.

> Far from the busy mart
> Deep in the woods, dear heart,
> He'll lie, and have no part
> In friendship or good cheer.
> The lyre, the flute so clear
> Shall sound, but he'll not hear.[1]

[1] *A Lost Friend* (from the Greek), by Denis Turner.

And 'the Power which wields the world with never-wearied love'—where then is the evidence of that love, of that affectionate solicitude for men, for the poet himself, cut off by cruel illness in his youth? If you read the story of his last days you will not, I think, come to the conclusion that it was a matter of indifference to Keats whether or not he continued to be a witness of all this wonderful beauty. And are not love and friendship a part of it? How, too, has it come about, if this Power created so marvellous and delectable a world, that multitudes who passed through it found existence there devoid of any worth, a betrayal of their youthful hopes, their birth a calamity and death a boon?

Through such a chaos of inconsistencies no philosopher could steer a course; in this wild sea of contradictions no ship of thought could swim. Resignation is not seldom described as a Christian doctrine and a mysterious doctrine, a turning away from earthly to heavenly things. But heaven in what sense? Is resignation itself the only heaven, and death a deliverance certainly from the ills of life, but at the same time 'the morningless and unawakening sleep'? And if this be the Christian's joyful hope, how does it differ from that of other men? All mankind may equally anticipate the blissful entry into the 'all-healing hospital of death', where they will join the happy company of those for ever dead, as dead as any stone. They, too,

> When all the tears of time are dry
> The night shall lighten from her tearless eye.

They, too,

> from the fetters of the light unbound,
> Healed from their wound of living shall sleep sound.

Religion, until our modern interpreters got to work upon it, rested upon the belief in another and a future world, with which our human destinies were somehow associated. If no such world exist interest in religion is, to my mind, of much the same order as an interest in the geography of Gulliver's travels, or the tribal customs of the Lilliputians. Religion has resigned in favour of ethics. In the eyes of most believers, to excise from Christian doctrine the hope of a life to come would be to extirpate its starry centre, its sublime expectation. I am not discussing the truth of Christian doctrine. I am speaking only of its interpretation. Is Christianity a religion for the stalls, and also a religion for the gallery, for the emancipated intellectuals, who take it in one sense, and the simple folk, who take it in quite another? Is there any doubt of the Christian promises? Is this much talked of better country a pious legend only, a pretty story for the children? What were the glad tidings which have brought comfort to so many millions of aching hearts? All men are not theologians or philosophers, and the question to which the simple folk desire an answer is as simple as themselves—Do the dead exist? If Christ's teaching gave no promise of individual life beyond the grave, His followers have been, one fears, sadly deceived, and the history of Christianity is the history of the greatest imposture ever practised upon suffering humanity. Christians may find philosophy a dangerous ally if it requires them to believe that the many mansions spoken of by Christ were so many graves; if it requires them to believe that when St. Paul exclaimed, 'O death, where is thy sting? O grave, where is thy victory?' he was indulging in a false and windy rhetoric.

What did Christ teach, and His followers believe these nineteen hundred years? It is not for me to say. I have read in the books of some theologians that a confirmation of the belief in a future life is undesirable. They are, I believe, mistaken. When they assure us further that human destiny, the fate of the soul, is not a religious interest at all, and claim merit for this remarkable discovery, they are not, I think, wise in their generation. They incur a widespread suspicion that they have profound misgivings, are far, indeed, from sure that for this ancient faith there is the slightest foundation. They proclaim that Christianity is not in need of this supporting pillar, and rests upon far more solid columns. It is an interesting speculation how long it would survive the extinction of the belief. In my judgment not long. The decay of this ancient hope, as old as the human race, is the worm at the root of all our creeds, and without it Christianity becomes what Arnold a generation ago declared it to be, 'Morality touched with emotion,' a gentle humanitarianism, associated with a time-honoured and beautiful ritual—humanitarianism, which that penetrating thinker, Dostoievsky, held to be the form of atheism most to be dreaded, the greatest anti-religious force in Europe. When Christianity ceases to stand, as it has stood hitherto, for the infinite and everlasting value of the individual, its sun will surely set. Let its guardians look to it. Men will not long distress themselves to save their souls when they know that save for the present hour they have no souls to save.   Nor will it long survive if it propose to make of resignation, of deliverance from the world, of abstention from its natural activities, of withdrawal and retreat, the end to be achieved.   'There is no gain in shutting out the world,' as Maeterlinck expresses it, 'though it be with walls of righteousness.'   If it offer no future and exalt dying above living, the time has come to look round for some other and more heroic religion, a religion of encouragement to put more heart into men. Time was when they supposed themselves upon an expedition of some interest and importance.   Such a time will come again, and with it a religion to suit the time, to

> give the world another heart
> And other pulses.

We have digressed.   Let us return to Newman's dilemma.   He was convinced of God's existence, and his conception of deity carried with it the attribute of goodness in the human sense, of kindness towards its creation, as well as of almighty power.   His own benevolent heart would have it so, and told him so.   A God to whom he might resign in perfect confidence his entire being, alone seemed worthy of that august title.   What is a God?   It was remarked by Blake that 'all deities reside in the human breast'. Or, in Spinoza's acid phrase, a community of triangles would worship a triangular God.   So each man seeks a deity after his own heart.   Your God is your ideal.   A community of logicians would ask for a First Cause, a community of mathematicians for a God who geometrises, while a community of Newmans would create for themselves a God of love.

Thus the Christian's God filled and satisfied to the exclusion of all others his affectionate and pious soul.   But how was this kindly Providence to be demonstrated?   Arguments for God's existence?   Yes, there were arguments, with which theologians had busied themselves since the world began, and still busy themselves. Unhappily they fell far short of the demonstration that Newman required.   At the most they demonstrated only a First Cause, Aristotle's Prime Mover, or Plato's 'self-subsistent Being'.   Of course the world is somehow supported.   It does not rest upon the back of an elephant.   And this you may also truly say, the archi-tect is present in the building, though not a trace of him is visibly present in its structure. But these arguments for God's existence were never advanced by the Founder of Christianity. The New Testament—a noteworthy omission—supplies no such arguments. The God whose existence could be proved by 'the correct use of reason' was not at all the divine Being of Newman's, or any Christian's desire. The God of love does not reside, and so will not be found, in the palace built for him by the metaphysicians. Of what use are such metaphysical gods? Or can any man take an interest in a deity who is uninterested in him? The arguments in support of such a Being, 'did not', as Newman himself said, 'warm or enlighten him,' or 'take away the winter of his desolation'. Despite their formidable array, their marches and campaigns, the army of the ontological, teleological, cosmological arguments has no victories inscribed upon its banners. Man asks for a helper. and it is the existence of an ever-present help in time of trouble that is in doubt. An enormous deception, an ugly insincerity infects this whole region of debate. Among the theologians you have Pantheism with a Christian varnish, and among the philosophers a 'darkness visible' no eye can pierce. You have the 'polite atheism' of Spinoza, for whom God is nature, and who yet calls upon his fellow creatures to love and worship this insensate power, a power as unconscious of their existence as the palm tree of the poet who sings its praise, and, still more absurdly, of its own existence. Conscious man prostrates himself before an unconscious God, unaware of the worship. What kind of bastard piety is this?

'Never propose to thyself', said Donne, 'such a God as thou wert not bound to imitate.' Yet once for all discard you may, and must, the doctrine that the God of love can be established by arguments, can be either proved or disproved. The only God of whom you can be sure is the God given in your own experience —'sure of the thing,' as Jeremy Taylor phrased it, 'though not sure of the argument'. Experience dispenses with proof; proof rests upon, and can rest upon nothing else than experiences, which speak for themselves. Is beauty ever in need of demonstration, or is goodness? Religion, like poetry, music and painting, requires an organ of vision. You may have a mathematical genius like Newton, or a musical genius like Bach, or a religious genius like St. Francis, or a poetic genius like Virgil, or a genius for action like Napoleon. You may also without genius have an appreciation of such things. The discovery of poetry is man's discovery, the discovery of music is man's discovery. The discovery of religion and morals are his discoveries. *Est Deus in nobis.* There is no other revelation than the revelation of his own soul. And what is the implication of these discoveries? That in the soul itself resides a divine principle of which these are the fruits. Like music and poetry, religion provides its own justification, like them is witness to its own worth. If I am happy, do I hurry round to the psychologists to assure me that it is so, that I am in fact happy? They are much more likely to assure me that I am miserable, and make me so. If you experience in a picture, a poem, a sonata, or in the companionship of a friend a sense of pleasure, or contentment or joy, should you make haste to consult the Royal Society whether in fact you have had or are justified in having any such experience? I do not advise it. You will be plunged in doubt, and presently—debauched by dialectic—cease to believe it. Men are mad enough, yet scarcely so mad as to indulge in such exalted lunacies. If you find, as millions have found, in thoughts of God, in prayer and worship a support and consolation, what more can arguments do for you? The power of religion to confer happiness, to give peace, has abundant testimony in its favour.

> Your music's power your music must disclose,
> For what light is 'tis only light that shows.

Definitions of God are not so much perilous as they are insane. Define God? As well attempt to place a ladder against the sky. He is incomprehensible, and if comprehensible were no longer God. 'We can know', as St. Augustine said, 'what God is not, but we cannot know what He is.' And though the intellect delights to try its wings in the ambient air of speculation, 'tis too chill and nipping for the soul. To enquire further for a better understanding into the nature of divine Being is to gaze at the sun. The greater the light the more the pupil of the eye contracts; it dazzles, and the excess of light becomes a darkness. Nor is there any value in a belief which fails to move us, which we accept without interest and go our ways without recalling. Only those which inflame the spirit have any virtue, or are worthy to be called beliefs at all, and the wise man holds by the faith which provides for him the strongest incentive to living, and rouses his highest powers.

How slippery is the ground over which we have travelled! So confused are we in these times amid the hubbub of contending voices that we have almost come to believe, in Fontenelle's words, that 'everything is possible, and everybody is right'. Can we be sure of anything? Yes, we may be sure that there are such things as obsolete and superannuated ideas, that have served their turn, and are no longer useful. And to quarrel with the conditions of existence, to crucify yourself, to look upon resignation as the key to religion are among them. There are also others. That either God or man must somehow be held to blame for the human situation, that the Fall of Man was the great aboriginal catastrophe—of these incoherent doctrines nothing can be made. What can be substituted? Well, there are alternatives. If we were to interpret the so-called Fall of Man as a fortunate rather than a lamentable occurrence, if we were to call it rather his coming of age, the moment at which he took upon himself his natural duties and responsibilities, matters might begin to wear a sensibly brighter appearance. If it were regarded as the moment at which a world of finite creatures came into being, providing for them a field of enterprise, we might look upon ourselves with less pity together with greater interest and respect. If we were to substitute for the idea of a lost paradise, in which there was no room for activity, since nothing could be done there without impairing its everlasting perfection, for the idea of human beings loitering for ever through fields of asphodel, the idea of a more honourable rôle assigned them, and a more adventurous journey through the Cosmos, and of the world as a family estate left us to do with as we please, if we could substitute for the thought of ourselves as timid children in a well-regulated nursery the conception of a resolute company of men, a band of vikings, standing on their own feet, and no longer afraid of what time or change might bring—would these be impious or dangerous thoughts? 'Why stand we here', enquired Blake, 'trembling around, calling on God for help, and not ourselves in whom God dwells?' To die upon the last rampart for the cause he holds most dear is the happiest death for any man. Or can you tell me of a better?

The gods may be interested to see what we can make of the world; and our business seems to be to make it what we should like it to be, if—as is not, indeed, impossible—we may have, ourselves, to return to it.   We must do our best, and yet not expect too much either of ourselves or our fellow creatures.   *Die Zeit ist unendlich lang*, and the journey no doubt will be a chequered one.   If we are foolish and stupid, it will make it all the easier to become wiser; if, as is certain, we are far from perfect, there will be all the more room for improvement.   And if it be asked, 'What assurance have we of final victory?' I answer, 'They are not soldiers who require to be assured of it before taking the field.' 'Upon the night-view of the world', as Fechner wrote, 'a day-view must follow, which will give foundation to the view of the natural man—not contradict it.'   The natural man?   Yes, he must be accepted.   And with him we must accept the things of time.   'All that the earth provides we must like'—'Nothing is superfluous, nothing is to be rejected.'   We must build on what we know and have, making of human experience and history a foundation for our efforts and ideals.   And if it be not our positive duty to give currency to the ideas in which we believe, to give them enduring form, to ensure their acceptance for the good of future generations, to fight for them, 'to adorn our Sparta'—if this be not our duty, I for my part cannot tell you where our duty is to be sought.

XIV

THE LAWS OF GOD, THE LAWS OF MAN

Make laws as though all men were good: the wicked triumph, the good are crushed. Make laws as though all men were evil: the wicked slip through them or circumvent them. Only the good obey them and suffer.

Maeterlinck

Moralists distinguish Magnanimity and Modesty by making the one the desire of greater, the other of less and inferior, honours. But in my apprehension there is more in Magnanimity. It includes all that belongs to a Great Soul: a high and mighty courage, an invincible Patience, an immoveable Grandeur which is above the reach of injuries, a contempt of all little and feeble enjoyments, and a certain kind of majesty that is conversant with great things; a high and lofty frame of spirit, allied with the sweetness of Courtesy and Respect; a deep and stable resolution founded on humility without any baseness; an infinite hope and a vast desire; a Divine, profound, uncontrollable sense of one's own capacity; a generous confidence, and a great inclination to heroical deeds; all these conspire to complete it, with a severe and mighty expectation of Bliss incomprehensible.

Traherne

XIV

THE LAWS OF GOD, THE LAWS OF MAN

Let us now adventure for an hour upon the still-vexed waters of
ethical theory, turn, that is, from the professors of knowledge, who tell us what we should believe, to the professors
of conduct, who tell us what we should do—and why. If you
have any hopes that they are likely to prove less peremptory with
us, you must, I fear, lay those hopes aside. The professors of
conduct have been in the main austere men, seldom genial, com-
placent or humorous. They have dealt more often in censure
than in praise. They have been for the most part men who prescribed for themselves a rigorous discipline, and, believing that
their fellows were at least equally in need of it, advocated the
same mode of life for their neighbours.

We have seen that the theologians have their troubles. The
moralists, too, have theirs, and you may be sure no slight ones.
'To preach morality is easy,' remarked Schopenhauer, 'to find a
foundation for morality is hard.' If philosophers agree upon anything they agree that the conduct of men is a matter of supreme
consequence. Good behaviour is the cement of society. Without it there neither is nor can be safety or order in the world.
How then is this desirable behaviour to be secured and maintained? Laws can of course be enacted and enforced, but on
what principle? Religion, true or false, with its attendant beliefs in God and a world to come, has been, on the whole, if not
its only, at least we may believe, a stout bulwark of morality.
With the decay of religion and its sanctions it becomes an urgent
question what can take its place, what support for ethics of equal
efficacy, indeed of any efficacy, can be substituted. To find a
basis for morality is a pressing necessity, but, as Schopenhauer said,
by no means easy.

And there is the further distressing enquiry which Sidgwick, a
professor of moral philosophy, put to himself—'the question,

281

whether to profess ethics without a basis?' 'It is beyond a doubt', wrote Pascal, 'that the mortality or the immortality of the soul must make an entire difference in morals; yet philosophers have treated morality as independent of the question. They discuss to pass the time.' This great man, you may think, exaggerates, yet a difference of some kind it must surely make. And Pascal is not alone in his opinion. 'In order that it may be concluded by a universal demonstration that everything honourable is beneficial, and that everything base is hurtful,' said Leibniz, 'we must assume the immortality of the soul, and the Ruler of the Universe, God.' Do you desire further testimony? Listen, then, to Rousseau. 'If the Deity does not exist, only the ill-disposed can be said to reason, the good are without sense.' Add still another from the numerous witnesses who might be called into court in support of Pascal's contention. Here is that of a living scholar and thinker, Mr. Joseph: 'It seems to me that as long as we hold the world and what happens in it really to be what physical science takes it for, we cannot talk the language of ethics, and must jettison conduct.'[1]

Would you be surprised to hear that this opinion, held by many men of the highest intelligence—the opinion that outside religion no firm basis for morals can be found—excites in others the utmost exasperation and repugnance? Who can they be? you enquire. I will tell you. They are the ethical idealists, who though they have nothing to say either upon immortality or a moral Governor of the universe, yet perceive the necessity—if human society is to be preserved from destruction—the crying need for moral standards. Do not be misled by their zeal for righteousness. It does not arise from any concern for the final destiny of the race. It arises from the gnawing, though undisclosed, anxiety, the well-grounded alarm that, religion apart, no binding laws, no well-knit principles of human conduct can be discovered. With them religion is valued, though they themselves dispense with it, for the support it lends to goodness and virtue. They would identify religion with ethics, make it, as Arnold did, 'morality touched with emotion,' seeing in good behaviour, as they think, the supreme interest of mankind, and the absolute pivot of civilisation. They tremble at the thought of the chaos that would accompany its disappearance, a wintry season for the virtues, and the final de-

[1]*Some Problems of Ethics*, p. 39.

moralisation of society, whose stability is their one, and, indeed, only concern.

For this reason the ethical idealists will go so far as to remain silent upon—even countenance—a creed they believe false, yield that pawn that they may win the queen. They are aware that human beings live long in the atmosphere of a faith which has lost its vitality, and with a physician's arts would prolong the life of a patient they believe to be in *articulo mortis*. Nietzsche ridiculed 'the English shallow-pates', who when they abandoned the Christian God illogically retained Christian morality; but what were they to do, if they could find no other?

Let me recall to you a moving poem by Matthew Arnold, which has for its subject the story told by Herodotus of a young king of Egypt, the best and justest of its rulers. To him came an oracle, foretelling that he had but six years more to live and reign. Was this, he asked himself, the recompense of the gods for virtuous living and duty done,—

> When on the strenuous just man Heaven bestows,
> Crown of his struggling life, an unjust close.
>
> Oh, wherefore cheat our youth, if thus it be,
> Of one short joy, one lust, one pleasant dream:
> Stringing vain words of powers we cannot see,
> Blind divinations of a will supreme;
> Lost labour! when the circumambient gloom
> But hides, if gods, gods careless of our doom?

And as he ponders the iniquity or indifference of the celestial powers, the young king resolves to throw aside the duties and the cares of state, and, in a forest retreat he loved, to give, with a group of friends, the brief remaining years to revelry and sensuous delights.

> Here came the King, holding high feast, at morn,
> Rose-crown'd; and ever when the sun went down
> A hundred lamps beam'd in the tranquil gloom,
> From tree to tree all through the twinkling grove,
> Revealing all the tumult of the feast—
> Flush'd guests, and golden goblets foam'd with wine;
> While the deep-burnished foliage overhead
> Splinter'd the silver arrows of the moon.

'And why not?' If you have the courage to utter the words, be prepared for the tempest of moral indignation that will burst

283

over your head. The best of men dislike being driven into a corner, and since there is absolutely no answer to this 'why not?' it is only natural that it should exasperate the ethical idealists. Nothing in their view approaches ethics in importance, and some means therefore of controlling the natural impulses of men is the imperative of imperatives. Yet where in the absence of religion to look for the authority to enforce upon human beings the binding moral principles?—how, indeed, to show that such principles exist, or are in any way binding at all?—there you have the unanswered riddle. There you have 'the philosopher's stone', the gem of price which has been sought with diligence, with anxiety, even with desperation, yet alas, also in vain.

Probably upon no subject ever discussed through the length and breadth of the globe has there been expended a fiercer hubbub of words than upon this—the foundations of morality. 'Why should I ask God to make me good when I want to be naughty?' asked the little girl. All the wise men of the world are put to silence by this childish query. A parliament of philosophers will not resolve it. When we set out in search of an answer we are, like the rebel angels in Milton's Pandemonium, 'in wand'ring mazes lost'. 'Pleasure is empty,' say the Puritans; 'it passes away.' Ah, yes, but the ascetic as well as the reveller goes, and who has the best of the bargain?

During an illness towards the close of his life Voltaire was visited by a priest, who summoned him to confession. 'From whom do you come?' enquired the sick man. 'From God,' was the reply. When Voltaire desired to see his visitor's credentials, the priest could go no further and withdrew. Is the moralist in better case? Unhappily no; he is in worse. He cannot speak in the name of any church, any accredited body of opinion, but only in his own. How many moral systems are there? It will take you some time to count them.

If philosophers have been suspected of lip service to religion in order to obtain its support in the service of morals, rulers of states have come under a similar suspicion. The gods they considered a useful fiction, and faith in them to be encouraged among their subjects. If gods did not exist it would have been necessary to invent them—or something else to take their place. Whatever else goes, the moral law must be preserved, and no harm if in the regalia of religion it could be made to look more imposing.

284

Otherwise the State itself had to be dressed up to look like God; in some cases presenting no very engaging or convincing portrait. Of this pious fraud even Plato was suspect. In his anxiety for righteousness he mingled, it was said, myths in his writings, inducing men to fancy that their conduct in this life might affect their fortunes in a life to come. Was Kant free from Plato's dread that in their own interests men might stray from the path of virtue? He, too, appears to have suffered from similar apprehensions, and gave to the moral imperative a higher certainty in the universe than God or immortality. They were postulates, far from demonstrable truths. Postulates cost nothing; postulates are cheap. There is no harm in postulates. But the moral law, the 'I ought, therefore, I can', could not safely be left in the air. It was raised to the dignity of an unchallengeable proposition, enthroned in awful majesty above the very gods themselves, immutable and eternal. Such was Kant's uneasiness lest in the interminable flux all foothold for virtue might be lost, that, as Schopenhauer said, he hurried back to the Decalogue, and took over the inviolable law, the categorical imperative, from the Mosaic tables of stone.

Lest men might be precipitated into the abyss, lest they might do as they pleased—from this frightful prospect even the most hardened rationalists recoil in consternation. Ethics are the sheet anchor of the Cosmos. In their view the world might get along pretty comfortably without God, but without rules of conduct it would become a total wreck. So perilous is the situation that in the attempt to find an indestructible basis for conduct even philosophers will flout every law of logic, and torture words out of every vestige of meaning. Listen to Socrates, the most admirable and most lovable of men. 'No evil', he told his judges, 'can befall a good man, neither in this life nor in that which is to come.' What meaning can be attached to these words? His statement is certainly false if the word 'evil' be used in the sense it has invariably borne throughout the whole of history, in all times and in every language under the sun. 'No evil can befall a good man.' How interesting a discovery! A good man, therefore, has never suffered in mind or body, never been bereaved of friends or children, never sickened at the sight of cruelty or injustice, at the miseries of the innocent. Epictetus talks in the same lofty strain. The good man is known by his complete indifference to all experiences of this kind. May we not say to Socrates and Epictetus, 'My good friends, we cannot sufficiently admire your constancy, your noble sentiments, but we should have preferred you to use words in a human and intelligible sense. And have you considered the case of the simple souls, or of children? Have they never suffered? Have evils never befallen them? Have they never been bewildered by misery they could not understand, never wept in the desolation of their gentle hearts? No doubt, like you, they should have reflected that all was well with them, that they were not in any way afflicted, and like you should have remained serene in the consciousness of their virtue. We fear, my dear Socrates and Epictetus, that it was hardly possible for them, and that in your commendable zeal for good conduct you have outstripped your wonderful wisdom, for which you have been so justly celebrated.'

To save morality men will deny the plainest facts, and cry out in horror against truths of which the whole world is vividly aware as indisputable. 'Everyone admits', wrote Machiavelli, 'how praiseworthy it is in princes to keep faith, and to live with integrity, and not with craft. Nevertheless our experience has been that those princes who have done great things have held good faith of little account, and have known how to circumvent the intellect of men by craft, and in the end have overcome those who have placed reliance on their word.' No historian would dare to contradict that bold assertion. Yet for his frank utterance of this, and similar irrefutable truths, Machiavelli has been execrated as a monster, and his name coupled with the Prince of Darkness. Schiller went a step further than Machiavelli. 'Not a single example can be shown of a people,' said he, 'where a high level and a wide universality of aesthetic culture went hand in hand with political freedom and civic virtue, or where beautiful manners went with good morals, or polished behaviour with truth.' We are, you see, still in the region of the contraries, of conflicting ideals. As the child is born of two parents, so the world of the two opposites. They make their way into the very heart of Christian doctrine.

Many Christians, like Pascal and Luther, held that the ethical ideal is irreconcilable with the religious—in our day a strange idea. They saw in the attachment to conduct as supreme a great danger, equivalent in their eyes to the doctrine of salvation by works, instead of by the grace of God alone. The moralists, they held, had set up a false god, the god of the heathen, in the place of the true and living God. And, however you permit yourself to confuse the issue, religion and ethics, though in the interests of the latter frequently identified, are, in their essence, poles apart.

For, in the first place, ethics never lifts its eyes from the present scene; it is earthbound, and thinks only of the prosperity and security of our daily lives. Society and its institutions are the sole objects of its interest and concern. Regard for the rule, which is ethics, and regard for the person, which is religion, are widely separated and often irreconcilable interests. The law, or the rule, knows no friends, cherishes no affectionate solicitude for the human soul, and offers no consolation to the individual man, 'created sick, commanded to be whole.' It presents, and must present to all alike, and at all times, an inflexible countenance. For the particular person it has not a spark of consideration. Whatever his heredity, environment, circumstances, the law is the law. For it the individual is a mere abstraction, and the community or State the true and only reality. The soul of the sinner, your soul or mine, has for ethics no more relevance than the sparks that fly upward. It has never heard of souls, and has nothing to do with them, if they happen to exist.

Religion, on the other hand, or so it claims, is based upon an affection for humanity. It extends hope, consolation and encouragement to weak and suffering mortals. It has pity for man in his outcast state, and for it, as St. Augustine will tell you, the individual human creature outweighs in his infinite preciousness all other values that can be placed in the scale against him. For religion man's destiny is the supreme issue. And who can dwell exclusively upon the faults of a beloved person, or be indifferent to his distresses or his fate? But the categorical imperative—is it kind? Does it minister to you in disease, or visit you in prison? Does it care whether you come to your end upon the gallows, or descend into hell? Is it prepared to do anything for you? Have you ever heard that the categorical imperative at any time offered anyone a drink, even so much as a cup of cold water? It is, then, neither human nor divine. I think perhaps that the best thing to do with the categorical imperative is to banish it to an uninhabited island, where it can contemplate throughout eternity its own unapproachable perfection.

It is told of Edmund Burke that upon one occasion he gave a shilling to a beggar. A young lady in his company ventured to remonstrate, remarking that it would probably be spent on gin. 'Madam,' said Burke, 'he is an old man, and if gin be his comfort, let him have gin.' How disrespectful to the categorical imperative! I share Burke's disrespect for it. I prefer the dictates of human kindness.

And this imperative, so famous and so awe-inspiring, does it in fact assist you to a knowledge of what is right in a particular time and place? Its secret is like that of the British Constitution. No one can tell you what it prescribes. You object that I have forgotten its single comprehensive behest—'So act that your action can be universalised, can apply to all men in a similar situation.' Very exalted, yes, and very useless. How many men throughout the whole history of humanity ever employed such a formula? And, unfortunately, in this vexing world situations are invariably unique, never exactly repeat themselves in respect of place, time, circumstances and the persons affected by them. Nor can any rule be framed applicable to a course of conduct in any and all circumstances, times and places. The touchstone of values is not everywhere among men the same. When Mrs. Rosita Forbes visited the penitentiary at San Paulo, she asked if there were many thieves among the inmates. The warder was shocked. 'Oh, no,' he replied, 'Brazilians are very honest. Nearly all these men are murderers.'

The ethical idealists, Puritans without being Christians, search without ceasing for the book entitled *The Eternal Law*. In these days of religious apathy they have their golden opportunity. Let them produce its credentials. They insist that it derives from a source higher than high heaven, that it came into existence at the same moment as the world itself, and is as old and fixed as the stars in their courses. The assertion has often been made. Well, let them now prove it. Never was there greater need. Nature will not, however, come to their aid. Is nature concerned whether we wash or not, have good manners or not, keep our promises or not? Is nature, or any principle in nature, concerned whether we are ambitious or not, musical or not, humorous or not? He has something on his hands who sets out to prove her preferences in such matters. Let us go further. Is she concerned if we live by thieving or honest toil, are pitiful or cruel, have many love affairs, few or none, prefer sport to study, delight in war, hunting, adventure, or shudder at them? She makes men of every pattern, and sends her rain upon the just and unjust alike. People talk as if nature should be better pleased with good than with bad men, as we judge good and bad. But they are equally her children, as are the fish of the sea and the fowls of the air— her creation, owing all they are and have to her bounty. We may well, indeed, extend our reverence to saints and heroes, but nature neither reveres nor admires. How could we think it possible? She creates saints, heroes, reverences and admirations, even gives birth to creatures that we, from our human standpoint, view, it may be, with abhorrence and disgust.

There is in all this no slight cause for amazement and bewildered dread of the world and life. Are we to trust the heart or the intellect, for they do not understand each other, and speak a different language? As you cannot prove the existence of a benevolent God, so you cannot prove the values of goodness or beauty. The testimony to God, goodness and beauty are in the affections of your own heart. In this pass ethics will not serve you. For ethics the battle is lost before it is joined. Ethics is in arms against the will-to-live, and proposes to cut off the right hand with the left. Ethics does not so much as attempt an explanation of things as we find them. It throws no light upon the great mystery. It cannot even produce its own birth certificate. Curious, is it not? that morality, as Plato, Sophocles and Cicero observed, never intrudes into our dreams. Nor does it make life worth living, or shed over it a beam of cheerfulness. It gives to the weary no encouragement. Is life a prison, and were we born to go about in fetters? Was man made for the Sabbath, for the sake of obeying the law? How utterly tiresome and unprofitable, then, is existence. The very word 'ethics' seems to cast a gloom over the human spirit. Is it necessary to have this skeleton at the feast? Is it necessary to enthrone a tyrant over us in order to be just and honest and friendly? We do it no honour, nor honour to the human race, when we distress ourselves over the foundations and future of goodness. While the human soul endures it will not perish out of the earth; commanded, however, it will not be. Not law, but love, say the poets. Friendliness is as natural as self-love. 'I see no difference', said Leopardi, 'between kindliness and what is called virtue.' Virtue is friendliness, an attempt to see our neighbours' point of view, to radiate cheerfulness, to make them happy. Blake saw very clearly that there is no such thing as general benevolence. Virtue in the abstract is a vain thing. There are only particular acts of kindness, personal, of a certain date and time, and the sooner we cease to think of virtue as separable from such actions the better.

There is an incident in the life of Socrates rarely recalled by the moralists. I quote Lecky's account of it. 'In one of the most remarkable of his pictures of Greek life Xenophon describes how Socrates, having heard of the beauty of the courtesan Theodota, went with his disciples to ascertain for himself whether the report was true; how with a quiet humour he questioned her about the sources of the luxury of her dwelling, and how he proceeded to sketch for her the qualities she should cultivate in order to attach her lovers. She ought, he tells her, to shut the door against the insolent, to watch her lovers in sickness, to rejoice greatly when they succeed in anything honourable, to love tenderly those who love her. Having carried on a cheerful and perfectly unembarrassed conversation with her, with no kind of reproach on his part, either expressed or implied, and with no trace either of the timidity or effrontery of conscious guilt upon hers, the best and wisest of the Greeks left his hostess with a graceful compliment to her beauty.'[1]

But for the impulse towards kindness already seated in the human heart the talkers talk in vain. Were it not already in our nature, as well imagine you could impart valour to a stone, or humour to an alligator, as plant it there. Nor will debate, however prolonged, determine whether the universe has claims upon our obedience, or deserves our affection. Have the gods a case against mankind, or mankind against the gods? Has the human race done wrong or suffered wrong? In this world of the opposites no deeper fissure has divided opinion. Men there have been in whom a sense of their sinfulness, of unworthiness to stand in God's presence has overwhelmed all other thoughts, and men there have also been of a wholly different fibre, in whom indignation took the place of penitence, and resentment of reverence—indignation and resentment that we poor pawns upon the chess board of existence should be subjected by the tyranny of heaven to lifelong miseries, and yet called upon to obey and worship our per-

[1]W. E. H. Lecky's *History of European Morals*, ii, p. 296.

290

secutor. Indignant such men have been that to the burden of life, hard enough to bear, there should be added the burden of the moral law, from which other creatures are free. For there is this matter of justice, which the theologians and moralists are prone to overlook, not the justice between man and man, but the justice due from heaven for men in the grasp of fate. Since they find it difficult to secure from the gods, is it surprising that they endeavour to secure it for themselves? And will you blame them for the disorders that follow? Is it better to see injustice done, or suffer it in one's own person, than attempt to redress it? The world is no mirror of justice. If men cannot find justice in the courts of heaven, you will not persuade them to accept God as their judge. An unjust God has nothing divine about him.

Before the Oriental despot men prostrated themselves in the dust. His might was right, and their God was made in his image. They saw nothing strange in his caprices, his tyranny or injustice. The Greek had a prouder heart and thought differently. Power was not in his eyes a synonym for justice. The despotism of the East met at Marathon, at Salamis and Plataea, men who would not consent to live in bondage. The Oriental stands for peace at the price of submission, the Greek for freedom at the price of combat. Take your choice, remembering that it is the choice between the slave and the freeman.

To me it sometimes seems that our moralists would do well to cease their upbraidings and apply themselves to the interesting problem—'How is goodness to be made the object of passionate desire, as attractive as fame, success, or even adventure?' If they could excite in men an enthusiasm for virtue, as the poets, musicians and artists excite in them enthusiasm for beauty, and the men of science for truth; if they could devise a morality that had power to charm, they would win all hearts. 'To be virtuous', said Aristotle, 'is to take pleasure in noble actions.' A poet does not tell you how happiness is to be secured, he gives you happiness. And our reformers might do a great service to humanity if they could explain to us why a diet of milk and water does not appear to suit the human race, why the milksop has never been the hero of the romancers, why the biographies of the peace-makers lack readers, why the lives of dare-devils, of buccaneers and smugglers and all manner of wild men captivate the youthful souls, the young folk so recently—if we are to believe

Plato and Wordsworth—arrived from heaven, trailing clouds of glory from their celestial home. There is a mystery for them, upon which to exercise their wits. Why should courage and reckless daring, even the adroitness and cunning of Ulysses, not conspicuously moral qualities, so entertain and delight us? Why, as Luther enquired, should the devil have all the best tunes? If the moralists made these obscure matters clear to us, they would earn our thanks. 'He had too much spirit to be a scholar,' said Aubrey. Must we add another to the commandments, 'Thou shalt not have high spirits'? Are we to put a premium upon low vitality? Something appears to have gone amissing in our moral code. Repression, renunciation, resignation, we have heard of their values and recognise their values. But how dispiriting, how slavish as a panacea for our ills! Mankind in these days appears in need of more rather than less life, of resolution, high-heartedness, and the star of hope in the heavens. If you desire to serve rather than desert the world, you must avoid the attempt to quench the flame of life, to destroy the energies nature has implanted in the race. You take the wrong path. You should make use of them, divert or deflect them to nobler ends, harness them to the chariot of your ideal. And not till we have rid ourselves of the monstrous notion that the sole human motive is self-interest need we hope to lay the foundations of a sane moral philosophy.

And something seems to have gone amiss with our ethics if the brightest proposal it can at the moment offer as a shining goal is either to turn ourselves to stone, as the Stoics advised, or accept some kind of human ant-heap or beehive as the model for the future human commonwealth, a recommendation to go back to the insects for our instruction—a miserable, an ignoble *Wiederverthierung*—and achieve a harmony by the enslavement of the individual. Men are to accept serfdom for the sake of peace and quiet, the content of the dungeon, where you have regular meals, and are in no danger from robbers. It is an agreeable prospect. For my part I should be much surprised and disappointed in my fellow creatures were they so poor in spirit as to prefer plenty in servitude to freedom with a diet of herbs, were they prepared to accept the 'base, dishonourable, vile submission', to lose all dignity and stateliness in their outlook upon both life and death. Time will tell. But when you hear these proposals made,

Then loosen the sword in the scabbard and settle the helm on thy
head,
For men betrayed are mighty, and great are the wrongfully dead.

We have no reason to believe 'God is a merely moral Being',
says Dean Inge. Certainly it were a giant folly so to contract
our vision, to suppose that regulations for human traffic through
the crowded world were the Be-all and the End-all of things, the
sum of existence, the sole aim and purpose of the illimitable
universe. No one thing is everything, and 'goodness', as Bradley
wrote, 'is not absolute or ultimate; it is but one side, one partial
aspect of the nature of things.' Virtue is indeed adorable, but
there is also truth, there is intelligence, there is strength, there is
grandeur, there is humour, there is magnanimity. There are
even such things as good scenery, good art, good health and good
looks—all worth some consideration, or the human race has been
much deceived. Why should we refuse to admit the infinite
complexity, the innumerable windows through which the soul
may view the astonishing landscape? Heaven save us from the
blindness of single vision, from the philosopher's confined to the
intellectual, the naturalist's to the physical, the moralist's to the
ethical, the artist's to the aesthetic view—

> Great God, I'd rather be
> A pagan suckled in a creed outworn:
> So might I, standing on this pleasant lea,
> Have glimpses that would make me less forlorn;
> Have sight of Proteus rising from the sea,
> Or hear old Triton blow his wreathèd horn.

There is not, never was and never will be a perfect world. A
perfect world there cannot be, yet an improving world is possible
and even probable; and as an unweeded garden may yet contain a
luxuriance of flower and fruit and fragrance, so an imperfect
world like ours may well contain ten thousand types of excel-
lence, of perfect or well-nigh perfect things—days, hours and
seasons to content the heart, beauty in nature, beauty in art,
splendour in man, in faith, in courage, in honour, in friends and
lovers. 'Tis our grief we cannot have them all together, and for
ever. Were that possible their values would vanish. Their
perfections would be without a foil, and we should pray for rain
and storms to diversify the celestial weather. The human soul
delights to walk in the dark as well as in the sunlit avenues. And

only infants in reflection could suppose that the warfare in which, whether we like it or not, we never lay down the sword, not even the 'pacifists', is the simple warfare between good and evil. Every good casts its dark shadow, every good is the enemy of another good. One type of perfection, one ideal, however exalted, is attainable only by the sacrifice of another. You cannot on the same site and at the same time erect a Greek temple in all its divine loveliness and a Gothic minster in its equally divine loveliness. The ascetic virtues cannot flourish side by side with the social and domestic. If you choose to be an anchorite you cannot be a statesman. A hermit can know nothing of love or friendship, nor can the social worker devote his strength to the advancement of knowledge. Contradictions swarm in the very air we breathe. And the world's sensitive and tired souls sicken at them, and avert their eyes, forgetting that the contradictions have given us a world to live in, and that we owe to them our birth and being.

I think ideas are the most mysterious things in a mysterious world. Not so long ago men were convinced that science would save us, or universal suffrage would save us, or education for everyone would save us. Now it is universal peace that will bring about the millennium. *O sancta simplicitas!* During the Middle Ages, the ages of the soul, men believed in God, in themselves as sinful and in need of salvation. They had no doctrine of progress, never supposed that by any human efforts could the world be saved. They put their trust in their Creator and a better world to come. Then arrived the Renaissance with a new and captivating bundle of ideas, which exalted the European mind to an ecstasy of delight. The previous ideas were amusingly crude and mistaken. Here at last was the final truth. Man was not by nature sinful, and consequently not in need of salvation. God was an unnecessary hypothesis. No other world than the present existed, which could by the proper use of reason be transformed by human exertions into an earthly paradise.

How unforeseen and startling are the alterations in opinion, how strange these secular revolutions! What changes in heaven or earth, you ask, or in the conditions of human life brought about this remarkable revolution? You may well ask. No change of any kind in the natural world. The sun and stars rose and set as they had ever done. The winds blew and ocean rolled; calms and tempests succeeded each other; heat and cold, health and disease, joy and sorrow, birth and death—all the circumstances of human life remained unaltered. The change, the astonishing transformation took place in the inner world of the mind or heart of humanity. An idea, a faith was inexplicably born. A thought took shape, and went forth conquering and to conquer. We talk of the origin of cultures and civilisations, but where have new and happy, or for that matter misleading thoughts their origin? Are they whispered by the winds, or do their seeds fall out of some other planet to take root in the soil of our souls? I find the origin of ideas as perplexing as the origin of mutations or species. They exhibit a similar suddenness. They are beyond prediction. They appear to have a life of their own, independent of space and time, and to come and go at their own good pleasure. 'A passion', said Hume, 'is an original existence.' We have natural histories of plants and animals, but the natural history of ideas remains to be written. It should be done. For they are living and powerful entities of some kind, and as infective as fevers. Some, like flowers, are the creatures of an hour; others of a prodigious vitality, root themselves, like oaks, in the soil of human nature for a thousand years. Ideas, like individuals, live and die. They flourish, according to their nature, in one soil or climate, and droop in another. They are the vegetation of the mental world.

Certain ideas go by the family name of concepts. What is a concept? It is an image or picture by which we endeavour to make things clearer to ourselves, or, as we say, to understand them. They are postulates, or lanterns, and have in science an instrumental value. But in regard to these postulates men of science have made the important discovery that you must not trust them too long or too completely. They are useful servants but bad masters. Unless periodically examined they may lead you astray. And in science, when her concepts, her working hypotheses cease to keep in step with observed facts they are ruthlessly discharged. I submit we might do well to follow the example of our scientific friends, and enquire whether a number of the concepts which have so long dominated ethical and religious thought are not in need of revision. Whether, for instance, when religion committed itself, in one breath, and with no distinctions drawn, to a denunciation of 'the world, the flesh and the devil', and ethics set forth to war down the will-to-live, they were not involved in fixations of thought, whose day was done, and in need of other and more encouraging concepts. It is certainly possible to go about in self-imposed fetters, and 'drag at each remove a lengthening chain'. It is certainly true that in the light of a new concept a situation may be transformed and wear a different countenance. Unexpected possibilities may be revealed, and a wholly new prospect come into view. And when a choice is offered, we should without hesitation exchange the thought that narrows and restricts for the thought that enlarges and stimulates the mind.

'I think', said Conrad, 'that the proper wisdom is to will what the gods will.' I would go further. I would say that to love life is to love the gods, and that in obeying the will-to-live we are fulfilling divine orders. Or why else is the instinct to be found in all creatures as they set forth on their great expedition? No doubt we are beset with difficulties. There are other beings in the world beside ourselves, to whom the same orders have been issued. The opportunity is the greater to exercise our brains. Birth is the sudden opening of a window, through which you look out upon a stupendous prospect. For what has happened? A miracle. You have exchanged nothing for the possibility of everything. This everything is, however, a bare possibility, and to implement it demands all the powers of body, mind and spirit at their highest tension. In life, the gift of the gods, you have in your hands the master key which unlocks all the doors of the universe. Existence has this advantage over non-existence: it denies nothing, and leaves room for experiences beyond imagining. The gods deal lavishly in surprises, and will spring, I fancy, a good many more on us. There will be misadventures and mischances among them, for existence is an oxymel, a bitter sweet. Yet an exhilaration accompanies all creatures, a zest for living wells up in them from the profoundest depths of being, which it is too monstrous a contradiction to suppose that nature or nature's God intended them to suppress or deny. We have energies, nature has seen to that. But upon what are they to be expended? That she appears to have left to us.

The connoisseurs of misery interpret the pervasive melancholy which also accompanies existence as a regret that ever they were born. I am not skilled in this variety of metaphysical diagnosis.

Do not forget, however, that if its pains exceeded its pleasures no life could endure. Do not forget that nature distributes her buffets: they are neither continuous nor cumulative, and have even their medicinal values. Our *de-luxe* pessimists, who have personally little to complain of, take upon their shoulders, omitting its satisfactions, the wretchedness of the whole creation, and find it an insupportable burden. You may judge them right. You may declare the cost of living too high. You may proclaim a surrender of individual consciousness, and re-absorption in the whole the finale to be most desired. Very possibly nature may meet your wishes. She has no need for, and no liking for unwilling recruits, and enrolls none but volunteers for the endless adventure. Let those who fear wounds, toils, sufferings, go their way and be for ever at rest. But how many, were the choice allowed them, would refuse another life?

This recurring mood of the soul is, we have seen, itself one of the contraries, the night which contradicts and yet is followed by the day. Give to the pessimist youth and health, a spring morning and a lover, and his mood will change. He will consent to postpone extinction, he will cling to the excruciating wheel of existence a little longer. With the present generation any form of optimism is, of course, a mere synonym for stupidity. How many writers of our time have made the discovery that the world is not wholly charming, that life is brutal, tiresome and vulgar, and that no decent person should have been invited to so squalid a party? How clever they are and how vocal! They display their cleverness by asking for better bread than can be made from wheat. It was, moreover, at their birth that intelligence entered the world. They first discovered that there were tears in mortal things, and go about pluming themselves upon their superior penetration. But neither their grandmothers, nor their great-grandmothers, though they wrote fewer books, were as ignorant as they suppose. They, too, knew something about life. There were, as the poet said, many brave men before Agamemnon, and there will be other brave men, and as clever as our contemporaries, born after them. And part of their cleverness will consist in making another discovery—that they can take it or leave it; and still another, that neither lamentation nor sneers are of much assistance, so that it would be wiser to save your breath to cool your porridge.

The struggle for existence?　What need further to dwell upon it?　Or of the struggle with nature, never ending, for a little bread and water?　True it is that

Not for golden fancies do iron truths make room.

Life, we know, has a double edge.　But neither science nor philosophy has put into our hands the touchstone whereby these iron truths can be distinguished.　And what, indeed, is truth, what goodness, and what beauty?　These, as I think, are among the things we have to discover.　Who has defined them for us, despite the cataract of words with which the world is deluged? The soul of man is not yet awake, not by millenniums.　And his religious and ethical codes are no more than stammering efforts to speak a language imperfectly known.　They reflect, indeed, some common experience.　There flows beneath them an under-current of agreement, but the expression of it cannot reach the lips, and the tongue falters when the heart would speak.　Yet it is possible through it all to accept Hegel's advice, 'Be a person.' Be a person and treat others as persons—if you must have a for-mula, there are not many better.　That, or the English one, 'Be a gentleman.'

The best religion for a man, said the oracle of Delphi, is the religion of his country.　And if you ask how, in the meantime, are we to order our lives, the answer is 'Exactly as our predeces-sors have ordered their lives, by the customs and traditions of their nation and country, by the best conceptions of their day and generation.'　Never, indeed, regarding them as final, but as pro-visional, till we can improve upon them.　Speaking of one of his own poems, Keats wrote—'I leaped headlong into the sea, and thereby have become better acquainted with the soundings, the quicksands and the rocks than if I had stayed upon the green shore, and piped a silly pipe, and took tea and comfortable advice.'

In creation is perpetual and unfailing delight.　Nature revels in it.　It is the goal of all desire, and upon creation of some sort every man is bent.　Nor is there anything of pleasure or of profit which he does not make for himself.　He is the eternal dreamer.　He creates his own ethics, as he creates his pictures, his poems and his worlds to come.　Out of his own experiences he builds them.　He has to live by his own rules, and knows his own needs, and of these no angel can tell him more than he already knows. He has business on his hands which will outlast things as they are, and the present arena of his activities. For there is nothing static in the universe, as there is nothing static in thought, either in science or philosophy, in religion or ethics. There is nothing static even in the laws of nature, which we fancy unchanging and eternal. Her ways were not always her present ways, and her present ways will not be her ways to everlasting. Is the thought too terrible that we are children, who know nothing, absolutely nothing, children trying to be happy, who have everything to learn? 'However early you rise', says the proverb, 'you cannot hasten the dawn.' Is it absurd to suppose that we have not yet learnt, and are far from knowing, standing as we do on the very edge of the world, anything of its inner recesses and resources? That we are far from knowing even what we fancy we know—the true nature of truth and beauty and goodness?

Mankind, as I fancy, is committed to a long journey. Knowledge and wisdom are of slow growth, as history is witness, and the universe offers an extensive field of enquiry. No one can say what awaits us. Not, we have found reason to believe, unbroken felicity, yet on the other hand the possibility of very great felicity. The omens are not all unfavourable. It was the fair ivory gate that sent forth the false, and the gate of horn the true dreams. You may insist that the present and visible world is the alpha and omega, the beginning and the end of all things as far as we ourselves are concerned. For that conclusion there are arguments in plenty. 'Death', said Aristotle, 'is a dreadful thing, for it is the end.' Take that view and you cannot but think poorly and despairingly of the whole creation. To many minds it appears so certain a truth as to require no demonstration, and the contrary so preposterous a fancy as not to be worth discussion —as not for a moment to be entertained. If you know of course you know. But there is knowledge and there is also a different thing, opinion. A fixed idea has great advantages. Your mind is at rest, and you are under no necessity either to defend it, or to consider further evidence on the matter. For myself I have no affection for fixed ideas. My distrust of them, as of all that appears certain and obvious, is profound. Had I been present at the birth of this planet I would probably not have believed on the word of an archangel that the blazing mass, the incandescent whirlpool there before our eyes at a temperature of fifty million degrees, would presently set about the establishment of empires and civilisations, that it was on its way to produce Greek art and Italian painting, would tolerate such things as music and mathematics, make room for optimists and pessimists, admit the arrival of Homers, Beethovens and Napoleons, or even the small fry of Gifford Lecturers. I would have listened most respectfully to the archangel, who predicted these singular occurrences, but I would have whispered to myself—'He is a romantic.' So it is that I have become a confirmed sceptic in respect of precipitate and headlong conclusions. I say to myself, 'If things half as improbable happen in time to come there will be plenty to talk about.'

The universe does not deal in things that mortals expect, and when a fixed idea makes its appearance, as Nietzsche would say, a great ass makes its appearance. The only incredibility, as it seems to me, and the only impossibility is that the Cosmos contradicts itself. If by the use of reason we declare it unreasonable we are thrust back upon the question 'How did this reason arrive in an unreasonable world?' Yet whatever our attachment to reason, and we cannot be too greatly attached to it, let us remember that the secret of the world's everlasting interest lies precisely here, that you cannot explain it, and never know what is going to happen next. This is the source of our unabating hope and never-dying expectation.

XV
ONCE UPON A TIME

And what than this can be more plain and clear?
What truth than this more evident appear!
    The Godhead cannot prize
   The sun at all, nor yet the skies
   Or air, or earth, or trees, or seas,
Or stars, unless the soul of man they please.
   He neither sees with human eyes,
     Nor needs Himself seas, skies,
   Or earth, or anything: He draws
No breath, nor eats or drinks by Nature's laws.

The joy and pleasure which His soul doth take
In all His works is for His creatures' sake.
    So great a certainty
   We in this holy doctrine see
   That there could be no worth at all
In any thing material, great or small,
   Were not some creature more alive,
    Whence it might worth derive.
   God is the spring whence things come forth;
Souls are the fountains of their real worth.

Traherne

XV

ONCE UPON A TIME

What is undeniable if anything be undeniable? Looking about him for an indisputable proposition, upon which to erect his house of thought, a recent brilliant metaphysician, the late Professor McTaggart, took for his foundation not the famous 'I think, therefore I am' of Descartes, but a more general proposition—'Something exists'. Let us, too, allow that 'something exists'. And let us assure ourselves that this something includes ourselves, that we also exist, at least momentarily, since we are here discussing the situation. To exist, when you reflect upon the matter, appears the most natural state imaginable, and yet the most puzzling. For if you make a resolute effort to grasp the idea, with all its implications, you become speechless. We awake at birth, you may say, upon a rocky islet in a waste of immeasurable waters. How did we arrive here, on this lonely spot? How did the island itself come to be there, the surrounding seas, the sun, moon and stars over our heads? A most peculiar situation when you come to think of it, which has provided the wise men of our species with an inexhaustible topic of conversation. 'Something exists', and here in some miraculous fashion we are. And our awareness of the situation, that is, our conscious life, first emerges in a distinction we draw between ourselves and our surroundings. 'Here am I', each of us comes to say to himself, 'and over there is something else.' 'Me and not me,' the distinction between subject and object, marks the first step on the long journey of every man's mind.

Later, when you and I look round the island upon which we are marooned, and begin to take stock of its features, we become aware of a motley assembly of shapes and colours, 'the ten thousand things', as the Chinese call them, or in philosophic language, 'the manifold', 'shot', as it were, 'out of a pistol at us', as Hegel said. We behold a variegated landscape of moving and stationary objects, we distinguish stars, clouds, trees, rivers, hills, valleys, flying, walking and creeping animals. Some of these animals are, we discover, like ourselves in a number of ways, and with them we establish communications of one kind and another, engage in common undertakings, eat and drink together, and become more or less quite friendly.

For this charming prospect, however, a species of the race, the true-blue philosophers, have no eye. Their thoughts wander elsewhere. They are consumed, you remember, with a professional passion, which does not trouble others in the least, for the invisible rather than the visible, for the *ensemble*, the totality, the whole, in their own phraseology the Absolute; in which the various objects, with all their distinctive peculiarities, that the rest of us are content to observe and admire, are, they tell us, included; from which they were originally derived; and of which, ourselves with the rest, all are the manifestations. With almost one voice the sages to whom we go for guidance in our difficulties proclaim that the world, which certainly appears as a multiplicity of separate things, extremely unlike each other, is fundamentally a unity.

How do they know this? Obviously not by inspection or observation. Such a conclusion does not leap to the eye. You would never reach it by simply looking round you. Nor is it a conclusion that can be proved. Yet the human mind when it sets to work, trying to account for its singular situation, persistently demands, and usually reaches this result. It is better pleased, as we have seen, with the idea of unity than plurality, better satisfied to think, whatever the appearances suggest, or however things now are, that, at all events in the beginning, once upon a time, everything emerged out of a single substance or state of being. Human thought is anxious to get rid of the multiplicity of separate objects, and to show that they are derived from and supported by a single underlying substance, more real, stable and permanent than the separate things, which are in a state of flux, always coming and going, arriving and departing.

Now it is a matter of very great interest and importance—quite apart from the truth or falsity of the opinion—to note this characteristic of the human mind. Why do we prefer to think in this way, to go behind and deny the plain evidence of our senses that there are numerous and very different things, in favour of a doctrine that they are ultimately one and the same? Why do our mortal minds demand this unity, which cannot be derived from observation? If it be a prejudice of the mind, and a prejudice it may certainly be called, it is an extremely curious prejudice, for it appears irresistible, a law or necessity of our logic, compelling intellectual consent. Reason, that is, opposes the testimony of the senses, and we reject the distinct information they give. Seeing, in short, is not believing.

Such then is the structure of our intellects. Matters appear to us easier to understand, more amenable and intelligible when the Many are reduced to One. Or, if we probe further, we discover that we think in this fashion because to do so meets some deep-seated emotional need of our natures. It conduces to our mental comfort. In daily life we are called upon to deal with all manner of things, to understand them, as we say, and we endeavour to identify them, to find them alike. In their similarity they present a more friendly appearance. 'So, this is like that', we tell ourselves, and thus simplify them.

And not only do we thus agreeably save ourselves trouble by economy in thought, bringing different things under the same category, but by pigeon-holing them we attain a sense of tranquillity and security. Human beings, like all animals, are nervous creatures, nervous, and rightly nervous, in unfamiliar surroundings. Dangers lurk in the shadowy places, in the forest gloom. Nothing is more repulsive to us or more alarming than the strange and unknown. From the strange and unknown, from anything of which we have no previous experience, and from which we do not know what to expect, we edge away. Unexplored lands are full of hazards. If on the other hand we can say, 'Ah, yes, this is like that', or 'We have seen this before', or 'This was to be expected', our natural apprehensiveness is diminished and light-heartedness engendered. Were one of our prehistoric ancestors to be introduced for the first time to a railway station, and see an express train emerge roaring from a tunnel, we may be sure he would be terrified out of his senses. We, who have seen this kind of monster before, remain calm and composed. To find resemblances or patterns in the world around us, to which its various strange appearances can be assigned, eases the mind, banishes our anxieties, and opens up the possibility of bringing unusual, eccentric and hazardous things under our own control—

in a word, of rising superior to circumstances, and mastering the general or universal principles at work in them.

Another peculiarity of the human intellect is its desire to see things clearly and distinctly, in the sharpest, most clean-cut outlines, so that there may be no mistaking what they are. The terms we apply to render the idea of intelligibility are all terms associated with ocular vision, with sight. The visible and the intelligible are, indeed, virtually interchangeable and synonymous terms. Light, without which the eye cannot function, is pleasant to us because it makes things clear and plain, and we speak of it as revealing or illuminating. Similarly with mental processes. We say 'I see that' in respect of an argument, or 'That is apparent', 'That is clear to me', 'How lucid', or 'As clear as daylight'. Conversely darkness is depressing and distasteful. It corresponds to the unintelligible. 'How obscure', we say, or 'One has to grope for his meaning', or 'He is blind to that view of the matter'.

The ideal in science, or any intellectual activity is, then, geometrical precision. Since geometry deals in figured spaces, in sharp outlines, in pictures, diagrams and patterns, the clearest mental life is that of the geometer, to which all science and philosophy aspire, where there is ocular demonstration, where the squares, triangles and circles provide proof beyond argument of what they are. Here everything is triumphantly certain and final. There are no intellectual remainders, no dubieties; no shadows are cast. There are no ragged edges, no imperceptible meltings of one thing into another, no uncertainties and no hesitations. What clearness and finality, what absolute perfection, what mental comfort there is in a circle, or the very idea of a circle.

So there is a similar clearness, finality, perfection in the idea of the One, the Whole, the all-containing Absolute. When it reaches that idea our thought reaches utter completeness and a haven of rest. It cannot go further, and there is no further to go. Its troubles are ended. And with the peace the idea provides is bound up the blessed sense of security. For the Whole is a closed system. Nothing can enter it from without, for there is no without. Nothing can escape from it to go elsewhere. There is no elsewhere. It is itself the all, the total assembly of things that are, or were or ever will be. Or if there be other universes, out of any relation with it, they can be no concern of ours. One can see, then, why this idea of the all-inclusive One, providing as it does the completeness and perfection so dear to the human mind, immensely attracts the philosophers. The monistic doctrine is their favourite creed, around which they flutter fascinated, as the moth around the shining lamp.

If now we accept this doctrine that everything derived originally from one source or one substance, we are involved in metaphysics—in an enquiry, that is, which goes beyond physics. We meet once more the vexatious puzzle of the One and the Many, to which, as the Rome, you might say, of philosophy, all roads eventually lead. And the puzzle is simply this—how between them can any reconciliation be effected? How can the Many be derived from the One, how did they come into existence? Even to appreciate the complicated and thorny nature of this conundrum involves tedious travelling. To a lady of my acquaintance, who said she liked the English, a Scotsman put the unusual query, 'Hae ye ever been able to get one of them into a metapheesical argument?' Scotsmen are by nature philosophers —the famous Kant had Scotch blood in his veins—and for them metaphysics is as much a necessity and as palatable as their daily bread; so we may perhaps proceed with confidence, and do our best with this ancient enigma.

I have said that it carries us beyond physics. For even if you have satisfied yourself that the world is a physical world, through and through made up of material particles, and trace all its varieties, physical and mental, to combinations of these particles or atoms, you have still to account for the atoms and the void in which they float, for their origin. You are faced, that is, with the problem of a first cause. Modern physics, leaning upon the law of entropy, asserts that the world must have had a beginning. 'There is no doubt', to quote Sir Arthur Eddington, 'that the scheme of physics, as it has stood for the last three-quarters of a century, postulates a date at which either the entities of the universe were created in a state of high organisation, or pre-existing entities were endowed with that organisation which they have been squandering ever since. Moreover, this organisation is admittedly the antithesis of chance. It is something which could not occur fortuitously.'

Could it possibly have arisen without a cause, out of a previous nothing? Hume and Kant professed to think it possible. But few of us can compass such a thought. Nothing can come from nothing, we think. Few of us are such master magicians as to be able, even in imagination, to conjure a whole universe, ourselves included, out of utter vacancy. And in any case it simply cannot be believed that it arose all at once, just as it is at present. If you begin with atoms, it is quite obvious that it took them a long time to arrange themselves into the world we see and the creatures it contains—a very long time. Miracles, some think—though I do not myself see why they should think so—are not quite so remarkable if you have millions upon millions of years in which to perform them. And you have still to begin with something—space and time, which, wherever they came from, when they got together had some heavy work before them to construct the universe. It is necessary to begin with something, and, if you take this line of explanation, you try to picture a gradual process of development, of evolution, from the original substance to the present state of things.

If your imagination fails before this conception, there are alternative theories. You may believe that the world never had a beginning, it was always there, always in some form in existence, and can never go out of existence, or you may believe that it was created by a supreme, eternal power, which existed prior to the world, and called it into being. Great issues depend upon your choice of answer. It is a metaphysical problem, which concerns the divine as much as the philosopher. With, however, a difference.

The difference is this, that the philosopher does not consider himself called upon to assign any peculiar status or dignity to the human race, to regard it as in any sense a separate kingdom or state within a greater. For him, you and I may be merely things among other things, more curious, perhaps, but without any privileged rank or position over stones, flowers or stars. The philosopher is merely at a loss to explain how and why all the separate, dissimilar things arose out of the One. The theologian, on the other hand, has more serious matters on his hands—two in particular. He desires to maintain the absolute perfection of the One, of God the Creator, who, as he holds, made the world, and to account at the same time for the evils and imperfections present in His creation; and preserving, moreover, the supreme unity of God, to provide a separate status for man, an independent existence and will, which confer upon him responsibility for his actions, without which he becomes the merest nonentity, with no firmer standing in the universe than a wave of the sea or grain of desert sand. If God is all in all, man, the theologian sees, is nothing. If man be in any sense an independent creature, his own master, who can go his own way, God has lost control of His world. Glorify the Whole, and the parts correspondingly lose their importance and significance. Exalt the parts, and you diminish the majesty of the Whole.

The philosopher, you observe, is free from the theologian's anxiety, not concerned to claim any importance for human beings. He is at liberty to assert, as he frequently does assert, that in respect of being or reality they are upon the same footing as chairs or tables. He is free also wholly to ignore the problem of evil. For nature, if it be a blind energy, or for Space-Time, good and evil have no meaning. We have no doubt our preferences, our ideas about them. If things meet with our approval we call them good, if they conflict with our aims and purposes we call them bad. If, however, we are unimportant our ideas and preferences are also unimportant. And the distinctions we draw between good and bad are manifestly not to be found in nature. There is no right or wrong in the tiger's leap upon the antelope, the rending of its prey by the shark, or the bite of Anopheles, the mosquito which carries malaria. There is nothing more natural in health than in disease, in the action of an anti-toxin than of a toxin. If, then, an indifferent, unthinking energy produced the universe, or, as Spinoza declared, a God whose thoughts are not like our thoughts, no explanation of good and evil is required. They are simply occurrences or events among other events.

With their differing dilemmas neither religion nor philosophy has successfully grappled. Must we then abandon the effort? The world is certainly beyond our comprehension, yet we cannot but entertain ideas about it. 'The true logic for this world', said that great mathematical genius, Clerk Maxwell, 'is the Calculus of Probabilities, the only mathematics for practical men.' Bishop Butler was in agreement with this standpoint. 'Probability', said he, 'is the guide of life.' When the man of science and the theologian are at one, we may, perhaps, accept their guidance and go forward.

And here, before entering upon debatable land, lest we be

trapped in a delusion which has afflicted so many poor souls, let us beware of supposing that materialism and idealism, so called, or the schools of thought represented by these terms, necessarily lead in respect of ourselves to different results, necessarily differ at all in their estimate of man, in their respect for his aspirations, or concern for his destiny. Idealism is often no more than an inverted materialism, and provides no better for man's spiritual welfare. Religion obtains no firmer support, however the terminology may differ, from the one than from the other. It matters not in the least whether you say 'All is matter' or 'All is mind', as far as human beings are concerned, if they be looked upon as mere passing manifestations of the universal process, either as ephemeral appearances of a conjectured universal mind or temporary atomic structures on the stage of nature. There is little to choose between these two schemes of thought save in their manner of execution. You may be shot or hanged; it matters nothing five minutes later. If you have a care for the individual man and his hopes, put not too hastily your trust in the word 'idealism', that wolf in sheep's clothing of the philosophic schools.

Well, then, beginning with the assumption of the One, or whole of Being, how should we regard the universe, what conclude as to its true nature? Is it, for example, material or spiritual, created or self-originated, temporary or everlasting? And again, how came it, whatever be its nature, to give birth to its multitudinous and very dissimilar products? Ask these questions, and you are plunged into an ocean of disputes and conjectures, from the idea of a divine creative intelligence, wisdom *in excelsis*, 'Zeus alone with his thoughts' a world-soul or God, to that of a vortex of material particles, out of whose continual clashing, accidental and interminable, there arose the astounding texture, of which we are ourselves the most astonishing portion.

We have, let us suppose for the moment, a unity. The One is all and the all is One. Our bodies, our minds, the external world—nothing anywhere has an independent existence, all are knit up in the same tapestry.

> They reckon ill, who leave me out;
> When me they fly I am the wings;
> I am the doubter and the doubt,
> And I the hymn the Brahmin sings.

Yes, but it still remains to be decided 'what kind of unity?' A conglomeration, an aggregation, a clashing, contending multitude, or a single enduring whole, of which the parts are but momentary, evanescent appearances, as Shelley seemed to think?

> The One remains, the many change and pass:
> Heaven's light for ever shines, earth's shadows fly:
> Life, like a dome of many-coloured glass,
> Stains the white radiance of eternity.

It sounds as plausible as it is undoubtedly poetical. Yet how came it about that this immaculate Whole, in its aboriginal lordly seclusion, so far forgot itself as to make war even in appearance upon its own perfection, to condescend to apparent parts and discords within itself? How came it to harbour battle, murder and misery, or what seem like them, within its gates? To call them appearances does not rid us of their unpleasant society. To change the name is not to change the thing. 'He who denies the real existence of nature', said Rouvier, 'has still to create a natural history of appearance and illusion.' He has still, in philosophic language, 'to save' the appearances, to account for them. Let us know, we ask, why they tell an independent story of their own, why the world should wear so false a countenance if in fact it be one, and only one. How came this pristine unity to be so violently disturbed and shattered into innumerable fragments? What kind of explosion produced these results? Why all this sublime futility? Logic tells you that all is one, but we common men are not, like the great system builders, so much in love with logic as to wipe ourselves off the slate for the sake of its bright eyes. We have our aches and pains as unpleasantly conclusive evidence of a vivid existence all our own. We are not, like you, on visiting terms with the Absolute. 'A philosopher', wrote Hamann, 'who admonishes me to look upon the whole sets before me a task as difficult as does he who bids me look into his heart. The Whole is as much concealed from me as is his heart. Does he think I am a god?'

In all its forms the monistic doctrine, that the great reality is an indivisible unity, encounters grave difficulties, so grave that we read in Plato, 'certain Ionian and Sicilian Muses agreed that it is safest to weave together both opinions, and to say that Being is Many and One (πολλά τε καὶ ἕν), and that it is controlled by

311

love and hate.' To that opinion we may have to return. Meanwhile the position appears to be either that the universe originally consisted of the Many, already from the first separate, independent and uncreated entities, or the One somehow became the Many, and so gave rise to a world, which could not otherwise have come into existence. And this latter view, by reason of its immense philosophical prestige, cannot, whatever the difficulties, lightly be dismissed. In what form, then, if adopted, can it be rendered most acceptable to the reason and the imagination?

However far into 'the dark backward and abysm of time' we travel to explain the present, we must suppose the past was of such a kind as to render the present possible. If we hold by the notion of causation at all the past necessarily contained the possibility of the present. Whether or not you call it God, if you are to ascribe to it the origin of all the worlds, the power within or behind the universe must have been of God-like quality. And we must also conclude that it could not express itself, or in any way manifest its attributes, save through some division or dissolution of its original unity. For a world whose parts—and to be a world it must have parts—are indistinguishable from each other, all perfectly alike, is a contradiction in terms. A world of any kind involves discontinuous and separate elements, differing from each other. And however supreme and perfect the One in its primal and majestic isolation might potentially be, how in a state of undiversified sameness could its qualities be displayed? They could not. Just as in the physical world there could be no events if an equal temperature everywhere prevailed, so in a Whole without differences nothing can take place. To be revealed or disclosed the primordial power, or any power, must meet with resistance. Yet, since it is itself the only reality, no such resistance necessary for the revelation of the Whole can anywhere beyond its own boundaries be encountered. The resistance, therefore, must be self-created. The One must itself release its powers, and provide the opposing principle, the resisting energy. It must engender the polarity, the mighty opposite, which will serve to display or manifest its omnipotence. As one may see a lake or reservoir among the hills, motionless and calm, exhibiting no sign of strength, yet give rise on the raising of a sluice, to a foaming cataract, a torrent of leaping plunging waters, so we may think of the unmoving and perfect One transformed by its own act into the turbulent Many, the angry, contending surges of a world at war. 'There would seem to be', as Professor Laurie said, 'no other way of creating a finite world save through the negation of the One of Being, and this again is inconceivable save as resistance to the One, and the conflict of each with all.'[1]

Thus, perhaps, if anything profitable can be thought or said on such a topic, if our frail minds are to form any conception of the inconceivable, of the beginning of things, which, as Socrates believed, demanded 'superhuman wisdom' to explore, we may think of the Cosmos as the 'awakening' of the Many in the One, as arising from a self-division within the Whole. And we may think of creation as the moment at which its duration passed into our time. During the reign of the undivided Absolute time was not, there were 'no days and nights, and months and years', as Plato said, and there was no story. History begins with time— *cum tempore*. A story is the unfolding of events in time, and for us there is no penetrating into eternity. God, then, as the mystics say, negates Himself, in order that there may be a world, and this negation or sundering is creation's dawn. '*In Ja und Nein bestehen alle Dinge*,' as Boehme expressed it. 'All things subsist in Yes and No.'

After this shadowy fashion we may essay to imagine the unimaginable, and suppose the separate, individual entities to have arrived on the stage of being, each carrying with it a portion of the spiritual energy, each reflecting from its personal and finite centre, in its own degree, the vitality, the fire, the light, the intelligence, the inexhaustible energy of the primordial source or fountain whence it sprang. But for the self-division which gave them birth the One had remained a tranquil, unruffled ocean,

> still as night
> Or summer's noon-tide air.

In some such metaphysical manner the appearances may be accounted for or 'saved'. But their status within the whole still remains uncertain. The appearances are of very varied types and grades, of longer and shorter life, differing as the tortoise differs from Achilles, or the mountain from the rainbow. Among them can the creatures drawing the breath of life be distinguished as of greater consequence than others, the grass of the fields, the

[1] *Synthetica*, vol. i, p. 219.

sunshine and the rain? And in particular can any eminent or unique standing be claimed for human beings, those remarkable rational creatures, stranded, or as some would say shipwrecked, on the shores of a minor planet? Are these nobler appearances, as they themselves fancy, of any more importance than the waves which tossed them there?

> Most men eddy about
> Here and there—eat and drink,
> Chatter and love and hate,
> Gather and squander, are raised
> Aloft, are hurl'd in the dust,
> Striving blindly, achieving
> Nothing; and then they die—
> Perish; and no one asks
> Who or what they have been,
> More than he asks what waves,
> In the moonlit solitudes mild
> Of the midmost Ocean, have swell'd,
> Foam'd for a moment, and gone.

Can they be 'saved' in any fuller sense, rescued from the flux of the eternal tides, or do they, like the waves, again subside into the ocean depths?

No philosophic system which begins with the One or Absolute has succeeded in discriminating among its emanations, or providing for some, as against others, any enduring value or significance. All are but as water drops, condensed out of the primal mist only to be absorbed, to lose again the identity or individual being they had temporarily experienced. If the One gives birth to the Many it ends by devouring its offspring. For the monistic doctrines the Many are the creatures of a day. They flower to fade and wither.

> The sun comes forth, and many reptiles spawn;
> He sets, and each ephemeral insect then
> Is gathered into death without a dawn,
> And the immortal stars awake again.
> So is it in the world of living men.

If now we decline to fly about the universe in search of the Absolute, of which knowledge is hard to obtain, we may take another and, as some think, a more promising route, beginning our philosophical journey with matters near at hand, and as we know them. We may take counsel with the pluralists, the friends or adherents of the Many. The One, they argue, is beyond our scrutiny, and therefore a profitless subject of discourse; 'the ten thousand things', on the other hand, are in possession of the visible field, and possession is nine points of the law, and of some consequence even in logic. But for these illusory appearances, being yourself one of them, they ironically remark, you would never have heard of the One or Absolute about which you are so anxious. However they arrived upon the scene, the appearances at least appear, which is something. They are, moreover, persistently and overwhelmingly in evidence, stand resolutely at bay, and decline to depart at the bidding either of monarchs or mystics. Let us begin then, advise the pluralists, with the evidence of common sense, with 'the furniture of the earth and the choir of heaven'.

If now we go to school with the *a posteriori* rather than the *a priori* thinkers, we find among them at least one philosopher of the first rank, Leibniz, the chief protagonist of their way of thinking, 'the greatest intellectual genius', it has been said, 'since Aristotle.' All knowledge was, like Aristotle's, his province, and though born in 1646, nearly three centuries ago, the scientific acumen and prescience of Leibniz enabled him to foresee, and even in a measure anticipate, many conclusions arrived at by the most recent science. He arrived, for example, by his own acute and original route, at the modern theory of 'the unconscious', 'changes in the soul', as he called them, *petites* and imperceptible, so slight as not to attract our attention, which, nevertheless, in combination —as many slight and hardly heard sounds may together make a great noise—exercise a profound influence upon our waking lives. In his denial that between conscious and unconscious states a hard and fast line could anywhere be drawn; in his declaration, supported by modern physics, that matter or substance is but another name for energy, since all substances are for ever in activity, and action is their characteristic quality; in his view that empty space is a fiction, and that space and time, however distinct, are inseparable—in these, as in his approach to philosophical problems by the mathematical route, in his idea resembling the modern cell theory of the organism as composed of lesser organisms, Leibniz appears as a bright prophetic star, forerunner and foreteller of new ways of thought.

In his view, in the view of this most suggestive and remarkable thinker, just as a nation is composed of persons, so the universe may best be understood as consisting of an infinite variety of living and active beings, monads, as he called them, each a separate and distinct centre of energy, monads of many grades and levels, the whole forming a *scala naturae*, a staircase of living creatures. 'The world', said Leibniz, 'is not a machine. Everything in it is force, life, thought, desire.' The monads reflect the universe, each from its own angle, each in its own degree. Each has its own energy and appetite, and each seeks, as men and animals seek, the fulfilment of its own peculiar needs. This great community extends both upwards and downwards from man through the whole creation. The world, in brief—a noble thought, and at least worthy of belief—is a living society.

Suppose we carry with us this thought, which has earlier authority behind it, and see what light it may throw upon our immediate experience. If that experience tells us anything, it reports that energy is operative throughout the length and breadth of the Cosmos, which is, indeed, a texture of energies. It reports with assurance that the realm of nature exhibits both order and disorder, sympathies and antipathies, purposes and cross-purposes, is fissured by such opposites as are to be found in human society and within ourselves. For the adherents of the perfect One or Absolute these contrary forces present a mystery, an enigma utterly beyond solution. How unpalatable the view that the history of the universe is merely that of an unfortunate episode, arising out of the inexplicable dissolution of a perfect Whole, which, doing only to undo, scattered itself abroad with lamentable and painful results only to repent, and to resume again its solitary reign—indulging in the childish game of building up merely to destroy. Or how strange and distasteful to suppose that God first created the world and then had to redeem it. Hard as they are to interpret, things wear for the pluralist an aspect far less forbidding and formidable. Of the contradictions and frictions everywhere present in the world some at least, to our knowledge, arise out of the simultaneous existence of innumerable creatures, struggling each upon its own account for more and fuller life, the satisfaction of its own independent aims and purposes. May it not be that a similar state of things prevails throughout the entire structure?

316

Accept for a moment the point of view. Suppose, with Leibniz, the world to be a congregation of separate entities, extending from the dust beneath our feet to the stars above us. A surprising fancy, you think, but let us give it rein. Suppose each individual particle within the Universe bent in its own mode and measure upon the expression and expansion of its separate being, all in a degree sentient, some below, some above what we call consciousness, 'less sunk in matter', as Leibniz expressed it, than others. Suppose the world's existing patterns the outcome of these striving selves. Suppose further—a crucial step—the division we habitually make between the animate and inanimate a needless dichotomy, and the minutest of existing things, the very constituents of the atoms themselves, charged with vital energy, each living and spiritual in its essential nature. We know, indeed, that life proceeds only from previous life, but who has drawn for us, as in the case of the viruses, the dividing line? So pervasive and ubiquitous is the will to live that we may well stretch the line of imagination, and suppose it to inform not only ourselves and all organic nature, but even what to us appears inanimate nature itself. Does science forbid the suggestion? On the contrary, it now inclines to support it. The wheel has come full circle. Whereas until yesterday physics dictated its concepts to biology, biological concepts are now invading the realm of chemistry and physics. The modern physiological view, we hear from Dr. Charles Myers, maintains 'that consciousness, however primitive, fulfilling however feebly the function of orderly direction and purpose, is primary, and that it has grown by distillation, differentiation and restriction to narrower, more dominating, higher levels within the organism', in a word, that throughout the Cosmos mind controls matter, and not matter mind. Nature teems with life. Let us be bold, and say where there is life there is intelligence, which all living things in some elementary form display. All are architects or builders on their own account, and all life in its individual centres is marked by movement and spontaneity, which, indeed, are its distinguishing features. And what appears to us inanimate matter is, too, in perpetual activity, and may be correctly described as motion become visible.

'Spontaneity', you say, possibly with some indignation, 'how can that be ascribed to inanimate things?' Let us meanwhile postpone this enquiry, and fortify ourselves with Plato's words, 'if only we adduce probabilities as likely as any others, that ought to be enough for us'. 'Why not admit', asked Zeno, 'that the world is a living and rational being since it produces animate and rational entities?'—a pertinent query.

And here is, as I think, another. If science has for twenty centuries thought and spoken without reproach in terms of dead atoms, which no eye has ever seen, why not we in terms of living atoms? It was held by Giordano Bruno, who lectured for a time at Oxford in the sixteenth century, the first philosopher to use the term 'monad', that life and mind flowed through and belonged to all things from the least to the greatest, that

> the multitudinous abyss
> Where secrecy remains in bliss,
> And wisdom hides her skill,

was alive and eternal in all its parts, and from pole to pole.

On this conception the Cosmos is 'a vast and complex web of life', a concourse or colony of creatures, for each of whom its environment, or forum of activities, is just the rest of the society. It is a hierarchy of innumerable minds, an ascending series of intelligences. In their association and after their several fashions they endeavour, one and all, to secure each for itself a *modus vivendi* and a better life. And the physical world in its various patterns is the outcome of their combined strivings to that end, the form their interaction takes for us. In their fellowships they find their opportunities, and from their intimacies and rivalries, from their ceaseless intercourse, arise the evolutions and processes which the passage of nature displays. They have made, as it were, terms with each other, settled down in groups, formed habits, as do communities of men and animals, in adaptation to circumstances, and achieved a certain stability, an adjustment and equilibrium, such as, despite its convulsions and disharmonies, appear in the regularity and uniformity, the stability and order of nature that we call her laws. Or how else are we to account for these laws? Who made them? How did they come into being? Did nature make her own laws, as we make resolutions?

'Mind', as Professor Stout wrote, 'is not produced at all, but is in some way involved as a primary factor in the creation of the universe.' Look round over the landscape of nature and observe its continuity, the almost insensible series of its gradations, and

318

you know not where to insert your dividing knife or draw your line. Overnight and in secret ways the minerals take counsel together and glide into plants, plants into animals and animals into men. Observe the organisations on land and water, in air and sky, federations in which the higher and more advanced among the monads make use of the lower, the growing things of the elements and minerals, the moving creatures of the growing things. Crude or mindless matter is not capable of organising a world. What hinders that we should accept the analogy offered by human society and human history? There, in that scene of action, as in what seems the inanimate creation, the striving individuals have formed tribes and federations, adapted themselves to surrounding circumstances, fallen into fixed customs, and ordered, as the creatures on the lower steps of nature's staircase have ordered, their ways of life.

Pursue the thought, and you find a thousand resemblances between the events of human history and the story of the physical world as related by science. Are we not then justified in regarding nature's ways as everywhere the same, in believing that in her higher patterns she repeats and reflects her lower and works to the same design throughout her whole domain? Rotate the arch and you have the dome. And whence comes our intelligence unless it already animates the whole? The world of our experience has two sides: the external world with which we are in contact through our senses—the bridges between soul and soul—and the internal realm of thoughts, desires, affections, a private realm of equal importance, not less insistent or less real. Of these two realms, the public and the private, we are somehow the citizens, and of both we must take account. Utterly dissimilar as they seem, they are somehow united, as if by miracle, yet an accomplished miracle. It is there and at work. If we regard the universe as a congregation of living beings, a spiritual assembly, the external world is the manifestation of their co-operation. And the resistances and oppositions it discloses are the oppositions and resistances of will to will, of thought to thought, of soul to soul among its innumerable members, exhibiting in the public arena, as in human society, each its individual will to live in its various intensities, degrees and forms. 'Each portion of matter', wrote Leibniz, 'may be conceived as a garden full of plants, and as a pond full of fish. But each branch of the plant, each member of the animal, each drop of its juices, is also some such garden or pond. And although the earth and air separating the plants of the garden, or the water separating the fish of the pond are neither plant nor fish, they also contain plants and fish, but, for the most part, too minute to be perceptible by us.'

Life and intelligence, then, are present throughout the entire universe, and shared by all the monads in their respective modes, and the world we see is the result of their collective activities. Governed they are, as Empedocles asserted, by sympathies and antipathies, as are the individuals in human society, and may be looked upon as members one of another, as sharers in a common existence—however undeveloped and primitive on its lower levels—in the same confederacy. Nature, we may say, has not given birth to life. She is life. The Universe is not the home of life only because it is itself alive. And the mind, although it has its centres in the individuals, develops only in the co-operations and frictions of society.

Such a view, if we take it, at least involves us in no denials and no manifest contradictions. Yet, it may be objected, if you paint such an atomic picture of the world, you must still find a meeting-place for the individual monads, a ground for their inter-action. They are somehow together. They cannot be wholly unrelated and solitary wanderers in the boundless void. If the One cannot in its unpartitioned, undivided unity produce a world, the Many are equally powerless without the One. 'Hegel maintained', wrote Professor McTaggart—'and there is much to be said for his theory—that finite existences can only be really individual and differentiated in proportion as they are united between themselves in a close unity. The organs of the human body are contained in a closer unity than the stones in a heap, and at the same time these organs have each a more individual nature than have the stones of a heap.' To complete the picture we may accept the argument, and allow the universe its ground, its unify-ing genius, and yet think of the whole as less a single splendour, like the sun, than a night of stars. None the less, though it is all too easy to lose oneself amid the endless galleries and perspectives of time, it is still easier to put upon reasoning more than reasoning can bear, to plunge into an abyss of speculation where nothing can be determined, there to court illusion and return with dis-ordered minds and empty hands.

Regions there are where for us enquiry ends. 'I do not think', wrote Harvey, 'we are greatly to dispute about the name by which the First Cause is to be called, whether it be God, Nature or the Soul of the universe; all still intend by it that which is the beginning and end of all things, which exists from eternity, which is author and creator, is omnipresent, and not less in the single and several operations of natural things than in the infinite universe.' That there is a source of life, a ground of things, sufficient to have produced all things, a foundation everlasting, self-existing, is consistent with reason, and I do not know that any better name than God, or any better definition of that Power than 'the Life of life' has yet been given. 'He who believes he knows it not, knows it,' says the *Sama Veda*, 'he who believes he knows it, knows it not at all. It is regarded as incomprehensible by those who know it most, and as perfectly known by those who are utterly ignorant of it.' Let no man speak of certainties, for at the best we but gaze into a great mirror, where the transient is for a moment seen—the birth of new ideas, or of faiths that serve their hour, the march of unpredictable events, armies that pass, kingdoms that rise to fall and princes riding by. Yet we may be sure our destiny is the world's destiny and our journey its journey; nothing less is to be believed. Life has its inexpugnable trials. They are our lot, and the law of its being, arising out of the conditions which made it possible. We must expect winters as well as springs, and seasons of wild weather.

The world is what it is, not for us alone. It exists, because it provides for the largest number of compatible patterns, is more comprehensive and inclusive than any other could be, and with wider present and future horizons. And God thought it good, you may say, better than none. 'I worship Him', said Goethe, 'who has infused into the world such a power of production that, when only a millionth part of it comes out into life the world swarms with creatures to such a degree that war, pestilence, fire and water cannot prevail against them.'

Goethe worshipped the omnipotent, continuously creative Spirit. And in His universe is everywhere to be found purpose. If you ask 'what purpose?' we come to a halt. For if we are to use the word 'purpose' in respect of the whole universe it must be in some different sense than in its application to ourselves and our finite ends. The supreme purpose at least includes and provides a scene or realm of purposes, of undertakings, of patterns on the loom of time, woven by the individual selves. These are our present and immediate concern. On this field you can grow your crop, or build your house or fight your battle. To each creature belongs a certain freedom in his own hour and place, and for his own dreams and preferences, such as was permitted the masons for their carvings in the great medieval cathedrals, within the larger design. And as the coral insects, occupied each with its own activities, at work upon they know not what, are yet the builders of new inhabitable lands, new worlds flowering into ocean paradises, so the individual entities have their share in the creative advance into novelty. Process is real and history is real, but the process will not be the process, nor the history the history we anticipate. There the deep opens beneath our feet and imagination fails. For although our private aims and ends are within our view and partially within our compass, the greater purpose and the cosmic history are not in our hands. They are taken up and overruled by the genius of the universe.

We must revise and enlarge our categories of thought, for the logic of yesterday will not serve us to-day and for ever, as Kant and many philosophers before and since, supposed. We are deceived if we fancy that the mind, which has had a long history, has no more to say, or that the universe, whose history is as long, has wound up its affairs. There is much to come. 'Modern science,' says a great physicist, Weyl, 'so far as I am familiar with it through my own scientific work, mathematics and physics, makes the world appear more and more as an open one, as a world not closed, but pointing beyond itself.'

> Leave the inferior minds and look at man!
> Is he, the strong, intelligent and good,
> Up to his own conceivable height? Nowise.

And if not, is it likely that he has exhausted in thought the depths and heights of the system to which he belongs? As science continually endeavours to reduce life to death, the body to a corpse, in order the better to understand it, so the philosophers, who desire to bring things to a standstill, prefer a static universe, as more amenable to their examination.

When we have a choice a spacious view is to be preferred, as best in keeping with a Cosmos we know to be spacious. I put to you a question. Are our thoughts too noble, too magnificent for the reality to compass? Are our cheques too large for the bank of the universe to honour? Can the mind, even in imagination, outrun or outrange the whole from which it sprang? For my part, I think not. 'The sun', said Anaxagoras, 'is larger than the Peloponnesus,' and people wondered at his saying. For my part I think the universe is wider and larger than the wisest even of philosophers have ever conceived. Let us then think imperially, for the more magnificent our thoughts the nearer the truth.

XVI

HERE AND NOW

LINES

Spirit of ice and snow,
Goddess, whose hands are laid
Upon the brows of men who needs must go
Seeking Thy loneliness, immortal Maid,
Within the fastness of Thy frozen place;
Dost Thou their toil behold?
Thine heart is dull with cold,
Cold is Thy shrine, and colder Thine embrace!

Whence do the deep spells rise,
Which draw men still to Thee?
Thou hast no warmth of summer in Thine eyes,
Like her who called across the Ægean Sea
Grave wayfarers to quaff her foaming wine,
Thou hast but frozen dew,
Thy worshippers are few,
But these, Thy chosen ones, hold Thee divine.

Thine is no wealth of flowers,
Thine are no feasts of youth,
But the deep passion of enduring hours,
And endless seeking after endless truth,
Are the strong chains which bind men to Thy seat,
Who, grappling with Thy strength,
Conquer Thy might at length
Or, failing, sleep contented at Thy feet.

Maud Holland

XVI

HERE AND NOW

Within the last thirty or forty years certain aspects of nature, inextricably associated with the familiar world of the senses, have more and more forced themselves upon the attention of men of science, and dragged them somewhat unwillingly into the presence of the most obstinate of our metaphysical problems, the great twin mysteries of time and space. Philosophers, indeed, long ago confronted them, but these aspects of nature are now seen to fall within the province of physics, and must somehow be incorporated into its account of the external world, its description of the extensions, durations, motions and boundaries of that world. Thus a more lively awareness of time has lately appeared in the thought of our age, together with new interpretations of space, and we have come, or suppose ourselves to have come, to closer quarters with these concepts, and have at least more vividly perceived their paramount, indeed overwhelming significance in the grand scheme of things. Metaphysics, once regarded as the queen of the sciences, advances a new claim to the throne, from which, according to Kant, she had unjustly in his day been deposed. 'My soul is on fire', wrote St. Augustine of time, 'to understand this most intricate enigma,' and it has been borne in upon us, as upon him, that until we can attain to some clear comprehension of the true nature of time and space, all the doors leading to any fuller knowledge than we already possess of the world's structure are firmly locked. In a word, they are seen to be in science, as in theology and philosophy, the guardians or warders of all the mysteries.

Yet what can we possibly discover about them or say about them? We speak of days, and nights, and months, and years, but what is it that we thus divide? We speak continually of 'Here' and 'Now', but where is 'Here', which goes about with us wherever we go, and when is 'Now', which is always slipping away to make room for another 'Now'? Has it, for instance, occurred to you that if there were no spectators of the moving scene of nature there would be no 'Heres' and no 'Nows'? 'Here' is 'here' for someone; 'Now' is 'now' for someone. Nature, which is everywhere at once, has no 'Heres' and no 'Nows'. For us space and time appear to contain all things: everything lies within space, and everything happens in time. Nothing lies outside, or is independent of them. They provide the framework of the world in which we live. Yet, familiar as they are, if you allow yourself to meditate upon time and space you enter a region of bewilderment, giddiness overtakes you, and what mental powers you possess shrink and fail before them. There they are perpetually present, the terrifying apparition of time, never beginning, never ending, 'the moving image of eternity,' in Plato's inspired phrase, and that other not less terrifying spectre, the abyss of space. Remove everything in thought, all the worlds, there remains the vast void, which refuses to go. Time and space provide the setting of our little lives, and in this horizonless expanse the whole history of mankind shrivels to nothingne‿s, becomes a mere flicker, a momentary flash of lightning in an unfathomable night. And yet how serenely this earth of ours glides, silently and without a ripple through the uncharted gulf. 'The great universe', it has been said, 'seems to sleep in its arms like a child in its cradle.' In the divine stillness of that limitless ocean it is at home. An ocean of what? Of nothing, it seems, nothing at all. How far does this emptiness extend through which the universe journeys, and whither can we suppose it to be journeying?

We may labour with words, but to what purpose amid these incomprehensibles? We can see that time and space are unlike anything else with which we have any acquaintance. There is nothing with which to compare them. Whatever they may be, they appear to include all material things with which our immaterial minds are somehow associated; yet this we may say with confidence, that things themselves in any sense of the word they cannot be. No tool of any kind bites on them. No rude hands can be laid upon these immortals. No chemical analysis can tell you their composition, no biology unfold their ancestry or relate the story of their evolution. There cannot be material bodies without the space they occupy, but we can imagine space which

328

contains no bodies. Time, too, without events—sometimes called 'duration'—we can indeed imagine, yet of empty, eventless time we could not be conscious. Of neither space nor time do our senses give us the slightest information. They cannot be seen, heard or depicted; space is not seen, nor time; there is nothing to see; and travel fast or slow, you approach no nearer the terminus of either; and if time flows it is a flowing without anything that flows.

Since, then, though omnipresent, they refuse to submit to laboratory methods, to be touched, handled or in any fashion made the subject of experiment, things or substances they clearly are not, nor yet the properties pertaining to things. How, then, can the insubstantial come into contact with, or have any relations with the substantial objects which surround us? How came material things to enter this shadowy framework?

The same insuperable problem meets us when we try to understand how thought can lay hold on substance. For the world of our understanding thoughts and the world of solid things are like two rivers, which flow side by side, yet seemingly never meet. 'Like can only act upon like', as Anaxagoras said. Neither we nor anyone else, declared Kant, can explain how this harmony between thought and things, 'as if nature had been arranged expressly to suit our powers of comprehension'—described by Leibniz as 'a pre-established harmony'—has been brought about. By some kind of natural magic the objects seen by the eye, the sounds heard by the ear, become those ghostly yet real things we call ideas. A *modus vivendi* somehow exists between the mind and the external world which baffles the philosophers.

Consider a little further, and you perceive that these curiosities, space and time, appear to have certain resemblances to each other, and also certain most interesting differences. Space possesses what we call three directions or dimensions, length, breadth and height. Everywhere, you may say, in space three ways meet. And time, also, has for us, though not for nature, three phases, three successive dimensions, past, present and future. Setting aside the very troublesome enquiry into the nature and meaning of 'dimension', let us note that the dimensions of space form an intimate society; they are simultaneous and never found apart from each other, while those of time, on the other hand, are never found together. When the future puts

329

in an appearance to become the present, the former present vanishes into the past. Past, present and future are most unfriendly and avoid each other, save for a nodding acquaintance during the period described by philosophers as 'the specious present', a peculiar feature of our perception. During this span of perception, estimated to last a few seconds, which intervenes between past and future, and varies in duration with different individuals, the flow of time is, as it were, arrested. We hold together what has just taken place with what is now present to us. We have standing ground, or what Professor James called 'a saddleback, on which we sit perched, and from which we look in two directions', momentarily, in the flowing stream. Does this stream flow to meet us, do you think, as we face it, or does it carry us onwards with it as it goes? If time flows at all, in what direction does it flow? Certainly not north, south, east or west. Does the future that is to be come towards us, or does the past flow forwards, swallowing the present and growing as it goes? Are we standing at a stationary point awaiting time's coming, as we await the arrival of an incoming train, or are we ourselves in the train, moving through unmoving scenery, for ever there? Is it conceivable that the future already exists? If that were so, if its contents were already determined, it could hardly be the result of the past, or caused by the past, and the whole idea of causation becomes unintelligible. As distinguished from space, which is for us stationary, time seems to move in one or other direction, unless, indeed, we are in some fashion deceived, and the whole scene of events that ever were or will be is unmoving, and it is we who break up into fragments, into days and years, the eternal 'Now'. 'What would happen', asks Maeterlinck, 'if time stopped?' 'Nothing,' he says; 'we should have no suspicion that it had stopped. There *is* no time; there are only imaginary measurements of a thing existing only in our imaginations.'

There is still, however, another way of regarding time, its 'before and after' aspects, not so easily dismissed, since they are not the equivalents, as we might carelessly think, of 'past and future'. As we have already observed, past, present and future are constructions of the mind, and have no meaning, apart from us and our experience, in the physical world. There, however, in the outer world you may speak of an earlier and later occurrence, of a succession of events, one taking place before or after another.

Professor McTaggart spoke of the Past, Present and Future, or subjective series, as the A series, the 'Before and After' aspect as the B series, and concluded after a long and difficult argument that there is also a C series, independent of both, of which the A and B series were misrepresentations due to ourselves. I would set forth this argument if I could persuade myself that I fully understood it.

Let us avoid confusing ourselves, and note briefly two among the theories of time, of which the first is usually called the theory of absolute time, something which exists quite apart from us, and from the events which take place in it, something independent of all other things, which flows majestically and steadily along, which has moments, to which moments events, when they occur, can be assigned. For the most part philosophers reject absolute time. Hume held that space was merely 'the manner in which objects exist', and nothing in itself. Berkeley described it as 'the absence of resistance'. So, too, thinkers, like Kant and Leibniz, held that time has no independent existence, and is merely the relation between phenomena or events. For Kant both space and time were subjective; they were the forms of our sensibility, which make experience possible for us, experience, however, of phenomena or appearances only, not of the reality which underlies them. So, too, for Leibniz, space and time were not independent things, but the order or arrangement of co-existing and successive events. Space, he held, is the order of co-existing events or phenomena, as time is the order of successive phenomena. Neither is, in fact, real, both are mental structures. They are right, yet time is something deeper than the mere relationship of events to each other, or our way of seeing them. It is, as is space, a component or factor in the scheme of nature. And we must bear in mind that time in itself—though often confused with our awareness of time—plays a part of its own in the Cosmos.

Whatever their true nature, it is now universally allowed that space and time are as much the concern of the man of science as of the metaphysician, and we face with him the perplexing situation, 'How can physics in any manner grapple with aspects of nature which are clearly not physical, which are wholly unsubstantial?' The method of science, as we know, is to analyse and measure. Now to analyse is to separate out the ingredients, the component parts, as for example, the oxygen and hydrogen of which water is composed. We can go further. Things unseen, like air, can be analysed and weighed. Of what then is space composed, or time—what are their ingredients? They have none. They are not, like the elements, atomic or molecular, they have no separable parts. Well, then, let us try measurement. To measure you need a point from which to begin your operation, and also a unit of measure. But where in time or space are you to fix your point of departure, and what unit in either case do you propose to apply? A yard of time has no meaning, and to measure distances in empty space containing no objects—if there be such a thing—is in fact impossible, for we have no means of determining any positions there. You cannot paint a portion of space red or green, or mark it in any way so as to distinguish it from any other portion. 'In space', as Maxwell said, 'there are no milestones; one part is precisely like any other part, so that we cannot know where we are. We find ourselves in a waveless sea, without stars, without compass or sun, without wind and tide, and cannot say in what direction we move.'

If you are of a naturalistic turn of mind you are plunged in still deeper distress. For you have to determine the position in space and time not only of material objects, but of your ideas and sentiments. How are they to be either located or measured? If I say I have no great opinion of Hitler or Mussolini, or of anyone nearer home, where is that opinion, where am I to look for it, and what is its length and breadth? Or let us ask ourselves: Where are the objects we see in dreams? If you wish something easier, you might try this: How far away is the picture you see reflected in a mirror from the same picture on the wall? In a word, 'How shall we represent in space an existence not in space, and in time an existence not in time?' We speak, indeed, of weighty opinions, but how many millions of them will depress a balance to the extent of a pennyweight?

These are not such ridiculous questions as they sound. They indicate the initial embarrassments awaiting the man of science who desires to incorporate space and time into his sketch or model of the universe, not to speak of the still more formidable problems which arise when he reminds himself that the concepts and terms he employs, his dimensions, intervals and durations, are in every case coinages of his own mind, mere symbols of his own making, with which he endeavours to interpret the structure of reality, of which he is himself an inseparable part.

Space and time, we have seen, appear to have some superficial resemblances, and clearly are somehow associated with each other, an association which has suggested many ingenious ideas and phrases. Time, for instance, has been described as 'fluid space', and space as 'motionless time'. When we speak of places as 'near' or 'far away' we mean points which it will take a shorter or a longer time to reach. We estimate space, that is, by the passage of time, and find them already associated in our minds. Yet there belong to each certain deep, distinguishing features, which cannot be overlooked. First, unlike space, for which we have no inner sense, time is appreciated by our minds in two ways. We have a double apprehension of it—a subjective and objective apprehension. There is, we are all aware, an inner, or private time, and an outer, or public time. Within ourselves we are conscious, in the succession of our thoughts, of the lapse of time. This inner, or psychological or soul time may, in relation to the outer, move slowly or quickly, and be more or less crowded with mental experiences, under, for example, the influence of certain stimulating drugs, like hashish, which startlingly magnifies durations and distances, or, as it is said, with drowning persons, before whose inner eye the scenes of their past lives flash by with inconceivable speed. With such variations in the appreciation of time everyone is familiar, as when we are bored or interested, happy or dejected, or lonely. In the society of some acquaintances, and I fear at some lectures, an hour seems quite interminable, on other occasions it flits past only too rapidly. 'Time travels', as Shakespere has it, 'in divers paces with divers persons.' However unconscious we may be of the passage of external or clock time, sitting it may be absorbed over a book, we are aware of the inner current of our thoughts and emotions. It is something felt. Upon this distinction between private and public time Bergson dwells in his *Time and Free Will*. The mind, he argues, has its own sense of the passage of time, of duration. But we substitute for this true time another, a concept due to the intrusion of space; we imagine an outer time, which science looks upon as measurable. We borrow, that is, from the outer world the notion of magnitude, a spatial idea, and confuse the inner subjective experience with the outer presentation, 'its ghost', as

333

Bergson calls it. We mistake it for reality. But true duration has nothing to do with space. This independent, homogeneous time is, he thinks, a pure fiction.

Nevertheless, between this, our inner appreciation of time, and the outer or public, usually called 'clock-time', some correspondence appears to exist. We know that under hypnosis a suggestion made to a subject that he will do something, write a letter, or go out for a walk, after the lapse of say 11,470 minutes, or 850 minutes, will be fulfilled with surprising accuracy. The subject can give no account of the manner in which he performs the necessary calculation, and is, indeed, quite unaware that any suggestion, which he appears to obey automatically, has been made to him. The extraordinary precision of the correspondence between the inner time determination and external time is in these cases undisputed and unexplained.

Again, on the other hand, in the mystic's trance, such as is recorded of Socrates, the sense of time seems wholly to disappear. A charming old medieval story tells of a holy abbot, who, meditating in the fields, and entranced by the singing of a lark, fell into adoration of God's glory and goodness. When he awoke and returned to his monastery he was recognised by no one. No abbot of his name had ruled there for three hundred years. So profound had been his ecstatic concentration that he had passed, we might say, into eternity, where time had no existence, and he was free of its fetters. Of such a state, where intensity of thought takes the place of duration, and brings time to a standstill, an immovable 'Now', most of us have in a far-off fashion tasted, when immersed in deep consideration of an absorbing problem or calculation. In such conditions the stream of time seems to be arrested and ceases to flow.

When we say, then, 'Time flies', do we mean inner or outer time? Is this subjective time the true time, or are we to regard the common or clock-time, by which, in concert with our neighbours, we carry on our affairs, as of superior reality or authority? And how are we to connect the one with the other? Eddington speaks somewhere of an 'entropy clock' within our minds, which enables us to correlate these inner phases of thought with the stream of external events. Whether or not we have such a calculating machine within us, this synchronisation of private and subjective time with outer and objective time is, in the opinion

334

of some thinkers, the question above all others, of first and crucial importance.

The sidereal heavens, the atom and the mind all appear to have time-scales of their own. Their times do not correspond and cannot be imposed upon one another. Public or sidereal or clock-time, to which the interest of astronomers and man in general is confined, is not applicable to what may be called electronic time, since the measures of radio-active movements within the atom cannot be brought into any relation with astronomic time. To these it seems we have now to add a 'biological time',[1] which governs the growth and the activities of the living organism. It is now known that a wound in such an organism heals more slowly, according to a determinable ratio, as the organism ages. That is to say, the principle of equal work in equal time, as exemplified in the measurement of sidereal motions, by the velocity of light, does not govern the operations of living things. Their chemistry has its own scale. An increase of temperature alters their appreciation of temporal intervals estimated by the clock, as less or greater intensity of feeling alters our estimate of time's flow similarly measured. A connection seems thus to be established between mental—or psychological—and physiological time as measured by bodily processes.

There is another and very notable peculiarity of time—its irreversibility.

> The moving finger writes, and having writ,
> Moves on, nor all your piety nor wit
> Can lure it back to cancel half a line,
> Nor all your tears wash out a word of it.

There is for us no going back in time, no undoing of what has once been done. *Fugit irreparabile tempus.* In space I have a certain liberty, I can move about, but not in time. Again, if I move fifty miles east or west in space, the movement makes no impression upon me. I myself remain unchanged. I am the same person here as in London or the United States. Not so with time. If fifty years pass over my head I am utterly changed. One can easily imagine any number of movements in space, backwards, forwards, up and down, as in a lift or aeroplane, which would in no way alter the things moved. But time, with its 'unimaginable

[1] See *Biological Time*, by L. du Loüy.

touch', in Wordsworth's phrase, alters everything both in the organic and inorganic worlds.   Growth, the growth of plants or animals, cannot proceed without the help of time, which, with its creative or destructive finger, is unceasingly and everywhere at work.   Time walks, that is to say, hand in hand with change, with a succession of events, whose order is irreversible.

And what is change?   It is the supreme fundamental feature, the governing principle of the universe, the terrible, unceasing restlessness, the continued Becoming, which is at the root of all our anxieties and woes.   We cry out for peace, for rest, for a cessation of this perpetual and distressing flux, for the eternity of changeless Being, the goal of the mystic's craving.   But the universe, ceaselessly in movement, whose very soul is movement, knows nothing of such a word, or such a state.   Time and change are its masters.   Stars and mountains, seas and continents bow themselves before His omnipotent serene majesty, Time.

We cannot but allow to time, then, a higher or archangelic throne in the creation, a metaphysical rank and dignity above space.   For space appears to be passive, time all-powerful and active, the charioteer of all the worlds.

Observe, however, this.   Of the irreversibility of time no account is taken by the mathematicians.   Geometry lies outside its domain, and all planetary movements, such as the earth's motion round the sun, might be reversed without altering in any way the existing situation, or the calculations involved.   In mathematics you have a science which is indifferent to time and is unaffected by its passage.   In mathematics time is accordingly represented simply as a line, going either to right or left, with a different sign, + or −.   In physics, on the other hand, this will not do.   For physics deals with energies and actions, and where there is action there is motion, together with the time in which it takes place.   Anything which moves in time takes time to move.   So that time becomes for physics 'the relation of motions'.

Again, although the total quantity of cosmic energy remains, according to that science, ever the same, there is a law, you remember, the famous Second Law of Thermodynamics, which, we are told, admits neither of doubt nor exception.   This law asserts that the available energy is continually decreasing, and in this decrease we have a direction post which points one way only. Heat passes from a hot to a cold body, never from a colder to a hotter; and when all bodies in the universe reach the same temperature, which is, according to this supreme law, inevitable, its total energy will be for ever locked up, and the Cosmos lapse into a trance, the everlasting trance of death. This irreversible process, known as Entropy, foretells the end of the material universe, for movement and change will cease. Time's irreversibility is the only physical criterion which enables us to distinguish the past from the future in the surrounding world; it is the arrow of which Eddington speaks, as showing the direction of time's flight. The arrow points to a downward slope into the gulf of a final and irremediable stagnation. However regarded, time thus presents an inexorable countenance. Something of profound significance is taking place, of which it is the index, with which human destiny is inseparably associated.

That science should find itself faced by formidable, even insurmountable difficulties in its dealings with space and time is in no respect surprising, and their roots are easily laid bare. The physical world is her province. But no physical key will fit the wards of nature's lock, with whose intricate mechanism are interwoven motion and number, life and growth, volition, memory and thought, to which the laboratory methods of science are obviously inapplicable. In this shadowy land, with its immaterial and intangible inhabitants, science has but one resource, to inject them, as we may say, with substantiality, to give body to the bodiless, to make them what they are not, solid, measurable things. Or you may put the matter in another way, and say that science resorts to the device of substitution. For the immaterial she substitutes the material. When she meets, for example, with thought or volition they are replaced by molecular movements in the brain, susceptible, or supposed to be susceptible of measurement. For space and time a similar substitution is made. If you ask what time it is, science refers you to a machine called a clock. Immaterial things, like space and time, are in science represented by understudies—in modern relativity theory by rigid rods and synchronised clocks. And to our astonishment we hear of space as curved or warped in the vicinity of objects, as if it were itself an object or substance. At first, you remember, it was the ether which served as a medium or carrier for the various waves of radiant energy, a peculiar kind of substance which finally became so highly charged with violent contradictions as to become comic, so much of a music hall grotesque that it endangered the dignity of science, and was quietly withdrawn from the stage. Space stepped gently and without ostentation into the breach, space whose existence no one doubted, which might, if left undefined and no more inconvenient questions asked, be supposed capable of sustaining the part. So nothing was said, and the play proceeded.

Or take motion. We speak of speed, a velocity of so many miles an hour. But this speed or velocity, what is it? The qualities of substances are largely determined by their velocities. From a jet of water projected at high speed an axe will rebound without passing through it, as if it had encountered a steel bar. Yet of absolute velocity, as of empty space, science knows nothing, and can know nothing. All motions in the universe are relative to other motions, with which they can be compared. Nor could we be so much as aware that we were moving at all were we in a vacant void, out of relation with other moving bodies. Motion in itself can neither be perceived nor measured. Nor, again, can energy be measured save by comparison with other energies. With none of these things, absolute energies or motions, empty space or empty time, has science any acquaintance. So, in order that she may deal with it at all, space is converted into an extended substance, crowded with physical events. It is composed, we gather, of electric fields, and it is of these fields, or what they contain, and not of space itself that science is in fact invariably speaking.

And if you ask how time, since it is not in any sense a dimension of space, can possibly be substantialised, as in the famous formula space-time, you meet with a most ingenious contrivance. The time of the physicist is not the philosopher's time. It has undergone a most interesting transformation. The physicist's time is an imaginary quantity, measured by adopting the speed of light as a limiting or maximum velocity. For the invisible and immeasurable flow of time Relativity theory substitutes a physical equivalent, or what passes for an equivalent, a peculiar, selected velocity, that of light, to which no acceleration can be given, and by this arbitrary device, which speciously objectifies time, science obtains a measuring rod, a kind of footrule. Time's true character is thus adroitly eluded and ignored. The problem is quietly dropped, and for measurement purposes a system of signalling installed. The signals employed are light signals, assumed to be the fastest possible. They must be so assumed, and for this reason. If a faster messenger than light were admitted to be possible, a speed, that is, greater than light's, let us suppose an instantaneous intuition, an observer so equipped might become aware of an event before, from the scientific point of view, it had happened, before, that is, the light signal, the scientific messenger, reached him with the news that the event had taken place—a possibility science does not care to contemplate. On reflection we see that the peculiar paradoxes with which Relativity theory is beset—the local times which replace simultaneity, the bulge or curvature in space-time—these paradoxes are due to the fact that modern physics is not dealing with space and time at all, but solely with things masquerading in their room.

All this, after many alarms and excursions, is now recognised. Not long since, the Wyld Reader in Psychology at Oxford asked Professor Einstein, 'What was his view as to the relationship between space-time and psychological time?' and received the answer that 'from his' (Professor Einstein's) 'point of view as a physicist there was no relationship'. The truth is that, philosophically considered, we have stumbled upon a mare's nest. The sensational advances in modern physics bring no light to our darkness, and leave the old enigmas of time and space precisely where they found them. It might have been foreseen that it would be so. If we assume phenomena, things as they appear, to be things in themselves, we are, as Kant pointed out, instantly involved in illusions. And sooner or later all physical enquiries come to their predestined end. If there be a world beyond the physical they cannot enter it. They cannot follow the ghost through the space-time wall. They can only point to the place where it disappeared, to some region beyond. In our day the space-time of science has 'devoured matter', and with this result physics reaches its inevitable end. Matter, with its various old familiar properties, has dissolved into radiant energy. Its atoms and molecules have been hotly pursued only to melt into electrons. These in turn evaporated into space-time, which marks the limit or final boundary of all our investigations—a world apparently condensed or crystallised out of nothing. The powers of science, apart from the applications of the knowledge gained, are exhausted. In the matter of explanation it can go no further. The ghost, matter, has disappeared through the wall. Physics, chemistry, biology have said all they have to say, and the rest is silence, the old silence under another name, or the old materialism. Space-time, that is to say, the wall itself, is now declared to be God, the Creator of all things, and how much wiser we have become. Unity or identity, the decision that all is one, the only goal with which the human intellect will rest satisfied, has on this line of enquiry been reached, 'the infinite', which, as Leibniz held, 'is always latent in things'. And the conclusion appears to emerge, that nothing has in reality ever happened; all change, as Parmenides taught, is an illusion, and the whole of Being imperishable and immutable.

Yet when this result has been arrived at we meet with an instant contradiction. To this unchangeableness, this unity and identity, is opposed the Becoming, to which the finger of time, the arrow of entropy, so steadily points, a real past, and a real future, as marked by the flow of events. The universe is not static, it is in process. Now, in this material energy, though, as the Second Law of Thermodynamics teaches, with the passage of time it is continually decreasing, we have, in fact, what we may call the power-house of the universe. It is not wasted energy, but somehow, while its strength lasts, is translated into the building of life and mind. There it is, laying the foundations of things to be on higher levels of existence, destined, it may be, to supersede its own. For it is indeed possible that the passage of the whole, the running down of the material universe, may be towards a transformation of the material into a mental world, giving birth to a new state or states of being unlike the present. Above the stream of motion and of change a genius presides, the genius of the universe. 'And there always remains in the abyss of things', as Leibniz said, 'slumbering parts, which have yet to be awakened, to grow in size and worth, and, in a word, to advance to a more perfect state. And hence no end of progress is ever reached.' Even to-day the world we know contains what its past ages never contained, and history will not repeat itself. Time, moving on its irreversible career, is unceasingly at work, giving birth to thoughts unharboured in the past, and undertakings never paralleled.

There is here something more than appearance; there is a process and a prophecy. 'It is impossible', as Professor Whitehead wrote, 'to meditate on time and the mystery of the creative passage of nature without an overwhelming emotion at the limitations of human intelligence.' Suppose now we admit them—admit, I mean, the limitations of our minds—should we be inconsolable? Is there any cause for lamentation? Charles Lamb confessed that he enjoyed, now and again, a ramble in imagination 'outside the diocese of the strict conscience'. I admit a similar schoolboy fancy for breaking bounds. Let us break them, and ask ourselves whether the satisfactions of a perfectly rational world, as polished and perfect as the circle drawn by Giotto's unerring hand, would be all that fancy paints them. Beyond the bounds of comprehension may there not lie a romantic, delectable and quite inhabitable country? 'Tis no doubt a philosophical impropriety, even impiety, to suggest that a defence of any kind can be offered for the inconceivable and astonishing, for the unbelievable and inexplicable. Yet why should we suppose things necessarily conformable to our notions of them, to the simplification our tender minds require? Why not expect the unexpected? May not our reason's incapacity to surprise the secrets of nature be a hint that they form an inexhaustible procession, and be, too, since there is so much the more to look forward to, a blessing in disguise?

Those who would have life logical, a pretty geometrical design, a kind of finished garden city, to which no additions can be made, must, indeed, view its confusions and irregularities with uneasy apprehension. To pattern lovers, to neat minds, who prefer things in their proper places, ticketed and pigeon-holed, it no doubt presents a shocking spectacle, an inextricable tangle, a wilderness without ways, aflame with conflicting energies, swarming with creatures of a hundred million habits, involuted and convoluted to an indescribable complexity. Let it be so, and let us take a holiday from the requirements of a static logic, asking ourselves whether such a holiday might not benefit our spiritual health. Half-hours with the irrational, the magical, the surprising, have they not a tonic quality, a charm of their own, the charm of the medieval as contrasted with the modern garden city? Have you observed how much those irresponsible beings, the poets, are in love with such wild things, and how much they are in demand among children? They would not give a fig for logic. Perhaps nature speaks through them as clearly as through reason. 'What shocks the virtuous philosophers', said Keats, 'delights the chameleon poet.' Might one not be happy all one's life long among miracles, with the mysterious and the incomprehensible? Would a world beyond understanding be utterly dismal, dreary, intolerable? More so than a perfectly understood world, geometrically exact, in which nothing lay round the next corner, all men were good and sensible and all governments unnecessary? I hardly think so. The illogical world remains eternally interesting. It seems, indeed, doubtful, whether what we call our newly acquired knowledge is more than a bringing what was already known into the clear light of consciousness. Doubtful also whether the present zone of human activities provides knowledge of the intellectual order. It seems rather a meeting of souls, a place of assembly, a public gathering, where friendships may be made, experiences compared, powers exercised and strengthened, possibilities of increased satisfaction explored, Becoming, in a very diversified universe, studied not in respect of intellectual requirements alone, but in all its range and opportunity. There appears something, however little, to be said for the world as a wonder or fairy-land, supernatural, full of marvels, with all the orthodox giants, dragons and enchantments, thrills, risks and adventures; for supposing nature clean beyond us, for believing the world the work of ever-active and inventive gods, whose ways and future designs are beyond knowing. Is there any need to be so much in love with logic, so hostile to the unique and amazing?

Yes, you answer, to his search after understanding belongs whatever dignity the human being possesses. No doubt. In knowledge, moreover, we acquire power, and the more of it the more ability to meet and master circumstances. Truth is certainly truth, and we need not be anxious about it, but in respect of any kind of final understanding, the lifting of the veil of Isis, would that be the crown of human happiness? 'Did the Almighty,' said Lessing, 'holding in His right hand *Truth*, and in His left *Search for Truth*, deign to offer me the one I might prefer— in all humility but without hesitation, I should request—*Search for Truth*.'

Now, no one has ever set out on an expedition to explore

Cloud-Cuckoo-Land. You assume, in other words, the existence of the thing for which you search. And science has always proceeded on the daring, the magnificent assumption that nature was intelligible, that it could be comprehended. Well now, is it? There's a question. To believe it you must believe in the uniformity of nature, believe that what she has done yesterday she will do to-day, and for ever. For if nature is continually changing her ways, producing novelties, you can never come to an end of them, never exhaust her purposes or her mind. Or you must speak of these novelties never seen before, as 'emergents', life 'emerges' somehow out of matter, mind 'emerges' somehow from life. That is to say two and two make five, which is hardly human arithmetic.

With the postulate that nature is comprehensible, science has beyond denial achieved many and startling successes. But what kind of successes? Successes by the way. Look narrowly at their character. Mining for gold, we may say, for the explanation of things, science has come upon a great number of most fascinating and glittering pebbles—electricity, the spectrum, X-rays and a-rays and γ-rays, besides a hundred other curiosities. Has she found the gold of which she went in search? Has she, in fact, explained anything? It would be much nearer the truth to say that she has deepened all the old mysteries, making more marvellous what was already marvellous, leaving us dumbfounded, and her own adventurous spirits amazed. And, in the end, though in herself so glorious a witness to human powers, see what she has omitted from the account.

Galileo described a friend of his whose way of painting was peculiar. This was his method. He wrote upon the canvas in chalks, 'Here I will have the Fountain with Diana and her Nymphs; there certain harriers; in this corner I will have a Huntsman with the head of a stag; the rest shall be Lanes, Woods and Hills.' In the scientific account of the world you have a similar picture. History and philosophy, the rise of kingdoms, churches and poems, the scientific ideals and structures themselves, life and death, the passions and devotions of men are not so much as mentioned. 'The universe is put into equations,' wrote Maeterlinck, 'as the history of France was put into madrigals.' The places they are to occupy, as in the picture by Galileo's friend, are left blank, indicated only by chalk marks. You do not recognise the scientific landscape as in any way resembling the world in which you live, any more than the words written on the canvas enable you to see Diana and her nymphs, or the Huntsman with his dogs. In this drifting mist of electrons, in this resolution of all things into aspects of space-curvatures, into equations, what have we more than chalk marks, and have we become more intelligible to ourselves as in bewilderment we contemplate them?

> The treacherous colours their fair art betray,
> And all the bright creation fades away.

All our natural human interests have utterly vanished. The mill grinds only what it is designed to grind, and of necessity only in its own manner of grinding. 'Does it ever occur to a physician', as Maeterlinck asks, 'to heal his patients with the help of algebraic symbols?'

Whatever truth these metrical aspects of the world contain, how remote, how far away it lies from what we, striving, hoping creatures, value most! Science is the view of life where everything human is excluded from the prospect. It is of intention inhuman, supposing, strange as it may seem, that the further we travel from ourselves the nearer we approach the truth, the further from our deepest sympathies, from all we care for, the nearer are we to reality, the stony heart of the scientific universe. Let us put away from us, therefore, all thoughts of ourselves and all that most concerns us. 'The free man', says Spinoza, 'thinks of nothing less than of death.' He deceived himself. He desired not to think of it, and never ceased to think of it. Lay aside your humanity, advises this mathematically-minded philosopher, if you would arrive at the truth. God does not think as you think, and you should instruct yourself to think as God. He does not ask much of us, only that. Are atoms and molecules, then, are electro-magnetic energies more real than we who invented these terms, more fundamental than our friends and families, our loves and hates, our wars and religions? Does God think in dead things more truly than in us, and is He better represented in them than in our living souls? Are they to be subordinated to the metrical aspects, the constructions of the Euclidean understanding, or whatever it be that lies beyond them? So the noble company of the intellectuals desires us to believe. And this in utter ignorance of what in fact does lie beyond them. Tearing a

344

page out of the book of nature, they puzzle over the meaning. But removed from its context nothing in man or nature is intelligible, or can be interpreted as having any meaning whatever. They place truth above the truth seeker and knowledge above the knower, without any information greater than yours or mine where these are to be found. Their interest even in truth, moreover, has its limits. From history, for example, since nothing can there be measured or analysed, from its imponderable elements, from the ideals and passions by which its course is swayed, from the thought of Socrates, the gospel of Christ, the rise and fall of empires, the Reformations and the Renaissances, the intellectual philosophies avert their eyes. Is there less of truth in them than in the neutrons and the positrons, in the influence of Aristotle or Buddha upon the world than in geology or biology, in the essences of the spirit than in the chemistry of the stars? Is $2 + 2 = 4$ the highest type of truth? God forbid.

There are truths of many kinds, of the senses, of inner and outer experience, of the heart as well as of the understanding. And truth of any and every kind derives its sole value and significance from its relation to ourselves, to human life and destiny. Nature has no values. Only when sentient creatures appear do values appear. If you set them and their appreciations aside, in effect you set everything aside, and reduce the universe to a whirlpool of nonsense. And if the world consists of selves, we are at once driven to regard their interests and values as supreme and above all mere events. Just as grammarians concerned only with their syntax and sentences pass by the inspirations of the poets, so the logicians and rationalists can make nothing of human motives, actions or ideals. They have nothing to tell us of the soul, the mother of logic and reason. Nor have they anything to say of chivalry or honour, of character or friendship, of heroism or justice, of beauty or sweetness, of magnanimity or refinement, of elegance or charm. Or what they have to say about such things and how they came into existence is merely laughable.

What kind of knowledge or truth is this which becomes paralysed in the region of the spirit? Surely inadequate, is it not, this landscape without the human figures, this play without Hamlet, when we come to talk of explanation and understanding? Something must be true, whether we know it or not. But

345

understanding is a different matter. We appear to need a new logic and a new reason when we attempt to deal with life and mind. Certainly what we possess and employ will never account for existence, for growth and change, for the eternal and transcendent. The self is incomprehensible as the world is incomprehensible, because neither will await the erection of our logical scaffolding, because our minds cannot lay hold of change, and they are perpetually changing. 'Whatever changes', said Kant, 'is permanent, and its conditions only change.' What is this permanent which permits of the possibility of change? The universe and the self. Reason is, indeed, the eye of the soul, but as the eye is associated with the spatial sense, submerging us in its peculiar domain of visible things, so our logic, modelled upon and following spatial measures and concepts, finds there the limits of its travel. It is not the deepest thing in us, nor can it bring us to the heart of life. We are ourselves already at its heart, and our souls understand what logic baulks at. 'If we consider the matter closely,' as Mr. Belfort Bax has written, 'we shall see that the conviction of the truth of a given philosophical formulation, or, in other words, the conviction of the adequacy of the formulation, as expressing in the terms of abstract thought the self-consistency of consciousness, rests in the last resort upon feeling—namely, the feeling of intellectual satisfaction it affords'.[1]

And whatever the soul may be, it is never found apart from a self, which, it seems to be frequently forgotten, is as necessary to thinking as to feeling or living. The only existent which includes all other existents is consciousness, the appanage of the self; and apart from the self, the centre of everything, there is neither consciousness nor thinking, neither desiring nor explaining, neither science nor logic, neither knowing nor being known. The attempt to derive the self from atoms and the void, from space and time, to deny it any constructive rôle in the system of nature, has not failed for lack of unceasing and desperate effort. It has failed because you cannot explain the self in terms of the not-self. The philosophies of the future will, I think, take another and more promising way. They will allow to the self its unique status, its standing as a factor, a primary factor and an organising factor in the universal whole. They will reinstate personality in its true place in the universe, and leave room for its expansion. They

[1] *The Real, the Rational and the Alogical*, by E. Belfort Bax, p. 235.

will abandon, too, the notion of a God who made the world, and then, being weary, went into retirement. God has not ceased to think. And when a God thinks he thinks to some purpose. The genius of the world will not flag in his inventiveness, or be content drowsily to repeat himself for the convenience of the men of science and the philosophers, who, breathless with running, cannot think comfortably, and would have him cease from his labours, in order that at their ease they might comprehend and judge the value of his completed design. He will not, I fear, accommodate them.

The world has a history, and man has a history. If they have had a past, which is certain, that they will have a future is equally certain; and certain, too, that it will contain no fewer unpredictable and surprising events.

XVII

THE WEB OF LIFE

In the meantime I was sometimes, though seldom, visited and inspired with new and more vigorous desires after that Bliss which Nature whispered and suggested to me. Every new thing quickened my curiosity, and raised my expectation. I remember once, the first time I came into a magnificent and noble dining-room and was left there alone, I rejoiced to see the gold and plate and carved imagery, but when all was dead and there was no motion, I was weary of it and departed dissatisfied. But afterwards when I saw it full of lords and ladies and music and dancing, the place which once seemed not to differ from a solitary den had now entertainment and nothing of tediousness in it. By which I perceived (upon a reflection made long after) that men and women are, when well understood, a principal part of our true felicity. By this I found that nothing that stood still could, by doing so, be a part of Happiness: and that affection, though it were invisible, was the best of motions.

Traherne

XVII

THE WEB OF LIFE

Truth in our time appears to be a receding rather than an approaching star. There is no end to the philosophical systems offered for our acceptance. To which, then, should we incline? If we are not to abandon speculation, all thought upon the matter, shrug our shoulders at the tilts and tournaments going on everywhere around us, and end where we began, the only course is to accept, till intellect and imagination amend it, that way of thought which seems to leave the fewest difficulties upon our hands, and to account for the greatest number of our experiences. We do well constantly to remind ourselves that we are learning merely the alphabet of reality, and can only proceed with 'a kind of hesitating confidence', as Plato described it, in our reason.

And for the favourite model of the universe, which thinks of it as a single substance, the Absolute, eternally making and re-making itself, a solitary Being, exhibiting now these, now other appearances for no ascertainable reason, we may substitute—I would myself substitute—a scene of action, wherein innumerable entities or selves, real and enduring agents, are at work, to whose interactions, meetings, partings, attractions and repulsions we owe the parti-coloured arena we call the world. Against neither model, for they are no more than adumbrations or fancy sketches, has logic anything final or decisive to say. And for my part I prefer the latter, since it seems in closer correspondence with the state of the universe as known to us in observation and reflection alike. I adhere to the model which is in accord with universal experience and takes account of the intermingled order and disorder, the negations and affirmations everywhere open and patent throughout organic and inorganic nature. This model takes account of time as we must ourselves in daily life take account of it, and accepts existence as a becoming. It contradicts none of the positive findings of science. It rejects the

351

suspicion that the world is in any sense a machine, incapable of expansion, or that we and the other agencies at work within the world are propelled by mechanical motions. It provides for all a certain measure of freedom, and a field of purposes, not wholly illusory. The agents within it are not utterly deceived in supposing themselves agents in a real process. I prefer it to the theory of a machine dead from the first, which has never in any of its parts, or in any true sense, come alive, which could not, indeed, come alive, since it was in effect at an end from the beginning, in which nothing ever happens, for its changes are no more than repetitions of pre-ordained movements. In this notion of the world as a machine, a sort of island, unrelated to time and yet occupying such and such an amount of space, in this notion, which has for long so captivated the human mind, we have, perhaps, its palmary obsession, the most pitiful and beggarly of the concepts with which mankind has approached the interpretation of the great mystery. That men should have supposed a concept derived from their own petty contrivances applicable to the mighty sum of things, to the Cosmos itself, undermines faith in human reason beyond all the arguments adduced to demonstrate its utter pauperdom. To this child-like conception anything is to be preferred. 'The most irrational theory of all', as said Plotinus, 'is that elements without intelligence should produce intelligence.'

What then is to be substituted? For the painful struggle, 'for the immortal conflict going on' around us, as 'if God had let go the helm of the universe', Plato perceived it necessary to assign a cause. To him it appeared a dramatic contest between good and evil—a notion also too simple for our acceptance to-day. For all goods have their attendant ills, and all ills their attendant goods. Good leads to evil and evil to good. Within our frame of reference, and we cannot go beyond it, good and evil are not found unalloyed or in isolation, but interwrought in a pattern or network, which is the world, and without which no world could be. To account for the irregularities and confusions, the defects and disorders, opposed, as Plato assumed, to the Creator's will, he found himself wholly at a loss. On such an assumption these discords could only be attributed to a maleficent soul or souls, later personified in Christian theology as Satan, the Adversary of God; an adversary unhappily so powerful, if we are to judge by the murky shadows the world displays, as to challenge the omnipotence of God, its creator. For the illogicalities and accidents of life, its casual encounters, its hazards, mischances, eccentricities and humours, some other explanation is required. And the pluralistic model finds in these no invincible difficulties: since, though the Many seek good and only good, evil as well as good is to be expected in the world of their making, in their diverse designs and conflicting ideals. Were its source a perfect Absolute no room had been left for errors or absurdities; and in the abounding errors and absurdities, in the human comedy— and I would not myself, if I could, banish them as indefensibly disgusting—we have, it seems to me, an irrefutable argument for a multiplicity of entities, at numerous levels and of many kinds. The world, as I see it, is hardly less a comedy than a tragedy, 'a comedy to the intellect, a tragedy to the heart,' and certainly includes both, as components of the pattern which arises from the multifarious aims and circumstances among the innumerable agencies there engaged.

If now we prefer this model and accept the world as a process, and a growing or becoming, how shall we describe these agencies to whose activities it owes its confused and complicated character? Manifestly they are, to begin with, of many varieties. There are self-conscious entities like ourselves; there are creatures with organisms not unlike our own, sensitive and intelligent, as are the higher animals. There are others again whose consciousness appears dim, indeed; and others in whom it can hardly, if at all, be discerned. And finally below the plants we reach entities which appear to be actuated entirely by forces external to themselves, to whom it seems altogether absurd to ascribe individual existence in or for themselves in any sense—the elements, and their minute particles or atomic components, as described by the physicists. And these, the inorganic constituents of this planet, not to speak of the universe, are by comparison with its living things so vast in quantity, and in the space they occupy, that life in any or all its forms appears beside them a negligible nothing, the merest shimmer on the surface of a stupendous mass of dead, insensate matter; not so much by comparison, so far as science can report, as a single nautilus afloat on the Pacific Ocean, or a butterfly adrift, if that could be, in stellar space.

To claim, therefore, within the material universe a place for life or mind at all, to think of either as more than a petty accident, a passing shadow in the everlasting procession of physical events, has seemed to many philosophers the merest lunacy. Yet mind does more than matter can, since it includes all things within the survey of its intelligence, seeks after the invisible to be discerned only by its visionary aid, and so takes the whole Cosmos within its ken. Accepting its unparalleled transcendence and priority, can we find any trace of mind's mysterious powers at the lower levels of sentience, or follow it into the inorganic realm? Impossible, you think. And certainly life and mind vanish utterly from our sight when we reach the lowest levels of that realm, when we study its simplest denizens and attempt to pass beyond them into microscopic lands. We draw, and feel compelled to draw the sharpest distinction between the animate and inanimate fields, and can discern no connecting bridge. Yet the failure may well be in us, in our discernment and imagination; and to dictate to nature is dangerous. She drops, moreover, hints it were best not to overlook. The metals themselves, as dead, we think, as dead can be, none the less display, like living things, fatigue, and can like them be excited or poisoned. They have a primitive mode of being, a hidden life of their own, an unimaginable sensitivity. And the very electrons and protons, to which we are introduced by science as the minutest of nature's creations, strangely repeat in their simpler attractions and repulsions our own emotional reactions. They, too, are very much alive, though their mode or way of existence differs from that of the plants, from that of the mosses and the lichens, for example, as theirs from ours. And everywhere the presence of energy argues the presence of life, and the presence of life argues the presence of will, and at least nascent intelligence. And 'this account', in the words of Plotinus, 'allows grades of living within the whole, grades to some of which we deny life only because they are not perceptibly self-moved. In truth, all these have a hidden life; the thing whose life is patent to sense is made up of things which do not patently live, but, none the less, confer upon their resultant total wonderful powers towards living.'

One crucial difference there seems, indeed, to be, between the inanimate and animate realms as we are accustomed to conceive them, a distinction which carries us into the heart of a metaphysical problem of the first order, the problem of motion. Does anything in fact ever move at all? A preposterous question, you may think it. Yet it has been debated by some of the acutest minds that ever pondered the great enigmas. It was maintained by Parmenides, a philosopher held in the highest veneration by the Greeks, both as a man and a thinker, that motion and change, beginnings and endings, were all illusions of our mortal minds, mere opinions, a doctrine supported by his disciple Zeno in a series of ingenious puzzles, the most famous riddles of the world, among them the riddles of Achilles and the Tortoise, and the Flying Arrow. Achilles, you remember, could not overtake the tortoise, nor could the arrow fly. Motion was an illusion. There was no such thing. Since the nature of both space and time are here involved, the elucidation of these riddles, even were I equal to it, lies beyond our present scope. Let us be brief, and say that, in common opinion, to living things only belongs the power of movement, of moving and of producing motion, a power denied to material things, which cannot move, we believe, save as the result of a communicated impulse from some other object, already itself in motion, as when one billiard ball strikes another. Impelled, pushed or pulled they may be, but of themselves to initiate or give rise to motions they are incapable.

Can this supposed crucial difference, say between ourselves and the elements, be eliminated or surmounted, and if surmounted will it not lead to the result that we are ourselves as devoid of freedom as they—like lifeless things unable to produce motion, being ourselves also merely parts of a great machine—rather than to the result that lifeless things resemble us in the power of creating movements *ab initio*? Are we not in their category in this respect, rather than they in ours, like them impelled by external forces, blown as dust is blown by the winds, and our belief that we have power within ourselves to act and change the course of natural events, like so many of our fancies, a curious hallucination? To prove it an hallucination many thinkers have laboured and many arguments have been to that end evolved. Proved, however, it has not been. I wish to write a letter. Who or what is this 'I'? And how does this unseen entity, this 'I' set my hand going? Before these questions the mechanical philosophers recoil in dread. We know, as positively as can be

355

known, if there be in the word knowledge any meaning whatever, that as Lucretius, the supreme, indeed the only poet of note among the materialists, allowed, the beginning of motion comes from the heart or will, and is thence transmitted to the body and the external world. Can this apparent freedom, this spontaneity, this genius be found in the material elements; can they be supposed, in any intelligible sense, alive? Can we, in short, allow nature to be a continuous system, without breaks or barriers, animated in some fashion and degree throughout, a society, as Bruno and Leibniz maintained, of intelligent monads?

Well, let us first ask ourselves, 'Can there be such a thing as a motiveless movement?' How can science, or how can we, account for mere random motions or undirected energy? To suppose it, is, of course, to quit the field of reason in despair. There can be no such energy. Matter in motion, whatever matter may be, is active and energetic either as the result of some previous motion, or from some hidden and to us unknown inner impulse. From which then? There can be no doubt, you answer. Since the dawn of physical science all movements throughout the universe, it has been held, are the result of previous movements. To this opinion La Place gave expression in his classic statement that every event in nature flowed by the strictest necessity from previous events, and that a supreme intelligence with a complete knowledge of the universe at any given moment could infallibly foretell all its future states till the end of time. Here are his words—'A spirit who knew at a given moment all the forces existing in nature, and the relative position of all existing things or elements composing it, would, if he were able to submit all these data to mathematical analysis, be able to comprehend in a single formula the motion of the greatest heavenly body and of the lightest atom: nothing would be uncertain for him, and future as well as past would be open before his eyes.' You are familiar with the statement of this creed in the poetic version of Omar Khayyám—

> With Earth's first Clay they did the last Man's knead,
> And then of the Last Harvest sowed the Seed;
> Yea, the first Morning of Creation wrote
> What the Last Dawn of Reckoning shall read.

The universe, in brief, was a clock, wound up once and for all at some unspecified moment in the past, and nothing occurs in the revolutions of its wheels that might not from that moment have been predicted.

That age-long opinion is not, however, the modern doctrine. For it appears that the electrons and protons of which matter is supposed to consist, the centres of electric energy, are entities whose fluctuations cannot be traced to any previous movements; and where prevision ends, science, by her own confession, has reached its terminus. To the embarrassment of the mechanical philosophers, who think of the world as a rigid and lifeless system of springs and levers, science has arrived at a point in its history of momentous significance, perhaps the most momentous since its day began. The 'Sir Absolutes', the determinists, no longer appeal to science for support. If you care to assert, however astonishing may seem the declaration, that every particle of matter moves, when it does move, from an inner and free impulse of its own, the new physics is not prepared to contradict you. For some reason, no doubt, the particles move, but you are free to imagine, if you like, that each is an elementary mode of life, and to regard its movement as the evidence of that life, an action as spontaneous as any of your own. 'How has our physical world picture changed in the last twenty years?' asks Planck, one of the most brilliant contributors to the new picture. 'Each of us knows', he tells us, 'that the transformation which has occurred is one of the most profound which has ever taken place in the development of science.' Many of our most ancient and most desperate problems now present a different countenance, among them that most teasing conundrum, our oldest friend, the pivot upon which all others turn, the relation of the body to the mind. A new possibility in respect of their relations has emerged. For it is no longer forbidden us to think of nature as a grand society, a hierarchy, and to say that everywhere mind acts not upon dead matter, but at all times directly upon mind.

Look now a little more closely into this famous affair of causation. What can be simpler? The whole edifice of our knowledge is supported by it. We trace habitually events to their causes. Day and night we think in terms of causation. The idea of cause is the great central pillar not only of scientific thought but of all thought. If it trembles the whole building of our knowledge trembles. Fortunately, we think, it cannot

357

tremble, for it is based upon the eternal granite. Of this you are sure. But listen to this—'The word cause', wrote William James, 'is an altar to an unknown God: an empty pedestal still marking the place of a hoped-for statue.' Or this saying of Planck—'The problem of causality, the roots of which have certainly not been reached hitherto'.

What is the meaning of this? Into what wood of error, what dark forest of bewilderment have we strayed? Nearly a hundred years ago a Scotsman, David Hume, threw a bombshell into the camp of the philosophers in his startling analysis of the causality concept. He asserted, which was nothing, but boldly proceeded to prove, that to find anywhere or at any time throughout nature the effect in its supposed cause was impossible. You observed, certainly, that one event was succeeded by another, that, for example, the impact of a moving billiard ball upon a second ball was followed somehow by the movement of the second ball. But no connecting link between the two motions could actually be observed, beyond the fact that the one movement followed the other. Nor could you, save through previous experience, predict by any process of reasoning what exact effect upon the second ball the impact of the first would in fact produce. No logic could tell you what would happen. The result, as far as unaided human thought could say, might have been to bring both balls to a standstill, or the first might have rebounded in a straight line from the second. How then do we know what to expect in nature? Only previous observation can tell us. No one, as Hume pointed out, could have discovered, or could now discover by pure thinking, that the crystal is the result of heat, or ice of cold, without previous experience of these qualities. Throughout nature all events are separate events, and between them no logical or necessary nexus can be discovered. The link or bond is established in our minds by our expectation, by our previous observations of such a conjunction. Though the first million men you examine have their hearts on the left side of their bodies, you are not entitled to conclude that it is invariably so. The next may have it, as occasionally happens, on the right side.

Hume's reasoning has never been met. So deeply and firmly, none the less, is the idea of causation seated in the human mind that his destructive analysis of the concept made little or no impression either upon plain men or men of science. It

358

appeared a piece of metaphysical jugglery, clever but unimportant. Before Hume causality had all the force of a divine law. It spanned the whole heaven of human thought, since without it the regularity and uniformity of nature could not, it was supposed, be accounted for, and would be endangered. Therein lay the sting of Hume's analysis. To maintain the idea of physical causation everywhere operative throughout the universe was an imperative necessity if the scheme of things as an iron-bound mechanism were to be preserved from ruin. Not till yesterday did science arrive by a strangely different route at the conclusion Hume had reached. The relation of cause and effect, as Schrödinger recently expressed it, 'is not something we find in nature but is rather a characteristic of the way in which we regard nature.'

So much for the idea of cause, which it is not our present business to examine. We are concerned only with the findings of modern physics, and their bearing upon our special problem. The law, as it seemed, of nature and of the mind, that every event throughout the physical universe is strictly determined, is now seen to be an assumption, a thing taken for granted, a habit or prejudice of our thought.

Look again at the situation. At the base of all accounts of physical nature lies the atomic theory. All that the universe contains is, on that theory, made up of atoms, and all movements are the movements of atoms. If you carry your analysis further you come to particles of which the atom is composed, and to their movements. What moves these lesser particles? Here yawns the gulf. No one knows; no cause can be ascertained for the motions of the electrons composing the atom. An atom in a radio-active substance disintegrates, but when it will do so, or why it does so science is ignorant. Its waywardness, like human waywardness, is its unique quality. For all that physics can tell, the constituents of the atom, the electrons, may be mental entities, moving on their own initiative when they feel so inclined. But if, you object, there be such freedom in the realm of nature how can we be sure what will happen next, be certain that the sun will rise to-morrow, or water at freezing-point turn to ice, or that the regular routine of events, upon whose uniformity our lives are built, may not at any moment be thrown into utter confusion and disorder? You need not be disturbed, replies our latest physics. For though nature's movements may

359

not be governed by the law of strict causation, they are controlled by laws equally efficacious. Her order and uniformity are preserved by statistical laws. Just as in a given community the number of births, deaths or marriages can be foretold beforehand, although no single and particular death or marriage can be predicted, so the fluctuations of particles, as, for example, in the Brownian movement, or the emission of energy from radioactive substances, can be quite well accounted for without reference to the supposed law of causation, for which, as a matter of fact, we can find no evidence in our investigations. A high degree of expectation meets all our requirements.

You may, indeed, once more object that the difficulty physics has encountered in discovering the cause of the atomic fluctuations is merely a practical difficulty—the unfortunate limitations of our powers of observation. Were these extended or increased we could find the cause of every movement of every particle, the push or pull that mechanics requires. You may argue that ignorance of the cause is no ground for denying its existence. No, but also, you must allow, no ground for asserting its existence, more especially when not called for by the facts. Quantum mechanics, asserts Heisenberg, 'definitely proves the invalidity of the causal law.' According to the Heisenberg 'principle of Indeterminacy' the behaviour of the particles, of which the physical world consists, is not causally controlled. Science has reached the unexpected and perplexing conclusion that identical conditions do not necessarily lead to identical results, that the same state of things may give rise to different consequences, and since various events may follow, what will actually take place cannot be foretold. Note, also, that colours, for example, which are similar to the eye, are not in every case similar in respect of their originating causes. For us, that is to say, different causes may produce the same result. Moreover, to predict the movements of particles you must know their initial velocities, and velocity involves units or moments of time, which cannot be correlated with defined positions in space. We have also to bear in mind that the measurement of physical movements involves a smooth continuity of motion on the initial trajectory, a continuity which is by Quantum mechanics expressly denied. So that the motion of particles is not merely unpredictable; it is discontinuous and therefore not uniform.

This is a pretty pass. Say what you please, the indeterminacy in nature cannot be eliminated. The mechanical world, the darling of the materialists, has been shattered beyond repair, and we have to conclude, with Weyl, 'that in nature itself, as physics constructs it theoretically, the dualism of object and subject, of law and freedom, is already most distinctly predesigned.'

We may sum up in Schrödinger's words: 'All chemical transformations, the velocity of chemical reactions, the processes of melting and evaporation, the laws of vapour pressure, everything, in short, with the possible exception of gravitation, is governed by laws of this kind'—statistical laws—'and all the *predictions* derived from these laws are of a statistical nature, and are true only within limits.' Or we may take the words of Sir Arthur Eddington—'The result of our analysis of physical phenomena up to the present is that we have nowhere found any evidence of the existence of deterministic law.'

From the immovable determinists, like Professor Einstein, distress and vexation with this strange conclusion were to be expected. Even men of science desire nature to conform to their pet conceptions of her ways and structure. They must be left to look after themselves. And yet one may enquire why all this outcry and astonishment, the annoyance which has followed the failure of physics to establish mechanical causation in the atomic realm? Everyone is aware, or should be aware, that the idea of force is derived from ourselves, from our personal experience that we can act in some measure upon the outside world, and produce effects in it when we so desire; from the simple knowledge that a living entity does, in fact, introduce changes in the course of natural events, for we ourselves act in order that such changes may be brought about. How it was possible, Kant confessed, he could not indeed imagine. How his will moved his arm was as incomprehensible to him as the notion that his arm could hold back the moon. Incomprehensible, no doubt. Indeed a natural miracle. We are, however, surrounded with miracles, with God's language of fundamental facts, which we can neither deny nor understand. And among them, as I believe, is the fact that everything that comes about, all that happens, is the result of will in some shape or form. And as all human history is simply the edifice erected by the aims and desires of mankind, of the individuals born into the world, so the universe itself has

361

taken its present structure, and will take throughout time to come whatever aspects it may assume, from the wills of its innumerable and constituent beings, at once its creatures and the creators of its history. All the energy, will, intelligence, purpose displayed throughout the universe is the energy, will, intelligence, purpose of real individual beings of which in its entirety it consists.

I would ask you to observe that this conclusion does not deny the principle of causation, that events have their causes. It does not abandon nature to the rule of chance, of random happenings. It assigns events to the activity of individual entities, to their unpredictable impulses. In their desiring or willing you must seek the causes of these events. Limited in power as individuals indeed they are, as are we ourselves, to make their wills effective in a world of multiform purposes and designs; yet ultimately it is to will that all events in the universe must be assigned. Just as men create the arts, adding to the flower-garden of the world new species, we may read the story of the universe as a story of creation, it may be without end—for which at least no term or finality can be foretold—ever advancing towards unimaginable diversity.

Consciousness and mind need not then any longer be thought of, after the impossible fashion of an earlier day, as a kind of rootless flower grafted upon an engine, where none could grow, since between them a natural relationship there was none. Rather we may adopt the language of Kant, that if we could know 'ourselves and other things as they really are', we should see ourselves in a world of spiritual natures, our connection with which did not begin at our birth, and will not cease with the destruction of the body.'

What bearing has all this—the indeterminism of modern physics—upon the problem of human freedom, so hotly debated from century to century by churchmen and philosophers alike? Some will answer 'the closest', others that it has 'none at all'. When Spinoza declared that a stone thrown into the air, if it possessed consciousness would suppose itself to fall to the ground of its own free will, how did he know this? He did not know it. He merely made the assertion. He desired to discredit and deride the notion of human freedom. How does the matter stand to-day? Exactly as it did, save in a single but important

362

particular. If physics cannot account for the activities within the atom, still less can it account for the activities of the organism. If determinism be set aside as unproven in the realm of nature, where evidence for it appeared overwhelming, where is warrant for it to be found in the more difficult region of the soul? If it be discarded in physics, it can hardly in the absence of evidence be adduced to buttress determinism in psychology, where it is in opposition the most flagrant to the universal, never-questioned conviction of the natural man. Denials of human freedom will no longer serve, save to betray the naked prejudice which gave the dogma birth. Something more will now be required of its adherents than pious opinion. The foundations of the doctrine have been undermined. The onus of proof lies with the determinists, for their cherished fancy has, one fears, and in the house of its quondam friends, received its death-wound.

And one may, perhaps, be allowed the hope that we have heard the last of this tiresome and unprofitable controversy, this spider's web of dialectic, and are permitted a return to common sense. The strictest determinists act as if they possessed the freedom they deny, and cling to it in practice as the pivot of human intercourse. And what is the point of asking men to mend their ways, and live better lives, if you at the same time insist that they are tethered animals, and all they do, or can do has been fore-ordained since the beginning of the world? Or will you issue to them a metaphysical manual which explains that, none the less, for all their actions they are responsible? We must continue to believe that the soul or self is not a piece upon the chessboard of time, moved as a wheel or lever is moved. Our thoughts are our own, mine mine, yours yours, and if our thoughts, then also our acts. The soul stands for itself, and is in its own nature a purposive mover, however limited and conditioned a factor in the origination and passage of events. The individual self, the finite centre of impulse is, as Nietzsche held, both determined and free, limited by the presence of the other individuals, in itself free and creative. It is related of Diogenes that when he heard arguments against motion his manner of refutation was not by means of words. He contented himself by doing what had been declared impossible—moving by walking away. In this workaday world there is at times something to be said for this fashion of refutation.

If now we have found inacceptable the doctrine that individual existences are illusory, mere modes or passing appearances of the One or Absolute, a single subject—a doctrine which Nietzsche also thought unnecessary—and found it inacceptable since that doctrine commits us to 'the view of Spinoza', as Leibniz expressed it, 'and of other similar authors, that there is only one substance, that is to say, God, who thinks, believes and wills one thing in me, and who thinks, believes and wills quite the opposite in some one else', and since it commits us also to the doctrine of time's unreality, and denies Becoming, the production, that is to say, of unique, unpredictable events, the emergence, for example, of new species, and of historical events and persons never exactly repeated, the Caesars and Luthers, the pyramids and the Reformations—if we set aside this opinion, we may turn to the other doctrine, which regards individual entities as metaphysical units, as monads, each in some degree a self or soul, and views the world as their scene of interaction.

This world of ours has a history, whose recent chapters, as in astronomy and geology, may in part be read. What may we believe of its earlier and missing chapters, of which we have no record? We may say with confidence that though impenetrable by us, an observer, had he been present, would have found in that history no actual hiatus, no impassable gap or gulf. What went before, we must believe, made possible what now is. A continuity of some kind, could we follow it, runs through the whole creation, and it is without doubt a spiritual continuity. For, and this is indisputable, a certain aspect of our existence, of things as they now are, cannot be explained, or even coherently imagined in any physical terms at all—that aspect which includes consciousness, thought, will, meanings and purposes. These cannot by any gymnastic be reduced to such terms, or conceived as material in origin or nature. Thinking, remembering, believing, feeling, willing are not electro-magnetic or spatial processes. Nerve movements cannot give rise to them, nor can the brain recognise itself as a brain, ask itself how it came to think, or examine its logical prejudices. Brain movements remain brain movements, physical movements not less than those of leaves moving in the wind or ripples on a stream, and to conjure them into thoughts, desires and feelings is a babble of rhetoric. And since the principle, whatever it be, underlying all life certainly contained the possibility of such activities, and permitted of them, reason refuses to accept them, to accept, that is, consciousness, thought and volition as arising out of electromagnetic fields, or as the aggregations of particles, particles of matter which somehow got together, and having got together explained to themselves how the thing was done. It is asking too much of us. For to think of the willing, aspiring and feeling soul as made up of many powers and parts is to invert the truth, that the soul provides the unity and is itself the bearer of its thoughts and feelings, its own unique experiences.

If then in the attempt to account for things as they are I have to choose between atoms and living monads, I have not a moment's hesitation. I choose the latter. Let us say, then, that the realm of nature may be better understood or comprehended if interpreted in terms of such will and purpose as we actually experience in ourselves, and of which we can form no intelligible conception save as belonging to individual selves or souls of a like nature. They do not belong, the monads, to the corporeal world, and are themselves, indeed, transcendent and unrepresentable as entities, or substances occupying space, in which region they are but partially represented. Their relations to space and time, like that of the electron to space and time, are obscure and unknown to us, but are there, in that region, similarly represented by their activities. We know them to be present where their influence is felt, or in evidence. A single soul or self sums up—since no two are alike, as no two flowers in nature are alike, and since their mode of existence is hidden from us—the whole unfathomed mystery of things. We may conclude, then, that mind is ultimate, and the cosmic system a manifestation of many minds.

But what is here meant by mind? Not the intellect taken by itself, 'the Euclidean understanding', but those faculties in us of which the self is the sole possessor. Let us recollect that the intellect is not the deepest thing in us, and the soul does more than think. It feels, desires and wills. The soul or 'I' is something for itself, a quintessence of primordial being beyond analysis, deeper sunk in reality than the intelligence or understanding, which within itself it brings to birth. Nor does the mind appear first in man, though it is there we have certain knowledge of it. We have no mirror in which we can view our souls as we do our bodies. We may, however, use the term mind in default of a better, agreeing with Hume, that 'the cause or causes of order in the universe probably bear some remote analogy to human intelligence', and agreeing further with Green that 'will is indistinguishably desire and thought', and with Coleridge that 'the will is the synonym of the word "I"', or the intelligence itself'. We may use the term mind, where all terms are inadequate, as synoptic, and regard it as the soul's representative, the ambassador of its volition, feeling and thought at their various levels in nature, as exhibited in living things, and extending to the unsearchable and, as it seems to us, inanimate world, with which living things are so intimately and so inseparably associated and interwoven. As light itself cannot be seen, and is never seen, for we see only the objects illuminated by its unseen ray, so the monads or selves are invisible save in their doings, are revealed to us in the public world of space, the theatre of their action. For even we ourselves know ourselves only as we appear to ourselves—what in reality we are we do not know—just as the scene presented to us in the outside world is also imperfectly and indirectly known as the mesh or network woven by the interactions among other selves. And it is exceedingly probable, if not certain, that all we perceive, either of ourselves or of the things of sense, are the shadows cast by the things behind the veil that truly are; projections upon the spatial screen, a Mercator's distorted map of the veritable world.

Let us be clear and positive upon this, that the body or organism with which the self is in our experience associated, is not and cannot be identified with the individual, since it is merely that individual's representative in the material world. Nor are the mental activities and faculties of the true self limited by the body or the brain, but extend, as we have abundant evidence, far beyond the range of the senses. Not only does the self direct and control the organism, but wholly transcends it in respect of its innate powers and capacities. As the pictures on a moving film represent living actors, not to be found in that time or place, and no examination of the film itself will lead to any further knowledge of these actors, exhibit more than a few hours of their lives, or tell you where now they are, or what they are, so we may say their corporeal bodies represent only the activities of the living spirits on the space-time screen during a single episode in their

366

careers, and are no more their true and complete selves than the moving pictures in the theatre are the actual actors. Nor will study the most minute and exhaustive of the body and its parts, any more than of a figure in the moving picture, reveal in his whole nature the agent which produced its motions. For as the plant has a life in its roots below the soil, and a life above it in the sunlight, so also the soul or self. If we perceived in plants not their external shapes, their leaves and flowers but the internal processes and principles at work within them, if we saw their souls, how different they would appear. And how different would our fellow creatures appear if you could shut off your physical senses and, endowed with other eyes, for example, opened them not on your neighbours' forms and faces, but upon their thoughts and motives, loves and hates. You would then behold things not less real than their shapes and movements, but much more real, their very roots and springs, the forces and the principles at work, as completely hidden from corporeal sight as are the energies in magnetic or electric fields, discoverable only in their issue and effects.

And now consider further the society of selves or monads we have pictured, of which the entire hierarchy consists. It is composed of lesser societies or partnerships, the communities or associations of sympathetic entities. Monads of the same level congregate or draw together. They seek and find, as in the elements, their natural homes, forming throughout the realm of nature, as in minerals, plants and animals, a great variety of groups and federations, such as animate nature displays in flocks and herds, in tribes and races; groups which arise out of the native sympathies of their constituent members, or at the lower levels from their corresponding and simpler attractions. The monads at the lowest levels, constituting the inorganic world, are, we might say, 'filter passers', in which the presence of life and intelligence in its most rudimentary forms cannot by our present measures or methods be detected. Yet there, as elsewhere, no monad is attracted to another monad, no soul loves another soul, unless there is already a bond between them. Life takes in them all the myriad forms we see. For what is matter? It is, physics tells us, simply energy. And what is energy? It is the expression of will or Being. It is action, which is just life itself. We can go no further. And whence is our idea of energy which gives rise to action derived? From ourselves, who can produce it by willing. Personality is, in its final analysis, simply will or cause. And since the soul is in our experience a unity which is also a multiplicity, the particles in the inorganic or apparently inanimate world represent in their various aggregations the activity of souls, whose organ is the diffuse system of the group, and whose life is mirrored in its loose association.

A species, as Aristotle divined, might be the body or organism of a single and directing soul. As among bees and ants the whole hive or colony is a close-knit bunch or cluster spatially separated in respect of its individual members, yet animated throughout by a common co-ordinated life, by a strange, inexplicable inner sympathy of aims, the soul of the swarm, so the particles or atoms of the physical or inorganic world in their respective assemblies have a joint or common base, are held together by a guiding principle, of which the entire assembly is the organism or body, the reflection in space and time of its inward life.

And if, as we may well believe, the universe is everywhere and in all its parts alive, the first act in the cosmic drama provided— in the manifestation of these monadic souls, which to us appears as the material world—the earliest and most numerous of its many federations, and became the ground upon which the more closely knit organisms, informed by later or succeeding monads, took their stand; the later life waves flowing through and mounting on the earlier. The laws of nature would then be their consolidated behaviour, their simple, automatic habits. The succeeding organisms, which in cosmic history represent and mirror monads in more complete control of their activities, are less the slaves of custom. They too, however, have a long journey before them, advancing towards intenser life, an awakened consciousness and intelligence, which may, indeed, take strange forms, and under the superintendence of time create worlds to come and natural kingdoms unlike our own. For we must think of souls or selves as continually becoming more than they already are, having within them a principle of growth. Nor can consciousness ever reach a saturation point, since it contains possibilities without end—through gathered experience and its fructifying seeds—of expansion within the Cosmos; through which the soul, its possessor, is alone equipped to travel, and to which, of necessity, it belongs. It appears, the conscious soul, when with time and the process of time conditions are such that it can associate with others and have relations with others.

You recall Wordsworth's creed:

> 'Tis my faith that every flower
> Enjoys the air it breathes—

a poetic faith, perhaps not so wide of scientific truth. For nature appears to have at heart, and as end in view, intenser life and universal consciousness throughout her myriad modes of being, in their individual forms. And the organisms we see around us, what are they? They are, we may say, the sounding boards of the souls in action, or instruments in tune with them, as one tuning-fork is with another. The body or organism associated with the individual self, through which its inner life is partially manifested, is, in the common world of all existences, at once its means of communication with other selves and its protection against the bewildering extent and multiplicity of their activities. The body is a kind of sorting place or telephone exchange. No listener could deal with the million messages passing at the same moment through such an exchange, and no finite being could sustain the impact of all the cosmic activities simultaneously discharged upon it. It would be overwhelmed in the cataract. 'Nature', as Professor Kemp Smith expressed it, 'must be adjusted to the dimensions of the animal and human consciousness.' So we may think of the body as a screen or resistance coil, which diminishes the pressure of these activities, or lowers their tension to the point at which they can be in some degree supported, and in some degree apprehended. The world, that is, by our bodies is scaled down or reduced to the measure of our powers. Within its immensity we can keep our feet, and hold our own. We can select and order our experiences.

And not only is the self thus brought by the body into simpler and working relations with the rest of the universe; it is provided also with a spiritual perspective. As the eye deals only with a certain limited series of wave-lengths, the body measures for the self the relations and intensities with which, gauging their respective values, the self is specially concerned, and has in its own immediate interests to deal. Not all reality but a simplified edition of its fundamental features is open to us. And the world of space and time thus resembles an artist's picture. There a part of the boundless and unrepresentable landscape of reality is reduced and separated from the whole and framed for our contemplation. All these, it may be said, are dreams. But they are dreams which reflect, as I think, the truth. And not less dreams were the myths of the divine Plato, or the visions of Plotinus, the eagle soaring, as it was said, above that master's tomb. The practical philosophers no doubt would have us abandon them, and cultivate our gardens.

> Return, they cry, ere yet your day
>   Set and the sky grow stern:
> Return, strayed souls, while yet ye may
>   Return.
>
> But heavens above us yearn;
> Yea, heights of heaven above the sway
>   Of stars that eyes discern.
>
> The soul whose wings from shoreward stray
>   Makes towards her viewless bourne
> Though trustless faith and unfaith say,
>   Return.

XVIII

OURSELVES

Animula vagula blandula,
Hospes comesque corporis,
Quae nunc abibis in loca
Pallidula, rigida, nudula,
Nec ut soles dabis jocos?
The dying Emperor, Hadrian, to his Soul

Little, winsome, wandering thing,
Bosom friend and guest to-day,
Whither now, my soul, away,
Wan, and cold, and unattended,
All our former frolics ended?

XVIII

OURSELVES

We are, no doubt, of some trifling importance to ourselves, but to attach any importance or significance to mankind at large is difficult. 'We burn', said Pascal, 'to find some firm foundation, some unshakable basis on which we may build the tower which reaches up to infinity.' We desire, that is, to think nobly of ourselves. But the ship of life is so small and the sea of circumstances so wide, that we are discouraged.

And nature, mother nature does not hasten to her children's material or spiritual assistance, nor view their efforts with smiling appreciation. She hardly seems to have had us in mind at all, and has made poor provision for our security and comfort. For consider, what Lucretius long ago observed, how small a part of the earth's surface is fit for human habitation. Insignificant enough to begin with, our planet is, as a dwelling-place, miserably contracted. Stormy oceans nature has provided in plenty, barren mountains, burning sands, long leagues of polar snow and ice. But how little for its inhabitants of salubrious climate or easy ways of life. Mankind has had a hard and harsh row to hoe. Consider, too, the variety of afflictions to which the race is exposed, the inclement seasons, the droughts and floods, the wild beasts and noxious insects, the fevers and pestilences, the frightful prevalence of mental disorders from idiocy to mania, the nauseous physical abnormalities, the part played in its affairs by chance and accident. The lower animals, many of them, are equipped with talents better suited to their conditions of life than we, and are, in a multitude of ways, our superiors. Or survey the infirmities of the human mind and note the failures which attend the efforts of the wisest and the best among men and nations—the cruelties, the surly, bitter tempers, the fault-finding and vituperation, the superstitions and foolery, the intrigues and deceptions, rivalries and envies, the swindling and the villainy,

373

the petty scandals, the absurd pursuits and ambitions, worst of all, perhaps, the outrageous injustices, so that

> It seems a story from the world of spirits
> When any one obtains that which he merits,
> Or any merits that which he obtains.

Our moralists and satirists have in human weaknesses a broad and easy target for their denunciations and derision. But to think well of ourselves, or with such materials to lay, as Pascal desired, the foundations of a tower reaching up to heaven, seems an undertaking rather for a tribe of demi-gods than mortal men. It was born, apparently, the human race, under an unlucky star. And never, I suppose, was there an era in which all things human were viewed by its intellectuals with such burning contempt as in ours, an era in which they so hated and despised the world and all that it contains.

What, if anything, is to be set over against these discouraging features? I can think of nothing but our contemptible selves. Personality comes first. Unless something of celestial origin and value can be discovered in the self or soul the situation is beyond repair, and its amelioration an idle dream. So it is that around the nature of the soul, as around the body of Patroclus in Homer's *Iliad*, the battle rages more fiercely than in any other part of the stricken field. It is here the main issue of human destiny is in the balance, and here it will be determined.

Of what importance, then, if any, is the individual self? On that point, in their estimate of it, you have the deepest, the most fundamental divergence between the rival schools of thought. Is it the greatest of values, this assessor or valuator, as it sets up to be, or no greater than the least of values in an undiscriminating universe? In this matter we must take man in the singular, not in the plural number. Upon the destiny of each rests the destiny of all. For you can advance no reason why nature should look more kindly upon human society as a whole than upon the least of its members. They stand or fall together. Measured by nature's scale they are indistinguishable; in her great balances they weigh alike. Though the race survive the individual, 'tis only for a season. The greedy waters will in the end suck it down, nor will a ripple on the surface of eternity show where the vessel sank. Of what significance or value, then, we ask, is the individual self?

Already, however, we have overshot the mark. To talk of values is premature. Before talking of values, let us be sure the self exists, for if, as we are not infrequently assured, it has in fact no existence, its value is not in question, and further enquiry is spared us.

The modern and shortest way with the soul or self is to deny it outright. Can we suppose—to employ a figure used by Bayle, the French philosopher, in a different setting—can we suppose 'that a ship might be constructed of such a kind that entirely by itself, without captain or crew, it could sail from place to place for years on end, accommodating itself to varying winds, avoiding shoals, casting and weighing anchor, seeking a haven when necessary, and doing all that a normal ship can?' Yes, we are told, in the human or animal body we have precisely such a ship, which handles itself admirably without captain or navigator.

You have heard of this curious doctrine, of this psychology which rejects the psyche and retains only the 'ology', the science of the self without the self. Its founder was that disconcerting sceptic, Hume. As he was unable to discover the nexus between cause and effect, so with the best will in the world he was unable, he assures us, to find the self. Introspection, he maintained, wholly fails to detect any such entity. It finds, to be sure, perceptions and events taking place within us, but no bond between them, no unifying principle there. The fondly imagined being, the supposed master or navigator of the vessel, never appears. Evidence for his existence there is none. So other and succeeding philosophers have also reported, as, for example, Professor William James. 'The passing thought is the only thinker that the facts require.' Such is his categorical declaration. It hardly seems to chime with common sense, but what has philosophy to do with common sense?

Thus, in summary fashion, these great authorities deny and dispose of us, and incidentally of themselves. Where we imagined the 'I' or self to be, there is only, they tell us, a series of fleeting impressions, sensations, fancies, pains and pleasures, which succeed each other with amazing rapidity, but without any support, any connection or tie between them, no entity over and above them that as centre or subject thinks, feels or desires. It is then a mirage or hallucination, this notion of the self. Bodies we have, but they are automata, and this 'I', with which we fancy

375

ourselves to have some acquaintance, is an illusion. And an interesting and peculiar illusion, which till yesterday successfully played the impostor's part upon the whole human race, philosophers included. And not only so, but imposed also upon itself, till in the end, after this prodigious feat of deception, it laid a snare for itself and caught itself out. This illusion, the most extraordinary that ever was, discovered itself to be an illusion. The phantom recognised itself as a phantom. So extraordinary, indeed, that we may perhaps say the discovery is of no consequence. An illusion that so successfully apes reality, and does all that reality could be expected to do, is, we may conclude, for all practical purposes sufficient. If with an illusory million of money I think myself a millionaire, am recognised by my neighbours as a Croesus and can purchase all that a Croesus can, what more in reason could anyone ask? If the self, even the philosopher's self, which has no existence, persuades others and remains persuaded of its own existence, rises each morning after sleep with the same undisturbed conviction, and performs through three score years and ten its apparent duties with efficiency, its true standing in reality may be set aside as irrelevant. Illusion or no, if it continue as it is—ah, there lies the point— if it be permanent, and never awakes to the real situation, it will serve all our needs. Universal and everlasting illusions are indistinguishable from reality. One is reminded of the story of the king who dreamt nightly that he was a beggar, and his captive who dreamt nightly that he was a king. There was little to choose between them.

Hume desired to alarm the pious folk of his day and generation. It amused him. That he was as deeply impressed by his own argument as some of his followers I decline to believe. His was no untutored mind. He was capable of more than he pretends, of the simple reflection, for example, that the hand cannot grasp itself, nor the eye, though the organ of vision, catch sight of itself.

We observed, you remember, that no one has ever seen light. Like the self, light, which brings the whole world into our presence, which makes all else visible, is itself invisible. Do we conclude by parity of reasoning that light also has no existence? Hume requires the subject of the experience to be its own object while it examines other objects—to be at the same time at both ends of the telescope. His effort recalls to us the absent-minded scholar using his spectacles to look for them, or the rustic, in the Spanish proverb, searching the country for the mule upon which he is riding. On this reasoning the existence of the self could only be maintained if it could be detected when idle, when it was doing nothing, neither thinking nor feeling, when it was vacant. When it is busy and occupied it has no time to give you an interview or to be photographed, and unfortunately it is always busy. Each of us, therefore, it appears, has a theatre in his mind, on whose stage the thoughts and feelings are continually dancing, but there is no watcher of the performance, no spectator of their evolutions. One is driven to wonder who in that case knew they were there, or told us about them.

We are asked then to believe that the self is 'an orchestra without a conductor'. I say nothing of the consequences of this doctrine. Truth, if it be indeed truth, can defy consequences. With speculative theory it is rather different. And you cannot overlook that such a declaration is destructive of all responsibility. If there be no self there can be no responsibility. 'Without personal identity', as Bradley said, 'responsibility is sheer nonsense.' Passing thoughts cannot be appealed to or denounced. They cannot be called to account, praised or blamed. They cannot even be spoken to.

If Hume convinced others by his polemic against the self, he failed to convince himself. For at a later date, with admirable candour, he wrote, 'Upon a more strict review of the section concerning *personal identity*, I find myself involved in such a labyrinth, that I must confess I neither know how to correct my former opinions, nor how to render them consistent. . . . All my hopes vanish, when I come to explain the principles, that unite our successive perceptions in our thought or consciousness. I cannot discover any theory which gives me satisfaction on this head.' He concludes with the admission that the matter is 'too hard for my understanding'. If too hard for Hume's brilliant intelligence, we need feel no surprise that it has proved too hard also for his less acute and penetrating successors.

There are more persuasive lines of attack upon the self than Hume's, founded upon the now familiar facts of alternation or dissociation of personality, upon the gaps or lapses in the continuity of consciousness during sleep or trance, the interruptions and intermittency to which our sense of personal identity is subject. There are few more interesting studies than that of sleep, so familiar and yet so mysterious, of which so little is known, and few more fascinating or perplexing than that of dual, or multiple personality; but conclusions in this region are difficult to draw and the subject is too vast and intricate for present examination. Beyond doubt there are times in which the sense of self is in abeyance, dormant, latent or suspended. The human soul appears in sleep, in trance, and it may well be similarly at death, to sink into its ground, to cease its activities, to leave the region where alone it can be by us observed and at work. Beyond question the body appears to permit at times of a change of masters, of separate memories, of conflicting wills and purposes. Of all this the future must be left to tell us what to think, to explore the realm of the subconscious and its relation to consciousness.[1]

It is an open secret that psychology has failed to unseat or dislodge the soul. The beleaguered fortress has not surrendered. The worst psychology can do, as Professor James allowed, is 'to rob it of its worth'. Its worth or value is now the matter in dispute, whether it be rooted in the universe of being with sufficient firmness to outlast the passing hour, or, like the other appearances by which we are surrounded, will presently vanish into 'the infinite azure of the past'. 'We live', said St. Augustine, 'beyond the limits of our bodies.' He touches the vital point. It is widely believed, and no unnatural thought, that the body is the only support of the soul, that the body is, you might say, the knife, and the soul its edge. When the knife is destroyed there can be no more talk of its edge. But analogies are easy and dangerous. If analogies could in a debate administer the *coup de grâce*, not many arguments would survive. And to identify the soul with its associated body is no more than to revive the old-fashioned materialism and assert a dogma. For the body is an organism, a mechanism which consists of many parts, and no union of these parts can provide it with a presiding consciousness, which is interested in itself, enquires of itself, debates with itself. The self in self-consciousness both is and knows itself to be—being, as it were, two persons in one. Nevertheless, 'Although a soul', as wrote Leibniz, 'may have a body composed of parts, each of which has a soul of its own, the soul or form of the whole is

[1] See Dr. Gustave Geley's *From the Unconscious to the Conscious*, and Dr. Carl du Prel's *The Philosophy of Mysticism*

378

not composed of the souls or forms of the parts.' Reflect for a moment, and you must allow that the whole, whether it be a machine or a living creature, may enable you to understand the parts, but the parts will never enable you, however deeply studied, to understand the whole. The soul has knowledge of its successive states or phases, a knowledge not coincident with the states themselves; neither is it a member of the procession, nor yet the procession itself. Sequences of states cannot of themselves constitute an individual. Every animal, moreover, like ourselves, acts teleologically, that is, with a purpose in its doings. It adjusts itself and adapts itself to the future.

Whose then is that purpose, or what is it that looks forward to the goal in view? The relationship of the self to time and the passage of time wholly differs from that of any mechanism, for which neither past nor future has any significance. Unless, indeed, we form a wholly different conception of matter, endowing it with a nature or qualities unknown to physics, matter, lifeless and inert, has not among its so far discovered gifts the power of learning from past experience; physical movements in the brain cannot give rise to purpose, nor does a machine keep a watchful eye on coming change. If you begin with the parts you will never reach the genius or spirit of the whole. 'Multiplicity does not contain a reason for unity.' You can see what the body is, an arrangement of tubes, springs, levers, lungs, heart, muscles. They do not regret lost opportunities, take courage and determine to do better next time. The soul is not individualised by the parts of the organism. It provides, not receives, the unity. And though you may after a fashion account for the body, you cannot account for the 'I's' attachment to that particular body. Why should this be my body, this among the ten thousand times ten thousand others? Why, in short, should we be ourselves? Why should my ego be in existence in this time or age, and not associated with some other body in the past, or a body to come, not yet born? That 'I' should be here now, in this region of time is beyond comprehension.

The 'I' is the window through which every man that ever was born looks out upon the scene of existence. Flung open at his birth, shuttered at his death, at this window through which no one else can ever look, this untransferable viewpoint, each one of us sits all his life long. A body he may have, but a body without intelligence, without speculation in its eyes, is a mere zero, a thing which can be observed but cannot itself observe. This 'I' of ours goes further than the observation of other existences; it can observe its own. And its association with a certain time in a certain place is an impenetrable mystery. That there should be a world is astonishing, but that 'I' should belong to it, or to this particular portion of the world, my body, which is in some sense mine as against all others—who will go about to make this clear?

Let us then stand our ground, and look a little further into these strange matters of consciousness and personal identity. For we may with perfect confidence, and without fear of contradiction, affirm many things. We may say, for example, that the self or subject is the only point of departure for any kind of enquiry, even the most philosophical. Apart from a self you cannot find a mind. You assume it in every debate, for it is the condition of all experience, at the base of all knowing and debating, necessary to their very existence. You assume it even when you deny it. If, as the conclusion of a train of reasoning, I reject the self, I am at the same time affirming what I deny in the reasoning of which the self alone is capable. And apart from it there is no such thing as consciousness, which is nowhere else to be found in nature; and without consciousness you could not be aware that there was an argument to ponder or a subject to discuss. We look with suspicion upon our most direct and immediate knowledge, the inner knowledge of ourselves, of all that takes place in our minds and souls. Thoughts, wishes, feelings appear to us pallid, unreal, insubstantial, shadowy nonentities. And we look with confidence upon our outer knowledge of things, of trees, men and houses as certain, quite forgetting that this outer knowledge comes to us by way of and through the avenue of our minds, and that, if our inner knowledge is in doubt, the outer must be still more deeply in doubt, mediated as it is by way of these very thoughts and perceptions of which we are suspicious. When you speak of experience you mean and can only mean the experience of a self, for there is no other kind of experience. When you say that anything appears you can mean nothing but appearance to a subject. Everything is in consciousness or you have no evidence for its existence, and nothing can be asserted that is not in some measure already in consciousness. Even in dreams it surveys the scene, even when the windows of sense are darkened.

There is then no perception of an object in the absence of a subject. A feeling of toothache is someone's feeling, a desire to eat or drink someone's desire, the intention to take a walk someone's intention. One and all these are activities of a self. They do not float about unattached in the void. Abolish the self, and you abolish all thoughts, pleasures, wishes that ever have been, now are, or ever will be. No one will say that there is no such thing as feeling. Yet there is no such thing except in the experience of a sentient subject. If you say it is the body that feels, ask the physiologists in what part of the body the feeling arises. They cannot tell you where it is, divide it into parts or measure its intensity. You, yourself only, can judge of that. Emotions, too, are states of the self and cannot be further analysed.

Or take memory, than which nothing is more inexplicable. When memory raises its head the sciences are dismayed, and fly before it. What is it that remembers, if not the self? You have a history of your own, a private diary, of which no one else can turn a single page, independent of and within the world's history. No one can recall my memories for me; if I perish my memories are lost for ever, and if I remember a face I saw a year ago, the subject that remembers must surely be the same subject, the continuing self that formerly observed the features now recalled. Who else could it be? What relation has this process to the brain? Of that neither physiology nor psychology can give any intelligible account. Memory has never been localised as a power within the brain, or shown to be associated with any neural process. No examination of the body or brain in health or disease yields any information on this faculty of recollection; no physical theory accounts for it. I look for a moment at a ship upon the sea and then turn away. I can still, however, if I wish, see it in the mind's eye. Where in the interval has been that picture, where is it now, how do I retain it and recall it, perhaps months later? You may ask, but you will not be answered. The image of the ship has not vanished for ever. I can compare it, when I please, with the image of some other ship I saw years ago.

Of images and their nature, where they reside, or of what they are made, nothing is known. Images are associated with emotions, and the same emotion may recall a former perception or image. Elementary optics will inform you that the reflections of external things are upside down on the retina of the eye. Why, then, do I not see them thus but upright? For the reason that the objects and their retinal images belong to the physical world, the world of space relationships, of what we call real space. But my knowledge or yours is not in that space at all. Knowledge has no spatial relationships. 'The light', as Fichte said, 'is not without me, but within me, and I am myself the light.' That is, I have in me something not given by sensation. I also am there with my knowledge. There is in the soul a 'stationary principle'. And this 'I', the self or subject, is not a denizen of the space to which the object is confined. 'We act forwards, but we know backwards.' And some men seem to bring with them into the world a prodigious amount of knowledge. Where did Pascal as a child acquire his knowledge of mathematics or Mozart his knowledge of music?

The physical world, science maintains, consists simply and solely of vibratory motions. It tells us that the nerves which convey the various sense messages, of sight, touch and hearing, are merely wires, alike and interchangeable. It is not in them, therefore, that the messages of sense are sorted out. The self is the sorter. We are the artists, and the pictures we see could not be found in the brain. They are ours and only ours. If you could take a stroll in the external world, and somehow unassisted by the apparatus of eye and ear look about you, you would find there, so science declares, a complicated web of movements and nothing else but movements, neither shaped nor coloured. As there is nothing in the word circle which has anything in common with or resembles a circle, or in the word fish which resembles a salmon or a whale, there is nothing in an event which has anything in common with or resembles our perception of it. Our nerves convey vibrations and only vibrations, of which we make the pictures we suppose ourselves to see. And the self apart, suppose we could see the cells that enable us to see, we should have that unimaginable state of things—cells looking at themselves.

And meaning, what is that? Have you ever pondered meanings? We talk of the import or meaning of this thing or that, the meaning of a poem, the meaning of a scientific concept, of a political event. Where are these to be found in nature? Only in us. They cannot be exhumed or distilled out of material movements. As well endeavour to extract the skylark's song out of granite rock, or honey from the salt seas. They are not resident in physical things, or to be expressed in the terminology of the laboratories. Meanings are the exclusive property of conscious selves and continuing selves. 'Though the universe encompasses me,' wrote Pascal, 'by thought I encompass the universe.' What are we to understand by this? Despite its stupendous immensity, the universe is not aware either of me or of itself. I, in my insignificance, am aware of myself and of the world.

Is it possible, this paradox, this preposterous, unbelievable thing? For it declares that you and I possess a supreme talent denied to the universe. We are awake as nothing else in creation is awake. The most enigmatical, indescribable, undeniable attribute of the self is its awareness. How can such an awakening ever at all or anywhere come about?

Can material things, oxygen, hydrogen, carbon, water, lead, stone, electrons or protons, or any combinations of such things become conscious of themselves? Can the stream rise above its source or the result outsoar its cause? Can carbon recognise itself as carbon, or say 'Ah, here is hydrogen'? If not, beside them we are as gods, looking down from the Olympian battlements of consciousness upon the senseless nonentities which neither know nor care to know what they are or what they do.

Before you dismiss the self as irrelevant you will do well to ponder this, its aristocratic prerogative, which makes all else by comparison a negligible cipher. For it can neither be explained nor set aside. How we arrived on Olympus, on this height from which all the kingdoms of heaven and earth may be surveyed, I do not profess to tell you. Ask the space-time philosophers, or the physiologists or bio-chemists. Perhaps the brain secretes this magical essence, consciousness, as the liver secretes bile. Ask those who are prepared to explain the process to you, in this or in some other way. You may chance to find, even among philosophers, people who see nothing remarkable about consciousness. For my part I hold that neither intellect nor imagination, neither science nor logic, can cross the threshold of this mystery, nor language lay hold of it. To regard the advent of consciousness, that is, the world's coming to a knowledge of itself, the awakening of a soul in nature, to take this unexampled overwhelming fact as of course and for granted, as no singular event, or anything out of the way noteworthy or surprising, or again as a thing of accident among other accidents, were for me no easier a thought than the notion of the Himalayas giving way to laughter, or the ocean writing its autobiography. When you begin to suppose such things you make a clown of reason and adorn it with a cap and bells.

Though surrounded by and imbedded in the world, this awareness, this unique appanage or endowment of the individual self, marks its absolute separation from the rest of creation. Through this selfhood of unknown origin we become full citizens of the commonwealth in which all living things have their status. It is I myself, opposing myself to the not-self, affirming and at the same time resisting the whole, in my resolution to be and continue to be what I am, thinking and willing for myself, viewing myself and expressing myself from a standpoint not to be identified with any other throughout the past or present history of the universe, lonely and unrepeatable, it is this I, this breakwater against which the waves of denial burst in vain.

Whatever it be, this entity, this I, this being that cares for truth and beauty, the haughty, exclusive, conscious soul, its sense of personal identity survives all assaults. You may analyse it, with Hume, into a series of disconnected thoughts and feelings, but its unity reasserts itself in reviewing the series into which you have attempted to dissect it. In Hegel's words, 'I have many ideas, a wealth of thoughts is in me, and yet I remain, in spite of this variety, one.' There is then something in us which nature has not given, for she had it not to give. Selfhood is not a contingent entity, but the representative of a metaphysical and necessary principle of the universe, a part of its essential nature, a constituent of reality, nor without it could the Cosmos have attained to recognition, to full consummation or true being. Experiencing souls were a necessity if a universe in any legitimate sense there was to be. Such is the soul's superlative standing in reality. Beyond logic and reason, its essence 'tends to existence', since the world, though it contains many things unnecessary to its continuance, could not without the appreciation of conscious selves have come to life or be what it is. In the absence of these sensitive points, it were of no account, and virtually nothing. It is from this ground that the towering importance of the soul can best be seen and estimated, as the only watch-tower from which creation throughout its circumference and in all its parts and qualities can be observed and known. In a word, it alone brings everything into view.

Here is a statement beyond dispute, which will bear repetition, upon which too great an emphasis cannot be laid. The knowledge that the world exists, that there is a world at all, rests upon the testimony of individual selves. There is no other evidence than they supply, no other possible evidence than theirs to its being here, there or anywhere. For we must agree that stars, seas and mountains, however conspicuous they seem to us, are not in any way conspicuous to themselves. They do not look around, take note of themselves, or admire themselves. They are incapable of knowing, or awaking to such knowledge, and do not even guess that they are there on view. With the removal, therefore, of conscious selves, were that possible, no witness of any kind that there was in fact a universe, supposing it to be in existence, could be cited or would remain. As a whole and in every particular it is utterly dependent upon the attestation of experiencing individuals. It is reflected in the mirror of the soul and only there. This position no argument can turn, no manœuvre outflank. It is impregnable.

When you proceed, therefore, as do the naturalists, to explain the self as arising out of the components of the world it reveals, you are saying that the mirror is constructed out of the objects it reflects. You ascribe the origin of consciousness to the elements which it brings to light. You say the knower emerges out of what he knows, the discoverer of the scenery out of the scenery he discovers. And in this case if there were no conscious or observing selves, there would be in effect no scenery, no world; for the world has no knowledge of itself, and could not without selfhood, without the assistance of the watching selves, swim into its own ken.

Those who would account for consciousness by a combination of unthinking particles, who ascribe it to the architectonic atoms, make two assumptions at the outset, and before the argument begins—the first, a material universe existing as they see it wholly apart from existing selves, in its own right, self-supporting and self-sufficient—a universe that idealism refuses to acknowledge: the second, that it contained the power to produce its own spectators, an imposing masterpiece of art, which would do honour to any god, which Zeus himself might envy and desire to fashion. You will say that the objects under its inspection are as necessary to consciousness as consciousness to the objects, since in and for itself it cannot exist. The awareness upon which this stress is laid must be awareness of something. No doubt. But it is the capacity of awareness, not the act, which is in question. How did this capacity come to birth?

Bring all the worlds in their impressive splendour into the presence of a marble statue, and you will wait for an eternity before it becomes conscious that they are there. They have been long—how long?—in their own presence, yet none in that great assembly has by a wink or nod betrayed its existence to the rest. How strange a reticence, how dark must be the secret they are in conspiracy to hide! That the universe became aware of itself by accident—there's a noteworthy accident, there's a mad thought for you! If it be true, and true it is, that a thing in any legitimate sense can be said to exist only on the evidence of the experience of a conscious subject, how vain is the attempt to explain consciousness by its own experiences, by its contents, the knowledge of whose very existence you owe to consciousness. How are we to turn round and derive the awareness from the things whose acquaintance we have made and could only have made by means of that awareness? The fallacy involved has been a thousand times exposed, and only philosophers in desperation could, one fancies, overlook it—philosophers whose animosity against the self burns with a brighter flame than the logic they employ.

How does it run, then, the new story of creation, the old materialism in its new guise? It would appear somewhat as follows. In the beginning was Space-time, whatever that may be, and Space-time finding eternity or half an eternity heavy on its hands, said 'Let there be substantial things'. And with the assistance of the elements, the electro-magnetic energies and the rest of its imaginary progeny, Space-time produced the great galaxies, the host of heaven. There they were in their magnificence, shining, in Aeschylean phrase, like princes in the sky. But lo! after the lapse of infinite ages it somehow dawned upon Space-time that it had toiled in vain, its glorious works remained, alas! unseen, unknown, utterly unnoticed, unrecognised, unaccepted anywhere throughout its imperial immensity. How disappointing, how intolerable a result after so mighty and prolonged a labour! To what end this fabulous wealth, this extravagant expenditure of power without an eye to see and to admire? The emperor, Space-time, found himself without a court, without so much as a single subject in all his wide yet desolate dominions. A deathly, melancholy silence everywhere prevailed. How barren this swelling state, this lordly pomp, without some sort of society, in the absence of a worshipping, applauding circle! So grotesque a situation called for a further and supreme effort, an effort, after untold exertions and experimental essays beyond enumeration, finally successful. Summoning all its resources, and by means of some dark incantation, for the spells employed have never been divulged, conscious selves were in the Space-time laboratories evolved, entities somehow magically constrained to admit the existence of the unknown monarch and his never-heard-of world gave them the desired recognition, the required social standing. Under the magical persuasions of Space-time they took notice of the universe. It was given an audience. It had climbed the ladder and arrived. It was received, though with no warm welcome on the part of some of the more aristocratic entities, and you may now read its name in Debrett.

Such is the new story of creation for philosophical children. If you are interested in heraldry, consult, for the conjectured lineage of this universe, its arms and fabricated quarterings, the appropriate scientific manuals. I read again the other day the older and superseded story in Genesis, and reflected upon the incomparable genius it displayed, the genius of an untutored age. How sanely it accepts the incomprehensible, how nobly it eschews explanations which are no explanations, with what proud intelligence refuses to indulge in an intoxicating drench of words.

These are your opinions, some one may very properly say, and I can name vastly better minds who do not share your doctrine of the soul, who find no difficulty in believing that 'beings which are conscious are the outcome of those which are not', that 'I have consciousness in the same sense as my body has flesh-tint or solidity', and that 'I am one thing alongside other things and interacting with them'. I admit your contention. It can, how-

387

ever, easily be met. For my part I can name still greater minds and more distinguished philosophers who decline assent to these propositions. Here is one. 'Nothing can be more clumsy', wrote Schopenhauer, 'than that, after the manner of the materialists, one should blindly take the objective as simply given, in order to derive everything from it without paying any regard to the subjective, through which, however, nay, in which alone the former exists'— 'a philosophy', he adds, 'well suited for barbers' and apothecaries' apprentices.' And here is a second: 'It is of itself so evident', said Descartes, 'that it is I who doubt, I who understand, and I who desire, that it is needless to add any explanations in order to make the point still clearer.'

Little is, however, to be gained, I fear, by such ranging of authorities, or pitting them against each other. What appears to one mind axiomatic, clear and certain as the moon and stars in their courses, appears to another a delirious imbecility. To reach agreement by way of argument you must take your departure from common premises. If I hold the soul to be unitary, and see in consciousness a transcendental principle, and you provide for them a plebeian ancestry, believing them spectral effects, or matter in disguise, you seem to me to debase the currency of reason, and I, in your opinion, have thrown logic to the winds. We are like bishops in chess on different colours, and can never meet. If I refuse to derive the mind, which not only presents to us the universe, but creates the whole range of intellectual and spiritual values,

> whose faculties can comprehend
> The wondrous architecture of the world,
> And measure every wandering planet's course,
> Still climbing after knowledge infinite,

if I decline to derive this princely and originating power from the baser elements, or if I ask, why should the world in its purposeless revolutions have taken an upward direction, climbed so steep and difficult a slope, travelled towards a knowledge of itself, and your bland reply is 'Why not?'—there appears to be nothing left but to bid each other a civil good-bye, to shake hands and part. We differ. I am content to differ. Let us differ.

Every thing ultimate, unique, exceptional—and nothing is more so than the individual soul—is anathema to scientific rationalism, and in consequence unmentionable. Every soul is a living idiosyncrasy, where good none better, where bad none worse; and for a scientific age, in either case, beyond measure exasperating. Not because it changes and yet remains the same; for all changes involve a permanent element that does not alter, as the plant is still the same plant in leaf and in flower. But for other reasons. Not only has this eccentricity an inner and an outer eye; not only does it look back in time and forward into futurity, with joy and sadness; not only does it know itself to be capable of action while it remains at rest, fitted for far-darting excursions throughout the realms of matter and of thought, to which no limits can be assigned; this insubordinate, wandering, ideoplastic anomaly, imperially aloof, solitary, withdrawn, unvisited, impenetrable, which has no counterpart in space or time, no brother among sublunary things, carries with it a train of attendant memories, ideas, emotions, wishes and sympathies that the cyclic seasons, if they run into eternity, cannot repeat, nor revive elsewhere its rich, peculiar, exclusive existence. Despite these its transcendent qualities, or rather because of them; despite the fact that the individual is the maker of history since there are no other doers of deeds than individual souls; none the less the soul is out of favour in our time, not acknowledged in the superior circles, an outcast, a slum-dweller, a beggar on charity. To 'think nobly of the soul' is now accounted a symptom of low intelligence. But few of to-day's opinions will be those of to-morrow, and fewer still of the day after. You may hate life and despise man, but 'the power of the mouth, the wisdom of the brow, the human comprehension of the eyes, and the outstriking vitality of the creature' remain to confound you.

If men mistrust rationalism they have reason for their mistrust. Rationalists are much too simple-minded to act as guides or interpreters in this uncanny and incalculable world. And when I am myself in doubt among the philosophers I turn to the consensus of human opinion, to the beliefs of the plain man, that strange, indefinable being, on the surface ridiculous, in the depths profound. If he had words in which to express himself he could tell us things worth knowing even about the greatest matters, even, I think, about the soul. You remember the curious and interesting Old Testament story of Balaam, a man of great reputation in his day, so great that the King of Moab sent

389

for him in extremity.　And he saddled his ass and went to meet Balak, King of Moab.　And the Lord sent an angel to prevent him, and the angel stood across his path.　And Balaam, though a man of high intelligence, did not see the angel of the Lord, but the ass saw him.

XIX
RETROSPECT

All things to Circulations owe
    Themselves; by which alone
They do exist; they cannot show
    A sigh, a word, a groan,
A colour or a glimpse of light;
The sparkle of a precious stone,
A virtue, or a smell; a lovely sight,
A fruit, a beam, an influence, a tear,
But they another's livery must wear:
    And borrow matter first,
Before they can communicate.
Whatever's empty is accurst;
And this doth shew that we must some estate
Possess, or never can communicate.

Traherne

XIX

RETROSPECT

In our search for a philosophy which would leave the fewest difficulties upon our hands we have come, be they right or wrong, to certain conclusions, of which I may now remind you.

That this world of ours is imperfect needs no supporting arguments. And we have reason to believe that, although we may hope for a better, we need not look for a perfect world either in the near or distant future. For it is imperfect of necessity. A universe uniform and without variety, static and unchanging, all colours and shapes alike, all creatures, thoughts and feelings in unison, could be no scene or home of life. Existence involves diversity and movement, and thus better and worse, light and darkness, good and evil. It has its risks, therefore, is dangerous and will remain so. It involves the contraries, the ups and downs, the tidal rhythms, which preserve it from stagnation, in whose absence we could not be conscious of existence, or know ourselves to be alive. The good, too, is, for growing and expanding entities—however they came to a knowledge of such a thing—the enemy of the best, for with what has been already attained they cannot rest content, having hopes within them of a still better state, which imagined 'better' is the eternal critic of the present and actual. Such, then, is our nature and destiny. A perfect world is, moreover, manifestly incompatible with myriads of beings seeking there each its own individual welfare. Their intercourse, since no two are exactly alike, since each is in some respect singular or unique and ever in search of its private and peculiar needs, entails loves and hates, collisions and oppositions. A world of any kind is, in a word, a synonym for what we have, with the philosophers, called 'the Many', and thus the antithesis or denial of whatever perfection Unity or 'the One' could be supposed to provide.

You recall also that we put aside as beyond hope of solution by ours, or any other minds, the nature of 'the One', the great Reality or Being, in which they are rooted—a knot which neither atomists nor idealists have been able to untie. In what manner God or the Absolute can be at the same time the One and the Many we cannot tell, nor could the relationship between unity and plurality in primordial Being be made clear or set forth in human terms. God is at once the One and the Many, and before that mystery all the philosophies bow their heads. This, however, may be said, that for us to ask that the differences which constitute the world of the Many should be eliminated, that movement should be replaced by rest, and that the One should be all in all is to ask, as Heraclitus said, that the universe, and we with it, should pass away. It is to express a preference for death over life. To escape the differences and the contraries, therefore, is for us impossible. They are our life blood. Life is movement, movement is life, and movement is disturbance.

We arrived, too, at the conclusion that the activities or energies which make the world limit and condition each other, and what seem to us material bodies are the events which emerge from the interaction of these activities. Self-existent matter must be ruled out as an impossible conception. To this conclusion we added another, that the source of these activities, the souls or monads, though in our restricted view they appear as incessantly going and coming, arriving and departing, neither enter nor leave the universe, for it consists of them, and is at the same time their scene of operations, where infinite Being is progressively mirrored in Becoming. In these souls or selves we have the unique, unfathomable, constitutive and indispensable factors in the fundamental order. An undifferentiated unity is incompatible with the existence of a world, and the only differentiation of primordial or creative Being, which we can conceive as adequate, is its actualisation in thinking, feeling, expanding selves. For in these experiencing entities, and in them alone, can the system of nature find its recognition, and thus without them it has no true existence, and neither dignity nor worth. What is anything without beings aware of themselves and of their surroundings? The answer can only be 'nothing'. In the absence of such beings nature had not risen to knowledge of herself, nor could the universe know itself, or be known as a universe.

We saw, too, that all manifested life is individual life,

394

throughout the whole realm of nature, in its own manner and degree purposive. And the problem of change and permanence finds in these individual souls or selves its solution. Like the streamers or ribbons of weed attached to the sea-girt rock, they sway to and fro in the tides of time, yet are rooted in the underlying and immutable reality. We must rid ourselves of the notion that the universe is something outside ourselves, to which we accidentally belong. We are the universe, in every fibre of our body and being, nerve and thought, as are all other souls, each a microcosm of that macrocosm. There is a saying attributed to Hippocrates and quoted by Leibniz, that 'animals are not born and do not die, and that the things which we suppose to come into Being merely appear and disappear'. And with this opinion we are in agreement. They form, the souls or monads, a vast society, a hierarchy of innumerable levels, of which in organic and inorganic nature we see a part, as represented in the elements, the plants, the animals; an association the most intimate, an interlocked and interwoven confederacy. So that the universe is an arena at once of conflicting and yet linked and united purposes, such as human society itself exhibits.

If it be said 'These are unwarranted opinions', we must reply, 'Do not trouble to refute them, provide us rather with better in their room: not with certainties, for which we do not ask; but with conclusions more firmly grounded, with a broader foundation in facts, or such experience as we possess; with a way of thought by which the whole system of things can be rendered more intelligible, and you shall have our unstinted gratitude and thanks.'

In the course of our meditations we were driven, you remember, to reject not only the doctrine of the atomists, but to dissent from the most haughty and uncompromising among the philosophical systems, that of the Absolutists, since for the plebeian concourse of the Many, among whom we were ourselves numbered, it could find no enduring value. They were illusions, flitting phantoms or transient modes of a transcendent whole, for whose appearance upon the stage no reason was vouchsafed. The omnipotent One, the fountain of all life, we were required to believe, was the weaver of a Penelope's web, ceaselessly occupied throughout eternity in aimless and unnecessary undertakings, in doing what need never have been done.

By this doctrine we were, moreover, required to ignore what

we most desire to have explained—the strange ironies and contradictions in nature, the miseries and tribulations of sentient creatures, the wounds and heartaches they were called upon to endure, neither in their own interests nor in that of the One which gave them birth. We were required to accept the thought of this all-inclusive Absolute, in the stainless perfection ascribed to it, as none the less the source of all manner of unpleasantness, as paradoxically distributing throughout the world of our experience plague and tempest as well as health and sunshine, as present in the disease as well as in the physician; of this majestic mind, if mind it were, as present in the idiot as in Plato, in the sensualist as in the ascetic, in the sadist as in the philanthropist. And if we were disposed to enquire for the why and wherefore of its random operations, to ask what this ineffable Whole was about, whether it were, indeed, about anything beyond the production of change, and change for no better reason than the production of change; to all such enquiries no intelligible answers were to be obtained. This Whole without intelligence unleashed the hounds of strife, misery and pain for no imaginable purpose, or to no other end than to hunt the creatures it had previously brought forth, till the crack of doom. It was the Hindu Siva, the god with the necklace of skulls, 'who slays for the joy of slaying.' If its sublime energy were put to some use or served some purpose, well; if not, it could only be viewed with disdain. To suppose it wandering blindly into the darkness without intention or aim of any kind seemed to place it in a lower category of wisdom than our poor selves, to suppose its sole employment the creation of ephemeral shadows, in order idly to watch their movements as one watches the dance of gnats on a summer evening.

Above all we were left to wonder how it happened that the wide universe which brought them into being and implanted in its creatures a desire for justice was itself unjust; that the One, which called forth in them affections, itself had no affections; which bade them follow reason was itself unreasonable. 'Twas, we contended, too easy a thesis that within the immensities of this Whole or Absolute the conscious self should be regarded as an insignificant trifle, a negligible cypher in the sum of things, of no greater dignity than a leaf or cloud. Certainly against the background of eternity anything might be set down as insignificant. But least insignificant, one would think, the only entities which had formed the concept of eternity. And again, in their absence, by whom could testimony to the sublimity of this almighty power be given, or how could its intellectual or moral superiority be established? Was theirs merely the part to testify to that superiority and be extinguished?

Or once more, how are we to find anywhere within the One and Absolute's domain something of greater significance and worth than the enquiring and aspiring minds, which had made discovery of this transcendent One, otherwise unknown? Where to look save in them for any importance or value anywhere? Was it to be found in stratified rocks or planetary rings? On any form of computation were souls and their destinies, were minds and their questing thoughts, of no more consequence than the things they contemplate, than vaporous condensations or spinning orbs? Of more worth surely, we argued, the students than the objects of their study, than the times and spaces, atoms or motions. Set over against this imagined reality, the Absolute, in its everlasting and insensate duration, the despised entities seemed to have much to say for themselves. Unless, indeed, we were to think of the Absolute as indifferent to all values, and none were therefore anywhere to be found.

In such a doctrine, propounded seemingly to meet the requirements of a static and antiquated logic, what could be discerned but a pretence of majesty, a hollow beating of great drums? If we were by nature rational beings, let us, we concluded, be rational, and avoid, if possible, the acceptance of the final foolishness of all things as truth supreme. To resolve its age-long perplexity mankind has need to seek, we suggested, new concepts, to search profounder depths for the source of the contradictions it deplores— which none the less the world displays. They are omnipresent, run through the whole extent of nature and the mind, must be accepted and should be welcomed. For we seem driven to look for their origin at a deeper level, in the very ground of Being itself. The old and simple antithesis to which humanity has clung, upon which it has built its so many philosophies and religions, which it has pictured as a conflict between the powers of light and darkness, of good and evil, between Ormuz and Ahriman, between God and Satan—that old antithesis has failed. It will not serve to untie the Gordian knot, to account either for the world's structure or the ironies of man's estate.

Hard as it is to lay hold of, hard to allow, the antagonistic principles we see at work reside in Reality itself, and must there be resolved and reconciled. They are its attributes, equal and complementary principles, neither subordinate to the other, the twin pillars of the world's structure. The centrifugal and centripetal forces—not to be identified simply with good and evil—may be discerned within the heart of the universe, the very source of its existence, of life's never-failing fountain. In their opposition is the tension without which were neither life nor consciousness, and in its absence no world at all. Theirs is the left and right, the calm and storm, the congruities and incongruities, the tragic and the humorous, the social and the anti-social, the material and the spiritual. And in such a world we may expect to find, as we do find, pessimists and optimists, lovers of life and haters of it, lovers of activity and of passivity, of Becoming and Being. There is room and verge enough for an infinite and inexpugnable variety.

XX
THE DIVINE ARTS

Beauty: the Vision whereunto,
    In joy, with pantings, from afar,
Through sound and odour, form and hue,
    And mind and clay, and worm and star—
Now touching goal, now backward hurled—
Toils the indomitable world.

Watson

La vie est un degré de l'échelle des mondes
Que nous devons franchir pour arriver ailleurs.

Lamartine

XX

THE DIVINE ARTS

Mankind at its best and most promising—I propose now
to take a glance at a more cheerful aspect of human
life. In the fine arts man has travelled farther from
the animals and nearer to the angels than in any other of his enterprises or accomplishments. He is there in some measure a
creator. And we shall not, I fancy, be required to argue the
proposition that of all his multifarious undertakings the production of music and poetry, of painting and sculpture have been the
least denounced and condemned. You may not be greatly interested in these forms of human activity, but you will let them pass,
you will not be enraged by them. They have not, indeed, altogether escaped the censure of the stricter moralists, but I have
never heard of a society for their suppression. It would, I think,
be difficult to prove that music and poetry, painting and sculpture
have been responsible for much infelicity; easy, on the contrary,
to show that they have added considerably to the sum of human
happiness. Artists have in their works given to their fellow
creatures the maximum of pleasure and the minimum of pain.

Now, if indisputable, this claim, in so carping and contentious
a world as ours, is, when we come to consider it, of singular
interest, and, it may be, of high importance. The peculiar
place of the arts in human esteem, if we understood aright the
reasons for it, should throw light on many dark matters, even the
most obscure. For it is in the exploration of human nature
rather than of the material world that we are likely to come to
some understanding of our most pressing problems. Its secrets
lie deeper than the secrets of the vault of heaven, and the astronomy of souls is a more difficult science than that of the stars.
And it almost seems as if nature had taken man into partnership
to carry on her creative design. For in the arts he has planted
new flowers in her garden, which some think fairer than any of
her own, since in the pictures, the music and the poems much has

been said that nature herself never so much as thought, and could not herself have said. What shall we conclude, then? To see where we stand we shall have, I fear, to go back to the beginning.

The universe has brought us into existence, which is, of course, the fundamental thing, the basis of everything. Life, however, we have discovered, is not enough. Simply to be, to exist, is not in itself sufficient. We ask for more than existence, we ask for a happy existence, free from all vexation—in a word, for heaven. For some reason nature, possibly because she had done all she could, probably for some other and profounder reason, having given us life, stayed her hand, with the unfortunate results we see. She produced a world, but thoughtlessly failed or neglected to produce a paradise, leaving that undertaking to us; the making of a heaven for ourselves—a difficult business. And the best we have been able to do so far is to create a dream world, a world of the imagination, superior in a number of ways to the world in which we actually live, much pleasanter if less substantial. The root of the satisfaction the arts provide is thus easily explained. In the imaginative representation of the world and life we are freed of their disagreeable features, which are, as everyone knows, pretty numerous. 'Since', said Bacon, 'the world is in proportion inferior to the soul, there is agreeable to the spirit of man a more ample greatness, a more exact goodness and a more absolute variety than can be found in the nature of things.'

Quite true, but how did we come to pitch our requirements so high? The other animals placidly accept things as they are. The soul of man, you might think, had strayed out of its native country into a dry and thirsty land, and recalls its happier childhood. Like the traveller lost in the desert, it revisits in dreams the country known in earlier days, or was it before birth? Since, then, in music and poetry the lost paradise is in a measure regained, where like birds we are free to fly whither we please, their appeal to human nature may, we think, easily be understood. The poet Blake, you remember, pertinently enquires:

> What do we here,
> In this land of unbelief and fear?
> The land of dreams is better far,
> Above the light of the Northern Star.

Very good, and all quite simple. You may say that dreams, and artists, who are the purveyors of dreams, with dreams to sell, reminding us of something lost and certainly in universal demand, a painless existence, have thus found favour in our eyes. But where is this bright paradise for which we pine, and how did we come to leave it? Meditate a little longer, recall the ancient fables of the Garden of Eden and of the Golden Age, those strange echoes from the depths of the human soul, and you presently find yourself at the heart of a great mystery, immersed in the metaphysics of Being and Becoming, surveying heights where there is no secure foothold for human reason, and only to be trodden by philosophical mountaineers. What are we to understand by these alarming terms?

Avoiding, as we must, the technical language of the academic schools, and putting upon them our own interpretation, let us begin by saying that there are two modes of existence, which we may call passive and active ways of existing, its positive and negative poles. As we have had so often to remind ourselves in speaking of the One and the Many, we are surrounded by a great multitude of things, to which in the aggregate we give the name, nature. Nature presents an astonishing scene of varied shapes and colours, and of creatures pursuing innumerable and diverse ways of life. As the support of these surroundings, of all we see, know and experience, human reason is driven to postulate some underlying foundation or principle upon which they rest, the ground of all that is, or appears, which is the

Form in all forms, and of all souls the soul.

This is Being, which exists in its own right: 'The One, without Predicates' of Plotinus, to which many names have been given— the Absolute, Mind or God. You may call it what you will. Let us call it simply *Being*, 'ageless and deathless', the all-pervading Spirit in whom 'our dark foundations rest', revealed in the world's existence and the surprising aspirations of the mind.

As we cannot doubt, though no eye has ever seen it, that the moon has another side than that she presents to the earth, so with this sustaining principle. Reason compels us to assume behind the visible scene its everlasting presence. Further, as we have previously agreed, Being in isolation, undisclosed or undistributed Being, is with difficulty, if at all, to be distinguished from Not-Being. A power never manifested, how could it be known?

The world with which we are acquainted is a manifold. It has many observable parts. By that airy syllable 'world' we mean an assemblage of particulars, a variety, a heterogeneous multiplicity, interlocked and most intimately associated, yet, in appearance and on the surface at least, infinitely diversified. Now Being is not open to our inspection, and if it is to exhibit or reveal itself, if it is to be explicitly known as a world, it must somehow pass into Becoming, an active state, or, you may say, be projected on a different plane, the plane of measurable extension and duration, of space and time, with which we have some little acquaintance. And this variegated, moving pageant we term the world is just this other mode or pole of Being, its progressive manifestation or creation, which thus declares itself, and becomes visible in action. 'What appears', as Anaxagoras said, 'is a vision of the unseen.'

The world of our acquaintance, the Many or nature, is, then, Being externalised, our view of it; and Becoming is, we might say, its revealed or lighted side. How this actualisation or manifestation has come about we need not ask. It is clean beyond our range. Somehow from pure Being has emerged the procession of the starry universe, and all that followed in its train. Somehow in Becoming, in this diversified scene, the true nature of Being is displayed.

Observe now, bearing in mind that the language we employ is necessarily metaphorical and figurative, that in these two modes of existence, the passive and the active, we have our own small share. We describe them as our sleeping and waking states. We may think of a man asleep as in Being, as alive, as a potential force, but if we are to think of him as his true self we must see him awake. Not when alone and asleep, but when at the opposite pole of his existence, when he has exchanged passivity for activity, does he reveal his true nature. When he is awake, when he is up and doing, we come to know him on his lighted side.

And what of the man himself, how is he affected? In his waking condition, in his state of active Becoming, he has sacrificed something, the sweet oblivion in which men forget their anxieties, the pauper his poverty, the diseased his sickness, the ruined man the loss of his wealth, the bereaved his bereavement. The man awake has left behind him the divine repose, the heavenly peace he enjoyed in the blissful condition simply of Being. He has, you might say, mounted the battlements, and is now perpetually on anxious guard. He looks out upon the battle in the plain beneath him, upon the conflicts, the antagonisms, the swaying tide of events, in which he has his own part to play. He is no longer alone with himself, but immersed in the seething flux of the public world, a man among innumerable other men and creatures, whose desires, aims and purposes run counter to his own. He has entered the turbulent arena of the contending opposites.

The waking state affords, indeed, opportunities denied him when alone in the quiet he has left, opportunities to see and be seen, occasions for the acquisition of experiences, the exercise of his energies, in which there is perpetual delight, opportunities for expansion, for becoming more than he has so far been. But all at a price, the price of unremitting anxiety, watchfulness, frustration, disappointment, wounds and pain. He gains, doubtless, much, yet he has relinquished the blessed ease of his former state. He is an exile from Nirvana, the Nirvana of pure Being. In the realm of Becoming we are busy among other creatures like ourselves. We enjoy the pursuit of our personal inclinations, the exertion of our powers. Its adventures and undertakings have their value. But they are only to be had in the society of the Many, the others like ourselves, bent equally upon their separate ends and individual needs. They are only to be enjoyed amid the crowd of jostling fellow travellers, pushing and elbowing their way through the streets and markets, a bustling, noisy, hearty, pleasure-seeking, love-making, jesting, quarrelling, competitive, making-the-best-of-it crowd.

The soul in solitude, the sleeping soul, is in seclusion and at peace, but it is at a standstill. In that quiescent state, however heavenly it be, there can be no fulfilment of its nature, nothing accomplished. A man asleep, what can he be said to be? All differences between him and other men are obliterated. He is neither a pagan nor a Christian. He belongs to no party and assists no cause. He is neither a lover of beauty nor a searcher for truth, neither a good nor a bad man. He is an occupant of space, but his existence has neither value nor significance, and his Being is hardly to be distinguished from Not-Being. Yet a touch may wake him, may transform him into a maker of history, a poet, a founder of states, an Alexander or

Napoleon storming through the world, a demi-god, worshipped by millions; a touch may transfigure him into the statesman, the saint, the thinker, whose force the world may feel, and by whose power the centuries may be shaken.

The soul, we may agree, exists for itself, and is concerned for itself. None the less for the growth and expansion of its native and latent powers it is in need of an arena, a world of souls. If I am to exist in any true sense it can only be in relation with other existences. You may say, indeed, if you like, that the realm of Being is the world of reality, the realm of Becoming a world of appearances. There is no more favourite thesis with philosophers. You may say with Shelley that, lost in its stormy visions, 'we keep' there 'with phantoms an unprofitable strife'; nevertheless, it is in the latter state, and there only, that experience is possible, or a realisation of the nature that to the soul essentially belongs. It was built for this voyage. And the company of others is as much a necessity for each living thing as the necessity of remaining simply itself alone.

Here, then, is the dilemma. Which is the better state, which to be preferred, Being or Becoming? In which is the soul's true home? Can we say either, or should we say both? We can only reply that the question was answered once upon a time by the many souls in the bosom of the One, the One of Being. They could find in its eternal tranquillity no field for development. Existence there did not suffice them. And the desire to be awake, to be abroad and at work for themselves, to be makers of their own world, that, or a creative fiat which launched them into Becoming, gave birth to the universe we see and know.

So we may most reasonably account, as it seems to me, for things as they are and our present state. I can think of no better way. For the universe is no unorganised conglomeration of senseless things. It has a structure which calls for explanation. We are certainly not to suppose the whole of Being as once and for all, and in its present actualisation, complete. Its resources are vast, and there will always remain more to be revealed. We must think of Being as manifesting in space and time all that it can be, displaying there its inexhaustible wealth, unfolding itself in the succeeding phases of a world without end. And that process is throughout periodic or rhythmical, exhibited to us in the lesser rhythms, echoes of the unseen and greater—in the seasonal pulsations of nature, the alternation of her phases of activity and repose. The undulations of whatever it be that underlies matter, or constitutes it, are invariably periodic. A molecule of hydrogen vibrates, we are told, 450 million times a second. The souls, too, in the universe similarly display their twofold nature, in that they are wayfarers, continually passing from quiescent Being into active Becoming, and from active Becoming into quiescent Being. In our pulses throbs the pulse of nature in her alternating phases.

> The running winds of springtime call
> For culmination and repose,
> And autumn, letting roses fall,
> Sighs for the spring that brings the rose.

Nor can we suppose ourselves here and now to have full knowledge of ourselves, or to be fully known. For as the whole of Being is displayed at any time on the plane of action only in process and in part, so also with its constituent souls.

Empedocles is cited as saying that 'of necessity Love and Strife control things and move them part of the time, and that they are at rest during the intervening time'. If the One reassemble the Many, it will send them forth again as before. No one has yet shown us, or can show us, that it will be a different Many, as some philosophies assume. Why should it be? The bonds of affection are as real as the sympathies between electrons and protons. All that exists, all reality, is permanent, and spaces and times are for the souls but the media of their intercommunication with each other. They will sleep out the nights, but the days will see them again. 'There is', as Sir Thomas Browne said, 'something in us that can be without us, and will be after us; though it is strange that it has no history of what it was before us, nor cannot tell us how it entered in us.' The souls which were in the beginning within the whole of Being 'last', in the words of Leibniz, 'as long as the universe', and 'go from better to better . . . although most of this takes place imperceptibly, and sometimes with great circuits backwards.'

And what could be more simple or reasonable, more agreeable to thought, than the balanced rhythm of repose and activity that nature exhibits in her ebb and flow, in the counterpoise or antiphony of sleep and waking, death and life, withdrawal and renewal? As a longing for activity and companionship, native to the soul, invades it in the sphere of Being, so its counterpart, a longing for release from the buffetings of Becoming, the sailor's longing for a haven, returns it to the peace of Being.

Sleepe after toyle, port after stormie seas,
Ease after warre, death after life does greatly please.

So rocked in nature's cradle we feel the motion of her rising and her falling tides. Whatever the varying shapes and alliances the vision of life presents, nothing can enter existence that was not for ever there, nothing passes out of existence. You cannot go in and out, enter or leave the universe as if it were a house amid surrounding scenery. And the vast assembly of which Being consists has in Becoming its scene of action. Theirs is the patterned world around us, theirs the figured tapestry on the loom of time. What else than overwhelming, what less than wonderful and terrible, could it be when we consider its extent, duration, and the myriad agencies and activities, 'the many operations of gods and men', as Plutarch has it, there represented?

We have fetched a wide compass. What, you may ask, have Being and Becoming, or the cosmic rhythms to do with the music and poetry, painting and sculpture, we set out to discuss? Here is the answer in the words of Hegel. 'It is in works of art that nations have deposited their profoundest intuitions, and ideas of their hearts; and fine art is frequently the key—with many nations there is no other—to the understanding of their wisdom and of their religion.' Yes, but why? Why in the fine arts? Why in them rather than in the religions themselves, in the sciences and philosophies, the civic structures, the political institutions should we have the key to the human soul, to the deepest strata of its intuitions, its innermost wisdom? For the simple reason, shall we not answer, that they speak in the language of the soul rather than of the intellect, in a universal language, universally understood?

'There seems', said Aristotle, 'to be a sort of relationship between the soul on the one hand, and harmonies and rhythms on the other.' There is, indeed, such a relationship. And there is an undeniable knowledge possessed by the soul, when it keeps silence and appears to be asleep. The human body contains, or consists of, a vast system of inter-related rhythmical processes. If that be so, and we are in no doubt that it is so, and if these pro-

408

cesses preserve it in an environment which is itself a system of rhythms, the accentuated, pulsing system of nature, whose swelling and subsiding waves are everywhere in their periods clearly in a thousand ways to be discerned—as, for example, even in the ripple which the distribution of the lines in the spectrum so exquisitely displays—if in sober fact we are from birth to death, in soul and body, in all our vital processes immersed in a pulsing ocean, it would, indeed, be surprising if in such a rhythmical universe we were left unmoved by the rhythmical arts, which reproduce its measures, and thus play upon the corresponding and fundamental strings of our nature. 'Whatever is harmonically disposed', in Sir Thomas Browne's words, 'delights in harmony', and music, he held, following the inspired thought of Pythagoras, 'is an Hieroglyphical and shadowed lesson of the whole World . . . such a melody as the whole World, well understood, would afford the understanding.' Schopenhauer was of the same opinion. 'We may regard the phenomenal world, or nature, and music as two different expressions of the same thing.'

Is this mere mystical rhetoric? I do not think so. Through rhythm we are in the closest, most vital and intimate relationship with the entire Cosmos, which in this, its primary and proper language, speaks to us in every fibre of our being. And with compelling authority, an authority the human race has from the earliest times and in all lands acknowledged. From prehistoric ages music appears in association with the magical, religious and medicinal rites of all primitive peoples, invariably accompanied, as they were, with an incantation, a song or chant. 'Tis, then, no unwarrantable thought that in the highest reaches of the rhythmical arts we are privileged to hear, however fitfully, utterances 'above a mortal mouth', when

'Tis scarce like sound, it tingles through the frame
As lightning tingles.

To the soul's instincts and intuitions, such as direct the lives of animals, by which they navigate their course, the talent of the spider, the genius of the bee, the occult chemistry by which the caterpillar transforms itself into a butterfly, to these mysterious powers that brilliant detective, the wide-awake intellect, has no vestige of a clue. Nor could it have. For consciousness is not thought, nor thought an activity of consciousness, nor possibly even assisted by it. Thought, noticed or unnoticed, proceeds like a subterranean stream on its unruffled course. The poor soul, despised, denied existence, laughed out of court by the rationalists, how much more it knows, how many more miracles it can perform; how it must smile to itself at their pride and blind, groping labours. So far, indeed—as they fondly imagine—from enlarging our vision in the brain and nervous system of the body, nature has there, and of deliberation, contracted and concentrated our conscious attention upon the outer world, as with a searchlight directed upon a selected situation, confining our observation to things of the present hour.. By them, its mortal instruments, the soul's horizon is narrowed, its sight confined. They are there, the nerves and brain, and of necessity, to contract, not to widen its field of attention, to anchor, to preoccupy its gaze. They focus, you may say, a single wave-length of its ray on mundane and material things. For the truth is that 'The ear, the eye doth make us deaf and blind.'

So it is that our conscious lives are our surface lives, and upon our association with nature at the deeper levels, upon our wider and true selves nature herself draws down the blind. She would have us, undistracted, attend only to this place and this moment, the events of here and now. By our bodily senses we are limited to the realm of Becoming, pre-engaged with a particular part of the universe, to the immediate surroundings of our daily lives, which are at this present our instant and direct concern. Our senses are our guides to action in a restricted field. For that field only nature has given us eyes and ears; and with it alone, that is with sensible things, the intellect and its servant the brain are qualified to deal.

Yet to conclude that field the beginning and the end of things were sheer delusion. Who is not aware that there are hours in which the soul sinks, as it were, beneath the threshold of its conscious and daily experiences, when its ties with the body are relaxed, when it stands at gaze within its spiritual environment. For, as we have seen, we must admit the possibility of supersensible knowledge. And it is to this wider field, haunted by such strange fleeting gleams as are not to be translated into the coinage of the brain, the speech adapted to the traffic of social life, that we are in happy moments afforded entrance by poetry and the other arts. Surprised and momentarily absorbed, as

Professor Stewart so well described in his *Myths of Plato*, by their imagery and rhythms, we are caught up into the abiding presence of 'That which was, and is and ever shall be', and it is then 'We feel that we are greater than we know'.

For rhythm appears to be the distinctive and peculiar dialect, or style of the soul, its idiom or vernacular—as ordinary language is the natural tongue of the workaday intelligence—a vernacular instantly acceptable, and by all men understood. Hence, as Emerson phrased it, 'You can speak truth uncontradicted in verse, you cannot in prose'. Imagery, too, has upon us an occult and arresting power. Of this staying or arresting influence, the momentary entrancement of attention an image induces, since we have not time to dwell upon it, take a single instance, from Browning's poem, *Colombe's Birthday*:

> I will keep your honour safe;
> With mine I trust you as the sculptor trusts
> Yon marble woman with the marble rose,
> Loose on her hand, she never will let fall.

Where lies the charm of such an image?' It checks the mind's hurrying motions, and in such moments of absorption we awake to an amazed and speculative wonder, and hear the overtones of existence.

If you are enamoured of theories of art you will not have far to go. They are legion, and for the most part as uninstructive as they are numerous. For they are without metaphysical roots. And, however the notion displeases you, theories without metaphysical roots are things of nought, bubbles blown to burst. No doubt, wherever we look, bewilderment is our portion. Nevertheless, though everything has by some philosopher been disproved, something must be true. And we are not, I believe, far from the truth when we say that Being is not to be separated from Becoming, nor Becoming from Being. Not from one principle, but from two opposing principles, were the worlds set in motion. In the sweep of their majestic alternation, the primary and original pulse of their oscillating phases, all existence partakes, and in their greater, the lesser rhythms, echoing through the universe, have their source.

You will not, I trust, accuse me of mounting the horse, obscurity, to escape the dragon, nonsense. I have no other aim than to

411

attain the intelligible while avoiding the absurd—no trivial task in this region of discourse. And if you think these opinions strange, it is not by reason of their strangeness they miss the truth, but much more probably because they are not strange enough. We might think and discourse of the divine arts in many and interesting ways, as, for example, of music and poetry as arts of time, of painting and sculpture as arts of space. But all are music in its Greek and widest sense, the ordered and shapely, the measured, the flowing, the melodious. They are a rhythmical sisterhood. And we are not deceived if we regard each as a species of divination, and the artist as a man feeling his way into reality, attempting, in his own medium and manner, to fathom the inner significance of life's experiences, to penetrate its secret depths, to see things in a wider perspective. In the presence of Turner's or Tintoretto's pictures Ruskin felt as a man might feel in the presence of some supernatural being.

Pause for a moment and consider what it is we in truth desire, of what we are in search. Nothing else, surely, than a reconciliation between ourselves and the world to which we belong, that is— may we not say?—an attunement or concord between Being and Becoming, which if attainable were pure felicity, a reconciliation or harmony which human wisdom and experience fail in the world they so anxiously contemplate either to perceive or to effect. Yet since in the arts they are in a manner found together, in essence one, for this reason human nature derives from the arts its deepest satisfactions. Poetry appears to be something we have always known in our hearts, but have never before had so vividly presented to us. In these arts of divination the waking consults the dreaming mind; the surface consciousness, in search of more favourable omens, enquires of the oracle, of the better informed and wiser soul. And the inspired priestess by whom the world is seen in the wider perspective answers, 'Your experience is real, but consult the god within you and know that this real is not the whole of reality.'

The happiness the arts provide is the happiness of life more truly divined, more fully understood. Face to face with the stupendous fact of existence, our sense of it quickened, we are startled into a recognition of its unsearchable depths and unfathomable significance. Not otherwise, as we have so often said, save for this everlasting Becoming, whose tossing waves and dizzying changes we bemoan, could there be a universe, or creatures like ourselves. And to contrast it to its disadvantage with the fancied perfections of some other state of unbroken felicity, to suppose that for this of ours some diviner form of existence might be substituted, were no wiser than the attempt to draw a circle without a centre, or to imagine a triangular planet. For what were Being without a corresponding Becoming or Heaven without a contrasting earth? How necessary is this Becoming to give to Being substance, reality, content, meaning. From earth and Becoming are derived all the values of paradise and Being—which but for them were 'faultily faultless, splendidly null'. No occupations there, no thoughts to think, no memories to recall, no desires to satisfy. From the fountain of life, from

> The slow sweet hours that bring us all things good,
> The slow sad hours that bring us all things ill,

are derived all our possessions, all the wealth and substance, all subjects and qualities, all that makes us what we are. But for Becoming and its imperfections there were nothing in that perfect world we talk of to give meaning to existence. There were neither aspirations nor visions, neither hopes to ponder nor proposals to entertain. This poor earth gives gifts to Heaven, which, destitute of the teeming experiences earth provides, were sunk in poverty. Heaven could make no Don Quixotes or Sancho Panzas, no Hamlets or Falstaffs, no heroes or martyrs, no Stoics or Epicureans, no Sapphos or Shelleys, no jesters or humorists, or indeed anything of interest, without the assistance of this our dear, painful and toiling lower world. A heaven without change, without events, neither gods nor men could long endure.

Look now at the nature of these engaging arts, which link Being and Becoming, the moving and the unmoving, the changeless and the changing, in which we taste the delight of activity while at rest, where order is imposed upon disorder, and discord melts into harmony, by whose transforming magic sadness is made sweet, the heartaches translated into loveliness, metamorphosed into melody, and music made of pain.

> With rue my heart is laden
> For golden friends I had,
> For many a rose-lipt maiden
> And many a light-foot lad.

By brooks too broad for leaping,
The light-foot boys are laid;
The rose-lipt girls are sleeping,
In fields where roses fade.

And however impossible in our eyes the reconciliation between Being and Becoming may seem, yet look back into history, into the past, and you perceive it in a sense already achieved. In our excursions into the past, in our intimacy with what has been, we taste a spiritual quality. We are no longer in communication with flesh and blood but with immortal essences. How perfect it is, the past, to which nothing can be added, and from which nothing can be taken away! It is no longer material, it has become a vision. To it belongs the statuesque dignity of repose, the quality of everlastingness, never more to be troubled by the restlessness of change. Over the past time has thrown a transfiguring veil. Its agitations are at an end. A great stillness reigns over the centuries that are gone. The battles and revolutions, the pains and pestilences, the frustrations and miseries have lost their power to wound. The thunderbolts have all been hurled.

For Hector Zeus took forth and bare him far
From dust, and dying and the storm of war.

Only on the canvas of history the pictures of it remain, the eternal fascination of all that men have thought, and desired, and suffered and done.

Yet the storm of Becoming, the furious gale by which the ship of the world has been driven on its voyage, what do we not owe to it? We owe it everything. What is to be wondered at, admired, regretted, loved and hated—the whole scene of things. Is the voyage, then, to be deplored or welcomed? That is for you to say. It has bequeathed to us the procession of events, the architecture of thought, the passions and ideals which constitute the tissue, fabric or stuff, the filling, the substance of existence. The tempest of Becoming which produced them has blown over, and they are merged in the tranquillity of Being. None the less we must allow their abiding presence. There they are on the canvas of the past, the Becoming and the Being harmonised, reconciled and at one. And there they are, the records of human industry and genius, stars shining in a quiet sky, the books, the statues and the pictures, which in their strange immobility

414

preserve the strong, passionate life of generations upon generations, so that we see with Homer's eyes, think the thoughts of Sophocles or Virgil, sit down to conversation with Cervantes and share the vision of Michael Angelo.

And may we not say that the charm of all aesthetic experience consists in this, that it, too, presents the storm in the golden frame of peace? That it reconciles the opposites in the arrest or staying of the flux? Nothing is there denied, nothing denied of the tyrannies and injustices, the frets and fevers, the injurious wrongs that tax the intelligence and freeze the heart. Nothing is denied, all is affirmed. Yet as time with its magic wand deals with the past, so the divine arts with the troubles of the world. They have done their worst, and have no longer any power to harm. They can be remembered and contemplated without the former and accompanying pain.

Thus in poetry and painting, music and sculpture, the necessary and complementary character of Being and Becoming can be in a measure perceived and understood. 'For nothing', as Plato thought, 'can have any sense except by reason of that of which it is the shadow.' And here the opposites, 'His Darkness and His Brightness' meet. None can deny that there is within us an unsubduable thirst for existence, the will to live, a need for activity only to be satisfied in the realm of Becoming, in reaching out to more than we already are. Nor can it be denied, such is the nature of the human soul, that it shares in the pulsations of the universe, its alternating periods of withdrawal and renewal, of action and repose. For refreshment, for the harvesting of its toils, it demands a seasonal ascent into Being. And since in the arts it perceives dimly and through a veil the attunement of the opposites, it judges the harvest worth the pains, finding the world, in Plutarch's phrase, 'more good than bad', as Plato argued and Aristotle, too, agreed.

In his essay on *Virgil* Frederick Myers notes how many Virgilian lines have a history. 'On this line', he writes, enumerating each as he tells its story, 'On this line the poet's own voice faltered as he read; at this Augustus and Octavia melted into passionate weeping. Here is the verse which Augustine quotes as typical in its majestic rhythm of all the pathos and the glory of pagan art, from which the Christian was bound to flee. This is the couplet which Fénelon could never read without admiring tears.

This line Filippo Strozzi scrawled on his prison wall, when he slew himself to avoid worse ill. These are the words which like a trumpet call roused Savonarola to seek the things that are above. And this line Dante heard on the lips of the Church Triumphant, at the opening of the Paradise of God.' Consider the significance of this passage. Here we have lines of verse with a history of their own, a separate life, which like individuals have gone out into the world with power upon it, moulded the minds of men, influenced the course of events, lines which have lived, and still live and move and have their powerful being. Walt Whitman made a profound remark when he said 'All music is what awakes in you when you are reminded by the instruments'. In vain would the harper harp to soulless things ; nor could this enlargement of the consciousness, this sudden widening of the horizon, this spiritual suggestiveness belong to art, were it without warrant in the ultimate facts of the universe and our responsive selves. Beethoven is reported to have said, 'I must despise the world which does not know that music is a higher revelation than all wisdom and philosophy . . . the one incorporeal entrance into the higher world which comprehends mankind but which mankind cannot comprehend'.

'What is thought', it has been said, 'takes the spatial form, what is felt takes the time form.' And, as Lessing pointed out, the poet, and we may add the composer, has to deal, such is his medium, with our appreciation of sequence in time, the painter and sculptor with our perception of space. The peculiarity of the arts of time lies here, that their measures are intensive, not dimensional, the measures of our inner sense of time, of an order in which past, present and future are associated—memory of a past note or chord in relationship with a present, and anticipating a resolving note or chord to come, each of which were of itself without significance or value.

Painting and sculpture take another route to the capture of the mind. As Bergson has shown, the intellect bent upon an understanding of the nature of things, dominated as it is by the idea of action, stays the ever-altering patterns to dwell upon them, and the better to appreciate their character. And in painting and sculpture, arts of space, with which the intellect is so closely associated, the movement of Becoming is stayed for our contemplation. And then a strange thing happens, a curious experience supervenes, with which you may be familiar. I have myself, for example, gazed with fascinated attention at the pediment sculptures at Olympia, which exhibit all types of action, until I seemed to become a part of their immobility, to have a share in their eternal calm, set free from all the pains and passions there presented, and now at rest. As Wilkie, the painter, stood in the Escurial, gazing at Titian's picture of the *Last Supper*, an aged monk said to him, 'I have sat daily in sight of that picture for nearly threescore years; during that time my companions have dropped off, one after another, more than one generation has passed away, and there the figures in that picture have remained unchanged. I look at them until I sometimes think that they are the realities, and we are but the shadows.'

It seems as if in these mysterious arts we become aware, not indeed that the world is a perfect harmony—neither art nor philosophy has provided for us that demonstration—but that it contains harmonies, rhythms with which we find ourselves intimately in tune. These arts seem to be in possession of a secret, which they half reveal, an answer to the question—'How comes it that existence with all its agitations, pains and anxieties, is somehow in itself a happiness?' They answer it in their reconciliation of Being and Becoming. As Professor Stewart puts it in his *Myths of Plato*, 'There', in the picture, 'are the horses galloping over the snow, under the sleigh-driver's lash, their bells jangling, and the wolves barking close behind: there they are, all motion and sound, in a strange world of rest and silence.'

It is Plato's doctrine, and none more defensible, that the soul before it entered the realm of Becoming existed in the universe of Being. Released from the region of time and space, it returns to its former abode, 'the Sabbath, or rest of souls', into communion with itself. After a season of quiet 'alone with the Alone', of assimilation of its earthly experiences and memories, refreshed and invigorated, it is seized again by the desire for further trials of its strength, further knowledge of the universe, the companionship of former friends, by the desire to keep in step and on the march with the moving world. There it seeks out and once more animates a body, the medium of communication with its fellow travellers, and sails forth in that vessel upon a new venture in the ocean of Becoming.

Many, no doubt, will be its ventures, many its voyages. For

not until all the possibilities of Being have been manifested in Becoming, not until all the good, beauty and happiness of which existence allows have, by the wayfaring soul, been experienced, not until it has become all that it is capable of becoming—and who can tell to what heights of power and vision it may climb?— is it fitted to choose for itself the state and society which best meets its many requirements, as its natural and enduring habitation.

XXI
THE VERDICT

TO NIGHT

Mysterious Night! when our first parent knew
  Thee from report divine, and heard thy name,
  Did he not tremble for this lovely frame,
This glorious canopy of light and blue?
Yet 'neath a curtain of translucent dew,
  Bathed in the rays of the great setting flame,
  Hesperus with the host of heaven came,
And lo!   Creation widened in man's view.

Who could have thought such darkness lay concealed
  Within thy beams, O Sun? or who could find,
Whilst flow'r and leaf and insect stood revealed,
  That to such countless orbs thou mad'st us blind!
    Why do we then shun Death with anxious strife?
    If Light can thus deceive, wherefore not Life?

Blanco White

XXI

THE VERDICT

Viewed from first to last, and all in all, who can deny to the architecture of nature a certain stateliness, or refuse to recognise in it a singular genius at work? However incomplete, however disappointing, however short it come of what idealists demand, his were surely a churlish heart which refused all admiration for a residence in so imperial a style. It is told of the architects of Seville cathedral that they desired to erect a building of such proud dimensions, so marvellously fair that succeeding generations should deem them mad. And allow we may that in the plan of the universe we have, if a folly, a royal folly, so imposing and exalted as to extort astonishment, if not approval, for its towering splendour. May we not praise it, and praise, too, the striving souls or monads, the masons, as we may call them, who in their various tribes and assemblies poured into its age-long construction so eager a will to live, so great a wealth of roving and brooding desire? May we not accept the building as it stands, and count its superb if bizarre magnificence its sufficient justification?

By no means, men and sages not a few have replied. It remains a folly, better never built. The story begins well enough, but look to the event. Before you applaud consider first its cost, its ruinous cost—and we care not whose the project or design—in

> Fear, sickness, age, losse, labour, sorrow, strife,
> Pain, hunger, cold.

Compute its price in broken hearts. Most assuredly that price has been paid. And next, out of your wisdom expound to us what end, save a barren spectacle, a mere gazing stock, has been served, what object attained by such a universe. More is needed, much more, to win our applause than a showy and figured façade. The shrine you so much admire is an empty shell, gigantic if you please, but purposeless, inane. Within it no statue of a God is to be found, a guardian of the right, or if any God a monarch who can hardly be said to have dealt very handsomely with his subjects. Do not frown upon us as presumptuous and superfluous nonentities. However insignificant, we have our claims. 'By suffering we buy the right to judge.' Men ask for nothing from the universe save justice, and they have not obtained it. Had human happiness, such as it is, been equally distributed—and who is ignorant it is not so distributed?—or had ours been an existence free from care, something in defence of the fabric you commend might possibly have been advanced. As things are you will not with all the eloquence of all the silver-tongued orators obtain from the incorruptible jury of humanity a verdict in its favour. Individual, separate, personal existence, the basis of the whole design, has not proved its worth. Nor can it be proved. There is poison in the cup. Your belauded universe, a mountain in labour, has produced in man at best a ridiculous, a dazed, a purblind mouse. Talk no more, good friends, you know it well. Look in your hearts, and read the ineluctable truth—the partnership of living things is but 'a partnership in all-disastrous fight'.

What answer, if any answer, can be given to this challenging *cui bono*? To clear the ground, and find a footing in this so great and crucial a debate, it must first be said that existence in itself cannot be thus arraigned. For life no creature ever had, or could have, a distaste. The quarrel, then, where there is a quarrel, can only be with its accompanying and painful conditions. Or rather, perhaps we may agree, not so much even with these as with the presence of another adversary, a more insidious foe, the profound unrest engendered by the apparent aimlessness of life's journey. To live is by universal consent to travel a rough road. And how can a rough road which leads nowhere be worth the travelling? Mere living, what a profitless performance; mere painful living, what an absurd! Men need an incentive for their efforts. Make, however, the enquiry,

What is there to strive for, live or keep alive for?

and an ominous silence reigns throughout creation. Tell us, say our pessimists, of a goal, however difficult or distant, give us a star to guide our course. But spare us your transparent mockery, and do not require of men to live, suffer and die for no other end than living, suffering and dying. Here is no cause for jubilation, for 'Hosannahs in the highest'. Existence has been misnamed a boon. 'Tis a jest carried too far. Your diamond is paste. And what need to summon witnesses for this certain and central truth? It is broad-based on universal experience. It is buttressed by reason. Its force has been admitted by philosophers as well as poets, by simple souls as well as wise. It reverberates through the thoughts of men in all regions and ages. It finds an echo in every human heart. 'One can go on living', as said Tolstoy, 'when one is intoxicated by life; as soon as one is sober it is impossible not to see that it is all a mere fraud. . . . I now see that if I did not kill myself it was due to some dim consciousness of the invalidity of my thoughts. I, my reason, has acknowledged life to be unreasonable. But how can reason, which (for me) is the creator of life, and (in reality) the child of life, deny life? There is something wrong here.'

Yes, there is something wrong. But how sharply and concisely Tolstoy summarises the situation. He has, you observe, a dim consciousness of the invalidity of his thoughts. Where lies the flaw? Not in his logic, but in his unstated premises. The conclusion he draws rests upon an assumption, as well grounded, maybe, as most that fly about the globe. Yet an assumption. What is that assumption? That we are in possession of all the relevant facts to form the judgment, that we know all we need to know to estimate the value of life. Last and chiefest, the included postulate that the skeleton, death, crowns at the last its emptiness with appropriate derision.

Accept this postulate, and to provide any justification for so senseless a pilgrimage, plodding on for the sake of plodding on, circling like a caged animal within its prison bars, would be an undertaking of great if not insuperable magnitude. If any life beyond the present be denied, you need go no further. The world condemns itself. For if, indeed, existence offers any values it can only be to the individual beings who have a share in existence. If there be any good, and if there be any beauty, it is in them and their perceptions of such things. Where else could it be? The rest is but mud and motion. And since if the valuators perish, all values, truth, goodness and the rest, go with them into the everlasting night, no theological or metaphysical twitterings can rebut the demonstrable hollowness of life, its inherent futility. The passing show may have its interest, but how slight and ephemeral, how painful an interest. We are offered, it seems, a sip from the cup of life, which is then for ever withdrawn. No very munificent gift from the exalted and almighty Absolute.

And how wide, how grotesquely wide of the mark are they who indulge in childish and insensitive chatter, babbling of the hope for a future existence as a petty, personal desire, born of selfishness. For what, to put no gloss on things, are the implications of its rejection? The story of humanity becomes the story of a long procession of sufferers, for whose sufferings no justification is offered, of poor souls intellectually and morally confounded, who entered existence blind to any reason for their coming and will leave it blind, who cannot so much as conjecture their origin, or the meaning of their lives, whose elevation above the lower creatures has been their direst misfortune, their ideals an accentuation of their griefs. And the revolt of reason against this happy consummation is labelled selfishness! What kind of selfishness is that which asks no more for oneself than for all men and creatures ever born? Let us have no more of this.

Only, then, on some other postulate can the case for existence be argued with success. If death be the gulf to which the whole creation moves, to what end

> All the sublime prerogatives of man?

What use can a caged bird make of its wings? Carlyle speaks somewhere of Southey's eyes as 'filled with gloomy bewilderment and incurable sorrow'. He describes the eyes of men condemned, the eyes of all mankind, helpless amid their illusions, lost in a wilderness of woes. Convince the world that all will finally be as if it had never been, and though men were angels they would resent the preposterous proposal, which asks from them spiritual effort when all efforts are in vain. Play with your toys, you may. Construct to pass the time your paste-board paradises, chirp your sovereign remedies for human ills. Distract your thoughts in pursuit of a bubble reputation or soon-fading wreath, forget yourself amid grammars and lexicons, drug your numbered hours with dice, or sport or foolish loves—all will not serve.

> Surgit amari aliquid, quod in ipsis floribus angat.

Think, if only for a moment, think. Proclaim to men that 'Death is the only immortal', and religion receives its mortal wound.

Announce to them that all human history is a mere scramble for wealth or power, all loves and loyalties time's broken pottery—it is ruin, and every man knows it. Men will not be easily consoled for so much courage, so much endurance, so much faith, so much affection, so much sweetness cast into the void, when they recall the faithful hearts, friendly faces, strong intelligences for ever gone, when they remember the mothers weeping for their children snatched away. And palsied slaves they would be if they accepted these enormities with pious resignation or praised the gods any more. If the world in its scientific wisdom banishes humanity's larger hope, for all your excellent inventions, your alleviations of discomfort and disease, for all your wise saws and platitudes, the 'Never, never, never, never, never' of Lear will make of earth's pleasures a make-believe, and a sense of suffocation invade all thoughtful breasts. 'I would not say to Humanity,' said Madame Akermann, '*Progress!* I would rather say *Die!* for no progress can ever take from you the miseries of earthly life.'

Whence come our present discontents? Unless I am greatly mistaken, from the collapse of the high-pitched expectations of a regenerated human society. Believe in it if you can, the land of earthly happiness that was to replace the old and now discarded paradise to come. You cannot believe it will be to-morrow, nor in a century, nor in ten. That bubble has burst. And what now is left? Neither the old dream nor the new. And the malady of our age is just the thought that nothing or next to nothing is in truth worth attempting or achieving. And no wonder. How should it be? 'What gain to watch for an hour the inscrutable pageant, to be summoned out of nothingness into illusion, and evolved but to aspire and to decay?'

If you have not here among men who reflect, however unwilling they are to acknowledge it, if you have not here among those who have heard

More than Olympian thunder on the sea,

the pivot of the human situation, the question upon the answer to which all turns, I know not where to look for it. If in the denial of any renewal of life beyond the grave we do not virtually deny all life's present values, I know not where to find a more resolute denial of them. Tolstoy, enumerating all his advantages, his

425

health, rank, fame, 'possessing all that men desire', asks 'Is there any meaning in my life, which will not be destroyed by the inevitable death awaiting me?' The question awaits an answer. It cannot be evaded by any sophistries, this interrogation in which all others are resumed, to which all others lead. For what matter the rest, if it can never be known what was true or false, right or wrong, if no questions of any moment will ever be answered, no justice ever done? 'If immortality be untrue', as Buckle wrote, 'it matters little whether anything else be true or not.'

The thought of death as the only cure for human ills paralyses the mind, and puts reason to flight. It denies the world's rationality. Not so, you may say, only our beggarly reason's notion of rationality. Precisely, I answer, or will you out of your kindness inform me where I am to find another and a better understanding, superior to our own. I cannot take the point of view of an insect, a fish or a god. Philosophers and even divines there have been and still are who talk of it, who profess to tell you where this so superior wisdom resides. They have had the good fortune to discover a loftier mind, and to be taken into its confidence. It thinks, they tell us, very differently from our own, and for some inscrutable end has implanted in us another and deceptive reason, which runs clean counter to its wiser and higher intelligence. It would appear to delight in our intellectual and moral confusion, for all we love and cherish is for that sublime understanding a bagatelle.

Cold comfort this. To their chosen god these mystagogues would sacrifice his sentient creatures, even the mercy and justice by these same creatures foolishly supposed to be eminently divine attributes, if by such sacrifices they could preserve the barren and singular existence of a deity, an ugly addition to the world's Pantheon, that one thinks we could well have spared. For in their sculpture the supreme Being presents a sinister, a Mephistophelian countenance. They toil, one fears, in vain, who talk in terms of eloquence of God and the love of God to the assembly of the living, who have suffered at His hands and, having suffered, are about to be extinguished at His decree.

Rational? What could be less rational than that his pen and paper should be more enduring than the saint, that we should have Shakespere's handwriting but not himself? Raphael's pictures but not the mind that conceived them? It is then as Spartans we should live and die—who died, but were by death undaunted—and be content to leave a world so foreign, so contrary to our natures as to scorn our humanity and lacerate our affections. Beyond all peradventure it is the thought that death appears to proclaim, the thought of frustration and final unreason at the heart of things, that is itself the root of the pessimist's despair. The soul must sink when told that human life is mere buffoonery, that the story is without a point, that men must leave the theatre in which they played their sad, incomprehensible parts with their instincts mocked, their understandings unenlightened.

Give them assurance that it is not so, and the scene is changed. The sky brightens, the door is left open for unimagined possibilities, things begin to fall into an intelligible pattern. Man and the universe may yet be reconciled.

> If this fail,
> The pillared firmament is rottenness,
> And earth's base built on stubble.

Hope is the breath of life, and when hope lies dead the final darkness settles down upon the world. There is, then, no food for surprise that Dante wrote in his *Convivio*, 'Of all brutal opinions that is the most foolish, vilest and most pestilent which holds that there is no life after this', and entombed in his *Inferno* the philosopher who taught it. Nor do I believe you will find a poet who could he have believed in immortality would have decried it, or who denied a future life for any other reason than despair of its possibility. Hatred of life is bred of this despair.

But can we in reason hold this faith? This, the most remarkable of human beliefs, is no doubt of great antiquity, and comes to us across the ages. Yet how can that help us? Can any satisfying conviction be based upon the mere antiquity of an extravagant fancy? How many idle dreams have been bred by the exuberance of the human imagination? Or can we overlook the horror with which so many philosophies and religions of Eastern origin regard the thought of continued existence, the religions which give to

> Dateless oblivion and divine repose,

to everlasting night the preference over the day, which speak of deliverance from the wheel of life as the highest good? Or are these creeds also the children of desperation and the doubtful issue of life's protracted warfare?

Our interest in the future, how strange it is if we can never hope to see the future. That interest rarely seems to desert us, and in itself appears inexplicable were we not possessed of an intuition which tells us that we shall have a part in it, that in some sense it already belongs to us, that we should bear it continually in mind, since it will be ours. So closely are all human ideals associated with futurity that, in the absence of the faith that man is an immortal being, it seems doubtful whether they could ever have come to birth.

To Wordsworth that faith appeared the very keystone of our affections. 'I confess with me', he wrote, 'the opinion is absolute that, if the impression and sense of death were not thus counterbalanced, such a hollowness would pervade the whole system of things, such a want of correspondence and consistency, a disproportion so astounding between means and ends, that there could be no repose, no joy.' He speaks the truth in its pure simplicity. Let us take some modern affirmations of the same opinion. 'Personally to me', said Malinowski, 'nothing really matters except the answer to the burning question, "Am I going to live, or shall I vanish as a bubble? What is the aim and issue of this strife and suffering?"' Here is another. 'If men', wrote Sully, 'are to abandon all hope of a future life, the loss in point of cheering and sustaining influence will be a vast one, and one not to be made good, as far as I can see, by any idea of services to collective humanity.' And here is yet another. 'Modern optimism, in my opinion, is doomed'—I quote Lowes Dickinson—'unless we believe that there is more significance in individual lives than appears upon the surface; that there is a destiny reserved for them more august than any to which they can attain in their life of threescore years and ten.' These are the sayings of thoughtful men speaking from their hearts. Nor need we add to their testimony. 'That man', as Goethe said, 'is dead even in this life who has no belief in another.'

I do not need to be told that this opinion, even were it universal, adds not a pennyweight to the case for a future existence. Counting heads will not demonstrate a truth, even if they be good heads. One does not decide by vote the distance of a planet from the sun. To what end, then, these citations? They

428

endorse the view, from which, I think, there are not many, and will be fewer, dissenters as the centuries go by. There are more suicides among civilised peoples than among savages. And once the world has reached the reflective stage of full self-consciousness, if then it holds that this earthly life is all, there can be no exit, however long it lasts, from its disquiet, no comfort anywhere. 'Tis hard to imagine a hopeless world, but men may, perhaps, learn to live if they must, without enthusiasm, to sup lightheartedly with grief, and accustom themselves to the companionship of despair. That, or else seek a way by which to bring the great essay of life, the experiment which has failed, to the earliest and least painful conclusion.

Come now to the vital point. Are there any indications in nature or human nature upon which to found this hope?—the hope that even Schopenhauer could with difficulty forgo, when he wrote, 'In the furthest depth of our being we are secretly conscious of our share in the inexhaustible spring of eternity, so that we can always hope to find life in it again.' Many things are hard to believe, and a future life, some say, is quite incredible, and the mere thought of it a sort of madness. But what hinders if we have already found a present? That great philosopher, Bacon, could not to the last believe that the earth revolved around the sun. The facts were too solidly opposed to such a fancy. It was incredible. The diamond appears the acme of stability, it is in fact a whirlpool of furious motions. Who could believe it? What is credible? Only the familiar. When the news of the invention of the telephone was reported to Professor Tait of Edinburgh, he said, 'It is all humbug, for such a discovery is physically impossible.' When the Abbé Moigno first showed Edison's phonograph to the Paris Academy of Sciences all the men of science present declared it impossible to reproduce the human voice by means of a metal disc, and the Abbé was accused, Sir William Barrett tells us, of having a ventriloquist concealed beneath the table. The thing was unbelievable. A future life is, you think, unbelievable? How clear it is that death is death for men as for all living things.

Well, I should myself put the matter rather differently. The present life is incredible, a future credible. 'Not to be twice-born, but once-born is wonderful.' To be alive, actually existing, to have emerged from darkness and silence, to be here to-day

429

is certainly incredible. A philosopher friend of mine could never, he told me, bring himself to believe in his own existence. A future life would be a miracle, and you find it difficult to believe in miracles? I, on the contrary, find it easy. They are to be expected. The starry worlds in time and space, the pageant of life, the processes of growth and reproduction, the instincts of animals, the inventiveness of nature, the rising and the setting sun, the affections and passions, the character of thought, of will, intuition, consciousness, these singly and together plunge the human mind into profound amazement to be in their midst. They are all utterly unbelievable, miracles piled upon miracles

> To o'ertop old Pelion or the skyish head
> Of blue Olympus.

If there be a sceptical star I was born under it, yet I have lived all my days in complete astonishment. What does this fine reason of ours tell me to believe or disbelieve? When you come to me with your explanations of all the world contains I am profoundly interested. Not, indeed, in your explanations, which are, of course, like all others, supremely ridiculous, but in the bright-eyed simplicity of the human mind, and its explanatory prattle. Explain to me, for I am all attention, some of the everyday familiar things; how, for example, a stimulus to a nerve produces a sensation, by what process we recall a name or a fact, 'how a peacock's tail builds up a series of perfect eyes out of hundreds of separate feathers, each with its thousands of separate branches.'

Miracles? For my part I see miracles everywhere. I see nothing but works of magic. Miracles are not rare birds. They fly in flocks, they darken the air in their multitudes. So much for miracles. Nature is not natural, but supernatural, delighting in marvels, in confounding us with the astounding and impossible. If, as I have done, you have in your leisure hours accompanied the naturalists in their studies of the lower animals—the very humblest—you will, I think, return with your capacity for believing in magic greatly enlarged, with your powers of astonishment exhausted beyond resuscitation. As well might a moth attempt to understand a man as a man a moth. Or if, as I have also done, you have looked with some attention into the field of human faculty, into its still unexplored resources, into the testimony for the marvels that the submerged portion of our being reveals, you will not, I think, return with less amazement, but if possible in a state of still greater stupefaction. What mean these premonitions and apparitions, levitations and hauntings, these tales of far sight in time and in space, of pre-cognition and retro-cognition, of stigmata and faith cures, of crystal vision and alternating personalities, of dowsing and divining rods, of telepathy and hyperaesthesia, of hypnosis and suggestion—of which, it is said, there are some seven hundred explanatory theories—of monitions and intuitions like those of Socrates and Joan of Arc? They meet you everywhere, in every age, in every literature, in every quarter of the globe. Is it all crazy abracadabra, and is the whole world a madhouse? Do not let us talk of the credible and the incredible until we have looked further into these among many other things; from which, if well understood, a new vision of truth might arise.

For the nature of mind, our own nature, the nature of every thing, of all reality, is here in the balance. We are deceived, indeed, if we fancy that our five senses exhaust the universe, or our present standpoint its many landscapes. In the soul's unvisited and sleeping parts it holds both faculties and powers not mentioned in the books of the historians, the manuals of the mathematicians or the physiologists. 'The sensitive soul', as Hegel wrote, 'oversteps the conditions of time and space; it beholds things remote, things long past and things to come.' That we stand in other relations to nature than in our open and familiar intercourse with her through eye and ear, relations of which we are wholly unconscious, is not debatable, it is certain. We are organically supported by motions and processes, as in the eight and sixty octaves of electro-magnetic waves, not to speak of those unknown, undiscernible, untraceable by the most earnest attention. There are things to be seen the eye has not seen, and things to be heard the ear has not heard. Exchange your present senses for others attuned to different wave-lengths and you enter a totally different world, where you might very possibly meet quite different company. Nor is it even certain that it is with the brain we think any more than that it is with the eye we see. You fancy I jest. Not in the least. They are both but instruments, means or *media* of communication with beings of like nature with ourselves in this particular world. They give us entrance to this only to exclude us from others no less real. 'To suppose', wrote that level-headed thinker, John Stuart Mill, 'that the eye is necessary to sight seems to me the notion of one immersed in matter. What we call our bodily sensations are all in the mind, and would not necessarily or probably cease because the body perishes.' We are not to assume that what we do not now know will never be known. Till a few years ago the vast reservoir of electric energy in the secret recesses of nature, under, we might say, our very hands, escaped the attention of all the generations of observant men. For the human race it did not exist, yet now it is all in all. 'The perfect observer', I quote Sir John Herschell, 'will have his eyes, as it were, opened, that they may be struck at once with any occurrences which, according to received opinion, *ought not to happen*, for these are the facts which serve as clues to new discoveries.'

The study to which I refer has nothing to do with spiritualism or with religion. It is simply an enquiry into such occurrences as should not on our present theory of knowledge take place at all. And as Schopenhauer insisted, 'the phenomena under consideration are incomparably the most important among all the facts presented to us by the whole of experience from a philosophical point of view; so it is the duty of every man of science to get acquainted with them, and to study them thoroughly.' How many of them, and how many of our divines are, in respect of this study, like the professor of Padua, who refused to look through Galileo's telescope, lest he might see what he did not wish to see, who dreaded its revelations. But what we prefer, like or dislike, alters nothing in nature. Palatable or unpalatable, we must accept whatever lies in the path of our destiny. And if a tenth, a hundredth part of what competent observers in this field report be true, the castle of our thought may need rebuilding from its foundations. Simple people talk glibly of telepathy, for example; yet if extra-sensory perception alone were established the whole scheme of modern thought crumbles into ruin. It would be nothing short of a scientific revolution. Science and philosophy would be under the necessity, for them a sad necessity, to seek new concepts for the interpretation of reality, to redraw their antiquated map of the human mind, and

Cast their kingdoms old
Into another mould.

432

'I would certainly *not* now say', wrote Bradley, the author of *Appearance and Reality*, in 1923, 'that a future life must be taken as decidedly improbable.' And again, 'I should certainly be willing to agree to the possibility of selves which after death would be perceptible by, and recognisable by one another, and would so far have something in the way of a body.' How interesting that the most modern philosophy should allow that Heraclitus may have been right when he said two thousand years ago, that 'there await men at death things they have neither looked for nor dreamt of'.

How many modes of existence are there? I cannot tell you, but I should imagine them to be very numerous. And what kind of immortality is at all conceivable? Of all doctrines of a future life palingenesis or rebirth, which carries with it the idea of pre-existence, is by far the most ancient and most widely held, 'the only system to which', as said Hume, 'philosophy can hearken.' 'The soul is eternal and migratory, say the Egyptians,' reports Laertius. In its existence birth and death are events. And though this doctrine has for European thought a strangeness, it is in fact the most natural and easily imagined, since what has been can be again. This belief, taught by Pythagoras, to which Plato and Plotinus were attached, has been held by Christian fathers as well as by many philosophers since the dawn of civilisation. It 'has made the tour of the world', and seems, indeed, to be in accordance with nature's own favourite way of thought, of which she so insistently reminds us, in her rhythms and recurrences, her cycles and revolving seasons. 'It presents itself', wrote Schopenhauer, 'as the natural conviction of man whenever he reflects at all in an unprejudiced manner.'

According to Plato's theory of reminiscence (ἀνάμνησις), our present knowledge is a recollection of what was learnt or known by the soul in a previous state. You will say, it has no knowledge of its previous lives. But what man remembers every day of his life? And lost memories, as the psychologists will tell you, are recoverable. For the memory appears to be a palimpsest, from which nothing is ever obliterated. If we have forgotten most days and incidents of our present lives it is natural that memories of previous lives should fail us. Yet from infancy every forgotten day and hour has added to our experiences, to our growth and capacity. All that a child was and did, though unremembered, is still a part of him and is knit up into his present nature. Every day and hour had its value and made its contribution to the mind and soul. So it may be with former lives, each of them but a day in our past history. The universe is wide, and life here or elsewhere might on this view be regarded as a self prescription, a venture willed by the soul for some end and through some prompting of its own, to enlarge its experience, learn more of the universe, recover lost friends, or resume a task begun but not fulfilled. The time has not come to close any of the avenues of thought into the mysteries surrounding us, and unless death finally triumph over life, it may never come. There may even be choices open to the souls in their eternal quest for the highest good.

Again it may be that in the realm of Being the soul lives with its memories. Then if we could talk with the dead they could speak of nothing but their recollections, and would have nothing to tell us—as in the stories we have of conversations with them, they have usually in fact nothing to tell us—of their present existence. If it ever became possible to get into touch with them we should presently take it all for granted, and perhaps only historians would disturb the sleeping dead for details of events on earth forgotten, in which they took a professional interest.

In all our speculation we have constantly to remind ourselves of the lock to which we do not possess the key, the true character of time and our relations to time, which have never been determined, and upon which all else hinges, the nature of time and change, of which we are wholly ignorant. To discuss here these profound problems would, indeed, be unprofitable and inconclusive. And all discourse would end did we not assume that our present relations with time will remain what they now are, wherever our destiny may take us. They may, certainly, be very different; but perforce we think and can only think in terms of the experience we have had, or can recall, in terms, that is, of time and space. If they hold here and now, on what grounds can we rest the proposition that they do not hold for beings like ourselves throughout the universe, or are incompatible with existence in some other state? The best we can do, and that not much, is with things as we know them. With a timeless world and with conditions elsewhere prevailing we have no acquaintance. If ignorance can deny nothing, it can assert nothing. We may, on the other hand, be sure that what now exists in our experience is consistent with all that anywhere exists, and can nowhere contradict or render that experience otiose, useless or irrelevant. From what we have we should therefore expect something in relation to what we shall have. If things as they are have not a feature in common with things as they will be, we have no basis for thought at all regarding that future. Nature, one thinks, however greatly what is to come may differ from what has been, will remain the same nature, unless we are to regard all with which we are now familiar as an empty dream. It may be we should; yet, as Leibniz said, 'a leap from one state to another infinitely different state could not be natural'. The experiences of time and of our present condition could, one feels, only be valuable in an existence not wholly unlike it; and any doctrine which insists upon a totally dissimilar existence, an indescribable spiritual life as a sequel to the present, makes of the present an insoluble enigma. If we are to be so changed as no longer to recognise anything about us, intellect, will, aims or affections, which make us what we are, nothing of our true selves, or of the men and women who have lived, would then remain. 'Tis hard to imagine a mode of existence, though such no doubt is possible, so unlike the present. Into what banishment, one wonders, would all that meets our present sight be sent? Into what will the suns and stars, the great galaxies be transformed? They are no doubt in process of continual change, and with them we too shall change. Our lives are part of the universe and will last as long, but we must wait for the secrets of the history to come. To say that all is mystery is no more than the truth, but to interpret it as leading to one conclusion rather than another is to deny your premise.

And before we can attain to that final harmony between the universe and ourselves, to which we look forward as the consummation of existence, how much we have to learn about both! In respect of our true natures, of what in truth we are and are capable of becoming, to what heights in knowledge, wisdom, power, the soul can climb, of all this science and philosophy have so far hardly yet spoken. Nor can any boundary be set, any 'Thus far and no farther' to the expansion of the mind. In our present life we have acquired at the most the alphabet of this knowledge; and as for the universe, of the modes of existence and happiness of which it permits, of its possibilities as an abode for progressive beings like ourselves, we know less than nothing, and no single life could teach us what they may be. Nor can any reason be advanced why we should not in the end become its masters, mould it to our hearts' desires, and make of it a home, the natural and happy estate of the immortal spirits to whom it indefeasibly belongs.

Immortality is a word which stands for the stability or permanence of that unique and precious quality we discern in the soul, which, if lost, leaves nothing worth preservation in the world. If you can find in it no such quality its preservation cannot of course interest you, and you can accept the thought of its destruction with equanimity. And in this tranquil acquiescence is-thus summed up your opinion of all existence as a worthless misery. You pay life the compliment of regarding it with horror, with hatred and contempt. When upon this issue, then, judgment is given, with it is given also a judgment upon the universe itself. I read some time ago of a Spanish girl in England for the first time. Approaching London in the train she looked out on the sea of houses, factories and chimneys. 'These people have no view,' she cried, and burst into tears. To have no view, how sad a lot. A grey mist descends upon the world.

> For who would lose,
> Though full of pain, this intellectual being,
> These thoughts that wander through eternity,
> To perish rather, swallow'd up and lost
> In the wide womb of uncreated night,
> Devoid of sense and motion?

There is, then, nothing to be hoped for, nothing to be expected and nothing to be done save to await our turn to mount the scaffold and bid farewell to that colossal blunder, the much-ado-about-nothing world—a piece of work whose defence from any human standpoint, if this be all, no advocate dare undertake.

To believe life an irremediable disaster, the heavens and earth an imbecility, is to my way of thinking hard indeed. Since I am not prepared to believe the world a misery-go-round, a torture-chamber, a furnace of senseless affliction; since I am not prepared to believe the fiery, invincible soul a by-blow, a lamentable accident; I prefer to put my trust in the larger vision of the poets. To fortify our minds it is to them we have to return, and yet again return. They alone have understood. 'It exceeds all imagination to conceive', wrote Shelley, 'what would have been the moral condition of the world if the poets had never been born.... What were our consolations on this side of the grave, and what were our aspirations beyond it—if poetry did not ascend to bring light and fire from those eternal regions where the owl-winged faculty of calculation dare not ever soar?' And it is to their inextinguishable sympathy with humanity that they owe their understanding. Not to science or philosophy, but to their profounder appreciation of the strange situation in which we find ourselves, to their sense of the pitiful estate of man who, with all the forces of nature proclaiming an alien creed, still holds to his intuitions, who knows and knows well that he cannot support himself otherwise than by clinging—as a sailor clings to his raft in angry seas—to his passion for justice, his trust in the affections of his heart, his love of the lovely, his lonely struggle for the best, however clumsy and mistaken he may be in his present estimates of what is indeed best.

These are the features and faculties in man that the poets love and admire, his endurance, his resolution, his heroisms, his quixotry. Yes, the quixotry, the inexplicable preference, even to his own hurt, for the noble and magnanimous, the high and honourable things. Miracles they are that outmiracle all others if atoms and the void produced these human qualities. It is in the exalted thoughts and still more soaring dreams of 'that wild swan the soul', the admirable lunacies, the sudden gleams that illuminate the sombre landscape of human life that the poets find the revelation of the vital truth. They issue no commandments, they censure not, they upbraid not. In the fierce turmoil they are not utterly discouraged. They sympathise with every creature. They know, and yet, *mirabile dictu*, love the world. Theirs is a postulate, if you like, yet a postulate we must all make, if we are to enter the region of meanings at all, that our natural capacities, our natural instincts are not the casual spindrift of time, but of an earlier birth and longer lineage. As in the darkness, in the organism not yet born, the eye is formed to correspond to things invisible, and thus with confidence anticipates a world to come, so the soul's faculties, for love, for joy, for admiration, for achievement, correspond to a reality which exists, and is by them foretold. The soul does not provide itself with a passport for an

437

imaginary country, and cannot vibrate to a note unsounded in the universe.

How simple then is our duty—loyalty to life, to the ship's company and to ourselves, that it may not be through our surrender that the great experiment of existence, whose issue remains in doubt, come to an end in nothingness. 'We must not obey', said Aristotle, 'those who urge us, because we are human and mortal, to think human and mortal thoughts; in so far as we may we should practise immortality, and omit no effort to live in accordance with the best that is in us.'

What a handful of dust is man to think such thoughts! Or is he, perchance, a prince in misfortune, whose speech at times betrays his birth? I like to think that, if men are machines, they are machines of a celestial pattern, which can rise above themselves, and, to the amazement of the watching gods, acquit themselves as men. I like to think that this singular race of indomitable, philosophising, poetical beings, resolute to carry the banner of Becoming to unimaginable heights, may be as interesting to the gods as they to us, and that they will stoop to admit these creatures of promise into their divine society.